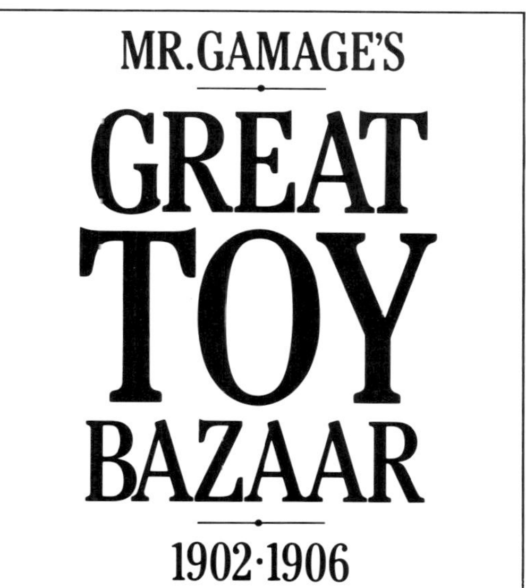

MR. GAMAGE'S

GREAT TOY BAZAAR

1902·1906

INTRODUCTION BY
CHARLOTTE PARRY-CROOKE

DENYS INGRAM PUBLISHERS, LONDON
HASTINGS HOUSE PUBLISHERS INC, NEW YORK

First published in the United Kingdom in 1982
by Denys Ingram Publishers
P.O. Box 287, London N1 1EU
ISBN 0 907724 01 9

First published in the United States of America in 1982
by Hastings House Publishers Inc
10 East 40th Street, New York, NY 10016
ISBN 8038 4745 9

Design: Ray Gautier
Editor: Charlotte Parry-Crooke
Research: Justin Knowles
French translation: Gilles Desmons
German translation: Agis Panagopolis
Photography: Graham Strong

Publishers' note
The publishers apologize for the poor quality of the reproduction of some items, particularly in the dolls section; this is due to the early letterpress process used in the original catalogues. However, given the relevance of the items concerned, it was felt important that they should remain included in the book.

Acknowledgements
The publishers gratefully acknowledge the kind help of all those who have contributed to the compilation of this book. They would particularly like to thank the following:
Alison Adburgham (for permission to include quotations from *Gamage's Christmas Bazaar – 1913*); Clifford and Heather Bond; Pierce Carlson; Gilles Hervé; Agis Panagopolis; Phillips, London (for the photograph on page 12); David Pressland (for loaning items for photography); Radio Times Hulton Picture Library (for the photographs on pages 4, 5 and 17); Sotheby's, London (for the photograph on page 13).

Introduction

The late 19th century and the early years of the 20th saw the creation of the department store, an institution that most of us nowadays take for granted. During the last quarter of the 19th century revolutions had taken place in manufacture and mass production methods, but retailing was still done in a relatively individual way, shops normally sticking to tried and trusted lines of trade. Soon, however, mass-produced goods of all descriptions became increasingly available, and improvements in the fast-growing areas of communications and marketing accelerated. Many astute businessmen were quick to spot the potential of these developments. In this new era of mass production the customer would no longer be quite so content to make do with what was available locally; and what about those millions of possible purchasers in the provinces and colonies whose buying power had to a large degree remained hitherto untapped? With an increasingly efficient service of ships and railways now at their disposal, many were quick to realize the rewards that a 'department' store might reap for them – particularly one with an organized mail order system. And for the customer such a store would provide the convenience of shopping for everything under one roof, even if only by post.

A mail order business, fraught with administrative complications, could, however, only be undertaken by organizations large enough to cope with orders flowing in from all corners of the world. But the impetus was there for the entrepreneurial retailer: if stock purchasing could be done direct from the manufacturers and in bulk at competitive prices, it would still be possible to cope with all the needs of the out-of-town customer, to sell goods at reasonable prices, and in addition be sure of a handsome profit at the end of the trading year. Of course, a large input of time and energy, and indeed business acumen, was needed to set this enormous ball rolling. But the manufacturers for their part were just as keen to be sure of guaranteed markets for substantial quantities of their products. It made sense to have an annual order for a bulk quantity, albeit at a lower unit cost, then to have to rely on higher priced orders for irregular numbers.

Of those businesses whose founders took advantage of this situation of enormous potential lucrative growth, some have withstood the ravages of time and economic recession; others have been felled by the pressures of the day. The names of their creators have, however, become legend: Mr Harrod, Mr Selfridge, Mr John Lewis, Mr Whiteley, among others in Britain; Mr Sears, Mr Roebuck, Mr Montgomery, Mr Ward, Messrs Butler, among many more, in the United States of America. No less colourful and innovative was the man whose 'emporium' in London was a household name throughout Britain and her colonies for decades: Arthur Walter Gamage, who in 1878 at the tender age of twenty started his 'empire' in a tiny shop in the London district of Holborn.

Introduction

La fin du 19ème siècle et le début du 20ème virent la naissance du grand magasin, institution reconnue aujourd'hui. Alors que durant le dernier quart du 19ème siècle les méthodes de production et de fabrication en série avaient vu plus d'une révolution, la vente au détail se faisait encore de façon très individuelle, les magasins se conformant à leur spécialité éprouvée au fil des ans. Cependant, avec l'arrivée sur le marché des produits de série, l'amélioration des moyens de transport et le développement du 'marketing' moderne, nombreux furent-ils à sentir le vent tourner et à profiter de ces changements. En ces temps nouveaux, le client n'allait plus se satisfaire aussi facilement des ressources locales; de plus, que faire de ces millions d'acheteurs potentiels résidant en province et dans les colonies, dont l'énorme pouvoir d'achat n'avait jamais vraiment été exploité? Avec un chemin de fer et une marine marchande de plus en plus efficaces (tant à l'èchelon national qu'international), beaucoup prirent rapidement conscience du fait qu'un 'grand magasin', doublé d'un service de vente par correspondance, possédait de nombreux atouts. Le client avait ainsi le loisir de faire tous ses achats sous le même toit, quand bien même ce n'était que sur catalogue.

Un service de vente par correspondance, inévitablement chargé de complications administratives, ne pouvait être mis sur pied que par de grandes organisations. Pour le détaillant audacieux, il était possible de tenter l'aventure: si les stocks pouvaient s'acheter directement, sans intermédiaire, chez le fabricant, en grand quantité et à prix concurrentiels, on pouvait alors satisfaire le client éloigné, vendre à des prix intéressants et réaliser des bénéfices conséquents. Bien entendu, temps, énergie et sens des affaires étaient essentiels pour mettre en marche l'énorme machine. Les fabricants, quant à eux, étaient tout aussi intéressés par la garantie de marchés substantiels; il était certes préférable d'avoir une grosse commande annuelle régulière, même avec une marge bénificiaire moindre, que de dépendre de commandes aux quantités incertaines, même si elles assuraient des bénéfices plus importants.

Parmi ces affaires dont les fondateurs bénéficièrent de la situation économique favorable, certaines ont tenu bon, contre les ravages du temps et des récessions économiques, d'autres on dû disparaître. Dans presque tous les cas cependant, les noms de leurs fondateurs sont aujourd'hui légende: Mr Harrod, Mr Selfridge, Mr John Lewis, Mr William Whiteley en Grande Bretagne; Mr Sears, Mr Roebuck, Mr Montgomery, Mr Ward, Messrs Butler, parmi beaucoup d'autres, aux Etats-Unis. Non moins pittoresque était Arthur Walter Gamage dont le nom était connu de tous les foyers de la Grande Bretagne et de ses colonies et qui en 1878, au jeune âge de 20 ans lança son 'magasin' à partir d'une petite boutique à Londres dans le quartier de Holborn.

Einleitung

Es war um die Jahrhundertwende, als ein uns heute längst vertrauter Geschäftstyp entstand: das Warenhaus. Im letzten Viertel des 19. Jahrhunderts, als die Massenproduktion bereits länger bekannt war, ging es im Einzelhandel noch relativ individuell zu, und die Geschäfte verkauften vorzugsweise bekannte und bewährte Artikel. Das immer umfassendere Angebot an Massenproduktionsgütern jedoch und die immer rasantere Entwicklung des Verkehrs- und Nachrichtenwesens regten bald viele kluge Geschäftsleute zum Nachdenken an. Sie erkannten die Möglichkeiten dieser Entwicklung und wurden sich bewußt, daß der Kunde im Massenproduktionszeitalter bald nicht mehr mit dem zufrieden sein würde, was er im Geschäft um die Ecke kaufen konnte, und daß es noch Millionen von Käufern auf dem Land und in den Kolonien gab, deren Kaufkraft noch größtenteils unbekannt war. Bald sahen viele – bei den jetzt zur Verfügung stehenden und weiter im Ausbau befindlichen Schiffs- und Eisenbahnverbindungen – den Vorteil des ,,Department store", wie es in England genannt wurde, besonders in Verbindung mit einer gut organisierten Versandabteilung. Auch für den Kunden war es von Vorteil, wenn er alles unter einem Dach und sogar auf dem Postweg kaufen konnte.

Das Problem bestand darin, daß ein Warenhaus, das alle verwaltungstechnischen Aufgaben erfüllen und Aufträge aus aller Welt ausführen konnte, nun im großen Stil zu betreiben war. Für den unternehmerischen Einzelhändler war jetzt der Anreiz gegeben, große Mengen preiswert direkt vom Hersteller zu beziehen und damit nicht nur sämtliche Bedürfnisse der Landkunden zu erfüllen, sondern auch konkurrenzfähig zu bleiben und am Jahresende mit einem schönen Gewinn zu rechnen. Um eine so große Idee vorwärts zu bringen, brauchte man allerdings viel Zeit, Energie und Geschäftstüchtigkeit.

Auch die Hersteller zogen einen gesicherten Absatzmarkt für ihre umfangreiche Warenpalette vor, indem sie große Aufträge für ein ganzes Jahr zu niedrigen Einheitspreisen abschließen konnten, anstatt ihr Spielzeug zu hohen Preisen, aber ohne jede Sicherheit verkaufen zu müssen. Manche Unternehmen, deren Gründer diese Zeit wirtschaftlichen Wachstums ausnutzten, haben sich – trotz schlechter Zeiten und Wirtschaftskrisen – bis heute gehalten; andere wieder mußten im Laufe der Zeit aufgeben. Aber die Namen der Gründer, wie z.B. Harrod, Selfridge, John Lewis in England oder Seas und Roebuck, Montgomery und Ward in den USA, sind bis zum heutigen Tag lebendig geblieben. Zu diesen großen Warenhausgründern gehörte auch ein Mann, dessen ,,Emporium" in London für Millionen von Menschen in Großbritannien und in den englischen Kolonien zu einem Begriff wurde: Arthur Walter Gamage, der im jungen Alter von 20 Jahren in einem winzigen Laden im Holborn-Bezirk von London sein ,,Empire" gründete.

The splendid Edwardian store front of A.W. Gamage Ltd in Holborn, seen from Fetter Lane before further expansion caused the incorporation of adjoining properties.

Given his minimal experience as a draper's assistant, and his lack of connections and backing, it must have seemed to many that the gamble that Mr Gamage took in leasing the shop was not at all wise. Indeed his original partner, Frank Spain, asked to be bought out, since even after several years, he was not confident that real success would come. But Arthur Walter Gamage's motto was not 'Tall oaks from little acorns grow' for nothing and he was determined to succeed. And succeed he certainly did: from his first *coup* of undercutting other retailers in the sale of hairbrushes with wire bristles set in rubber, for which there was a craze at the time, his modest business grew and expanded, both physically and in reputation, at an incredible rate. Relentlessly he pursued a policy of offering quality goods at prices that were significantly low, a strategy that gave him great popularity with the customers, though understandably less with his rivals. Relentlessly he pursued manufacturers in all areas who could give him goods at prices he wished to pay. And relentlessly he pursued the acquisition of properties adjacent to his premises in which to house his ever-growing stock.

Indeed, by the years immediately following the turn of the century the store had certainly grown into a 'tall oak'. It claimed to sell 'everything' and this does actually seem to have been the case. Apart from ammunition and explosives, all goods could be ordered by mail, a service which formed an important and remunerative part of the business. Through-

La splendide devanture d'A.W. Gamage Ltd à Holborn vue ici de Fetter Lane, avant l'agrandissement et l'incorporation des immeubles voisins, est un exemple d'architecture Edouardienne.

Vu sa courte expérience d'assistant chez un drapier et son manque de relations et de soutien financier, le pari que fit Mr Gamage en prenant un bail sur sa boutique dut sembler pure folie à beaucoup. De fait, son associé Frank Spain, après quelques années, manqua de confiance et demanda que sa part lui fut rachetée. Mais Arthur Walter Gamage avait pour devise: 'du petit gland croît le grand chêne'. Il était résolu du réussir. Le succès viendrait certainement: du jour où il se mit à vendre moins cher que ses concurrents un type de brosse à cheveux alors fort à la mode, son modeste magasin grandit et s'élargit à une vitesse incroyable, à la fois en taille et en réputation. Dès lors, avec détermination, il se mit à offrir des articles de qualité à des prix inférieurs à ceux pratiqués par ses rivaux, politique qui, si elle était appréciée de ses clients, l'était bien moins des autres marchands. Avec la même détermination il contacta fabricants et fournisseurs qui pouvaient lui procurer la marchandise qu'il désirait au prix qu'il souhaitait. Avec la même détermination il acheta les bâtiments qui jouxtaient sa boutique afin d'abriter un stock toujours croissant.

Au début de ce siècle le magasin était devenu un 'grand chêne'. Mr Gamage se targuait du fait que l'on y vende de tout, et il semble en effet que tel ait été le cas. Munitions et explosifs mis à part, toute la marchandise pouvait être achetée par correspondance, ce service formant une partie importante et rémunératrice de l'enterprise. En tous

Blick aus der Fetter Lane auf die prächtige edwardianische Fassade des Warenhauses A.W. Gamage Ltd. in Holborn. Später wurden die angrenzenden Bauten übernommen und in das Warenhaus mit einbezogen.

Seine ganze Erfahrung hatte er als Verkäufer in einem Tuchladen gesammelt. Das Risiko, das Gamage – ohne irgendwelche Verbindungen, Rückhalt oder konkrete Zielvorstellungen – einging, erschien vielen sehr unklug. Selbst sein ursprünglicher Partner, Frank Spain, trat nach einigen Jahren aus, da ein Erfolg keineswegs sicher schien. Nicht umsonst lautete das Motto von Gamage: Aus kleinen Eicheln werden große Eichen. Er war fest entschlossen, sein Ziel zu erreichen, und seine Arbeit trug Früchte. Nach seinem ersten Coup, als er die Konkurrenz in Haarbürsten mit Drahtborsten – die eine Zeit lang ein großer Verkaufsschlager waren – unterbot, entwickelte sich sein bescheidenes Unternehmen unglaublich schnell und wuchs an Größe und Ansehen. Treu hielt er zu seinem Grundsatz, Waren guter Qualität billiger als seine Konkurrenten zu verkaufen. Dies machte ihn zwar bei jenen nicht so beliebt, dafür aber natürlich um so mehr bei seinen Kunden. Auch seine Haltung den Lieferanten gegenüber änderte sich nicht, indem er denen den Vorzug gab, die seinen Preisvorstellungen entsprachen. Keine Gelegenheit ließ er aus, sein Geschäft in Holborn durch Zukauf angrenzender Gebäude zu vergrößern, um darin sein ständig wachsendes Lager unterbringen zu können.

Obwohl Gamage im Gegensatz zu Warenhäusern wie Harrods oder Whiteley's keine gesellschaftlichen Ambitionen hatte, sondern es vorzog, sein ,,Emporium'' für den ,,Kleinen Mann'' offen zu halten, zeigte er doch genau

Enjoying a game of clock golf (a line sold in the store), Arthur Walter Gamage is seen here at home at Finchley Manor in north London with family and friends in August 1908.

C'est Arthur Walter Gamage que l'on voit ici jouer au 'jeu de l'horloge' (gamme de jeux vendue par le magasin) avec famille et enfants, chez lui, à Finchley Manor au nord de Londres.

Arthur Walter Gamage mit seiner Familie und Freunden im August 1908 in seinem Heim Finchley Manor in Nordlondon beim ,,Clock Golf", einem auch in seinem Warenhaus verkauften Spiel.

out, Mr Gamage's principles of merchandise buying, promoting and selling were followed. He did not go in for manufacturing his own lines, but by concentrating on goods provided by manufacturers who made up large orders to be sold exclusively in his store he was able to undercut other retailers dramatically.

Though he never aspired to the social cachet of such stores as Harrod's or Whiteley's, preferring to stick to being the *'People's* Emporium', Mr Gamage most definitely had just as much flair for spotting new trends and fashions as the buyers at the smarter stores. From the earliest days of the bristle hairbrush, he made sure he was able to offer his customers the latest. From household goods to fashion, scouts' equipment (Gamage's were the official outfitters) to bicycles, picnic baskets to typewriters, Gamage's could be relied on to provide an incredible range of up-to-date goods at reasonable prices. A Gamage motorcycle was first sold in 1902. Mr Gamage offered 'everything', but he would not have been human if he had not had some favourite areas of interest.

As Alison Adburgham points out in *Gamage's Christmas Bazaar – 1913*, both Arthur Walter and his son, Eric, were 'mad about toys'. 'From the quite early days Mr Gamage specialized in unusual toys. There are legendary tales of his travels in search of them: of being confronted by a blizzard in the wilds of Michigan when looking for the makers of an ingenious toy gun; of having his ears frostbitten when travelling to a trade fair in

domaines les principes éprouvés de Mr Gamage étaient suivis: il préférait ne pas fabriquer ses propres articles, se concentrant au contraire sur les marchandises sans marque qu'il achetait directement chez le fabricant, celui-ci vendant en gros et exclusivement à son magasin. Il avait ainsi la possibilité de vendre beaucoup moins cher que les autres détaillants.

Quoiqu'il n'ait jamais aspiré à la réputation de magasin du 'grande monde' que possédaient par exemple Harrods, Whiteley's ou Schoolbreds Mr Gamage, se contentant d'être le 'magasin du peuple', avait tout autant de flair que les acheteurs des magasins plus élégants pour sentir les modes nouvelles. Depuis l'époque de la brosse à cheveux, il s'était fait une règle de toujours offrir le dernier cri à sa clientèle. De l'article ménager à la mode, de l'uniforme de scout à la bicyclette, du panier pique-nique à la machine à écrire, on pouvait faire confiance à Gamage pour présenter une gamme étonnante d'articles à des prix tout à fait raisonnables. Mr Gamage vendait de tout mais il n'aurait pas vraiment été 'homme', si, dans cette vaste diversité, il n'avait eu des domaines de prédilection. Ainsi qu'Alison Adburgham le souligne dans son introduction à *Gamage's Christmas Bazaar – 1913*, Arthur Walter et son fils, Eric, qui le rejoignit dans l'affaire après avoir terminé ses études, raffolaient tous deux de jouets.

"Très tôt Mr Gamage se spécialisa dans les jouets insolites. Il existe nombre histoires légendaires de ses voyages: comment il affronta un blizzard en plein Michigan afin de

so viel Flair beim Entdecken neuer Trends und Moden, wie die Einkäufer der vornehmeren Warenhäuser. Gleich von Anfang an – wie bei den Haarbürsten – gelang es ihm, seinen Kunden immer das Allerneuste zu bieten. Egal ob Haushaltsartikel, Mode, Pfadfinder-Ausrüstungen, Fahrräder, Picknickkörbe oder Schreibmaschinen, man konnte sich darauf verlassen, daß man seine Wünsche bei Gamages zu vernünftigen Preisen erfüllen konnte. Im Gegensatz zu anderen Warenhäusern verkaufte er keine Waren unter seinem Namen, sondern konzentrierte sich statt dessen auf Artikel ohne Namensbezeichnung, die ausschließlich für ihn hergestellt wurden. Er verkaufte alles, und darunter waren auch einige Dinge, die ihn persönlich besonders interessierten.

Wie Alison Adburgham in ihrer Einleitung zu ,,*Gamage's Christmas Bazaar – 1913*" erwähnt, waren sowohl Arthur Gamage als auch sein Sohn Erich, der sofort nach seinem Schulabschluß in das väterliche Geschäft eintrat, in Spielzeug vernarrt. Von Anfang an spezialisierte sich Gamage auf ungewöhnliches Spielzeug und es gibt lustige Geschichten darüber, was bei der Suche nach diesen alles passierte. Einmal geriet er in der Wildnis von Michigan, wo der Hersteller einer originellen Spielzeugpistole wohnte, in einen Schneesturm. Ein anderes Mal erfroren ihm auf der Reise zu einer Fachmesse in Chicago beide Ohren. Bei einer anderen Gelegenheit suchte er zwei Tage lang in einer abgelegenen Gegend von Österreich nach dem Hersteller eines

Two versions of Bing's 'Spider Motor Car' are shown here; one is driven by clockwork, the other by steam. The steam driven 'Spider' was offered by Gamage's in 1902. (See page 68.)

On voit ici deux versions de la 'Spider Motor Car' de Bing; l'une est mécanique, l'autre marche à la vapeur. La 'Spider' à vapeur se vendait chez Gamage en 1902 (voir page 68).

Zwei Ausführungen des „Spider Motor Car" von Bing. Eine wird durch ein Federwerk angetrieben, die andere durch Dampf. Der dampfbetriebene „Spider" wurde 1902 von Gamage's verkauft (s. Seite 68).

Chicago; of searching two days off the beaten track in Austria to find the maker of a toy he had seen in a Vienna shop. He visited Frau Steiff's doll and soft toy factory in the Black Forest, and became the largest British importer of her famous stuffed animals...'

From this extract we can see that no efforts were spared in the attempt to offer his youthful customers the best toys the world could provide – even at the cost of frostbitten ears and wild goose chases! Most of the details of Mr Gamage's business arrangements with the toy manufacturers of the day, and indeed the visits to and from them, have been lost in time but much of his energetic enthusiasm for all aspects of the toy trade is evident from such sparse documentation as does remain. This mostly takes the form of literature from the manufacturers and well-thumbed copies of the staggeringly comprehensive catalogues produced for Gamage's mail order customers, in which the toy department stock is amusingly described and delightfully depicted.

As collectors and ephemerists well know, such publications are mines of information. Supposition can at last be replaced by fact: prices, dates, makers, original condition of individual items can be confirmed; shifts of fashion and topical interest observed; the rise and fall of different manufacturers noted. For the serious enthusiast such sources are unparalleled; for the layman a whole bygone world is unfolded; for the social historian a wealth of documentation is provided.

The drawback, of course, is that nowadays

rendre visite à un farbicant de carabines pour enfants; comment il eut les oreilles gelées en se rendant à une foire du jouet à Chicago, comment il passa deux jours sur les routes autrichiennes à chercher le fabricant d'un jouet qu'il avait aperçu dans une boutique viennoise. Il visita également l'usine de poupées et d'animaux en peluche de Frau Steiff en Forêt Noire et devint l'importateur anglais le plus important de sa célèbre production. . ."

Cette citation montre qu'Arthur Walter Gamage ne ménageait pas sa peine pour que ses jeunes clients aient à leur disposition les plus beaux jouets du monde, même s'il devait avoir les oreilles gelées! Bien que la plupart des détails précis concernant les relations de Mr Gamage avec les fabricants de jouets se soient perdus dans la nuit des temps, son enthousiasme pour son métier et le monde du jouet transparait dans le peu de documentation qui nous reste. Celle-ci prend essentiellement la forme des écrits promotionnels faits par les fabricants eux-mêmes, et des catalogues de vente par correspondance, dans lesquels le rayon des jouets est décrit et illustré de façon tout à fait délicieuse.

Les collectionneurs le savent bien, de telles publications sont des mines d'information. Des faits solides remplaçant les suppositions étayent enfin notre connaissance: prix, dates, fabricants, condition d'origine peuvent être ainsi confirmés; ascension et chute de tel ou tel fabricant constatées. Pour le collectionneur, de telles sources n'ont pas leur pareil; pour

Spielzeugs, das er in einem Geschäft in Wien gesehen hatte. Bei einer dieser Reisen besuchte er auch die Fabrik von Steiff im Schwarzwald und wurde zum größten britischen Importeur der bekannten Stofftiere. Wie man sieht, scheute er keine noch so große Mühe, um seinen kleinen Kunden die besten Spielzeuge der Welt bieten zu können – selbst auf Kosten erfrorener Ohren und längerer Irrfahrten.

Die meisten Unterlagen über seine Geschäftsabschlüsse mit den damaligen Spielzeug-Herstellern und seine Reisen zu ihnen sind leider verlorengegangen; nur noch einige Lieferanten-Prospekte und stark beschädigte Versand-Kataloge, in denen sein Spielzeugangebot amüsant und detailliert beschrieben und abgebildet ist, sind Zeugnis seiner großen Begeisterung. Diese Kataloge sind nicht nur für den Sammler eine wahre Fundgrube. Hier werden Vermutungen zur Gewißheit: Man kann Preise, Daten, Herstellernamen und die ursprüngliche Ausführung einzelner Artikel nachschlagen und beobachten, wie sich Mode und aktuelle Interessen verändert haben und wer von den verschiedenen Lieferanten noch aktuell war. Für den Sammler ist dies eine einmalige Informationsquelle, für den Laien ist es das Tor zu einer längst versunkenen Welt, während der Sozialhistoriker hier eine Fülle von Beweisen findet.

Leider sind diese so gesuchten Informationsquellen nur noch selten zu finden. Während Lieferantenkataloge noch häufiger auftauchen – vielleicht weil bessere Archive geführt wurden – warf der Kunde gewöhnlich

these sought-after sources of information are rarely found; while manufacturers' catalogues are somewhat more frequently seen (perhaps more efficient records were kept), those from the great stores were usually disposed of when finished with by the customer. Who, after all, would keep for ever the annual offerings produced by many of the department stores of today? And with a store such as Gamage's, whose demise at Holborn in 1972 caused the dispersal and possibly the destruction of most of the firm's records and file copies of catalogues, the finding of treasures in this line is that much more unlikely.

Thus the discovery of two major Gamage's toy catalogues, hitherto unseen by today's collectors, is indeed an event of significance. The importance of these two catalogues, fine selections from which are reproduced here for the very first time, should not be underestimated. Produced respectively in 1902 and 1906 (in a decade when the toy industry was at its height), they provide categorical proof of Mr Gamage's contribution to the international toy industry. Reflecting his tireless and innovative approach to the buying and marketing of all types of toy, these pages offer to the child of the 1900s an extraordinary range of playthings culled from the showrooms of the great manufacturers of the era, as well as from those of a selection of smaller companies. Because of the variety of both products and makers contained between their covers, these catalogues encapsulate the golden age of toys.

It is not, of course, possible within the

l'amateur éclairé un monde disparu s'ouvre à ses yeux; pour le sociologue une richesse d'information lui est offerte.

L'inconvénient bien sûr est que de nos jours ces publications recherchées sont difficiles à trouver; alors que l'on voit de temps à autres les catalogues de fabricants, ceux des grands magasins sont beaucoup plus rares car ils étaient souvent jetés une fois utilisés. Qui après tout conserverait aujourd'hui ce genre de publication annuelle? Avec un magasin comme Gamage, dont le siège à Holborn fut démoli en 1972, provoquant ainsi la dispersion, voire la destruction, de ses dossiers (et donc des exemplaires de catalogues que l'on peut présumer avoir été conservés aux archives), la possibilité de dénicher des trésors semble bien limitée.

C'est ainsi que la découverte de deux importants catalogues de jouets de Gamage, inconnus jusqu'à présent des collectionneurs, est un évènement qui mérite d'être salué. L'importance de ces catalogues dont une large sélection a été ici reproduite pour la première fois ne doit pas être sous-estimée. Produits respectivement en 1902 et en 1906, durant une décennie pendant laquelle l'industrie du jouet, que ce soit en terme de compétence technique ou de créativité, était à son faîte, ils fournissent une preuve indubitable de la contribution de Mr Gamage. Reflétant son approche infatigable et innovatrice de l'achat et de la vente, ces pages offrent à l'enfant du début du siècle une merveilleuse gamme de jouets choisis chez la plupart des grands fabricants de

Versandkataloge nach Gebrauch weg. Besonders unwahrscheinlich war es, noch Schätze dieser Art von Gamages zu finden, da beim Untergange des Warenhauses in Holborn 1972 fast sämtliche Firmenunterlagen verloren gingen oder zerstört wurden.

Die Entdeckung von zwei großen, bisher noch völlig unbekannten Spielzeugkatalogen von Gamages, von denen hier erstmalig einige schöne Auszüge wiedergegeben sind, ist daher von um so größerer Bedeutung. Sie stammen aus den Jahren 1902 und 1906 – also aus einem Jahrzehnt, in dem die Spielzeugindustrie in jeder Beziehung auf dem Höhepunkt stand – und sind ein einmaliges Zeugnis von Gamages Beitrag zur Spielzeugindustrie der Welt. Beim Durchblättern dieser Seiten gewinnt man nicht nur Einblick in seine unermüdlichen Bemühungen, jede Art von Spielzeug einzukaufen und zu verkaufen, sondern man erkennt auch, welch ungewöhnliche Vielfalt von Spielzeug den Kindern um die Jahrhundertwende geboten wurde, und daß er dieses nicht nur von namhaften Firmen, sondern auch von kleineren Unternehmen bezog. Diese beiden Kataloge vor allen anderen aus jener Zeit verkörpern das „Goldene Zeitalter" des Spielzeugs. Es ist natürlich unmöglich, auf diesen wenigen Seiten jedes beachtenswerte Spielzeug zu beschreiben, das Gamage seinen Kunden zwischen 1902 und 1906 anbot, aber es ist interessant, einige Beobachtungen wiederzugeben, die sich beim Vergleich der beiden Kataloge unter Berücksichtigung weiterer

Märklin toys from Gamage's 1902 catalogue: the train appears on page 21, the 'Circus Caravan' on page 37 and the 'Ambulance Car' (equipped with wounded figures, stretchers etc) on page 36.

Quelques jouets Märklin que l'on peut trouver dans le catalogue de 1902; le train apparait page 21, la roulotte de cirque page 37 et l'ambulance, équipée de blessés, brancards, etc., page 36.

Märklin-Spielzeug aus dem Gamage's-Katalog von 1902. Der Zug wird auf Seite 21 gezeigt, der „Circus Caravan" auf Seite 37 und der mit Verwundeten, Bahren usw. bestückte Sanitätswagen auf Seite 36.

One of a range of steam driven toys offered by Gamage's in 1902. The steam boiler on this 'Motor Omnibus' from Bing is located in front of the passenger compartment. (See page 68.)

L'un parmi de nombreux jouets à vapeur vendus chez Gamage en 1902; la chaudière de ce 'Motor Omnibus' fabriqué par Bing est située à l'avant du compartiment passager (voir page 68).

Eines von mehreren dampfbetriebenen Spielzeugen, die 1902 von Gamage's angeboten wurden. Der Dampfkessel auf diesem ,,Motoromnibus" von Bing befindet sich vor dem Fahrgastraum (s. Seite 68).

confines of these few pages to describe and identify in detail every toy of note on sale to Gamage's customers in 1902 and 1906; it is however important to record some general observations drawn from the study of these two catalogues in relation to one another and other documented material already available.

In the manufacture of toys at this date, the great German firms without doubt led the field, especially in the tin toy area. Their superiority stemmed from a combination of technical skill, efficient organization, willingness to embrace mass production and the use of new methods, competitive prices, go-ahead marketing strategies, and inventiveness, initiative and hard work in all areas. Perhaps their awareness was their greatest asset; always quick on the uptake, each new fad or invention was quickly reincarnated in toy form by the Germans. Whether it was machines from the 'age of steam', motors cars, planes or current delights such as characters from the circus, their craftsmen could be relied upon to produce faithfully and realistically depicted characterizations. More than this, the Germans were acutely aware of the enormous potential of the export market. Makers such as Märklin, Plank, Bing and Carette had especially large export sales, as did Lehmann in the novelty toy line.

In France, the story was somewhat different. French tin toy makers appear to have been very good at getting the ball rolling, but not so good at seeing the ultimate potential of their inventions, and thus reaping the

l'époque, mais aussi chez quelques maisons plus modestes. Par la grande variété des produits et des fabricants contenus dans leurs pages, ces deux catalogues plus qu'aucun autre de même date, sont exemplaires de l'âge d'or du jouet. Il est impossible bien sûr, en quelques pages, de décrire et d'identifier en détail chaque jouet d'importance en vente chez Gamage en 1902 et en 1906; il est cependant utile de faire quelques observations générales fondées sur l'étude de ces deux catalogues et sur d'autres sources disponibles.

Sans nul doute les grandes firmes allemandes à cette époque règnaient en maître sur la fabrication des jouets et plus spécialement sur ceux en fer-blanc. Leur supériorité trouvait son origine dans une combinaison de haute technicité, une organisation efficace, un désir de se convertir à la production en série et aux méthodes nouvelles, des prix compétitifs, une stratégie commerciale rigoureuse, un esprit travailleur et un sens d'initiative et de création. Leur plus grand atout tenait peut-être à leur vigilance: toute nouvelle mode ou invention se trouvait rapidement réincarnée en jouet. Que ce soient machines de l'âge de la vapeur, automobiles, avions ou personnages de cirque, on pouvait fair confiance à leurs artisans pour reproduire de façon fidèle et réaliste de charmants modèles. De plus, les Allemands possédaient un sens aigu de l'énorme potential à l'exportation. Les fabricants tels Märklin, Plank, Bing, Lehmann et Carette réalisaient de grandes ventes à l'étranger.

En France les choses se passaient différem-

Unterlagen ergeben.

An der Spitze der Spielzeughersteller lagen damals zweifellos die großen deutschen Firmen, besonders beim Blechspielzeug. Die Gründe hierfür sind: handwerkliches Können, gut organisierte Betriebe, Bereitschaft zur Massenproduktion, Verwendung neuer Methoden, konkurrenzfähige Preise sowie eine zukunftsorientierte Marktpolitik, erfinderisches Talent, Initiative und Fleiß. Die Deutschen waren allem Neuen gegenüber aufgeschlossen und griffen jede noch so ausgefallene Idee oder Erfindung auf und brachten sie als Spielzeug wieder. Dampfmaschinen jeder Art, Autos, Flugzeuge und aktuelle Attraktionen wie Zirkusfiguren wurden immer naturgetreu nachgebildet. Und noch eines hatten die deutschen Hersteller den anderen Ländern voraus: Sie hatten die Möglichkeiten des Exports entdeckt und waren auf diesem Gebiet entsprechend aktiv, wie die hohen Exportumsätze von Märklin, Plank, Bing, Carette und Lehmann zeigen.

In Frankreich lagen die Dinge anders. Die französischen Blechspielzeughersteller hatten zwar einen guten Start, erkannten dann aber nicht die Möglichkeiten ihrer Erfindungen bzw. der Massenproduktion. Selbst ein so renommierter Hersteller wie Fernand Martin nutzte das günstige Wirtschaftsklima nicht. Nur die französischen Puppenhersteller machten den deutschen Konkurrenz. Viele Jahre lang behaupteten Jumeau und die anderen französischen Puppenhersteller die Marktspitze und hielten diese Stellung den

As well as the better known toy soldiers, William Britain's produced a few novelties, including this 'Equestrienne'. Flywheel driven, the fairy vaults over the bar as her horse races round. (See page 66.)

William Britain est plus connu pour ses soldats de plomb, mais il produisait aussi quelques nouveautés, telle cette 'écuyère' à volant qui saute au dessus de la barre alors que son cheval galoppe (page 66).

Neben Spielzeugsoldaten brachte William Britain auch einige Neuheiten wie diese ,,Equestrienne" heraus. Die Tänzerin schwingt um die Stange, während das Pferd im Kreise trabt (s. Seite 66).

benefits. And they certainly did not recognize the possibilities of mass marketing. Even such remarkable makers as Fernand Martin did not take advantage of the climate of economic expansion. This attitude was not shared by the doll makers of France, however, whose competitiveness compared with that of the Germans. For many years Jumeau and his fellow doll manufacturers led in the doll field and fought tooth and nail to retain supremacy over their teutonic rivals.

Elsewhere, notably in Britain and the United States, manufacturers tended to pursue more specialized lines generally on a somewhat smaller scale. In the United Kingdom the outstanding figure was William Britain, who made his greatest impact with ranges of toy soldiers and a small selection of fly wheel and friction driven novelties. In the United States George Brown, Ives and J & E Stevens made their mark, exporting their wares to a degree, and Schoenhut, who was continuing the toymaking traditions of his native Germany in Philadelphia, was famed for his toy pianos and the Humpty Dumpty Circus.

Given this state of affairs, it was not surprising that the qualities and attitudes which appealed most to Mr Gamage were those of the German manufacturers. In fact, as can be seen from the brief mention of Mr Gamage's business philosophy, the aims of both manufacturers and retailer were almost identical – what better grounds on which to set up a trading relationship that promised success to both parties. The success they together

ment. Il semble que les ferblantiers français aient été excellents pour lancer un nouveau jouet, mais beaucoup moins pour voir les potentialités de leur inventions et en récolter ainsi les bénéfices. Ils ne virent certainement par les possibilités d'une commercialisation en grande série. Même un fabricant aussi remarquable que Fernand Martin ne profitait guère du climat d'expansion économique. Cette attitude toutefois, n'était pas partagée par les fabricants français de poupées dont la compétitévité valait bien celle des Allemands. Pendant de nombreuses années, Jumeau et les autres entreprises français dominèrent le marché et se battirent avec acharnement contre leurs concurrents d'outre-Rhin.

Ailleurs, notamment en Grande Bretagne et aux Etats-Unis, les fabricants tendaient, et sur une plus petite échelle, à se spécialiser. C'est ainsi qu'en Grande Bretagne William Britain s'implanta en développant ses gammes de soldats de plomb et une petite sélection de jouets à volant et à friction. Aux Etats-Unis, George Brown, Ives et J & E Stevens gagnèrent une certaine réputation et Schoenhut, perpétuant les traditions de manufacture de son Allemagne natale, se rendit justement célèbre par ses pianos-jouets et son cirque 'Humpty Dumpty'.

Etant donné cet état de choses, il n'est guère suprenant que les qualités qu'appréciaient le plus Mr Gamage étaient celles des fabricants allemands. En fait, comme on peut le constater d'après la brève mention qui a été faite de la philosophie de Mr Gamage, les buts des fabri-

Deutschen gegenüber.

In anderen Ländern, besonders in England und den USA, war man mehr auf bestimmte Artikel spezialisiert, die in einem etwas kleineren Umfang hergestellt werden konnten. In England ist vor allem William Britain zu erwähnen, dessen Zinnsoldaten und mechanisches Spielzeug mit Schwungrad-bzw. Friktionsantrieb besonderes Aufsehen erregten. In den USA wurden George Brown, Ives and J. & E. Stevens durch ihre Exportaktivitäten bekannt und auch Schoenhut, der die Tradition seiner deutschen Heimat in Philadelphia fortführte und durch seine Spielzeug-Klaviere und den ,,Humpty-Dumpty" Zirkus berühmt wurde.

Es war daher nicht verwunderlich, daß Gamage die deutschen Hersteller bevorzugte. Seine Zielsetzungen waren mit denen seiner Lieferanten identisch und die beste Grundlage für den Aufbau einer für beide Teile gewinnbringenden Geschäftsbeziehung. Die hier wiedergegebenen Katalogseiten liefern den besten Bewes für diesen gemeinsamen Erfolg.

Gleich von Anfang an pflegte Gamage seine Beziehungen zu den deutschen Firmen, deren Erzeugnisse und Einstellung er bewunderte, besonders bei den exportorientierten Firmen. Diese waren bereit, Qualität zu angemessenen Preisen zu liefern, so daß Sonderabschlüsse und Exklusivverträge zustande kamen. Zum Schluß wurde Gamage mit speziell für den britischen Markt entworfenem Spielzeug beliefert. Mit den Firmen, die seinen Erwartungen voll und ganz entsprachen, blieb

achieved is conclusively documented for all to see in the catalogue pages reproduced here.

From the start Mr Gamage cultivated his relationship with the German firms whose products and attitudes he admired, particularly those who looked abroad for a major part of their business. They in turn fostered his aims of providing the best at reasonable cost by agreeing to special deals, exclusive contracts and ultimately the provision of toys designed specifically for the British market. For those who more than fulfilled their side of the bargain there was the assurance of continued long-term business. For those who could not live up to Mr Gamage's exacting standards and whose toys failed to achieve their selling targets there was only the ruthless chop of Mr Gamage's axe to look forward to. The products of those firms that lived up to expectations fill the pages of the 1902 catalogue, reappear in 1906 and even in 1913.

Märklin, Hess, Carette, Issmayer and Bing were the predominant suppliers of locomotives in 1902, with some examples by Schoenner. A vast array of static steam engines came from Plank, who also provided boats. Other nautical toys came from Carette, Bing and Märklin. This last firm appears in the pages of automobiles, as do Hess, Günthermann and Bing. The supply of novelty toys was mostly the responsibility of the two classic novelty makers, Lehmann and Günthermann. Celluloid toys, which made their first appearance on the market in 1902, also came from Germany, from Rheinischer Gummi of the Rhine area.

cants et du détaillant étaient quasiment identiques; n'était-ce pas ainsi le meilleur terrain d'entente sur lequel fonder une relation d'affaires avec succès? Ce succès, qu'ils atteignirent ensemble, est largement illustré dans les pages des catalogues ici reproduites.

Dès le début, Mr Gamage cultiva des relations privilégiées avec les firmes allemandes dont il admirait la production et l'attitude, particulièrement celles qui cherchaient à dévolopper leur marché à l'extérieur. Elles, à leur tour, l'encourageaient à vendre ce qu'il y avait de meilleur à des prix raisonnables, signant des accords spéciaux et des contrats exclusifs et, finalement, fabriquant des jouets uniquement destinés au marché britannique. Celles qui remplissaient leur part de contrat étaient assurées d'affaires à long terme. Leur production s'étale dans les pages des deux catalogues de 1902 et 1906. Quant à celles qui ne pouvaient se conformer aux conditions élevées de Mr Gamage et dont les jouets ne se vendaient pas selon les objectifs fixés, il ne leur restait plus qu'à attendre un coup de hâche sans pitié et inévitable.

Märklin, Hess, Carette, Issmayer et Bing étaient les principaux fournisseurs de locomotives en 1902, avec quelques exemplaires de chez Schoenner. Une grande quantité de machines à vapeur venait de chez Plank, qui fournissait aussi les bateaux. D'autres jouets nautiques provenaient aussi de chez Carette, Bing et Märklin. Cette dernière maison apparait également dans les pages consacrées à l'automobile avec Hess, Günthermann et Bing.

Gamage in einer dauerhaften Geschäftsverbindung, während die anderen Firmen, deren Erzeugnisse die Absatzquoten nicht erreichten, damit rechnen mußten, daß Gamage diese Verbindung nicht fortsetzte. Die Erzeugnisse der erstgenannten Firmen sind auf den Katalogseiten von 1902, 1906 und sogar von 1913 zu finden.

1902 lieferten hauptsächlich Märklin, Hess, Carette, Issmayer, Bing und vereinzelt auch Schoenner die Lokomotiven. Hauptlieferant für alle möglichen Dampfmaschinen sowie für Schiffe war Plank. Anderes nautisches Spielzeug kam von Carette, Bing und Märklin. Autos wurden von Märklin zusammen mit Hess, Günthermann und Bing geliefert. Für mechanisches Spielzeug waren hauptsächlich die Firmen Lehmann und Günthermann zuständig. Im selben Jahr kam auch zum ersten Mal Zelluloid-Spielzeug auf den Markt, und zwar von der Firma Rheinische Gummi- und Celluloid-Fabrik, Neckarau-Mannheim.

Außer diesen deutschen Firmen sind aber auch Lieferanten anderer Länder erwähnenswert. Damals war noch Jumeau führend auf dem Puppenmarkt, obwohl die meisten angebotenen Puppen aus den neunziger Jahren stammten. Wachspuppen kamen aus England, und zwar hauptsächlich von der Familie Pierotti, die sich in diesem Land ein Geschäft aufbaute. Bei Zinnsoldaten lag W. Britain an der Spitze. Andere Firmen traten trotz ihres Renommées nur vorübergehend auf. Ein typisches Beispiel hierfür war Fernand Martin, dessen „kleiner Pianist" (s. Seite 67) als

Märklin's vast 'Man of War' was adapted for different national markets. 'Maina', shown here, was for the American market; 'Siegfried', the German version, is illustrated in Gamage's catalogue (page 54).

Ce splendide vaisseau Märklin fut adapté aux différents marchés nationaux. 'Maina' que l'on voit ici était destiné au marché américain; 'Siegfried', la version allemande se trouve page 54 du catalogue.

Das Kriegsschiff von Märklin wurde nach nationalen Märkten variiert. Die hier gezeigte „Maina" war für die USA bestimmt. Die deutsche „Siegfried" wird auf Seite 54 gezeigt.

Günthermann's 'Handsome Clockwork Motor' *(Vis-à-vis)* was inspired by an 1890s Peugeot car. Made in four different sizes, the version shown here sold in 1902 at Gamage's for 3/6d. (See page 68.)

Un modèle Peugeot de 1890 inspira à Günthermann son 'Vis-à-vis' mécanique. Fabriqué en quatre tailles différentes, la version vue ici se vendait en 1902 chez Gamage's pour 3 shillings et 6 pence (voir page 68).

Die Anregung für Günthermanns ,,Handsome Clockwork Motor" (gegenüber) gab ein Peugeot von ca. 1890. Er wurde in vier Größen angeboten. Die hier gezeigte Version wird auf Seite 68 gezeigt.

Despite the overwhelming predominance of German makers, those from other nations do feature. At this date Jumeau was obviously still the leader in the doll market (though most of the dolls on sale were made in the 1890s). Wax dolls were of English make, mainly from the Pierotti family who had established their business in England. And William Britain's dominate in the toy soldier field. Others, despite their retrospective reputations, make only fleeting appearances. One notable example is Fernand Martin whose 'Little Pianist' (see page 67) stands alone in 1902 as the representative of the *oeuvre* of this great maker. There are toys from the United States too, mostly of the cast-iron variety.

But it was with the German makers that Mr Gamage set up his special, and often exclusive, contracts. He became Märklin's sole importer in Britain and had special arrangements with Issmayer and Plank. As can be seen on page 50, he bought up Plank's stock of 'Steam Model Screw Boats' and was able to market these at extremely low prices. There are even examples in the pages of the 1902 catalogue of toys, such as buoys and boats, which do not appear in Plank's own factory catalogues of the corresponding date. And it is highly probable that the same kinds of arrangements were made with the other large German makers. Certainly, Gamage's had a large workshop to which toys, particularly the German ones, could be sent for repair and the supply of spare parts.

It is hardly a surprise therefore to find in

Lehmann et Günthermann s'étaient fait une spécialité des nouveautés. Les jouets en celluloides, qui firent leur apparition sur le marché en 1902, étaient aussi fournis par l'Allemagne, à savoir Rheinischer Gummi dans la région du Rhin.

Malgré l'écrasante prédominance des Allemands, on trouve tout de même des fabricants étrangers. A cette époque Jumeau dominait encore nettement le marché de la poupée (quoique la plupart des poupées en vente aient été fabriquées dans les années 1890). Les poupées de cire étaient de fabrication anglaise, principalement des Peirotti qui s'étaient installés dans le Royaume Uni. Quant à William Britain, il règnait sur le marché du soldat de plomb. D'autres, malgré leur réputation ne font que de courtes apparitions, tel Fernand Martin dont le 'Petit Pianiste' (voir page 67) est seul à représenter son oeuvre. On trouve aussi des jouets en provenance des Etats-Unis, essentiellement en fer forgé.

Mais c'était avec les fabricants allemands que Mr Gamage eut des contrats particuliers, souvent exclusifs. Il devint l'unique importateur de Märklin et eut des arrangements spéciaux avec Issmayer et Plank. Comme on peut le voir page 50 il acheta à Plank tout son stock de bateaux à hélices à vapeur et eut ainsi la possibilité de les vendre à des prix défiant toute concurrence. Il y a même dans les pages du catalogue de 1902, des jouets tels bouées et bateaux qui n'apparaissent pas dans les catalogues de Plank publiés à la même époque. Il est hautement probable que de tels arrange-

einziges Stück dieses großen Spielzeugherstellers im Gamages-Katalog vertreten ist. Auch aus den USA ist Spielzeug zu finden, und zwar vorwiegend aus Gußeisen.

Mit den deutschen Herstellern aber tätigte Gamage seine Sonderabschlüsse, und zwar oft in Form von Exklusivverträgen. Er übernahm das Importmonopol für Märklin in Großbritannien und hatte Sondervereinbarungen mit Issmayer und Plank. Wie aus Seite 50 hervorgeht, kaufte er Plank den gesamten Vorrat an ,,Schraubendampfern" ab und konnte diese daher zu äußerst niedrigen Preisen anbieten. Der Katalog von 1902 enhält sogar Beispiele von Spielzeug, wie z.B. Bojen und Schiffe, das in dem Plank-Katalog entsprechender Zeit nicht erscheint. Es ist anzunehmen, daß ähnliche Abkommen mit anderen deutschen Herstellern getroffen wurden. Gamages unterhielt auch eine große Werkstatt, bei der man vor allem deutsches Spielzeug reparieren lassen konnte und die auch Ersatzteile lieferte.

Es ist daher kaum verwunderlich, daß auf den Seiten des Kataloges von 1906 fast genau dieselben Namen auftauchen wie in der Ausgabe von 1902. Nur hatte Gamage 1906 sein Angebot konsolidiert und erweitert. Carette tritt mehr in Erscheinung, während Issmayers Beitrag auf die Lieferung von Lokomotiven unter dem Namen von Carette Beschränkt ist. William Britains Angebot umfaßt jetzt auch ein paar Kräne sowie eine bedeutend größere Auswahl an Zinnsoldaten. Der Katalog von 1906 hat einige bemerkenswerte

William Britain's were renowned for their lead soldiers; a wide variety is depicted in Gamage's catalogues for both 1902 and 1906. The Gordon and Cameron Highlanders shown here are Set 89 from page 58.

La réputation de William Britain était fondée sur ses soldats de plomb; les catalogues de 1902 et 1906 en illustrent une grande variété. Ici les Gordon and Cameron Highlanders (page 58).

William Britain war für seine Zinnsoldaten berühmt, und die Gamage's-Kataloge von 1902 und 1906 zeigen eine breite Auswahl. Die hier gezeigten sind der Satz 89 auf Seite 58.

the pages of the 1906 catalogue very nearly the same cast of makers as in the edition of 1902. By this later date Mr Gamage had consolidated and expanded his range. Carette makes a more marked appearance and Issmayer's contribution is relegated to the production of locomotives marketed under the Carette banner. William Britain's range has widened to include a few cranes and there is a notable increase in their range of toy soldiers.

There are several important new inclusions this year. Among the soft toys from Fräulein Steiff is one of the early examples of the now immortal teddy bear (originally Teddy's bear, from Teddy Roosevelt) which she first showed at the Leipzig Fair of 1904; Mr Gamage was one of her first customers. Another first is the inclusion of Albert Schoenhut's 'Humpty Dumpty Circus'. This marvellously adaptable set of toys had such success that it was one of the few American made items to be exported in large numbers. Patents for the circus would appear to be later than 1906, so here again Mr Gamage was one of the first to stock it. The inclusion of both the teddy and the circus are further proof of Mr Gamage's eye for spotting potential winners. 'For', as Alison Adburgham points out, 'Gamage's were always abreast of the times in toys, if not a little ahead.'

Mr Gamage's axe has however fallen in 1906 on several of his 1902 suppliers: gone amongst others are the American cast-iron toys, the lead soldiers from Heyde which in 1902 provided competition for William Britain, and the steam locomotives from the

ments étaient également conclus avec les autres grands fabricants allemands. Nous savons que Gamage possédait un atelier où l'on pouvait envoyer les jouets à réparer (surtout les jouets allemands).

Ce n'est donc pas vraiment une surprise de voir dans le catalogue de 1906 presque la même liste de fabricants. A cette date Mr Gamage avait consolidé sa position et étendu sa gamme. Carette fait une apparition plus marquée, alors qu'Issmayer doit se contenter de produire des locomotives qui seront vendues sous l'étiquette Carette. William Britain a élargi sa gamme, en y incluant des grues, et agrandi sa collection de soldats de plomb. Mais on compte aussi de nombreux nouveaux venus cette année. Parmi les animaux en peluche venant de chez Fraulein Steiff, il ya a l'un premiers exemplaires du célébres ours qu'elle exhiba pour la première fois à la foire de Leipzig en 1904; Mr Gamage fut l'un de ses premiers clients. Le cirque 'Humpty Dumpty' d'Albert Schoenhut est une autre nouveauté. Ce merveilleux jouet fut l'un des rares jouets américains à être exporté en grande quantité. Il semble que les brevets pour le cirque datent d'après 1906; mais une fois encore Mr Gamage fut l'un des premiers à l'offrir. L'introduction de l'ours et du cirque nous offre une nouvelle preuve du flair de Mr Gamage à dénicher les meilleurs ventes. ''Gamage'', remarque Alison Adburgham, ''allait toujours de pair avec son temps en ce qui concerne le jouet. Il était même souvent légèrement en avance''.

Le couperet de Mr Gamage était cependant

Neuerscheinungen zu verzeichnen. Unter den Stofftieren von Steiff gibt es einige frühe Beispiele des heute unsterblichen Teddybären (ursprünglich Teddys Bär, nach Teddy Roosevelt), der erstmalig 1904 auf der Leipziger Messe gezeigt wurde. Gamage war einer der ersten Kunden. Eine weitere Neuerscheinung ist der ,,Humpty Dumpty'' Zirkus von Albert Schoenhut. Dieser schöne und vielseitig verwendbare Spielzeugsatz war so beliebt, daß er in großen Mengen exportiert wurde, was bei den Amerikanern sehr selten vorkam. Die Patente für den Zirkus datieren nach 1906 und Gamage war einer der ersten, die diesen Artikel führten. Teddybär und Zirkus sind auch ein Beispiel dafür, daß Gamage eine gute Nase für Verkaufsschlager hatte. Immer lag er mit seinen Spielzeugen an der Spitze und war den anderen oft voraus.

1906 hatte sich Gamage jedoch bereits von verschiedenen seiner Lieferanten von 1902 getrennt. Kein amerikanisches gußeisernes Spielzeug, keine Zinnsoldaten von Heyde, die 1902 mit Britains Erzeugnissen konkurrierten, keine Dampflokomotiven von Stevens Model Dockyard; von Martin nur ein Spielzeug als höfliche Geste: den ,,Zauberball'' (s. Seite 135). Die Puppenkonkurrenz ist stärker geworden, Jumeau/SFBJ (Société Française de Fabrication de Bébés et Jouets, ein Zusammenschluß der französischen Puppenmacher, um die Oberherrschaft der Franzosen auf diesem Sektor zu sichern) hat jetzt einen deutschen Konkurrenten namens Halbig, berühmt durch seine Charakterpuppen. Eine

British firm of Stevens Model Dockyard. Again only a token gesture is made in the direction of Monsieur Martin, this time the inclusion of his 'Magic Ball' toy (see page 135). Competition in the doll field has become more marked. The position of Jumeau/SFBJ (the Société Française de Fabrication de Bébés et Jouets, founded to band together the French doll makers in an effort to maintain French supremacy in the field) is being challenged by Halbig of Germany, renowned for their character dolls; a good Halbig doll sold for a third less than a good Jumeau. 1906 also saw the introduction of baby dolls – the *bébés*.

Fascinating as these changes are, by far the most remarkable shift is to be seen not in the choice of manufacturers but in the choice of subjects selected for depiction in toy form in the later catalogue. When one compares the two catalogues it becomes very obvious that the period between their respective publication dates represented a turning point in marketing philosophy on the part of both the manufacturers and the powerful wholesaler/retailer. By 1906 almost all the toys appear to be designed specifically for the English market. One wonders indeed just how instrumental the strategy-conscious Mr Gamage was in causing this new direction of catering to individual national markets.

In the 1902 catalogue a large number of toys, particularly the locomotives and their accessories, bought up from the major German manufacturers, were obviously stock lines from the factory catalogues; almost all

tombé sur plusieurs de ses fournisseurs de 1902: disparus sont les jouets américains en fer forgé, les soldats de plomb de Heyde qui faisaient concurrence à William Britain, et les locomotives à vapeur de la firme britannique Stevens Model Dockyard. A nouveau, Monsieur Martin n'a le droit qu'à un geste des plus symboliques, cette fois avec la présence de sa 'Boule Mystérieuse' (voir page 135). La compétition dans le domaine de la poupée est devenue plus intense: Jumeau/SFBJ (Société française de Fabrication de Bébés et Jouets fondée afin de rassembler les divers fabricants français pour maintenir leur suprématie sur le marché) se trouvent fortement concurrencés, voire défiés, par Halbig, une firme allemande, renommée pour ses poupées de genre; une bonne poupée Halbig se vendait le tiers d'une Jumeau. C'est en 1906 aussi que furent introduits les Bébés.

Quelques fascinants que soient ces changements, l'évolution la plus remarquable ne se situe pas tant dans le choix des fabricants que dans le choix des sujets sélectionnés pour devenir des jouets. Lorsque l'on compare les deux catalogues il devient vite évident que la période qui se situe entre leurs dates respectives de publication marqua un tournant dans la philosophie des fabricants et des marchands. En 1906 presque tous les jouets semblent être fabriqués spécialement pour le marché anglais. Et l'on peut se demander quelle influence eut Mr Gamage sur ce changement d'orientation.

Dans le catalogue de 1902 un grand nombre de jouets achetés chez les fabricants allemands,

gute Halbig-Puppe war ein Drittel billiger als eine gute von Jumeau. Auch Baby-Puppen kamen 1906 auf (zum besseren Verständnis: 1905 hatte 1 Schilling den Gegenwert von DM 1,03).

So faszinierend diese Veränderungen auch sein mögen, am meisten springt nicht die neue Auswahl der Hersteller ins Auge, sondern die in diesem späteren Katalog abgebildeten Spielzeugthemen. Vergleicht man diese beiden Kataloge, so wird einem klar, daß zwischen den beiden Erscheinungsjahren nicht nur bei den Herstellern, sondern auch bei den bedeutenden Groß- und Einzelhändlern ein Umdenken erfolgte. Fast alles im Jahre 1906 angebotene Spielzeug war speziell für den englischen Markt. Man fragt sich dabei, welche Rolle wohl der Taktiker Gamage bei dieser Entwicklung gespielt hat.

Im Katalog von 1902 handelt es sich bei dem meisten Spielzeug, insbesondere bei den Lokomotiven und Zubehörteilen der großen deutschen Firmen, ganz offensichtlich um gewöhnliche Serienartikel aus den Werkskatalogen. Fast alle Züge haben deutsche Formgebung und tragen kaum Aufschriften. Die Bahnhöfe und Zubehörteile gleichen den Vorbildern auf dem europäischen Kontinent, und die Schilder wie ,,Ausgang'', ,,Eingang'' usw. sind in deutscher Sprache. Es gibt einige markante Ausnahmen: ein entzückender englischer Bahnhof von Bing (Seite 43), beschrieben als ,,exakte Nachahmung mit ... Reklamen in korrekten Farben, Schildern, Sitzen und Lampen ...'' und eine kleine

Gamage's catalogues reflect the importance of French doll makers. Shown here are a Jumeau (No. 11), an SFBJ (No.11) and a *Bébé Mascotte* (M.10) – dolls of the kind sold at Gamage's in the 1900s.

Les catalogues de Gamage se font l'écho de l'importance des fabricants français de poupées. Ici une Jumeau (No. 11), une SFBJ (No.11) et un 'Bébé Mascotte' (M.10).

Die Gamage's-Kataloge beweisen die Bedeutung französischer Puppen. Beispiele der um 1900 bei Gamage's verkauften Puppen sind eine Jumeau (Nr. 11), eine SFBJ (Nr.11) und eine *Bébé Mascotte* (M.10).

Märklin's innovative approach is shown here in toys for sale in England: a rare 'Armoured Train' based on a Boer War original, an 'Electric Tramway' and a 'Central London Railway Engine'. (Pages 23 and 32.)

On perçoit ici l'approche innovatrice de Märklin dans ses jouets pour le marché anglais: un rare train blindé (convoi des Boers), un tramway électrique et une Central London Railway Engine (pages 23 et 32).

Märklins Gespür für Neuerungen zeigen diese Spielzeuge für den Verkauf in England: ein Panzerzug, eine elektrische Straßenbahn und eine Lok der Central London Railway (s. Seiten 23 und 32).

the trains are German in outline and few bear livery of any sort. Accessories and stations again are continental in design and feature signs for exits, entrances and so on in German. A few exceptions stand out: a delightful English station made by Bing (page 43) and described as an 'exact representation with... advertisements finely painted in correct colours, sign boards, seat and lamp...', and a small collection of locomotives bearing the English railway liveries or made in American outline with ubiquitous cow-catcher.

Turn then to the equivalent pages of the 1906 catalogue to witness an almost complete transformation in depiction and styling: gone are the ranks of locomotives, carriages, accessories, stations and even automobiles of German inspiration; in their place is displayed an overwhelming variety of authentically characterized toys of immediate appeal to the English child. Here are the liveries of the companies that made up the network of the Victorian and Edwardian British railway service: GWR, LNWR, LSWR, GNR, GER, NER and the Midland Railway; here too is a grand range of English country stations, one (on page 105) for the Great Northern Railway by Märklin even used as a further advertisement for Gamage's, since all but two of the enamel signs displayed on it promote the store's other departments! The functions of the different carriages are now proclaimed in English, and there is even a Märklin model of Stephenson's 'Rocket Steam Train' (page 89), as well as Schoenner's 'GWR Express Loco-

et plus particulièrement les chemins de fer, viennent évidemment tout droit de stocks; presque tous les trains ont une ligne germanique et peu portent les armes des compagnies ferroviaires. Gares et accessoires aussi ont un air continental et les panneaux de sortie, entrée, etc., sont en allemand. Il y a cependant quelques exceptions: ainsi une délicieuse gare britannique fabriquée par Bing (voir page 43) est décrite comme étant "une repésentation fidèle...avec les publicités peintes aux couleurs exactes, les sièges et les lampes..."; de même une petite collection de locomotives porte les armes de compagnies ferroviaires anglaises, et d'autres celles de lignes américaines avec le singulier chasse-boeufs.

Tournons maintenant les pages du catalogue de 1906 et nous assistons à une transformation de style et de dessin presque complète: les locomotives, wagons, accessoires, gares et automobiles d'inspiration germanique ont disparus. A leur place, nous trouvons une variété écrasante de jouets fidèlement reproduits et d'un attrait immédiat pour l'enfant anglais: ici les armes des compagnies qui constituaient le réseau ferroviaire britannique au temps de la reine Victoria et d'Edouard VII: GRW, LNWR, LSWR, GNR, GER, NER et le Midland Railway; là, un grand nombre de gares de campagne typiquement anglaises. L'une (page 105) conçue par Märklin pour le chemin de fer 'Great Northern Railway' faisait même de la publicité pour Gamage (tout les panneaux, à deux exceptions, vantant les mérites des autres rayons du

Lokomotiven-Auswahl mit Beschriftungen der englischen Eisenbahn-Gesellschaften oder – nach amerikanischem Vorbild – mit Kuhfänger.

Die gleichen Katalog-Seiten von 1906 dagegen weisen große Veränderungen auf. Die Nachahmungen von deutschen Lokomotiven, Wagen, Zubehör, Bahnhöfen und sogar Autos sind verschwunden Dafür findet man eine überwältigende Vielfalt von Spielzeug mit englischen Beschriftungen, die speziell das englische Kind ansprechen sollten. Die Züge sind nach dem Vorbild englischer Eisenbahn-Gesellschaften beschriftet, die Bahnhöfe sind Nachbildungen wirklicher englischer Vorbilder, und die verschiedenen Wagen sind ihrer Funktion entsprechend englisch beschriftet. Märklin baute sogar die „Rocket" Dampflokomotive von Stephenson (Seite 89) und einen GWR „Expresszug" mit einer „La France" Lokomotive (Seite 95) nach, ebenso Günthermann das neue Gordon Bennett Rennauto (Seite 140); Spielzeug, das man heute nur noch selten findet. Damit war die Umstellung auf den Export vollzogen.

1906 findet man schon Spielzeug mit Gamages-Warenzeichen. Es war Gamage nicht nur gelungen, seine Lieferanten zu überreden, sich auf seinen Markt umzustellen, sondern er hatte auch bei einigen langjährigen Lieferanten erreicht, daß sie für ihn billige Artikel herstellten, die er unter seinem eigenen Namen verkaufte. Dabei sind verschiedene Blechspielzeuge sowie eine Reihe von Puppen, die wahrscheinlich von Jumeau stammen. Hierbei war

motive' with its rare 'La France' engine, the original of which was bought by GWR in order for them to study French locomotive design (see page 95). And we should not forget the Gordon Bennett racing car by Günthermann on page 140. Thus was completed the transition from stock lines to export ranges.

Notable also in 1906 is the appearance of toys bearing a Gamage's trademark. As well as directing the attention of the manufacturers towards his national market, Mr Gamage had also persuaded some of his long-term suppliers to make up cheaper lines of toys to be sold under Gamage's own label. Several of the tin toy makers were prevailed upon, and there is evidence that Jumeau too was persuaded to produce a series of cheaper dolls for exclusive sale at Gamage's. This was presumably rather a *coup*, since Jumeau usually insisted that their identity be advertised in every way.

This question of makers' identity comes to the fore in the pages of both the catalogues shown here. The illustrations of some toys, notably those of Ernst Plank (EP), prominently display the manufacturer's trademark. Occasionally the trademark of Bing (GBN) is to be seen, and more frequently that of Günthermann (ASGW), especially in the 1906 catalogue. (By this date Gamage's had a special arrangement with Günthermann for the supply of novelties and were probably their distributor in Britain; Günthermann toys predominate in the pages of clockwork clowns, jumping rabbits, conjurors and so on.) Some manufacturers, on the other hand, did not

magasin!). Les divers types de wagon sont aussi conçus dans le style anglais. De même on trouve la 'fusée' ('Rocket Steam Train') de Stephenson (page 89), la 'Locomotive Expresse GWR' de Schoenner avec son moteur, 'La France' que GWR avait acheté afin d'étudier les locomotives françaises. Et nous ne devons pas oublier l'arrivée de la voiture de course ('Gordon Bennett racing car') fabriquée par Günthermann (en page 140).

A noter aussi cette année là l'apparition de jouets portant la marque de Mr Gamage. Tout en dirigeant l'attention des fabricants sur les besoins de son marché, Mr Gamage avait persuadé certains de ses fournisseurs de longue date de lui fournir des séries de jouets qu'il vendrait moins chers sous sa propre marque. Plusieurs fabricants de jouets en fer-blanc furent contactés, et il semble bien aussi que Jumeau fut amené à produire une série de poupées destinées à être vendues exclusivement chez Gamage. De la part de Mr Gamage, ceci fut un coup de maître car Jumeau insistait d'habitude pour que sa marque obtienne le plus de publicité possible.

Cette question de l'identité des fabricants est soulevée dans les pages des deux catalogues reproduits ici. Les illustrations de certains jouets, notamment ceux d'Ernst Plank, affichent avec ostentation la marque du fabricant. On voit à l'occasion la marque de Bing (GBN) et plus fréquemment celle de Günthermann (ASGW) surtout dans le catalogue de 1906. (Soulignons qu'à cette date Gamage avait des arrangements spéciaux avec

ihm ein Kunststück gelungen, denn Jumeau bestand gewöhnlich darauf, seine Produkte nur unter seinem eigenen Warenzeichen zu verkaufen.

Zum Schluß noch einige Einzelheiten zu den Herstellern, deren Erzeugnisse auf den Katalogseiten abgebildet sind: Bei verschiedenen Spielzeugabbildungen, insbesondere von Ernst Plank (EP), ist deutlich die Marke zu erkennen, manchmal auch die von Bing (GBN) and häufiger von Günthermann (ASGW), vor allem im Katalog von 1906. Um diese Zeit bestand bereits ein Sonderabkommen mit Günthermann über die Lieferung von mechanischem Spielzeug, und Gamage hatte wahrscheinlich den Vertrieb für Großbritannien übernommen. Günthermann Erzeugnisse findet man hauptsächlich auf den Seiten mit Uhrwerkspielzeug, wie Clowns, springenden Hasen, Zauberern usw. Es gab aber auch Hersteller, die keinen Wert auf eine Kennzeichnung ihrer Erzeugnisse mit ihren Markenzeichen legten, erst recht nicht bei den einzelnen Spielzeugabbildungen. Dies betrifft z.B. Märklin. Da es sich aber kaum gelohnt hätte, jeden Artikel einzeln nachzuzeichnen, verwandte Gamage auch Abbildungen mit Markenzeichen aus den Lieferanten-Katalogen, so daß kein Rückschluß auf die Einstellung des Herstellers hierzu gegeben ist. Für den heutigen Sammler ist es von großem Interesse und sehr wertvoll, wenn er aus diesen Warenzeichen den Hersteller erkennen kann.

Niemand wird mehr nach Kenntnis dieser Kataloge und der Geschäftstüchtigkeit von

A typical Märklin station of German outline on sale in 1902. In Gamage's catalogue (page 42) signs are in German; here the French version is seen. By 1906 stations at Gamage's were mostly of the English type.

Gare Märklin d'inspiration allemande en vente en 1902. Dans le catalogue (page 42) les inscriptions sont en allemand; ici c'est la version française qui est présentée. En 1906 les gares sont surtout anglaises.

Ein 1902 verkaufter typischer Märklin-Bahnhof nach deutschem Vorbild. Im Gamage's-Katalog (Seite 42) sind die Beschriftungen deutsch. Hier wird die französische Variante gezeigt.

bother to trademark their products, let alone each individual illustration in their factory catalogues; this was the case with Märklin. If Gamage's compiled their own catalogues from reproductions from the makers' catalogues, in some of which every illustration bore the company logo, (and this seems highly likely, since it was hardly worth their while to redraw each object), then the inclusion of these trademarks in Gamage's pages does not truly reflect the makers' attitudes on this point. Whatever the whys and wherefores, the inclusion of a trademark is of interest and value to the present day collector.

From what we have seen of Mr Gamage's business acumen, a strong claim can be made for him to be held the ultimate retailer in the toy field. He was doubtless of this opinion himself! Certainly his catalogues abound with grandiose descriptions of his supremacy: 'the largest assortment in the world of working railway accessories...', 'the largest collection of toy soldiers ... in Great Britain', 'largest collection in the world – all the latest novelties', 'Gamage's doll department – the best and largest assortment in London' he boasts in 1902. By 1906 customers are exhorted to see 'the grandest bazaar ever seen', 'the whole toy collection from the Austrian Exhibition', 'absolutely the largest exhibition of toys and games in the world' and 'our doll department' which 'will be found to be the most complete in Europe'.

Strong words indeed, but comparison with the catalogues of rival stores issued at much

Günthermann pour l'approvisionnement de nouveautés, qu'il était probablement son distributeur en Grande Bretagne et que les jouets Günthermann dominent dans les pages de clowns mécaniques, lapins sauteurs, magiciens, etc.) D'autres fabricants par contre ne se souciaient guère de signer leurs produits, et encore moins les illustrations de leurs catalogues. Tel était le cas de Märklin. Comme redessiner chaque article n'en valait pas la peine, il semblerait que Mr Gamage ait composé ses propres catalogues à partir des reproductions des catalogues de fabricants dans lesquels chaque illustration ne portait pas systématiquement la marque. L'apparition de ces marques ne reflète donc pas vraiment l'attitude du fabricant. Quoiqu'il en soit, celles-ci présentent un vif intérèt pour le collectioneur contemporain.

Mr Gamage se considérait comme le roi des détaillants. Avec ce que nous avons vu de son sens des affaires, nous pouvons probablement lui accorder ce titre. Il est certain que ses catalogues abondent en descriptions grandioses et dityrambiques de sa suprématie: "le plus grand assortiment au monde d'accessoires de chemin de fer ...", "la plus grande collection au monde – toutes les dernières nouveautés", "le rayon de poupées de Gamage – le meilleur et le plus grand assortiment à Londres", voilà ce qu'il clame en 1902. En 1906 les clients sont invités à aller voir 'le plus grand bazar jamais vu', 'toute la collection de jouets et jeux de l'exposition autrichienne', 'la plus grande collection de jouets au

Gamage daran zweifeln, daß er der König der Spielzeughändler war. Das war auch seine Ansicht. Seine Kataloge fließen über von überschwenglichen Beschreibungen und Superlativen, wie „das größte Sortiment der Welt an Eisenbahn-Zubehör", „die größte Sammlung der Welt von mechanischem Spielzeug", „die größte Sammlung von Zinnsoldaten ... in Großbritannien" usw. Wenn man diese Beschreibungen jedoch mit den Katalogen der Konkurrenz aus dieser Zeit vergleicht, muß man zugeben, daß es sich hierbei nicht um leere Phrasen handelte. Im Gegenteil, das Angebot der anderen konnte nicht mit dem verglichen werden, was Gamage zu bieten hate. Selbst Harrods, der größte Verfechter von Qualität, konnte sich nicht mit ihm messen; auch nicht zu Weihnachten, wenn der Spielzeugverkauf seinen Höhepunkt erreichte und Gamages seine alljährliche großartige Spielzeugausstellung, den sog. „Christmas Bazaar" veranstaltete.

Was wir über Einkauf, Ausstellung und Verkauf des wenigen, hier erwähnten Spielzeugs gesagt haben, gilt natürlich auch für die Vielzahl der anderen Freuden, die in Gamages Spielzeug-Abteilungen und Katalogen vor dem Ersten Weltkrieg zu finden waren: Puppenhäuser, Kaufmannsläden, Pferdeställe, Schaukelpferde, Spielzeugwagen, Wasserspielzeug, Pistolen, Puppenzubehör, Puppenherde (z.B. von Märklin, dessen Fabrik mit der Produktion von Küchenartikeln anfing), Magnetspielzeug, Kreisel, Archen Noah, optisches Spielzeug, Spardosen, Kasperletheater usw.

Among the stranger toys offered by Gamage's was Bing's 'Model Thrashing Machine'. Made to be driven by a steam engine, it was apparently equipped with a moving sieve and a corn elevator. (See page 48.)

La 'batteuse sur roues' de Bing était parmi les jouets les plus étranges vendus chez Gamage. Elle marchait à la vapeur et était apparemment équipée d'un tamis mobile et d'un élévateur à grains (voir page 48).

Unter den ausgefalleneren Spielzeugen bot Gamage's diese Dreschmaschine von Bing an. Sie war für den Dampfbetrieb vorgesehen und besaß ein bewegliches Sieb und einen Getreideheber (Seite 48).

Two of Gamage's impressive seasonal displays, both of which were for Christmas 1911. On the left, a superb range of soft toys from Steiff; on the right, dolls of the Jumeau type dressed in coronation robes.

Deux des étalages saisonniers de Gamage, tous deux pour Noël 1911. A gauche une remarquable gamme de jouets en peluche de chez Steiff, à droite des poupées Jumeau en robe de couronnement.

Zwei der eindrucksvollen Saisonauslagen von Gamage's zu Weihnachten 1911. Links eine prächtige Auslage von Steiff-Spielzeugen, rechts Puppen nach Art Jumeaus in Krönungsroben.

the same date does prove conclusively that these claims were not, as might be supposed, indulgent copywriters' fantasies. Far from it: the meagre pages of the rivals' offerings are sparse indeed. Even Harrod's, that great purveyor of quality, could not live up to Gamage's standards. Nor could they manage the scale of the superb special set-piece displays Gamage's promoted annually at Christmas, the most important time of year for toy sales.

Needless to say, Mr Gamage's high standards were applied not only to the purchase, display and sale of the ranges of toys and the few individual items we have had space to mention here. They were, of course, equally applicable to the other myriad delights to be found in Gamage's toy department and catalogues before the First World War: dolls' houses, model shops and stables, rocking horses, toy wagons, water toys, guns, dolls' accessories, miniature stoves (including those produced by Märklin, the line with which the firm entered the toy field), magnetic toys, tops, Noah's arks, optical toys, money banks, theatres and Punch and Judy shows, among many others. Endless pleasure will be found by all in the exploration of the fascinating pages of these catalogues, a fitting tribute to the memory of Arthur Walter Gamage, whose enthusiasm and energy caused a revolution in the toy world at its peak.

monde' et 'notre rayon poupées' qui 'on le verra est le plus complet d'Europe'.

Fortes paroles en vérité. Mais une comparaison avec les catalogues des magasins concurrents produits aux alentours de la même époque montre qu'en fait les prétentions de Mr Gamage étaient plus que de simples rodomontades. Même Harrods, ce grand fournisseur de produits de qualité, ne pouvait atteindre les critères établis par Mr Gamage. Ils ne pouvaient pas non plus rivaliser avec les incroyables étalages que Mr Gamage faisait installer chaque année à Noël, l'époque la plus importante pour la vente des jouets.

Nul besoin de dire que les hautes exigences de Mr Gamage n'étaient pas limitées aux quelques jouets mentionnés dans ces pages. Elles étaient bien sûr appliquées à la myriade de délices vendus dans le magasin avant la première guerre mondiale: maisons de poupée, boutiques, chevaux à bascule, charettes, carabines, accessoires pour poupées, fours miniatures (y compris ceux produits par Märklin, articles avec lesquels la firme pénétra sur le marché de jouet), jeux magnétiques et optiques, établis, arches de Noé, tire-lires, théâtres et marionnettes parmi beaucoup d'autres. Des plaisirs sans fin sont à découvrir dans l'exploration des pages fascinantes de ces catalogues qui demeurent un vibrant hommage à la mémoire d'Arthur Walter Gamage, dont l'enthousiasme et l'énergie causèrent une révolution dans le monde du jouet.

Beim Betrachten dieser faszinierenden Katalogseiten werden alle Spielzeugliebhaber sicher großes Vergnügen empfinden und den Namen Arthur Walter Gamage, der mit seiner Begeisterung, Energie und Tatkraft die Spielzeugwelt revolutionierte, auch unter den deutschen Sammlern zu einem Begriff machen.

—1902—
CATALOGUE

THE NOVELTIES ON VIEW AT GAMAGE'S 'XMAS BAZAAR WILL BE More Attractive!

THAN IN ANY OF THEIR PREVIOUS EXHIBITIONS.

MINIATURE RAILWAYS in all gauges, Mountain, Suspension and Overhead Railways, &c., will be kept continually in motion on a **MOST ELABORATE SCALE,** never before attempted, the groundwork being most **Realistic,** with Stations, Signals, Tunnels, Bridges, arranged to deceive the most critical eye. Bridges will span a lake on which Sailing, Clockwork and Steam Boats will be working, in

GAMAGE'S NEW BUILDING, over 300 ft. in length.

The whole will be lighted by Electric Light in miniature.

NO CHARGE FOR ADMISSION.

Don't fail to come yourself and bring your Children. ☞ **Open early in December.**

RAILWAYS.

A. W. Gamage, Ltd., have *considerably increased* their collection of **CLOCKWORK, STEAM TRAINS** and complete **RAILWAY SYSTEMS.** The **largest assortment in the World** of **Working Railway Accessories, lines** in all **gauges,** Switches, Junctions, Signals, Locomotives, Carriages and Pullman Cars as used on the L. & N.W.R., G.E.R., G.W.R., and M. Railway Systems, Stations, Tunnels, Bridges, Platform Barrows, Ticket Boxes, Punches, &c., &c., will be found **THE MOST COMPLETE** and **VARIED** in Great Britain.

Gamage's . . . Electric Mountain . . Railway complete.

THE NOVELTY OF THE SEASON!

TO BE SEEN IN MOTION AT GAMAGE'S BAZAAR.

No. 0 Gauge Electric Railway and Mountain, complete as illustration, including Electric Engine, Switches Insulated Rails, &c.

PRICE–

£9. 9. 0.

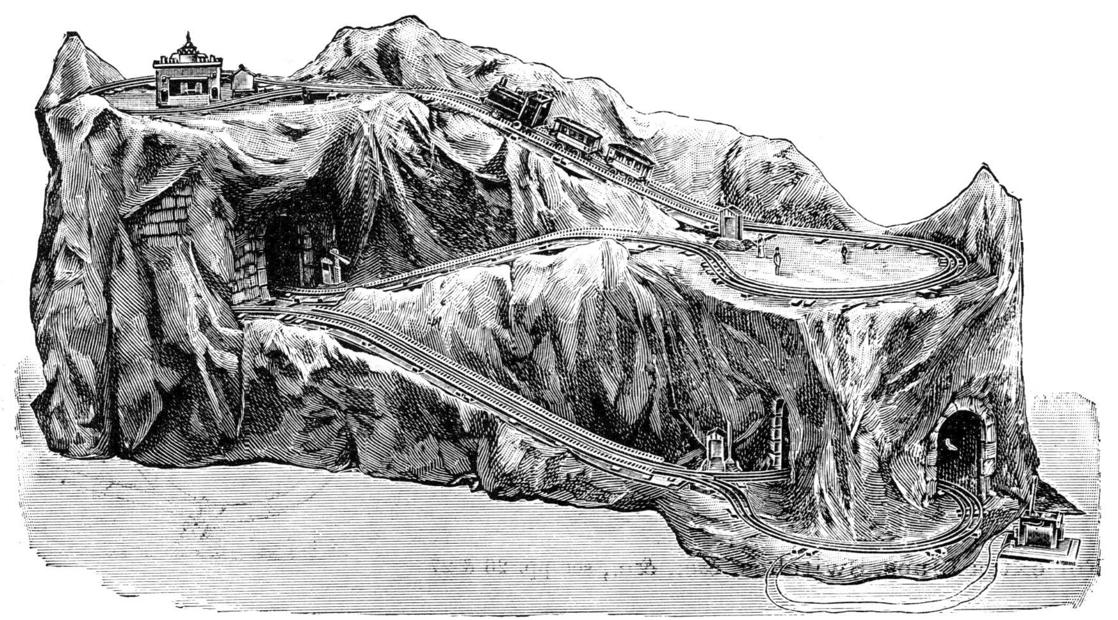

Gamage's Best Quality Clockwork Trains and Sets.

No. O Gauge.

BEAUTIFULLY ENAMELLED.

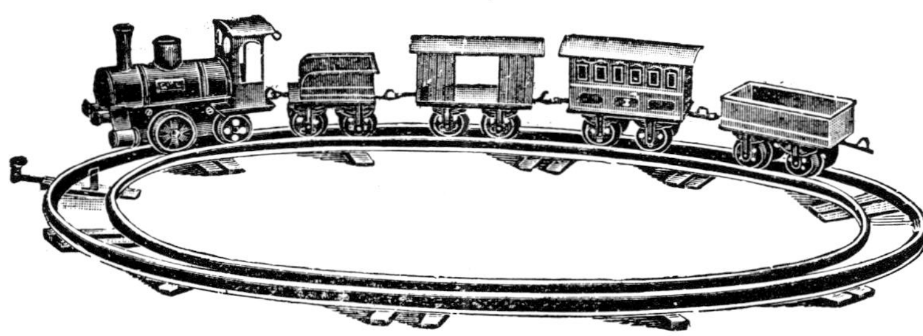

No. 20.

All Trains on this page have Heavy Engines, fitted with best Clockwork Movements. Cannot get out of order.

Clockwork Trains:

No. 20. No. 0 Gauge. Engine, Tender, Luggage Van, Passenger Carriage and Guard's Van, Set of Circular Rails.

Complete in strong box, ... **12/6**

No. 21. As No. 20, Engine fitted with brake, Oval Rails, also to form figure 8, and fitted with pin for putting on brake automatically. Price .. **17/6**

No. 22. Same as No. 20, Rails fitted with 2 Junctions.

Price **22/6**

No. 50. 0 Gauge Set, complete (as illustration) fitted with best quality Engine, Tender, 2 Carriages, &c.

Price **21/-**

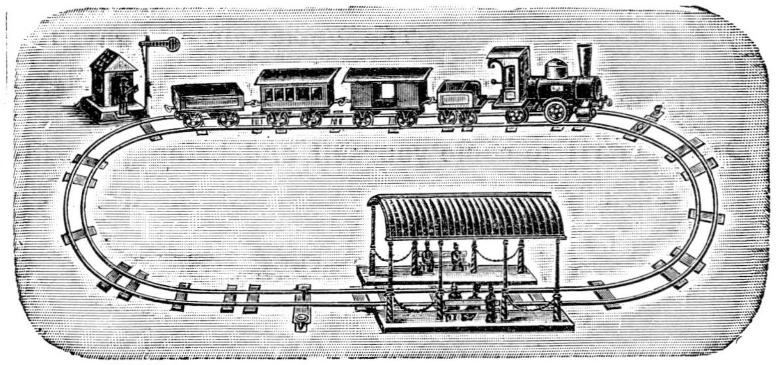

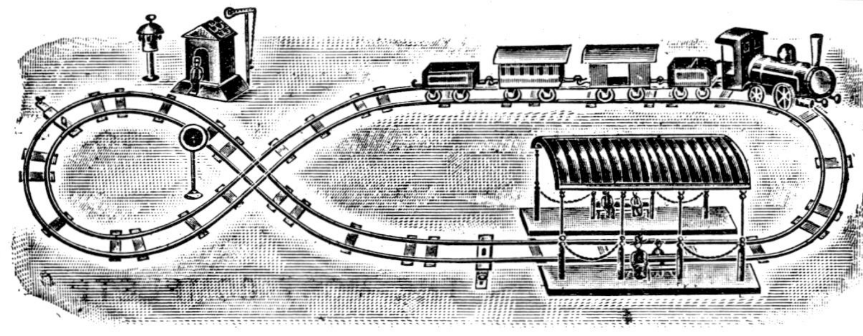

Railway System.

No. 51. No. 0 Gauge (as illustration), Strong Engine, fitted with best Clockwork Movements.

Tender, Carriage, 1 each covered, and open Truck, Station, &c.

Complete in Strong wooden box, **25/6**

No. 71. No. 0 Guage American Train, complete with Rails, Engine, fitted with best Clockwork movements and made to run forwards and backwards.

Price **24/6**

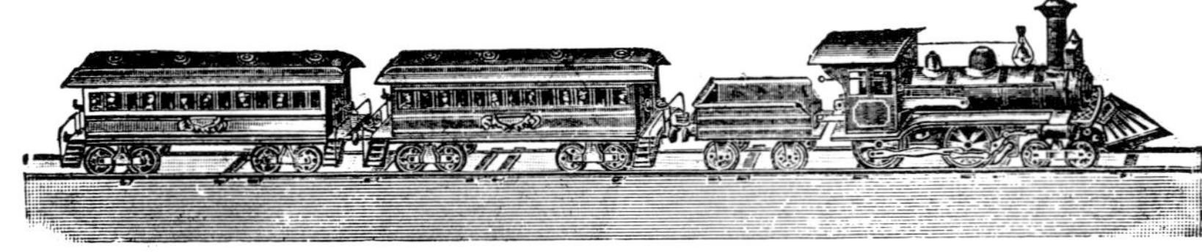

No. 71.

Railway System.

No. 70. No. 0 Gauge (as illustration), a complete system beautifully enamelled and very realistic.

Packed in strong wooden box **55/-**

No. 70.

Gamages Best Quality Clockwork Trains & Sets, *cont.*

No. 1 Gauge.

No. 23

Clockwork Train.

No. 23. Complete (as illustration). Engine with brake packed in strong wooden box. No. 1 Gauge.

Price **25/-**

Clockwork Train

No. 24. No. 1. Gauge No 23. Engine fitted wit brake and fast & slow levers. Extra lines and switches to form circle, oval, figure 8, &c.

Price **33/6**

Clockwork Train.

No. 26. No. 1 Gauge as No. 23. Engine with brake and fast and slow levers, extra lines and switches to form circle, figure 8, oval, oval with 2 switches and various other designs.

Price **45/-**

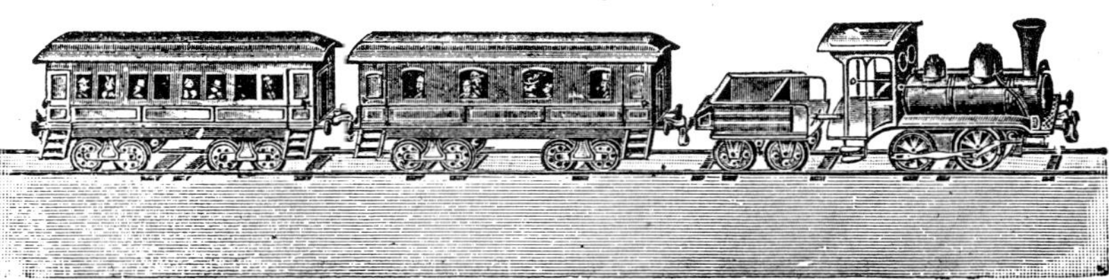

Clockwork Express Train.

No. 55. No. 1. Gauge. (As illustration).

Powerful Engine fitted with brake best clockwork movements, tender, 2 express pullman Cars, oval lines complete in strong wooden box.

Price **57/6**

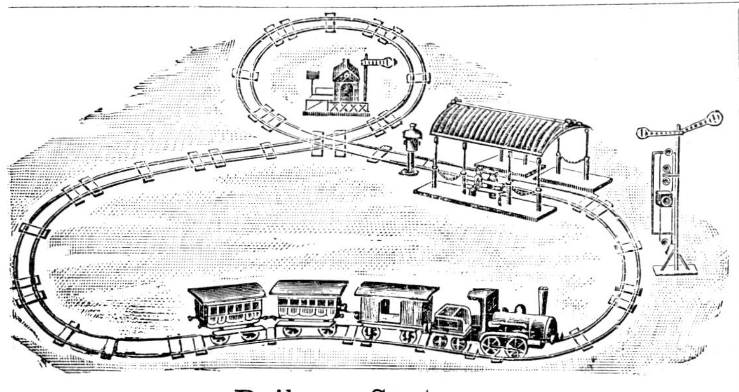

Railway System.

No. 54. No. 1 Gauge.

Powerful Engine with best Clockwork Movements.

Tender, Carriages, Truck, Station, Signals, Crossing, &c.,

In strong wooden box, price **55/-**

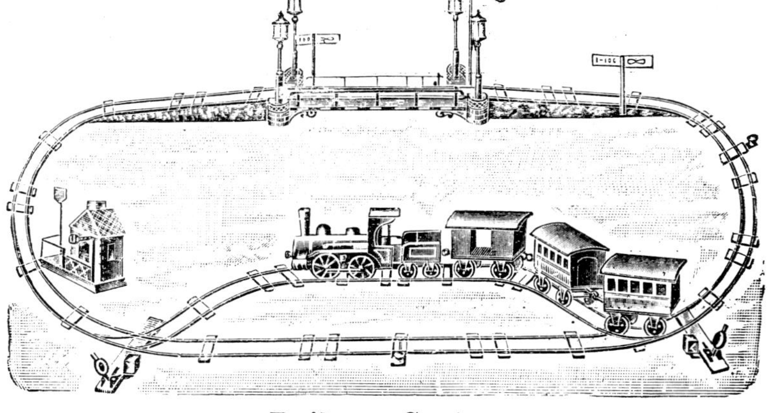

Railway System.

No. 72. No. 1 Gauge. Powerful Engine with best clockwork movements. Train (as illustration), bridge, crossings, signals, &c., complete in strong wooden box, **70/-**

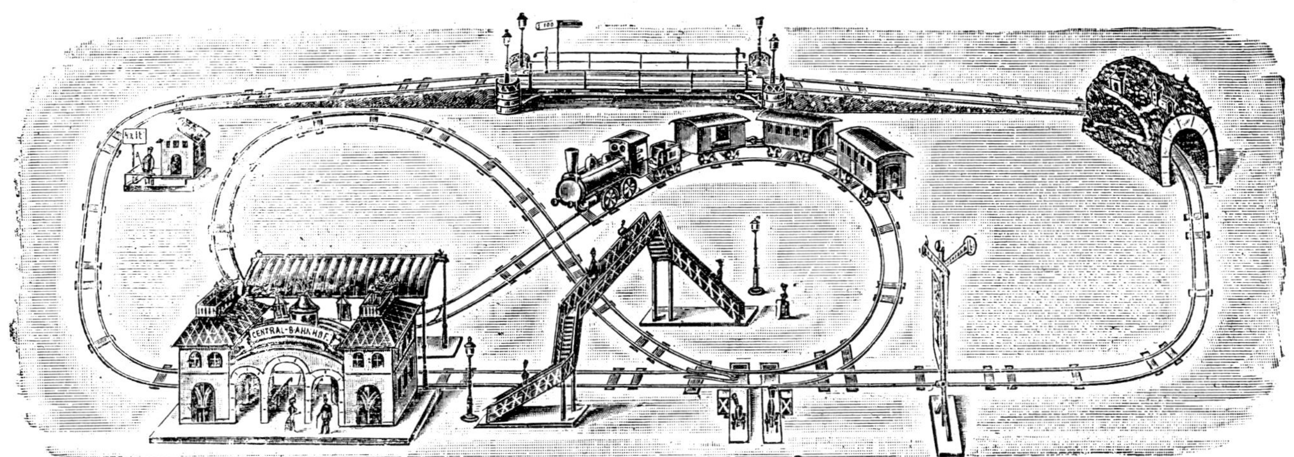

No. 66. **Complete Railway System,** (as illustration) No. 1 Gauge. Powerful Engine fitted with best clockwork movements, tender, 2 carriages, 1 truck, station, railway bridge, foot bridge, tunnel, signals, crossings, &c.

Packed in strong wooden box, price .. .. **£6 10s. 0d.** *Carriage paid.*

Gamage's Best Clockwork Trains and Sets, *continued.*

Nos. 2 & 3 Gauge.

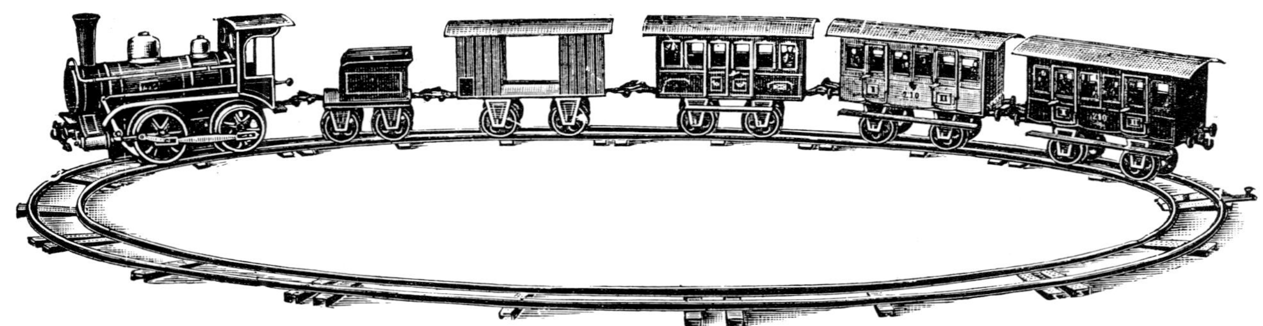

No. 26.

No. 26A. **Clockwork Railway.** No. 2 Gauge, Engine fitted with extra strong Spring, Automatic Brake, Rail and Carriages complete (as illustration) packed in strong wooden box. Price **40/-**

Large Powerful Engines fitted with Best Quality Clockwork Movements.

56. **Clockwork Express Train.** No. 2. Gauge, very Powerful Engine fitted with Best Clockwork Movements, Tender and 3 Corridor Carriages, Oval Lines, &c., complete in strong wooden box. Price **60/-**

No. 58. No. 3 Gauge.

Clockwork Pullman Train.

Complete with Oval Lines, 2 Switches, &c., runs forwards and backwards, fast and slow, and is fitted with Automatic Brake.

Packed in strong wooden box

£5 10 0

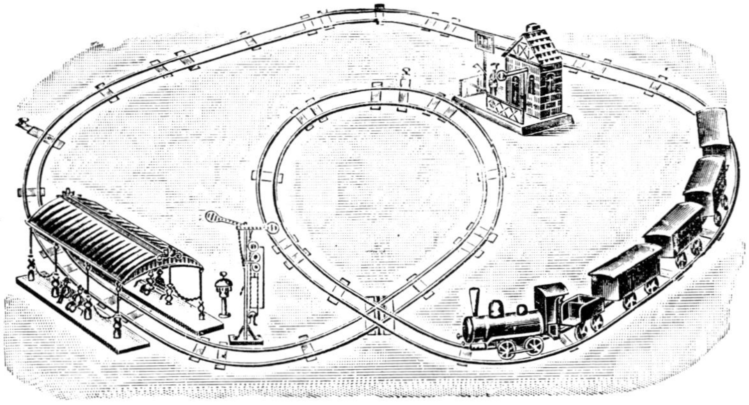

No. 26.

No. 26.

Complete Railway System.

No. 2 Gauge, (as illustration)

Price .. **£4 4 0**

Powerful Engine, fitted with best Clockwork Movements, Tender, Carriages, Trucks, Station, Signals, &c. Packed in strong wooden box.

No. 61.

Clockwork Train.

No. 3 Gauge. Large Powerful Engine fitted with best Clockwork Movements, Fast and Slow, and Tender, 2 Passenger Carriages and 2 Goods Trucks, Oval Lines, complete in strong wooden box. Price **63/-**

Gamage's complete Railway Systems.

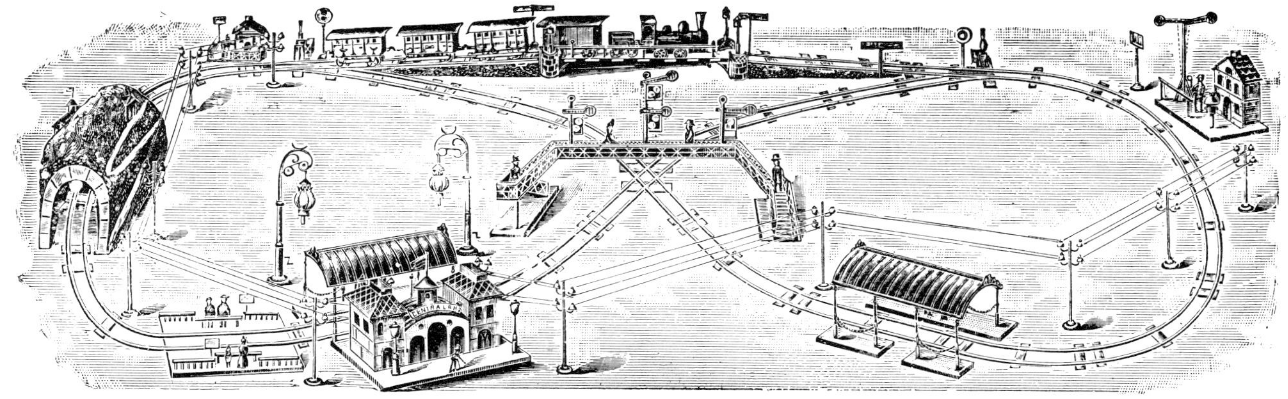

No. 65. **Complete Railway System,** as illustration, No. 2 Gauge, Powerful Engine, fitted with best Clockwork Movements, runs forward and backward, fast and slow, and fitted with Automatic Brake, Tender, 3 Carriages, 1 Truck, Railway Bridge, Signal Bridge, Station, Tunnel, Crossings, &c.

Packed in strong wooden box, price **£10. 10. 0.** Carriage paid.

Clockwork Armoured Trains, A GREAT NOVELTY!!!

GUNS
For Mounting Armoured Trains from 3d. each.
See Pages 55-58

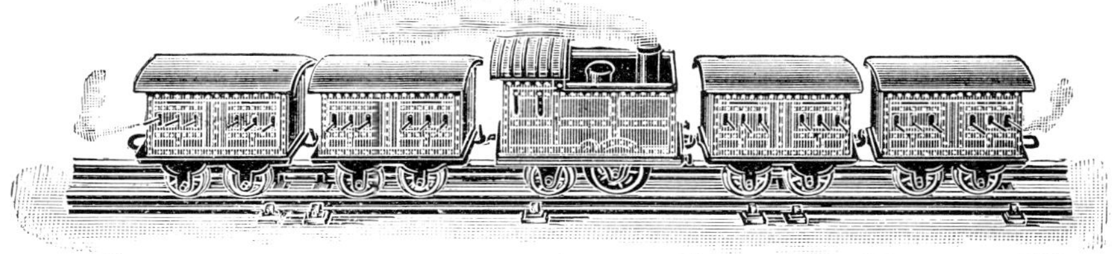

SOLDIERS
For Armoured Trains, From 4½d. Box.
See Pages 51-53.

No A.	Armoured Train complete, Engine, 2 Armoured Carriages, enamelled Khaki, with Circular Rails in Box ..	**3/6**	Postage 4d.
No. B.	Ditto, ditto 3 ditto ditto ditto ditto ditto ..	**4/6**	,, 4d.
No. C.	Ditto, ditto 4 ditto ditto ditto with Oval and Cross Pieces Rails in Box	**6/6**	,, 6d.

Armoured Trains with Cannon Wagons.

Armoured Trains with Heavy Engines fitted. Best Quality. Clockwork Movements.

CANNON WAGON.

No. D. No. 0 Gauge, Clockwork Armoured Train as illustration. Engine and 2 Gun Wagons, fitted with Guns and made to fire automatically when Train is in motion. Complete with Rails in Strong Wooden Box .. .. .. Price **35/-**

No. E. No. 1 Gauge, Clockwork Armoured Train. Engine fitted with strong spring reversing lever, full and half-speed Brakes, Tender with Coal, 2 Gun Wagons fitted with 3 Guns which fire automatically when Train is in motion. Complete with Oval Rails .. .. Price **55/-**

No. F. No. 1 Gauge, Clockwork Armoured Train, ditto, larger size .. .. ,, **63/-**

Cannon Wagons.

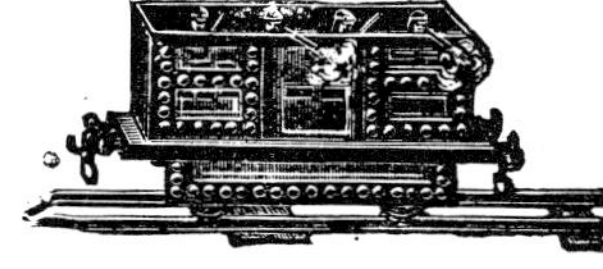

Fitted with Guns which fire Rubber Pellets and make a loud report when in motion.

No. 0 Gauge, with Guns ..	Price **6/6**	Postage 6d.
No. 1 ,, ,, ,, ..	,, **10/6**	,, 6d.
No. 2 ,, ,, ,, ..	,, **12/6**	,, 8d.

AMORCES (or Paper Caps) for Cannon Wagons.
Price .. **3**d. per dozen boxes.

Central London Railway Sets. (2d. TUBE).

No. 2420 Clockwork Motor, fitted with reversing gear, and automatic brake, fast and slow speed, complete with corridor carriages and passengers, oval lines with 2 brake levers.

No. 0 gauge, **27/6** No. 1 gauge, **42/-**
No. 2 gauge .. **60/-**

Gamage's Popular Clockwork Trains and Sets.

No. O Gauge.

No. 9.

No. 8A. Clockwork Train with 2 Carriages, Circular rails, &c. Packed in box.

Price .. **2/6** Postage 3d.

No. 9. Clockwork Train (as illustration), Oval Rails. Packed in box.

Price .. **3/6** Postage 4d.

No. 10. Clockwork Train, complete with 10 Curved Rails, Crossing, 2 Carriages, Engine & Tender.

Price .. **4/11** Postage 4d.

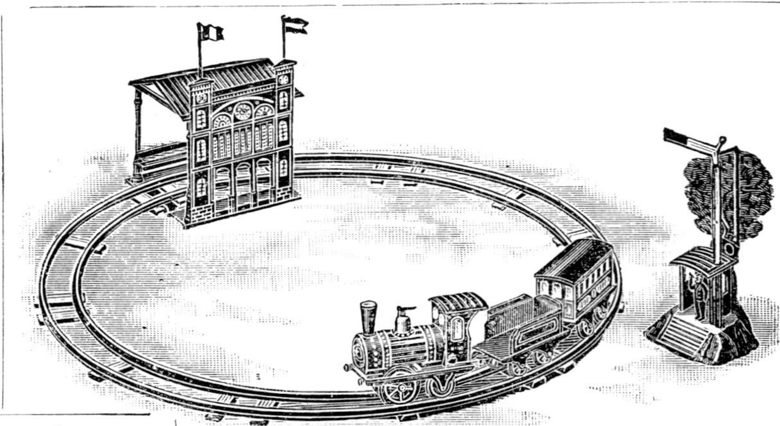

No. 12.

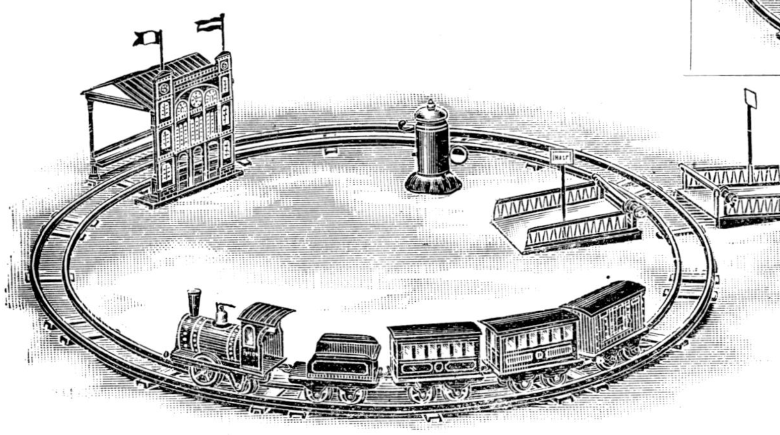

No. 18.

Clockwork Railway.

No. 12. Engine, Tender, Carriage, Circular Rails, Station and Signal Box. Complete in box.

Price .. .. **4/6** Postage 6d.

Clockwork Railway.

No. 18. Complete with Crossings, Station, &c. (As illustration) Price, **7/6** Postage 9d.

Engine House.

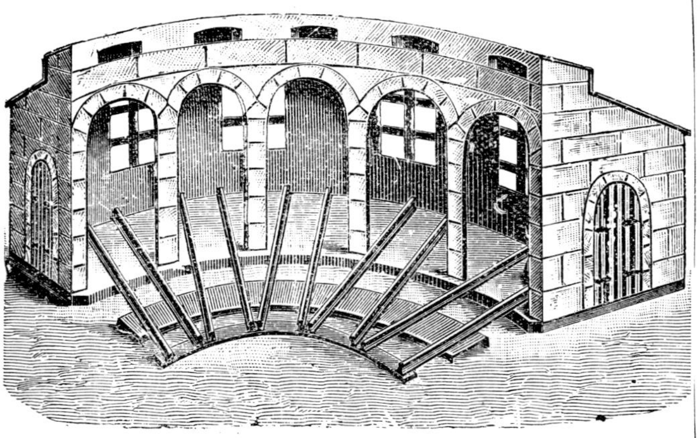

Engine House (as illustration) beautifully enamelled.

No. 0 Gauge, **16/6** No. 1 Gauge, **22/6**

EXTRA RAILS FOR TRAINS ON THIS PAGE.

Rails, Straight or Curved **2½d.** length. Crossings, **9d.** each. Switches, **2/6** pair.

POSTAGE EXTRA

No. 11. Clockwork Train, complete with 22 Rails, Crossing, Engine, Tender, 2 Carriages and Truck. Price, **6/6** Postage 4d.

No. 11.

Gamage's Popular Railway Sets—*continued.*

NO. O GAUGE.

No. 17A

Clockwork Railway System,

consisting of Pullman Train, Station, Tunnel, Lines with Switches, as illustration.

Price .. **18/6**

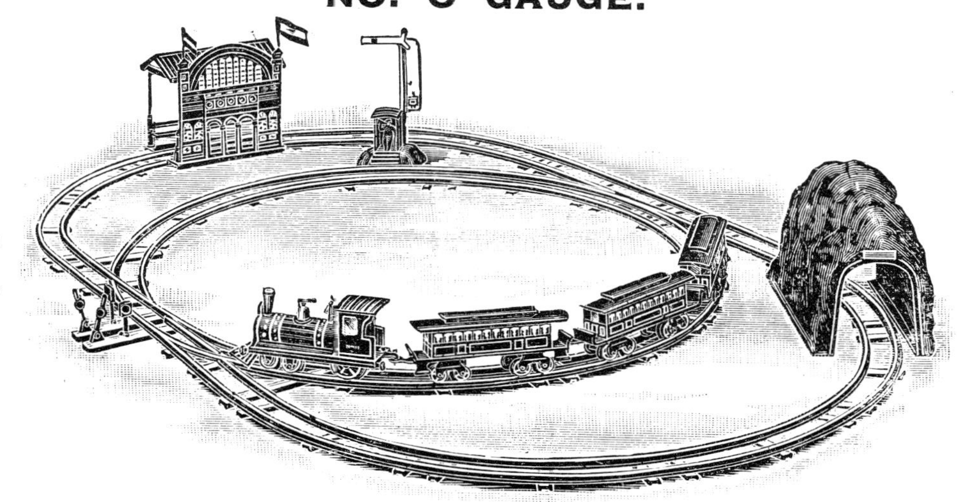

EXTRAS.

Straight or curved lines, **2½d.** a length.

Cross-lines, **9d.** each

Switches, **2/6** a pa

GAMAGE'S No. 15 RAILWAY SET.

Clockwork Railway System, complete with Train, Large Station, Signals, and Rails, in box.

Price .. **11/6**

Bridge .. **2/9** extra.

GAMAGE'S No. 16 SPECIAL RAILWAY SYSTEM.

Clockwork Railway System, consisting of Engine with Tender, **3** Carriages, Station, Covered Platform, Tunnel, Signal Hut, Bell Signal, and Rails, in box.

Price .. **17/6**

EXTRAS.

Straight or curved lines, **2½d.** a length.

Cross-lines, **9d.** each.

Switches, **2/6** a pair.

Postage Extr

Gamage's Tin and Clockwork Trains.

No. 4. Clockwork Train (as illustration), packed in box. Price **10½d.** Postage 3d.

No. 4a Clockwork Train, complete, packed in box. Price **1/6** Postage 3d.

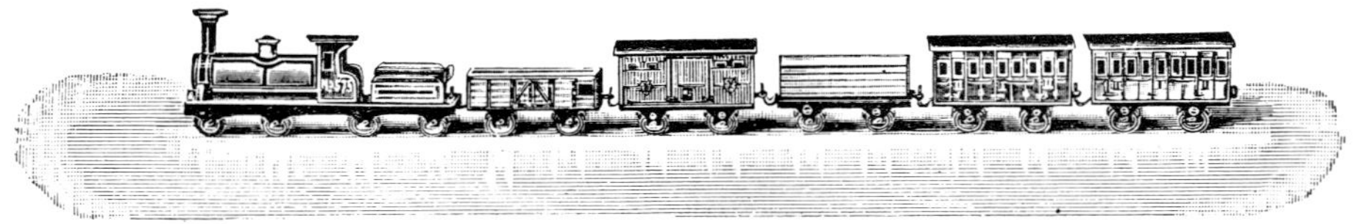

No. 1. Tin Train (as illustration) in enamelled tin; strong, packed in box. Price **10½d.** Postage 3d.

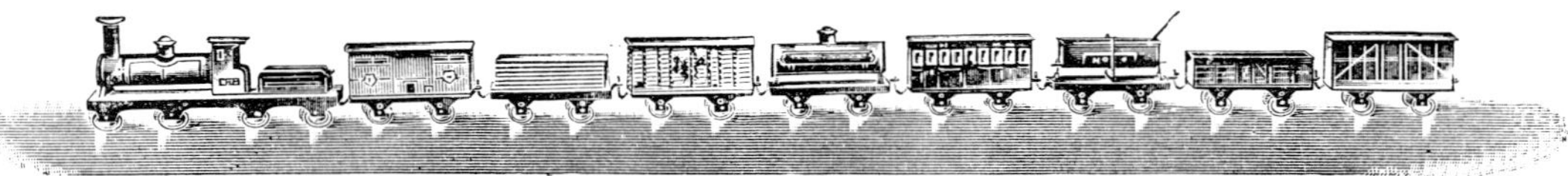

No. 2. Tin Train, (as illustration), enamelled tin, packed in box. Price .. .. **1/4½** Postage 3d.

No. 3. Tin Train, 4 corridor carriages and 1 ordinary carriage; packed in box. Price **1/11** Postage 3d.

No 6.

All Railways are packed in boxes.

Clockwork Railways, complete with Engine, carriage, station and rails.

No. 6 .. .. .. **1/-** each.
,, 7, with 2 carriages .. **1/6** ,,
,, 8, with tunnel and station, as illustration **2/6**

Postage 4d.

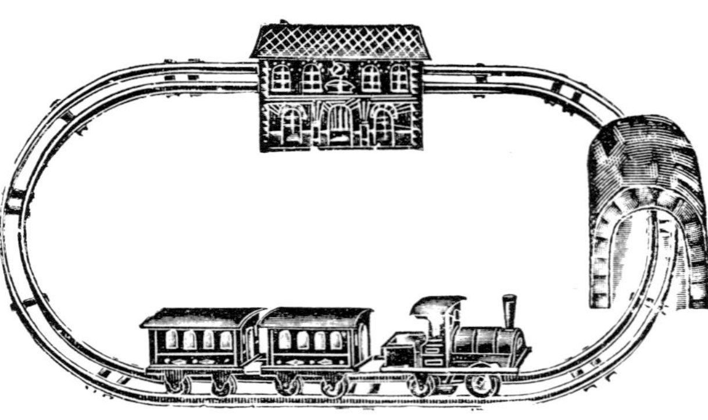

No. 8.

New Elevated Railway.

Consisting of Clockwork Engine, tender, carriage and elevated rails, (as illustration).

Price .. **2/6** Postage 3d.

Gamage's Malleable Iron & Steel Toys, THE ONLY - - UNBREAKABLE TRAIN

No. 13. Passenger Train, Engine and 3 Carriages, length 21 in. 1/- each. Carriage extra.

No. 14. Do., with 4 Carriages, length 26 in. .. .. 1/3 each. Carriage extra.

No. 600. Nickelled with 2 Coaches, length 15½ in. .. 10½d Carriage extra.

No. 78. Passenger Train, Engine and 2 Carriages length 20½ in. .. 1/9 Carriage extra.

No. 77. Passenger Train, Engine & 4 Carriages, length 33 in. .. 2/6 Carriage extra.

Nickelled Passenger Train, 3 Coaches, (as illustration), length 27 in. .. .. 2/6 Carriage extra.

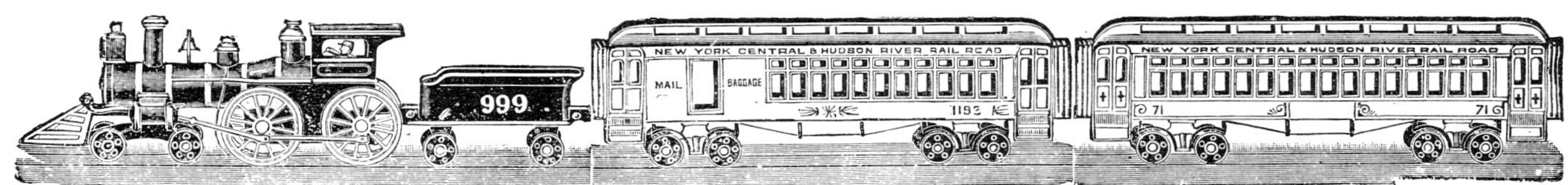

No. 118. Corridor Train, with 2 Coaches, nicely finished in colors, lengh 43 in. .. .. .. 7/11 Carriage extra.
No. 117. Do., with 3 Coaches, length 56½ in. .. .. 9/11 ,,

No. 205. Passenger Train, with 1 Steel Coach, length 14¼ in. .. .. 1/- Carriage extra.
No. 207. ,, 3 Steel Coaches, (as illustration), length 28 in. .. .. 2/3 ,,

No. 209. Passenger Train, with 1 Steel Coach, length 21 in. .. .. 2/3 Carriage extra.
,, 211. ,, 3 ,, Coaches, ,, 40¼ in. .. .. 4/6 ,,
,, 212. ,, 4 ,, ,, ,, 59 in. .. .. 5/11 ,,

Mixed Train with 1 Steel Car and 1 Coach, length 30½ in. .. .. 2/6 Carriage extra.

Gamage's Steam Railway Sets.

All Guages.

No. A.

Steam Railway Set.

No. A. Gauge 0 Steam Loco, with Brass Boiler, Oscillating Brass Cylinder, Steam Whistle and Safety Valve, 2 Carriages, 10 Oval rails, complete in box.

Price **11/6**

Steam Railway Set.

No. B. Gauge 0, Steam Loco with Oxydised Brass Boiler, 2 Oscillating Brass Cylinders, Whistle and Safety Valve, 2 Carriages and 10 Rails to form oval. Complete in box, **14/6**

No. B.

No. C.

Steam Railway Set.

No. 979. Gauge 0, Steam Loco, with Tender, beautifully Japanned Engine, fitted with 2 Oscillating Brass Cylinders Oxydised Brass Boiler, Nickelled Flanged Wheels, Steam Whistle and Safety Valve, 2 Carriages and Luggage Van, and 10 Rails to form oval.

Price **16/6**

No. 964. **Steam Railway Set**. No. 1 Gauge, consisting of Strong Steam Locomotive, with Oxydized Boiler, 2 Oscillating Brass Cylinders, Steam Dome, Whistle, Safety Valve (all Fittings nickelled), Tender, 2 American Passenger Cars, Oval Lines, **35/-**

Steam Railway Set.

Gauge 1. Midland Railway Model Steam Loco, finely Japannd. with Oxydised Brass Boiler, 2 Oscillating Brass Cylinders, Japanned, Flanged Wheels, Brass Dome, &c. Complete in strong wooden box.

Price .. **37/6**

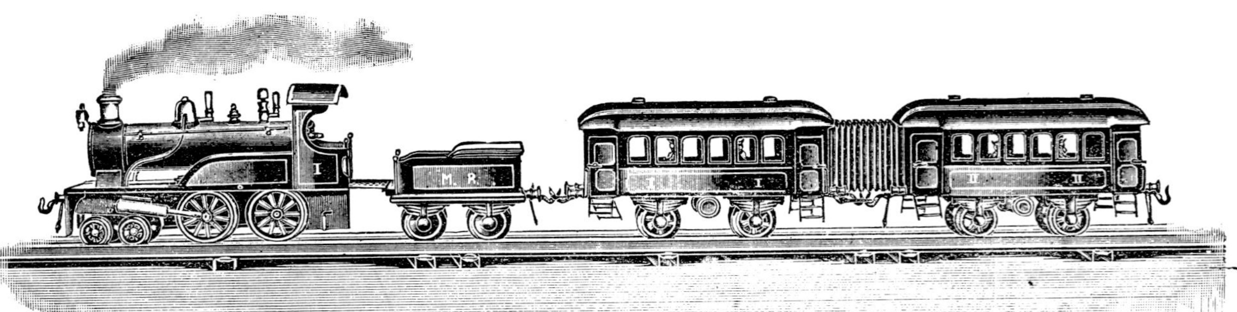
No. 45.

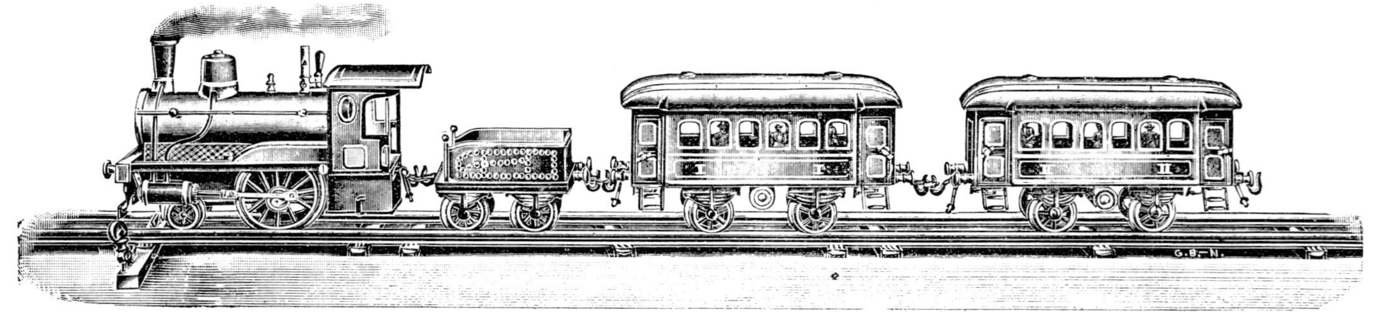

No. D. **Steam Railway Set**. Consisting of beautifully finished Loco, with 2 Double Action Slide Valve Cylinders, also fitted with Reversing Gear, exhausts into funnel giving the appearance of smoke, Tender, 2 Carriages, Rails, &c. Complete in box, **45/-**

GAMAGE'S STEAM LOCOMOTIVES. ALL GAUGES.

No. 39.

Gauge 0. Steam Locomotive, finely Japanned, polished brass boiler, oscillating brass cylinder, brass steam whistle and safety valve.

6-in. long .. .. Price **4/6.** Postage 3d.

No. 69.

Gauge 0. Steam Locomotive, finely Japanned, oxydized brass boiler, 2 oscillating brass cylinders, steam whistle and safety valve.

7-in. long .. .. Price **6/6.** Postage 4d.

No. 73.

Gauge 1. Steam Locomotive, finely Japanned, oxydized brass boiler, 2 oscillating brass cylinders, steam whistle and safety valve. Nickel-plated fittings.

8-in. long .. .. Price **12/6.**

No. 502.

Steam Locomotive with Tender, No. 1 Gauge, Polished Brass Boiler, 2 oxydized brass cylinders, whistle and safety valve.

12-in. long .. .. Price **8/6.** Postage 6d.

No. 504.

Steam Locomotive with Tender, No. 1 Gauge, nickelled brass flanged wheels, oscillating nickelled brass cylinders, oxydized brass boiler, steam whistle and safety valve, and fitted with reversing gear. Price **21/-**

No. 45.

Gauge 1. Midland Railway Steam Locomotive with oxydized brass cylinders, brass dome with starting cock, safety valve, brass hand rails and bell whistle, exhaust steam passing through funnel.

Japanned tender, beautifully finished.

Price **25/-**

No. 42.

Gauge 1. Steam Locomotive and Tender, accurately finished, with automatic reversing gear, 2 double action slide valve cylinders, oxydized brass boiler, steam dome, bell whistle, safety valve.

All fittings well nickelled, with flame guard and exhaust steam passing through funnel.

Price .. .. ..**25/6.**

Gamage's Steam Locomotives.

Model Locomotive.

No. 200. Steam Locomotive, all brass with 2 cylinders, steam tap and whistle.
Price 11/6

Steam Locomotive.

No. 4020. No. 0 Gauge. No brake.

These Locos. have the burner in the cabin, and the flame is, by forced air, spread through the boiler, generating steam quickly and giving great power.

Complete with Tender. Nickel plated parts.

A VERY FINE MODEL.

Price 25/-

Steam Locomotive.

No. 171. With bright brass boiler, brass frame and copperside tender, water and steam taps, bell whistle.

English make. 7 in. long.

Price 6/6

No. 36. Scale model of famous Caledonian Railway Engine "Dunalstair." English made Engine has brass tube boiler, 8 wheels (4 coupled), leading bogie, inside cylinders, whistle and dome, steam and water taps. Tender has 8 wheels on 2 bogies and tank to store spirits for loco. 21 in. long. Price 35/-
72 ft. of rail forming oval for above 18/6

Steam Locomotive and Tender.

No. 4021. No. 1 Gauge. Will run forwards and backwards, fast and slow, fitted with brake. Price 42/- No. 2 Gauge 47/6 No. 3 Gauge 75/-

Model Locomotive.

No. 395. Locomotive Engine, on 6 brass wheels; boiler $2\frac{1}{2}$ in. diam., $8\frac{1}{2}$ in. long, fitted with starting lever, 2 gauge taps, wind guard, 2 steam domes, safety valve, whistle, $\frac{5}{8}$ in. bore, $1\frac{1}{4}$ in. stroke, 2 eccentrics, waste steam to blow through funnel; entire length 14 in. To run either backwards or forwards.
Price 65/-

No. 396. Slightly larger than 395, with fire and smoke boxes, internal flame.
Price £4 10 0

Railway Lines 9d. foot. English make.

STEAM LOCOMOTIVE.

No. 159.

Bright cast frame, brass bronzed and relieved boiler, hand rails, buffers, buffer board steam and water taps, dome, whistle, and bogie with reversing motion.

$7\frac{1}{2}$ in. long.
English make.

Price 17/6

Gamage's Steam Locomotives—*continued.*

Superior Steam Locomotive with Tender.

No. 8373. Gauge 3. Finely japanned, with 2 Oscillating, Double Action Brass Cylinders, Oxydized Brass Boiler, finely nickelled Flanged Wheels, Brass Hand Rails, Steam Whistle, Safety Valve, Water Gauge, Starting Cock and 3 Head Lights, all Fittings finely nickelled, with Flame Guard and Japanned Tender.

21 inch long including tender.

Price **40/-**

No. 8373.

No. 42A.

Superior Steam Locomotives with Reversing Gear.

No. 42A. Gauge 2. Accurately finished, with Automatic Reversing Gear, 2 Double Action Slide Valve Cylinders, Oxydized Brass Boiler, finely nickelled Flanged Wheels, Steam Dome, Bell Whistle, and Safety Valve, all Fittings finely nickelled, with Flame Guard exhaust steam passing through the funnel, with Japanned Tender. 17½ inch long including tender.

Price **30/-**

Superior Steam Locomotives with Reversing Gear.

No. 42B. Gauge 3. Accurately finished, with Automatic Reversing Gear, 2 Double Action Slide Valve Cylinders, Oxydized Brass Boiler, finely nickelled Flanged Wheels, Steam Dome, Bell Whistle and Safety Valve, all Fittings finely nickelled, with Flame Guard, exhaust steam passing through the funnel, with Japanned Tender.

Fitted with 3 Head Light and Starting Cock.

21½ inch long including tender.

Price **50/-**

No. 42B.

Gamage's Clockwork Locomotives and Tenders.

All best quality and thoroughly tested before leaving Works.

No. A. Gauge 0.
Heavy Clockwork Engine, best movements, with brake.
7/11 each.

No. AA. Gauge 0
Do., fitted with 6 wheels, stronger spring, **10/6**

No. 0 Gauge Tender.
9d. each.
Postage 2d.

No. 1 Gauge Tender.
1/3 each.
Postage 2d.

No. L. Gauge 0.
Beautifully Enamelled Clockwork Engine, superior movements, extra strong spring, complete with brake and tender.
Price **17/6**
Model G.N.R., G.E.R. and L. & N.W. Railway Locos.
Gauge 0 .. 17/6 Gauge 1 .. 30/-

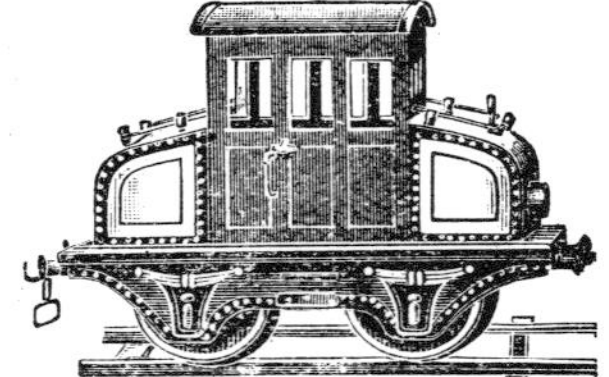

No. G. Gauge 0
Model Central London Railway Engine, best clockwork movements, **14/6**

Gauge 1, ditto .. **25/-**
For C.L.R. Sets complete, see p. 5.

No. C. Gauge 1. Heavy Clockwork Engine with brake and regulator, **12/6**
Tender **1/3**

No. F. Gauge 1. Powerful Express Clockwork Locomotive and Tender, goes forwards and backwards, fast and slow, and fitted with automatic brake.
Price **21/-**

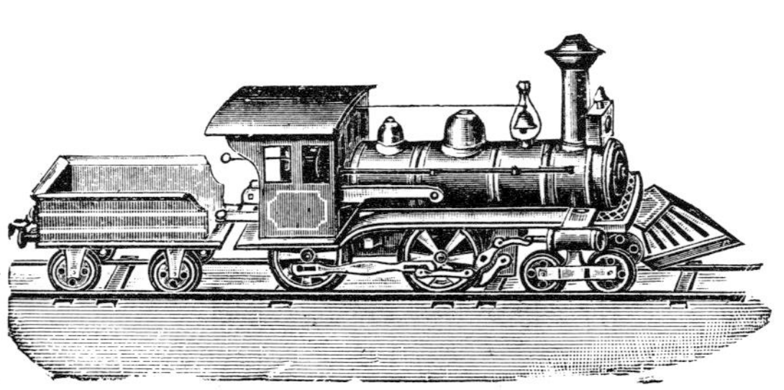

No. H. Gauge 1.
American Locomotive Engine and Tender, best clockwork movements and fitted with brake.

Price **20/-**

No. D. Gauge 1.
Whistling Locomotive, best clockwork movements, brake, &c. Whistles when in motion .. **17/6**

No. DD. Gauge 0. Do., Do. .. **11/6**

No. E. Gauge 2. Heavy Clockwork Engine with brake, **18/6**

No. P.
Clockwork Engine with bell which rings when in motion, fitted with best clockwork movements.

No. 0 Gauge **10/6**
„ 1 „ **15/-**

No. M. & N.

No M. Gauge 1.
Express Clockwork Locomotive, finely enamelled, bogey wheels, and fitted with superior clockwork movements. Price .. **32/6**

No. N. Gauge 2.
Express Clockwork Locomotive, finely enamelled, bogey wheels, and fitted with superior clockwork movements. Price .. **37/6**

GAMAGE'S MODELS OF ENGLISH LOCOMOTIVES (Steam).

Great Central Locomotive with Tender.

No. 7090. Gauge 2.

Beautifully japanned, with oxydized brass boiler, 2 oscillating brass cylinders inside frame, brass flanged wheels, brass dome with starting cock, safety valve, bell whistle, brass outlet tap, with practical frame guard and brass hand rails, exhaust steam passing through funnel, japanned tender.

21 ins. long including tender; 6 ins. high.

Price **42/-**

Great Northern Railway Locomotive with Tender.

With Fixed Cylinders and Reversing Gear.

No. 7094. Gauge 2.

Finely japanned, with strong oxydized brass boiler, double action slide valve cylinders, with reversing gear, smoke box, brass steam dome with starting cock, bell whistle, safety valve, and outlet tap, exhaust steam passing through the funnel, Tender mounted on 2 four-wheeled bogie carriages, finely finished.

22 ins. long including Tender.

Price **63/-**

London & South Western Railway Locomotive with Tender.

No. 7096. Gauge 3.

With Fixed Cylinders and Reversing Gear.

Finely finished, with oxydized brass boiler, double action slide valve cylinders, reversing gear, flame guard, nickelled flanged wheels, and connecting rods, smoke box, brass domes, safety valve, bell whistle, water gauge, brass starting cock, outlet tap, hand rails and brass spring buffers, exhaust steam passing through funnel. Tender, finely japanned and elegantly finished, with spring buffers. 28 in. long including Tender. 8 ins. high. Price **£4 17. 6.**

Gamage's Clockwork Locomotives—*continued.*

Clockwork Engine.

No. R. Gauge 3.

Beautifully enamelled fitted with very strong spring, automatic brake, &c.

Price **32/6**

Express Clockwork Engine.

No. S. Gauge 3.

A large and powerful Engine and fitted with very best movements, thoroughly tested.

Price **50/-**

No. R.

No. J.

Superior Express Locomotive with Tender.

English Model.

No. J. Gauge 1.

Fine japanned with extra strong clockwork with superforce and patent regulator with brake, reversing gear and running slowly and quickly with 4 coupled driving wheels and bogie carriage elegantly finished.

18 in. long including Tender.

Price **32/6**

Superior Express Locomotive with Tender.

American Model.

No. K. Finely japanned with extra strong clockwork with superforce and patent regulator with brake, reversing gear and running slowly and quickly with 4 coupled driving wheels and bogie carriage, elegantly finished.

19 in. long including Tender.

Price **32/6**

No. K.

NOVELTY! Clockwork Velocipede, with Driver and Railway Inspector, for running over Railway Track, fitted with Patent Speed Regulator. Gauge 0, **16/6** Gauge 1, **25/-**

Gamage's Traction Engines, Steam Rollers, Fire Engines, etc.

TRACTION ENGINE.

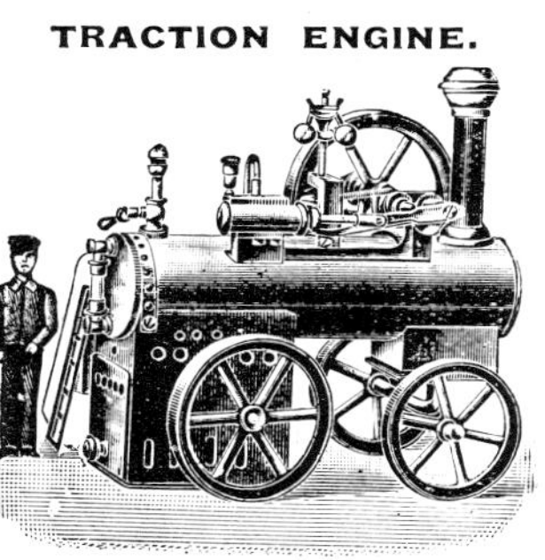

No. 4119.
Price **17/6**

TRACTION ENGINES.

Traction Engines, with double action slide valve cylinder, safety valve, solid oxydized brass boiler, water gauge, bell whistle and flame guard.

No. 1—8½ in. long, 4 in. wide, 9 in. high **15/-**
No. 2—10 in. long, 5¾ in. wide, 10½ in. high **20/-**

No. 1.

No. 2.

FIRE ESCAPE.

Mechanical Fire Escape, very strong, and beautifully Japanned, 23 in. high.

Price ... **4/11.** Postage 3d.

FIRE ESCAPE.

No. 3—Mechanical Fire Escape, adjustable, with Rubber Hose, with mouth piece, 25½ in. high. Price ... **8/-.** Postage 4d.

CLOCKWORK TRAM.

Price **27/6** Guage 1.

FIRE ENGINE.

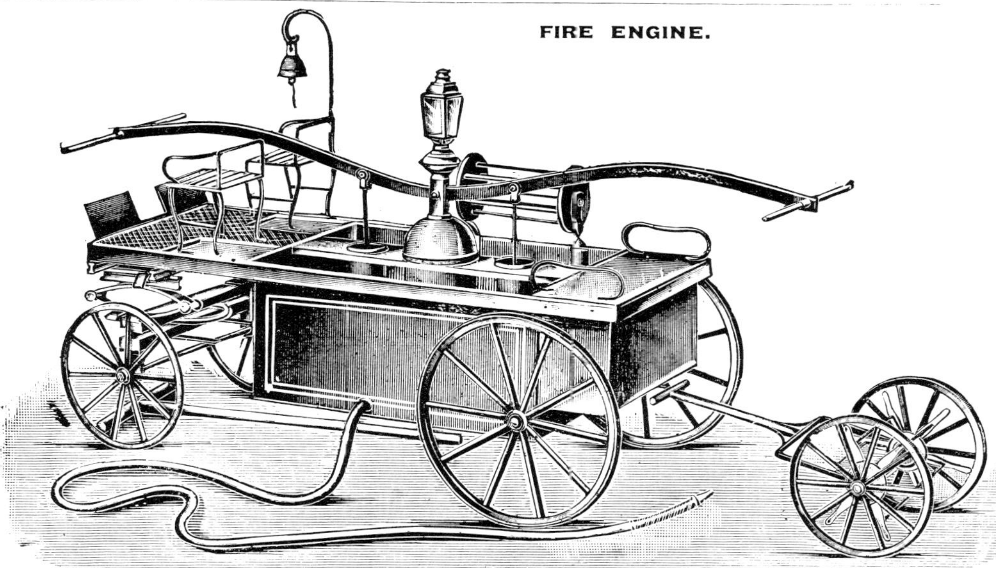

No. 13319.

Superior Fire Pumps.—Solid finish and finely japanned, with continual jet, with excellent ground brass pump work, strong work, with lantern to burn, windlass for hose and india rubber hose with mouth piece.

No. 1.	Length of Waggon (without shaft)	14½ in.,	height 10 in.	**16/6**
,, 2.	,, ,, ,,	18½ ,,	,, 11½ ,,	**21/-**
,, 3.	,, ,, ,,	22½ ,,	,, 13 ,,	**27/6**

FIRE ESCAPE.

No. 2.

Mechanical Fire Escape, very strong and beautifully Japanned, 31 in. high.

Price ... **7/6.** Postage 4d.

Carriages, Trucks, &c.,

For Clockwork and Steam Railways, all of best quality only.

Well enamelled in suitable colours. Very strongly made.

No. 05.

Passenger Carriage.

No. 0, **10½d.** 1, **1/3**
,, 2, **2/-** 3, **3/6**

Postage 3d.

Passenger Carriage.

No. 06. Super Quality

Best make and finish.

No. 0, **1/6** No. 1, **2/11**
No. 2, **4/6** No. 3, **7/6**

Postage 3d. & 4d.

No. 07.

Corridor Carriage.

No. 0 Gauge **1/6** each.
,, 1 ,, **2/11** ,,
,, 2 ,, **3/11** ,,

Postage 3d.

No. 02.

Royal Mail Van.

No. 0 Gauge **1/6** each.
No. 1 ,, **2/11** ,,
No. 2 ,, **3/11** ,,

Postage 3d.

Corridor Carriage.

Best make and finish, with passengers.

No. 0 Gauge **2/11** 1, **4/6**
No. 2 Gauge **6/6**

Postage 3d.

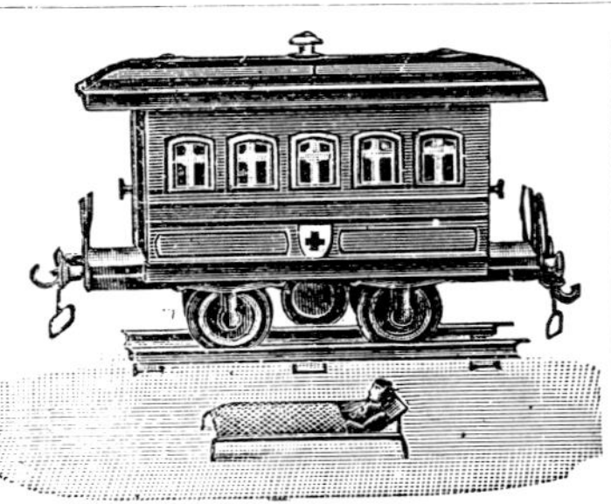

Railway Ambulance Carriage

No. 28.

No. 0 Gauge **3/11** each.
No 1 ,, **6/11** ,,

Postage 3d.

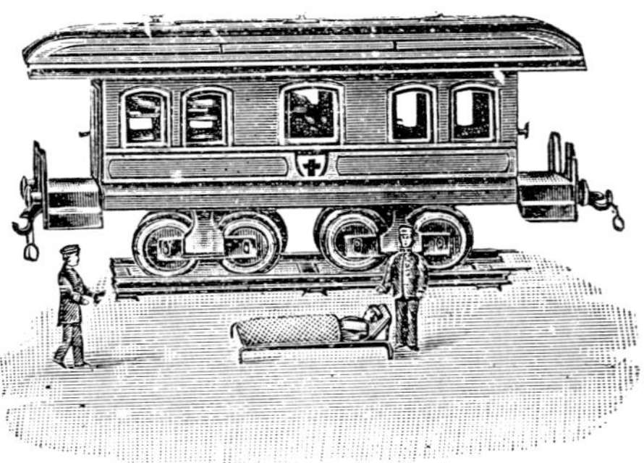

Railway Ambulance Car.

No. 48. Superior finish on bogie wheels.

No. 0 Gauge **7/11** each. Postage 3d.
,, 1 ,, **13/6** ,, Postage free.

Corridor Carriage.

Model of L. & N. W. Rly.

No. 0 Gauge, **3/6** ea.
No. 1 ,, **4/6** ea.

G. E. R. or G. N. R.

2/11 **4/3** ea.

Postage 3d.

Corridor Dining Car.

No. 42.

On bogie wheels, very Handsome Cars.

No. 0 Gauge .. .. .. **7/6** each.
No. 1 ,, ... **12/6** ,,
No. 2 ,, ... **15/6** ,,

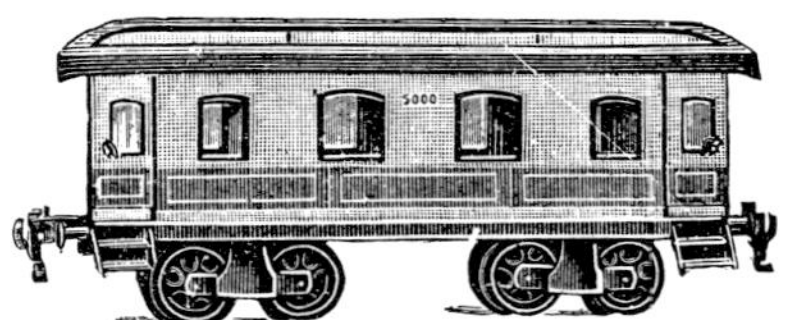

Corridor Dining Car.

Models of L. & W. N. R., G. E. R. or G. N. R.

No. 0 Gauge **7/6**
,, 1 ,, ... **12/6**

SLEEPING CARS, Same Price.

Corridor Sleeping Cars.

No. 43.

On bogie wheels, beautifully enamelled.

No. 0 Gauge .. .. .. **7/6** each.
No. 1 ,, ... **12/6** ,,
No. 2 ,, ... **15/6** ,,

Gamage's Latest Novelty—Railway Smash.

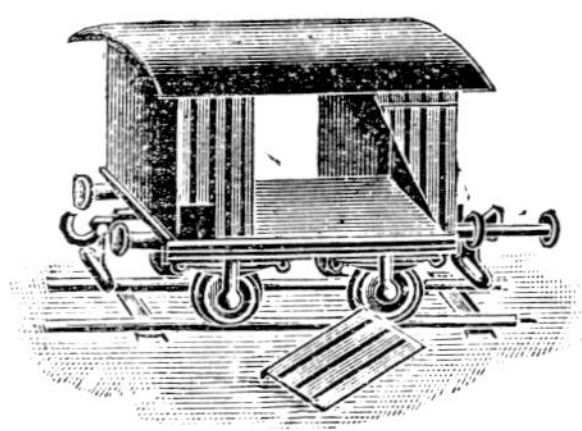

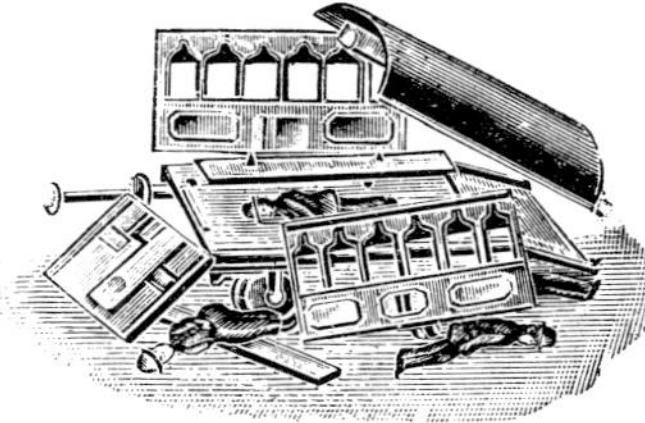

Accident Set.

No. 40.

Consisting of two carriages, one goods van; so constructed that when the train is in motion an accident occurs—one carriage being entirely smashed, the second one having two sides and top knocked out, and the goods van one side.

No. 0 Gauge **5/11** set of three. Postage 3d. No. 1 Gauge **7/6** set of three. Postage 4d. No. 2 Gauge **10/6** set of three. Postage free.

GAMAGE'S GOODS TRUCKS, WAGGONS, &c. *For Clockwork and Steam Railways.*

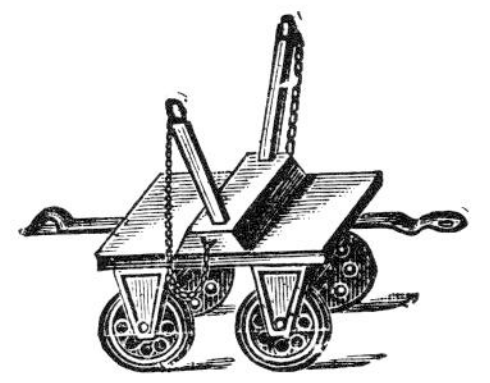

Timber Waggon.

Gauge
No. 0, 2/- 1, 3/- pair.

Tipping Truck.

Gauge
No. 0, 2/11 No. 1, 3/11 ea.

Tipping Waggon.

Gauge
No. 0, 1/- 1, 1/11 2, 2/6 each.

Open Coal Truck.

Gauge
No. 0, 10½d. 1, 1/- 2, 1/6 each

Open Coal Truck.

Gauge. With Brake House.
No. 0, 1/- 1, 1/6, 2, 2/6 each.

Covered Truck.

No. 0 gauge, 1/6 1, 1/11 2, 2/6 ea.

Luggage Van.

Gauge. With Brake House.
No. 0, 1/6 1, 2/6 2, 2/11 3, 5/6 ea.

Cattle Truck.

No. 0 gauge, 1/- 1, 2/6 each.

Holborn Brewery Van.

No. 0 gauge, 1/- 1, 1/9 2, 2/6 each.

Petroleum Tank Truck.

No. 0 gauge, 1/9 1, 2/6 each

Gas Truck.

No. 0 gauge, 1/6 1, 1/11 each

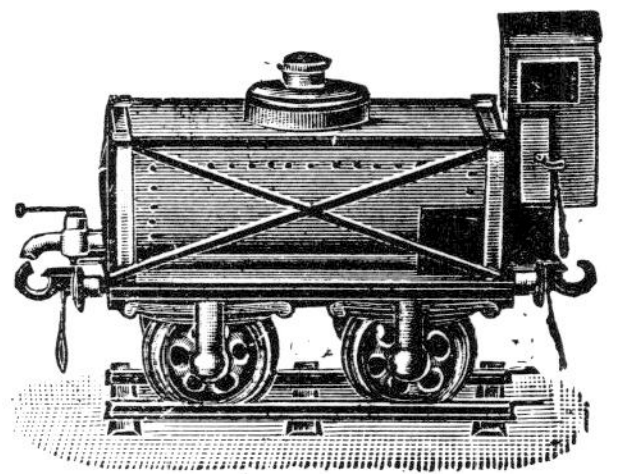

Tar Waggon.

No. 0 gauge, 2/6 1, 3/6 each

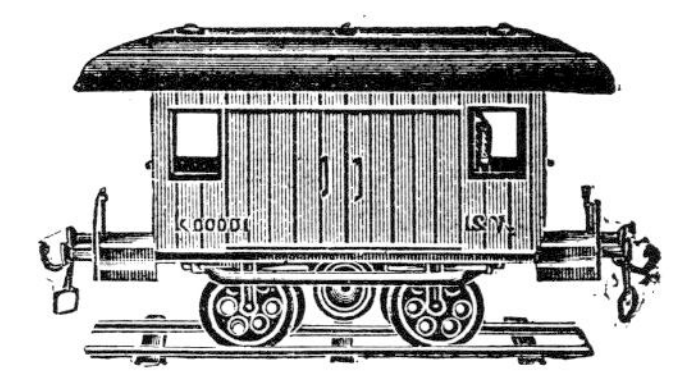

Long Luggage Van.

No. 0 gauge, 2/11 1, 4/6 2, 7/6 ea.

Postage 3d. extra on all above.

Transport Waggon.

No. 0 gauge, 1/11 1, 2/11 2, 3/11 Postage 3d.

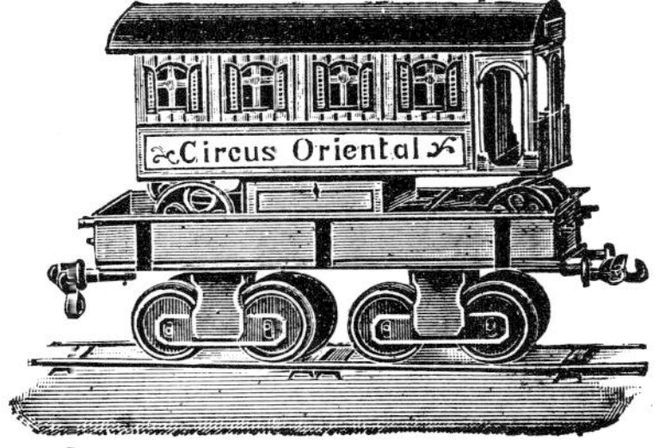

Circus Caravan on Truck.

No. 78. Complete as illustration.

No. 0 gauge .. 7/11 each. Postage 3d.
" 1 " .. 10/6 " Post free.

Pantechnicon and Truck.

No. 77. Complete.

No. 0 gauge .. 6/6 each. Postage
" 1 " .. 8/6 " 4d.

Platform Barrow

Strongly made 1/3

Postage 2d.

Luggage Trolly.

Well finished .. 1/- Postage 2d.

Platform Barrow.

Complete with Luggage.

Price .. 2/9 Postage 3d.

Gamage's Railway Crossings, Huts, etc.

Platelayer's Box.

Best Enamel.

Price **1/6** Postage 2d.

Railway Signal & Box

Price **10½**d. Postage 2d.

Railway Crossing, Signal and House

Best Enamel. Price **1/9** Postage 3d.

Railway Crossing

and

House

Best Enamel. Price **3/3**

Postage 3d.

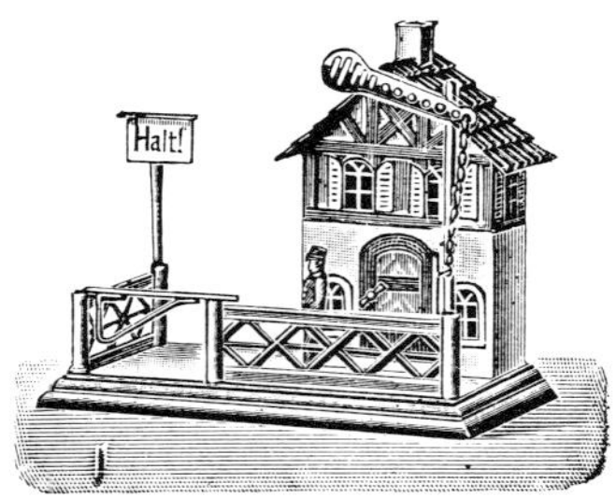

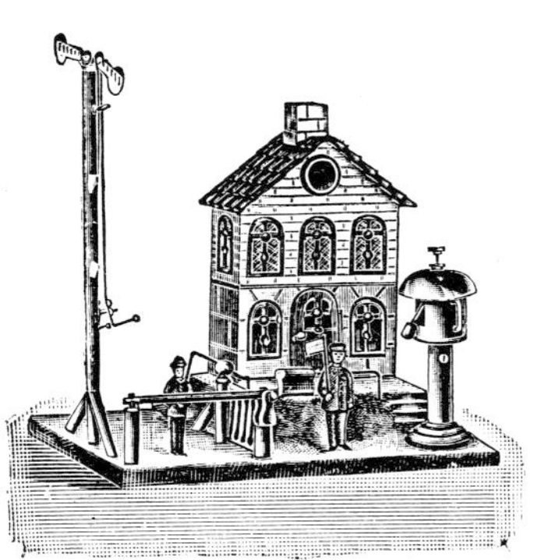

Railway Signal, Bell & House

Can be illuminated at night.

Price ... **7/6** Postage 3d.

Railway Crossing, House and Signal

Can be illuminated with Candles.

Price ... ... **5/6** Postage 3d.

Railway Crossing, House and Signals.

For 1 or 2-gauge trains. Made to lift up, as illustration. ... Price **15/-**

Bell Crossing.

The bell rings when train passes.
Best quality.

Price ... **7/6** Postage 3d.

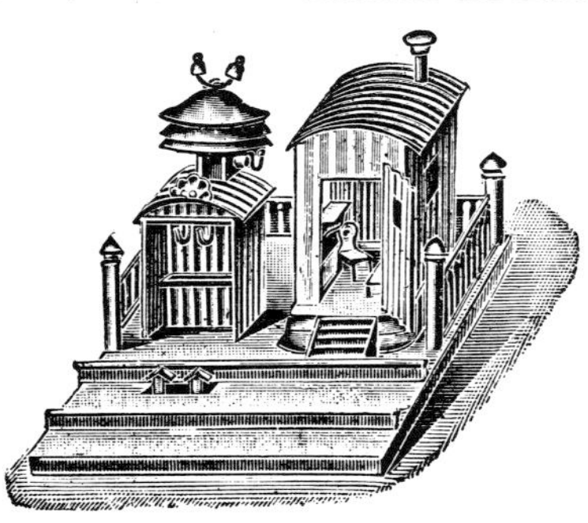

Clockwork Bell Crossing.

The bell rings when train passes. Best quality.

Price **9/11**

Postage 3d.

Railway Signal, Bell and Box.

Price ... **1/-**

Postage 3d.

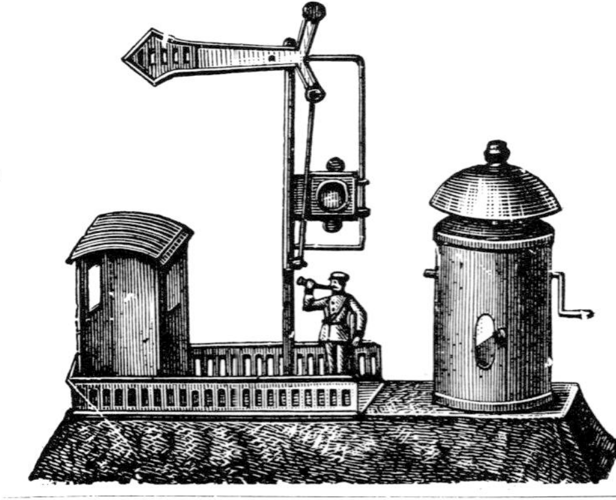

Railway Crossing, Signal,

Moveable Barriers, etc. Beautifully Enamelled.

Price **12/6**

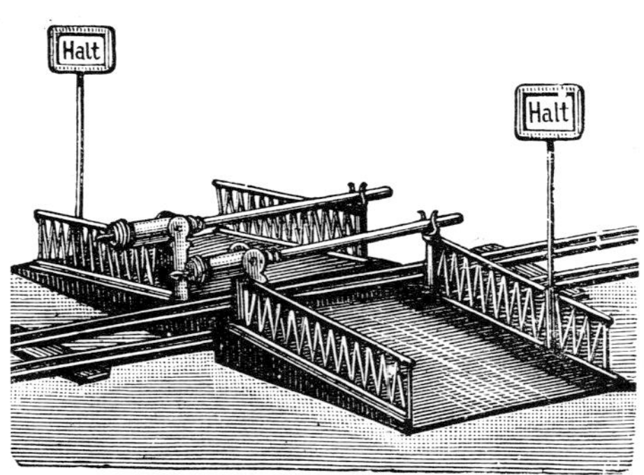

Railway Crossing

Moveable barriers.

Price ... **1/6** Postage 3d.

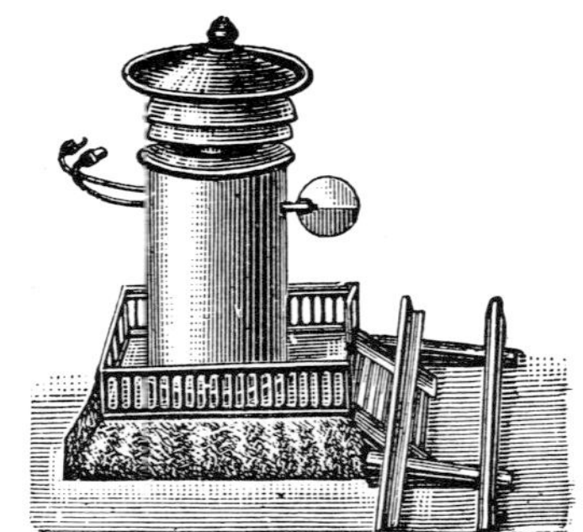

Bell Signal

Bell rings when train passes.

Price ... ... **2/6** Postage 3d.

Gamage's Railway Bridges.

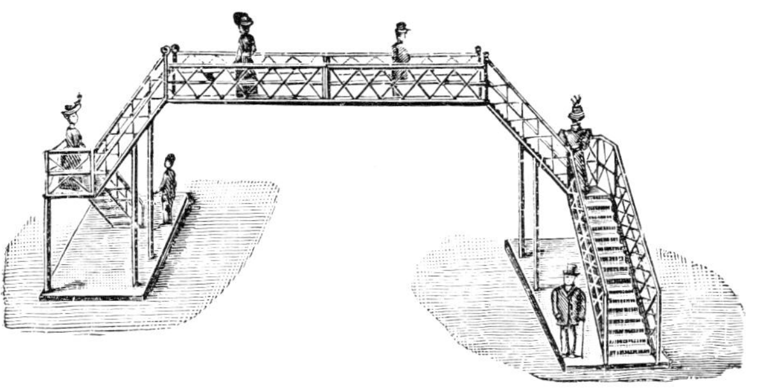

Railway Foot Bridge.

Well enamelled .. .. Price **3/3**

Postage 3d.

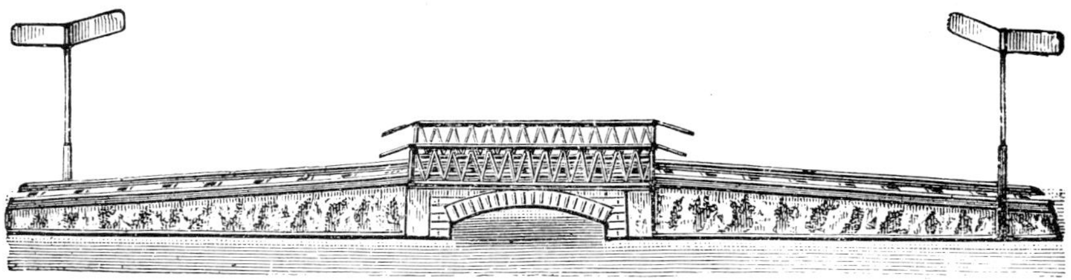

Railway Bridge for 0 Gauge Line.

Enamelled. Price .. .. **2/6** Postage 3d.

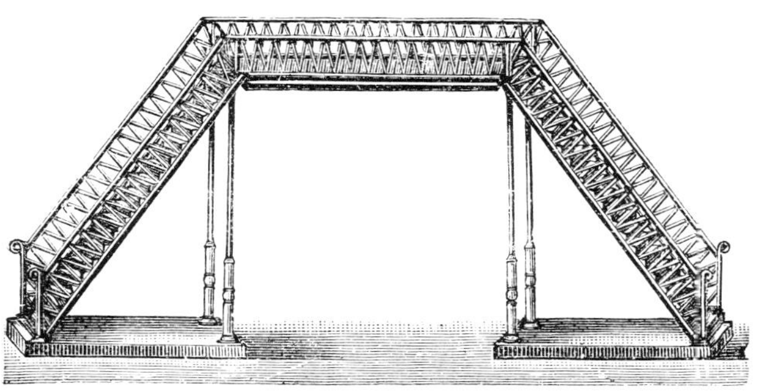

Railway Foot Bridge.

As illustration.

Price .. .. **1/6** Postage 3d.

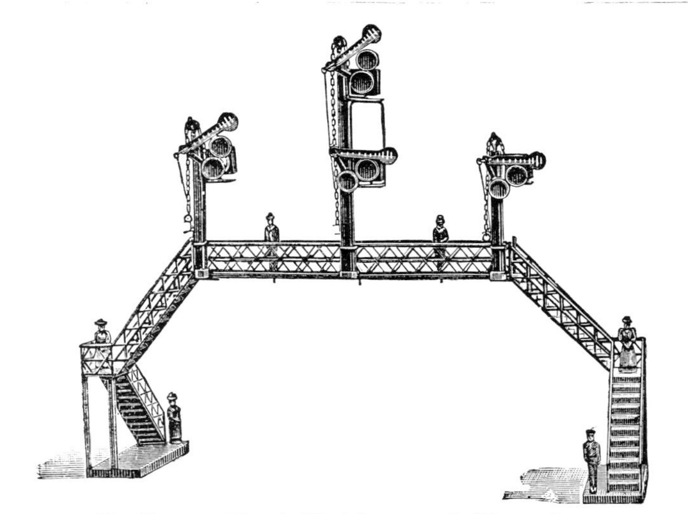

Railway Foot Bridge and Signals.

Beautifully Enamelled. Price .. **5/11** Postage 3d.

As illustration, **8/11** Postage 3d. Larger Size, **9/11** Postage 3d.

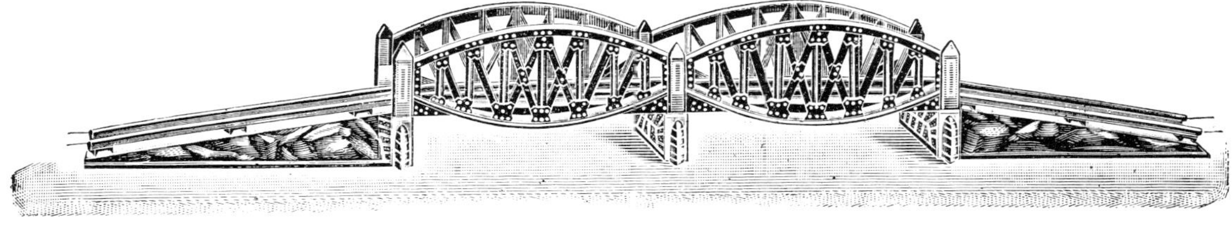

Railway Bridge,

New Style,

Beautifully Enamelled.

Made to take a-part.

0 gauge, **8/6** Postage 3d.

1 gauge, **12/6** 2 gauge **14/6**

No. 4.

RAILWAY BRIDGE

No. 0 gauge. Price **25/-**

Splendid Model, Superior Bridge, enamelled in several colours, complete as illustration. Can be used for No. 1 or 2 Gauge Railways

Price **42/-**

GAMAGE'S RAILWAY SIGNALS AND LAMPS.

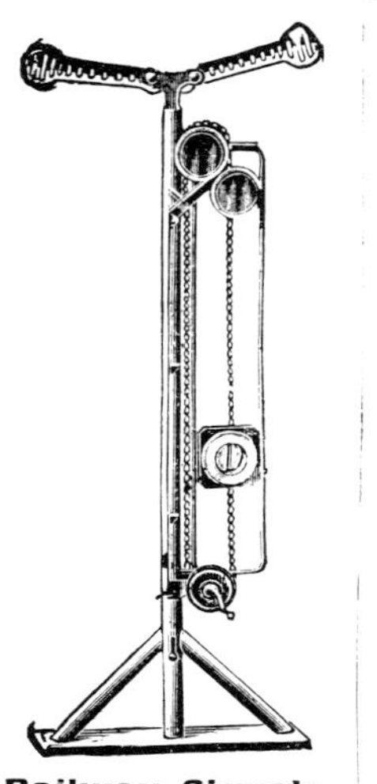

Railway Signals.

Price .. .. 6½d.
Postage 2d.

Do., (as illustration)
Price 2/11
Postage 3d.

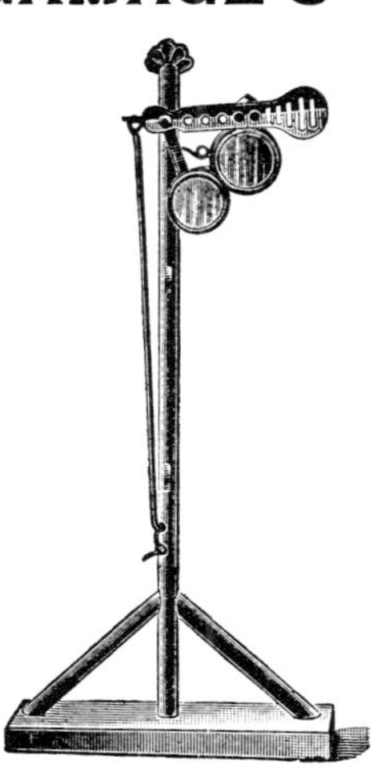

Railway Signals.

Best enamelled.

Price 1/6

Postage 2d.

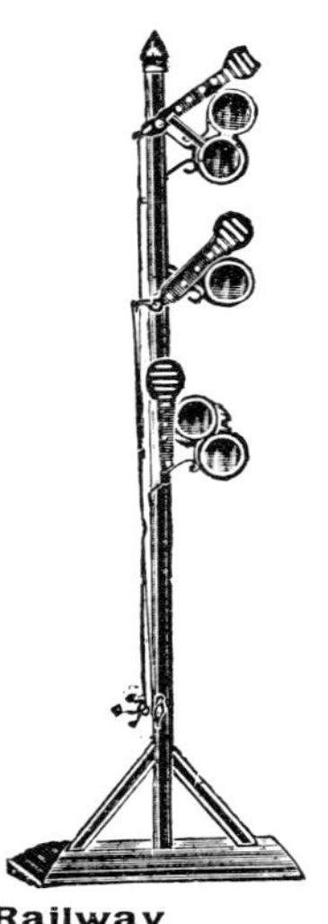

Railway Signals.

(As illustration)

Price .. 3/8

Postage 3d.

SIGNALS.

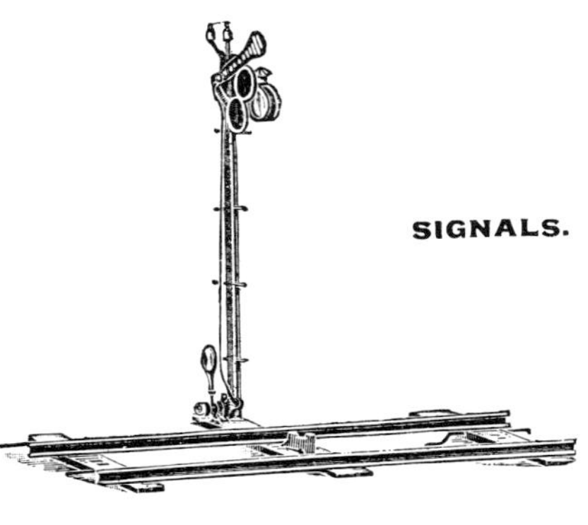

Railway Stop Signals.

(As illustration)

No. 0.	.. .. ..	1/11 each.
,, 1.	.. .. ..	2/6 ,,
,, 2.	.. .. ..	2/11 ,,

Postage 3d.

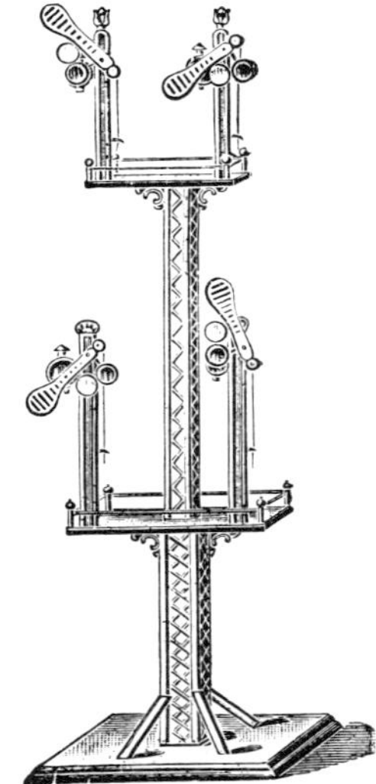

Railway Signals.

(As illustration)

Price 9/11 set.

Postage 3d.

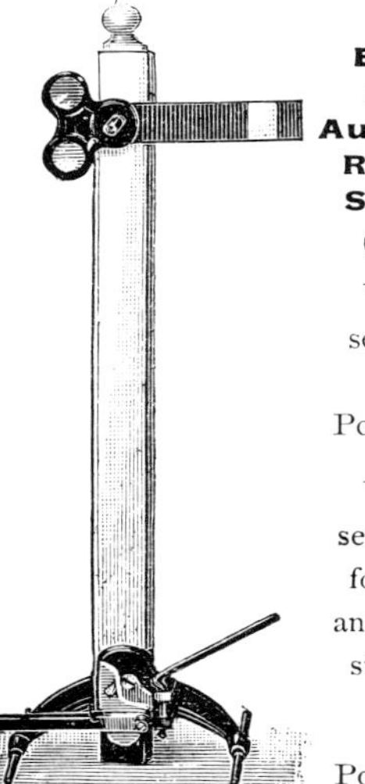

English Made Automatic Railway Signals.

(Patent)

With 1 semaphore
10½d.
Postage 2d.

With 2 semaphores for home and distant signalling.
1/4½
Postage 2d.

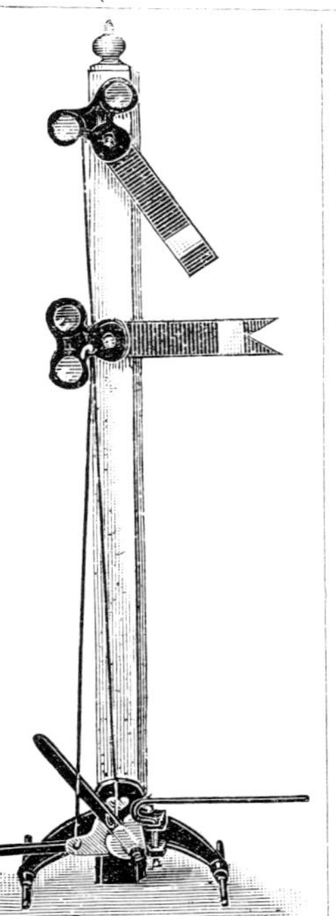

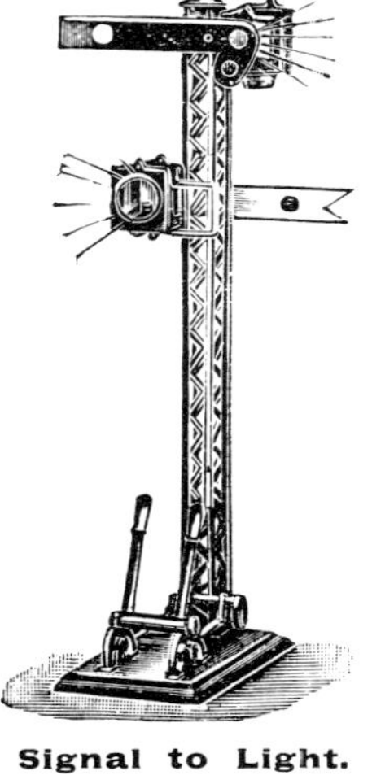

Signal to Light.

Midland Railway Model.

"Up" and "Down" arms, red and green spectacles, weighted motion, lamps fitted for burning and motion rods from framed levers to work each arm. 12½ in. high.

Price .. 3/11

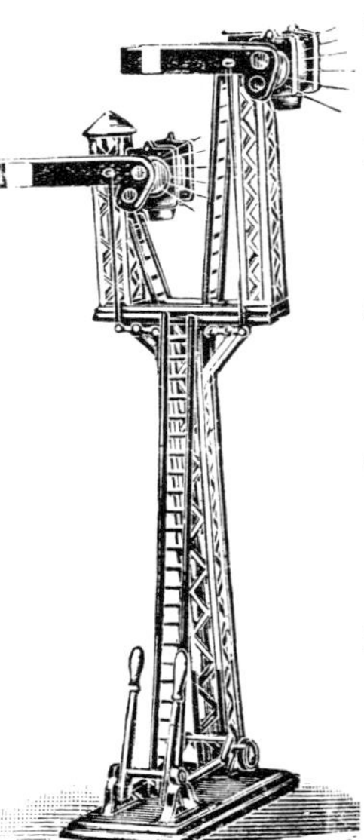

Signal to Light.

L. & N. W. R. Model.

Main and Branch line, 2 posts rising from one ground with lamps, fitted for burning, red and green spectacles, weighted motion, and motion rods from framed levers to work each arm.

15 in. high.

Price 6/11

Postage 3d.

Station Lamps.

Illuminated with Petroleum.

Price ... 1/9

With red glass 2/-

Postage 2d.

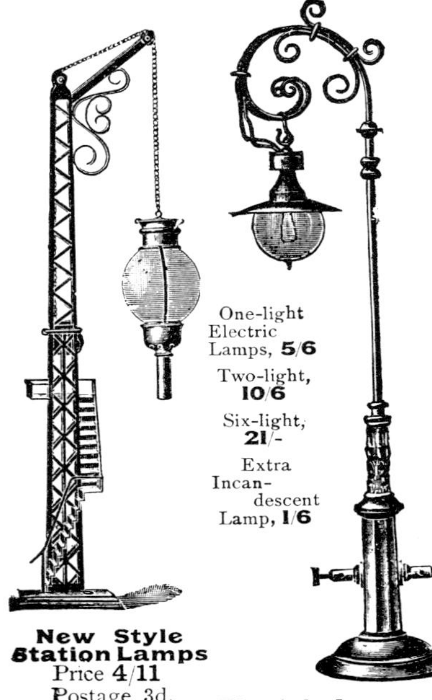

New Style Station Lamps
Price 4/11
Postage 3d.

One-light Electric Lamps, 5/6
Two-light, 10/6
Six-light, 21/-
Extra Incan-descent Lamp, 1/6

Electric Lamps.

'Lamps.

Suitable for Railway Stations, 6d. each.

Complete with candle.

Postage 2d.

Imitation Arc Lamps.

Illuminated with candles.

Price 4/6

Postage 2d.

Imitation Electric Arc Lamps.

Illuminated with Petroleum.

Price 2/11

Postage 2d.

Station or Street Lamps.

Illuminated with Petroleum.

Price—
3-arm ... 5/6
5 arm ... 7/6

Postage 3d.

Gamage's Tunnels and Sidings.

TUNNEL No. 2A.

No. 2. **Railway Tunnel.**

Enamelled, as illustration. Price **2/9** Postage 3d.
No. 2A, ,, ,, ,, **3/3** ,,
No. 2B, ,, ,, ,, **4/6** ,,

TUNNEL No. 1.

No. 1. **Railway Tunnel.**

Enamelled as illustration. Price **1/6** Postage 3d.

TUNNEL No. 3

No. 3. **Railway Tunnel.**

Beautifully Enamelled as illustration.
Price **4/6** Postage 3d.
No. 4. Ditto, Larger, **8/6** Postage 3d.

TUNNEL No. 6.

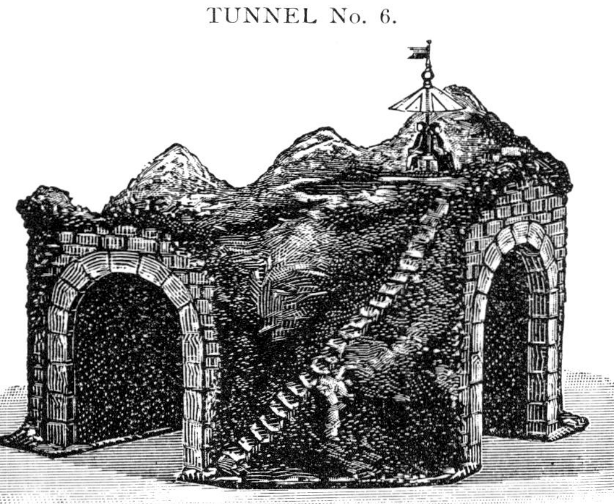

New Style, **Rockwork Tunnel,** beautifully Enamelled.
No. 6, **7/6**, postage 3d. No. 6A, **11/6**

TUNNEL, No. 7

Artistic

Railway Tunnel,

Best Finish.

No. 7 .. **8/11**
Postage 4d.

No. 7A .. **14/6**

TUNNEL No. 5.

No. 5. **Railway Tunnel,** Beautifully Enamelled, Large Size.
Price **8/6** Postage 4d.

House and Siding.

Goods Siding with Buffers and Slope.
No. 0 Gauge .. **12/6** No. 1 Gauge .. **16/6**

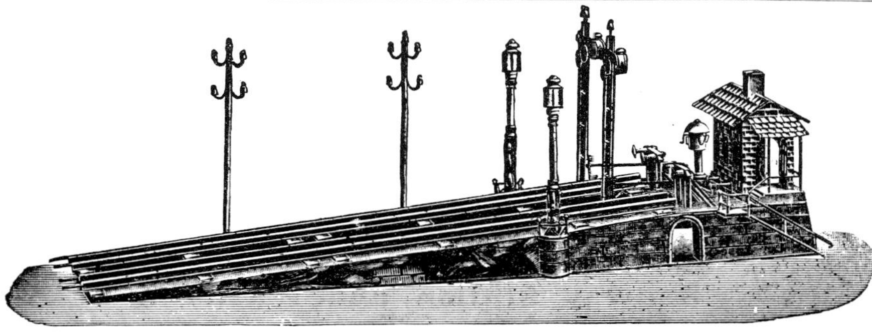

Shunting Siding.

Shunting Siding, Buffers and House.

No. 0 Gauge **33/6**

Gamage's Railway Stations, &c.

ALL NEW MODELS.

Railway Station.

Beautifully enamelled (as illustration).

Price **8/6**

Postage 3d.

Railway Platform Restaurant.

As illustration. Beautifully finished in enamel.

Price **12/6**

Railway Station with Platform.

Platform at side, beautifully finished.

Price **12/6**

Handsome Enamelled Railway Station.

As illustration.

Price **22/6**

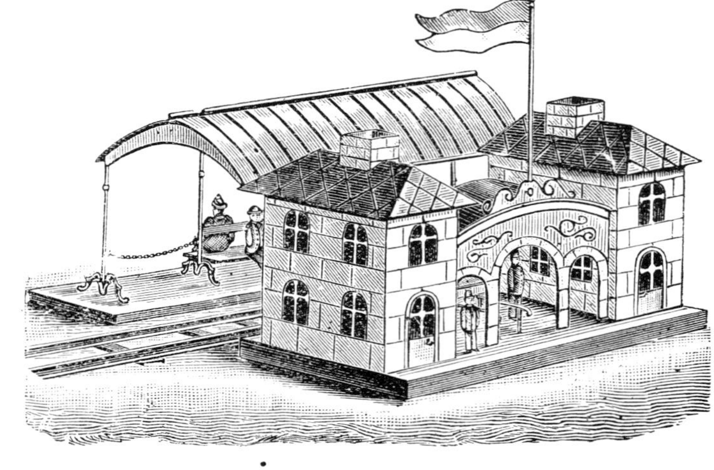

Railway Station.

No. 5. Best quality, enamelled (as illustration) Price **10/6**

Enamelled Railway Station.

Beautifully finished. Price .. **17/6**

Railway Station and Platform.

Enamelled and finished in best style. Price .. **45/-**

Gamage's Railway Stations, &c.—*continued.*

English Type. **Latest Novelty.**

Wayside Railway Station.

In fine Polychromic japanning. Exact representation with stamped roof, corrugated shelter, imitation arc lamps, advertisements finely painted in correct colours, sign boards, seat and lamp, finely finished 50 in. long, 10 in. wide 10 in. high. Price **20/-**

Railway Station and Platform.

Complete (as 2 illustrations) beautifully enamelled.

Price **45/-**

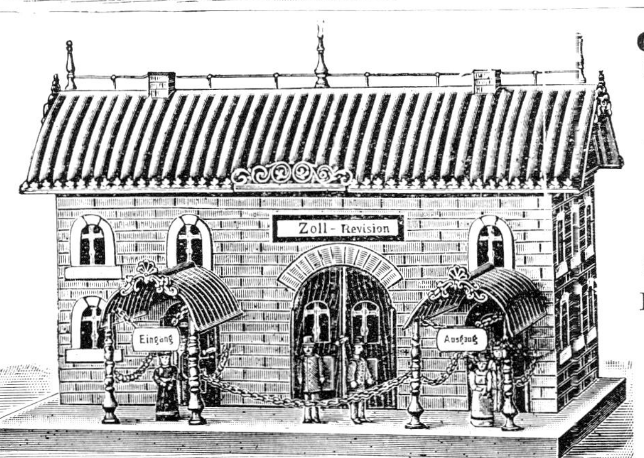

Custom House.

No. 8.

Enamelled and finished in best style, as illustration

Price **25/-**

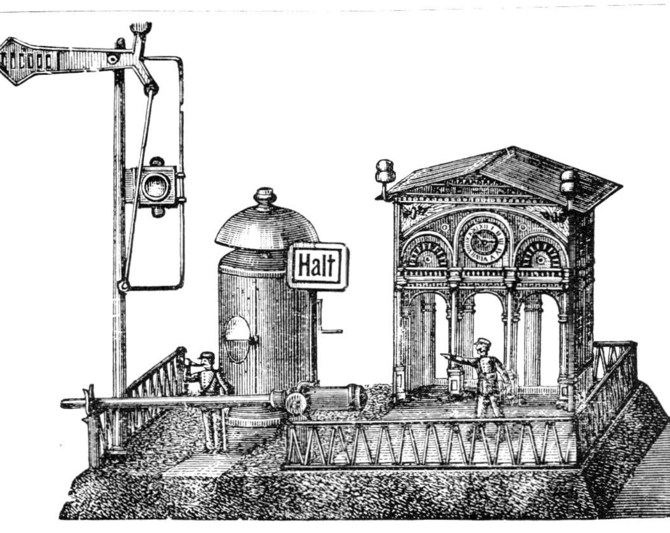

Railway Station.

Crossing bell and signal, complete, Price **3/-** postage 3d.

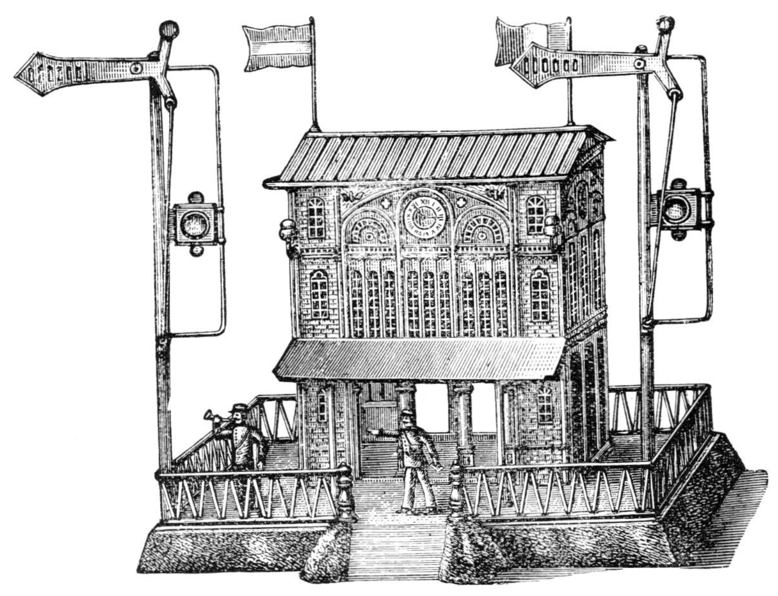

Enamelled Railway Station.

And signals, complete. Price .. **3/3**

Postage 3d.

GAMAGE'S STEAM ENGINES AND TURBINES

A. W. GAMAGE, Ltd.,
Having made an exceptionally large purchase of Steam Engines are enabled to offer them to the public at extremely low prices. Those marked "Special Quotation" are from **20 to 33⅓ per cent. less than usual prices.**

All are Reliable Engines and thoroughly tested before leaving the Factory.

No. 326 **The Ideal Steam Engine.**
A Powerful and well-finished Engine, as illustration.
Special Quotation.
No. 5, **25/-** No. 6, **30/-**

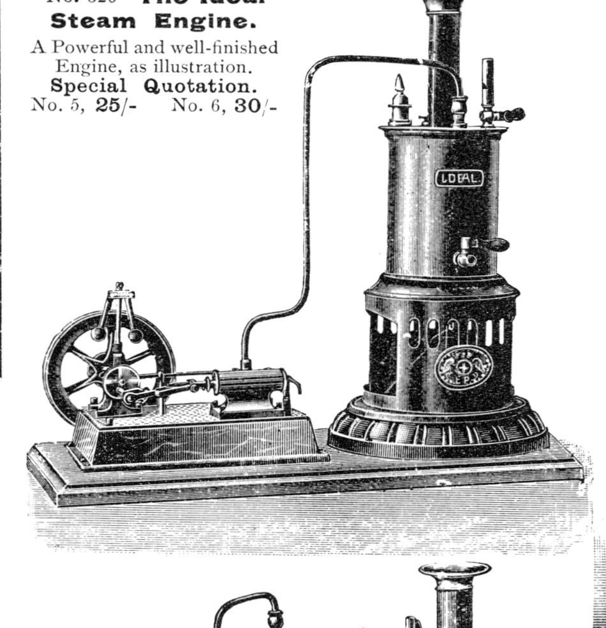

The "Viaduct" Horizontal Steam Engine.
Best make, thoroughly tested Oxydized Steel Boilers, **high** chimney, safety valve.
No. 4, **2/11** Postage **3d.**

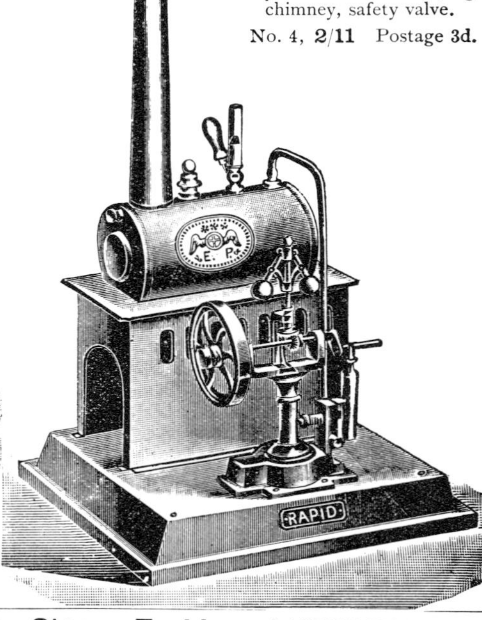

No. 158. **NEW MODEL Horizontal Steam Engine.**
Very strongly built fixed Cylinders.
The Cylinders employed in these engines are the latest construction, with closed valve box and eccentric valve motion.
This new Cylinder operates firmly and exactly; the power is correspondingly great and sufficient to drive several models.
Oxydized Brass Boilers.

No. 158, as illustration	**4/6**
No. 158A ..	**6/6**

Postage 3d.

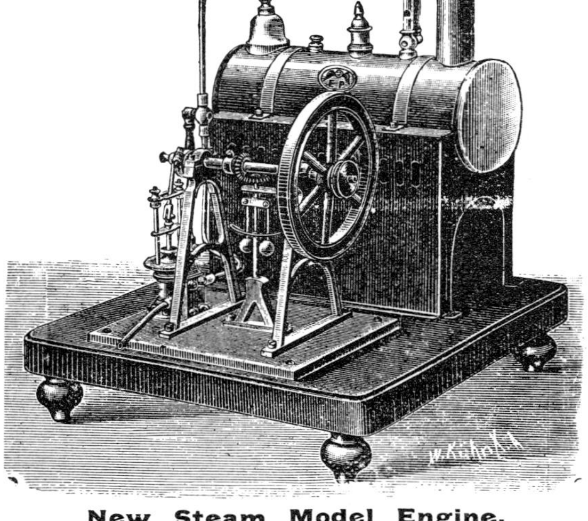

New Steam Model Engine.
No. 27. As illustration, Fitted with Governors with Slide Valve .. Price **65/-**

Steam Turbine. LATEST NOVELTY.
Our Turbines are distinguishable by their Special Construction, and like the large original machines they make an enormous number of revolutions. This number of revolutions, however, is reduced by a practical transmission in order to give greater force, and in this way the Turbines produce a very increased power. Our make in consequence represents an entirely new type of Steam Turbines of original and elegant finish. The Boiler is fitted with safety valve, accurate pressure gauge, whistle, and water **gauge**; the waste steam passes through the chimney (imitating smoke). The Turbine drum is fitted with an outlet for condensed water.

No. 1.—Steam Turbine with about 10,000 revolutions per minute, 10½ inches long, 9 inches wide, 13½ in. high (with chimney) .. **30/-**

No. 2.—Steam Turbine with about 8,000 revolutions per minute, 15 in. long, 11½ in. wide, 16 in. high (with chimney) .. **45/-**

Large Steam Engine.
Best Finish. A very fine Model.
Special Quotation.

No. 23	23A	23B
25/-	**30/-**	**37/6**

GAMAGE'S STEAM ENGINES. *ALL THOROUGHLY TESTED BEFORE LEAVING WORKS.*

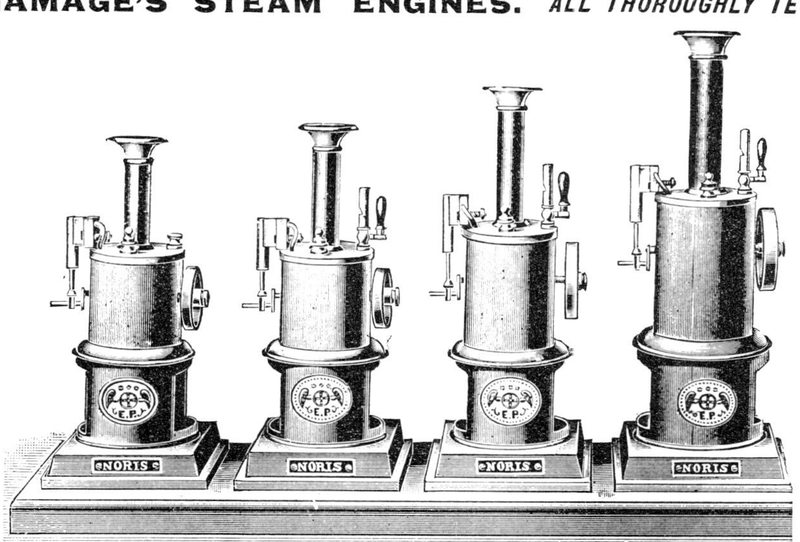

Upright Steam Engine, Oxydized Boilers, High Chimney, Safety Valve and Whistle, Best make and finish, as illustration. No. 10 **1/9** No. 11 **2/6** No. 12 **3/6** No. 13 with Tap **5/6**
Postage 4d. No. 12 and 13 with Whistle.

Upright Steam Engine
Fitted with Safety Valve and all latest improvements.
4112A **21/-** 4112B ... **27/6**

THE "MARVEL."

Upright Steam Engine

Will burn Spirit or Petroleum.

No. 9A ... **1/-**
No. 6A with whistle **1/6**
No. 7A ,, **2/6**
Postage 3d.

No. 8A, Do., and New Safety Valve ... **3/6**
No. 9A, Do..... **4/6**
Postage 4d.

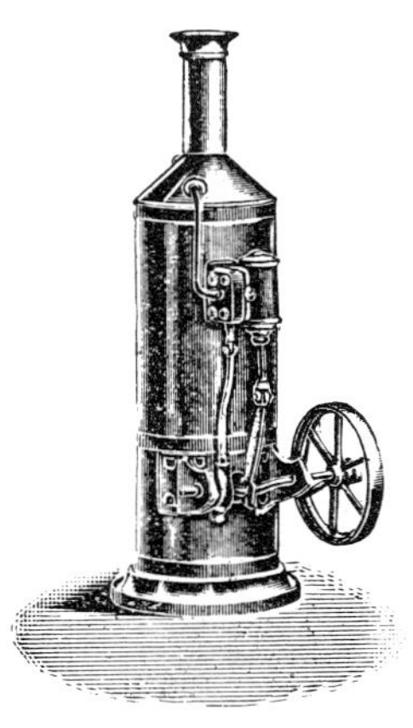

No. 14. **"Referee" Steam Engine**
¾ Full Size. New Model.
New Model Steam Engine, fitted with Safety Valve, Steam Gauge, Whistle and High Chimney.
No. 14 ... **5/11** No. 15 ... **7/11**
Postage 4d.

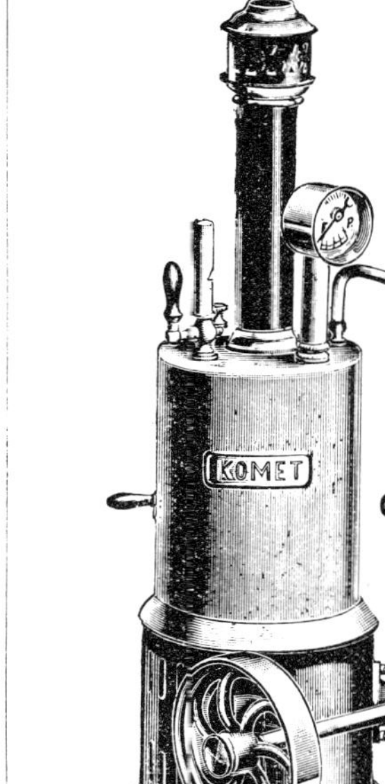

Upright Steam Engine
Special Quotations.
215, as illustration, **7/6** 216 **10/6** 217 **13/6**
Postage 3d.

Special Line.—No. 580 Vertical Steam Engine with reversing gear, **2/6** Postage 3d

No. 16. **"Referee Engine**
¾ Full Size. Quality as No. 14.
No. 16, as illustration **10/6**
No. 17, Large Size **13/6**
Post Free.

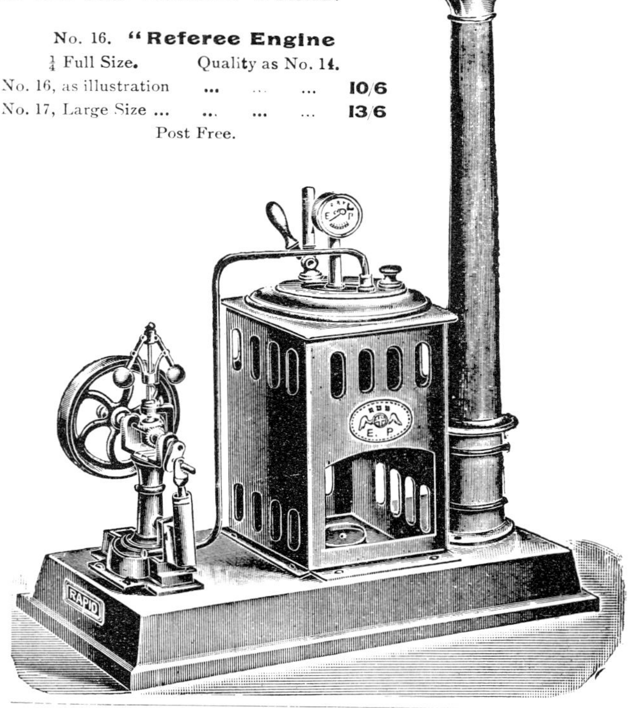

"Duplex" Steam Engine

Large Size, fitted with Double Action Oscillating Cylinder,

Best Quality Oxydized Steel Boilers, all one piece.

Special Quotations,
No. 19 **15/-** 19A **18/6** 19B **22/6**

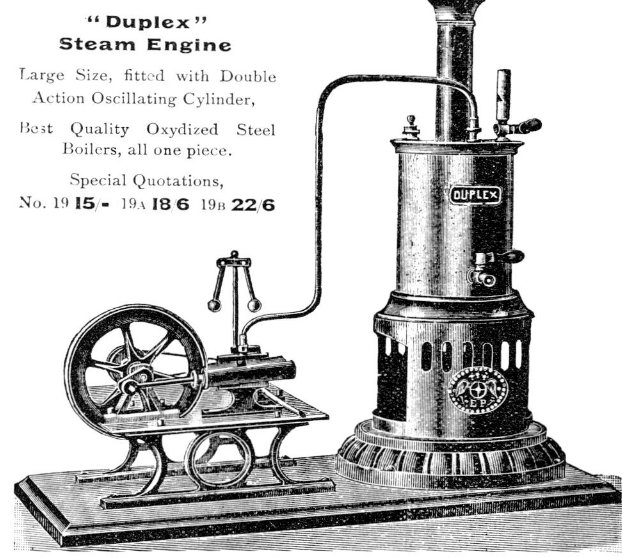

The "Ideal" Steam Engine

As illustrated.

Well Made and Thoroughly Tested.

Special Quotations,

No. 1	2	3	4
7/6	**9/6**	**12/6**	**15/-**

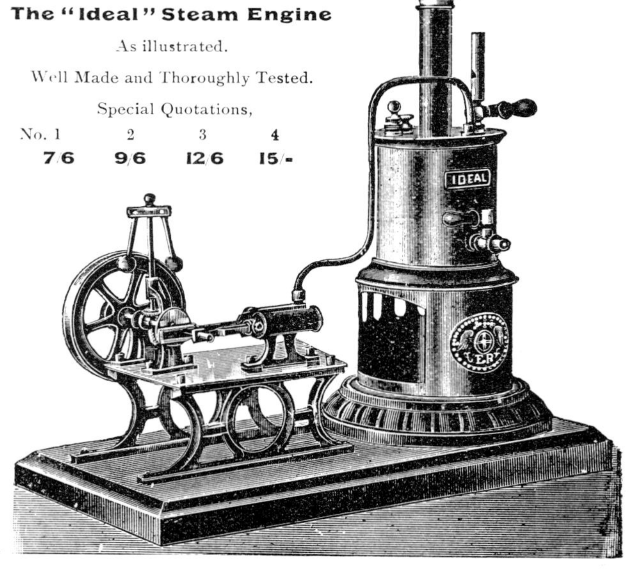

Gamage's Hot Air Engines, etc.

Fine Vertical Hot Air Motor,

For Spirit Heating, No Cooling necessary, extra strong and elegant finish, with new Gas Generating Spirit Lamp, large reservoir, solid cast iron, finely japanned, with nickelled fittings and flame guard, mounted on wood stand.

8020/0 with 1 pressure and 1 acting cylinder, and 1 fly wheel (lamp to burn about 1½ hour, entire height of motor 10¼ inches ... ... **17/6** each.

8020/1 with 1 pressure and 2 acting cylinders, and 2 fly wheels (lamp to burn about 2½ hours), entire height of motor 11½ inches... ... ... **42/-** each.

8020/2 Very Powerful, with Gearing, 1 pressure and 2 acting cylinders, and 2 fly wheels (lamp to burn about 2½ hours), with free conic pulley wheels (3 speeds), entire height of motor 11½ inches ... **50/-** each.

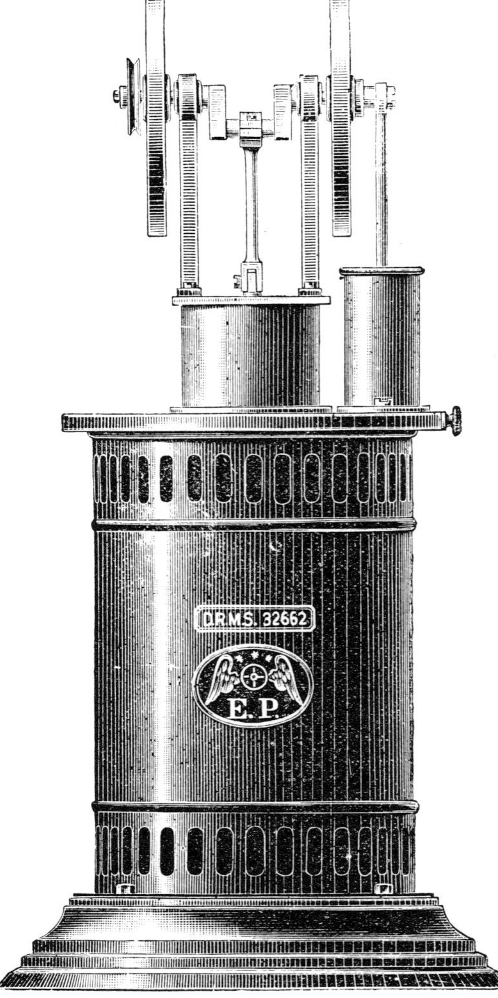

HOT AIR ENGINE.

Well made Hot Air Horizontal Engine with High Chimney.

Price **2/11** Postage 3d.

Upright Hot Air Engines.

Hot Air Engines suitable for Driving Models, &c.

No Water Required.

No.	331	332	332A	332B	
Height					in.
Price	**23/6**	**37/6**	**55/-**	**95/-**	

Hot Air Motors.

Elegant strong finish, reliahle working, no cooling necessary, fittings highly nickelled, mounted on wood stand with metal plate.

	in long.		
No. 1	9½	...	**12/6**
No. 2	11½	...	**16/6**
No. 3	14	...	**21/-**

No. 106.

The WATT Beam Steam Engine.

Beam Steam Engine built on the Watt system. Made of brass, oxydized boiler, all parts threaded easily taken to pieces.

Price ... **35/-**

No. 336.

HORIZONTAL

HOT AIR ENGINE.

Improved Hot Air Engine.

No water required.

No 334A ... **6/6** Postage 3d.

No. 334 ...**10/6** Post Free.

No. 336 .. **18/6** Post Free.

No. 338 ...**27/6** Post Free.

Gamage's Model Workshops, Engine Houses, etc.

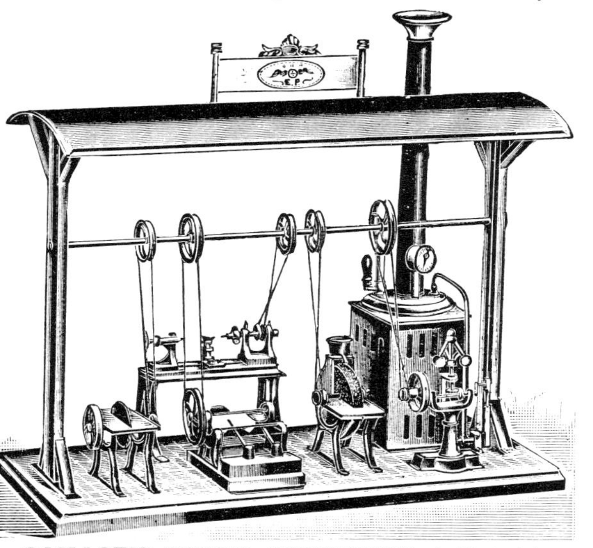

GAMAGE'S STEAM WORKSHOP As illustrated. Consisting of a Powerful Steam Engine, connected by shafting to 4 models, mounted on strong wooden base. Price **21/-**

MODEL WORKSHOP

Complete Workshop in Box.

No. 501A Consisting of Steam Engine and 3 Models,
Price **9/11** Postage 6d.

No. 501 Consisting of Steam Engine and 5 Models, as illustration.
Price **14/6**

No. 502 Consisting of Steam Engine with round Boiler and 7 Models.
Price **19/6**

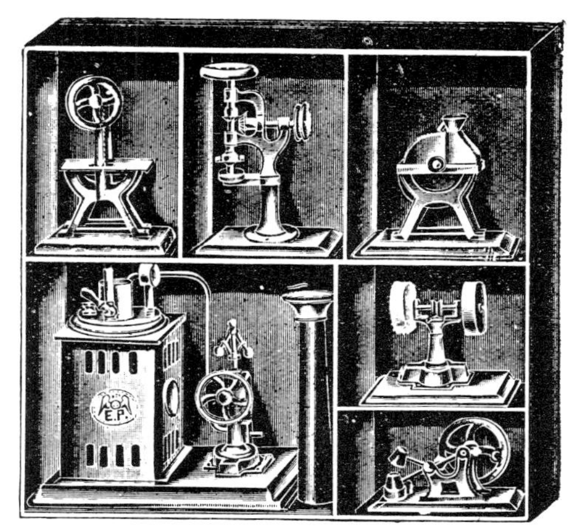

HORIZONTAL ENGINE

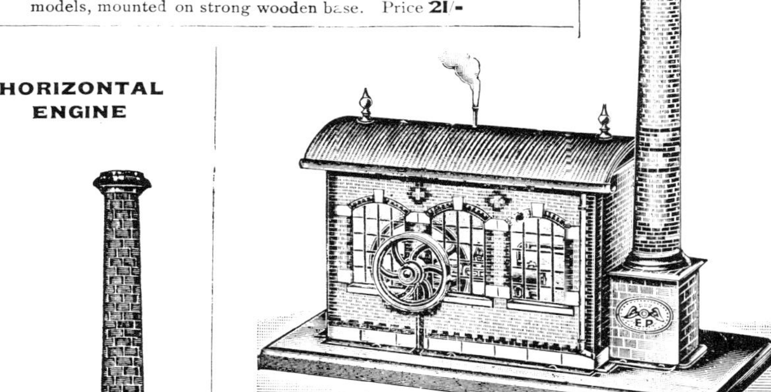

ENGINE HOUSE. Metal Engine House, with Steam Engine complete, with fly wheel outside house for connecting models. Exhaust steam passes through chimney to imitate smoke. Price **5/6** Postage 4d.

Powerful Steam Engine, with Brass Boiler, fitted with Safety Valve, Water Gauge, Steam Whistle, &c., &c., as illustrated. Superior make and finish.
Price ... **65/-**

HORIZONTAL ENGINE

Horizontal Steam Engine of best make and finish.

Nickel Plated parts, very handsome model.

No. 4115 ... **42/-**

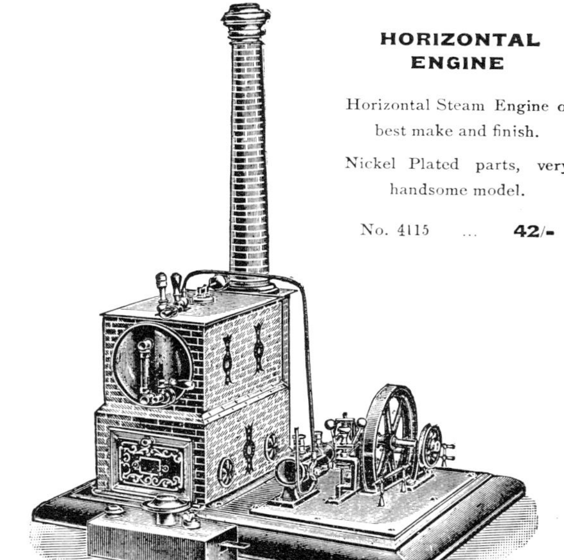

Gamage's Steam Workshop.

No. 120A Engine Shop, connected by shafting to 6 models, on strong wooden base, exhaust steam comes out of the chimney to imitate smoke.

Price 42/-

No. 120B Ditto Engine Shop of larger construction with a more powerful steam engine connected to 9 models, mounted on strong wooden base, movable skylight.

Price 75/-

Special Steam Workshop.

WITH TWO MODELS.

Price 9/11

Postage 4d.

Gamage's Working Models, For connecting to Steam and Hot air Engine and Electric Motors.

No. 7. **Model Lathe.**

Price ... ... **1/9** Postage 3d.

No. 5. **Model Grindstone**

Price ... **1/3** Postage 3d.

No. 10. **Model Circular Saw**

Price **2/-**

Postage 3d.

No. 9. **Model Hammer**

Price **2/-**

Postage 3d.

Model Chopping Machine

With moveable choppers and turning chopping board.

$5\frac{1}{2}$ in. by 5 in. wide.

Price ... **3/-**

Postage 3d.

Model Mincing Machine

With turning mincing knives.

$4\frac{1}{4}$ in. long, $5\frac{1}{2}$ in. high

Price ... **1/9**

Postage 3d.

No. 108.

Model Thrashing Machine

With moving sieve and corn elevator.

$9\frac{1}{2}$ in. long, 6 in. high

Price ... **6/11**

Postage 3d.

No. 103.

Model Turnip Cutter

$4\frac{1}{4}$ in. wide by 5 in. high.

Price ... **2/3**

Postage 3d.

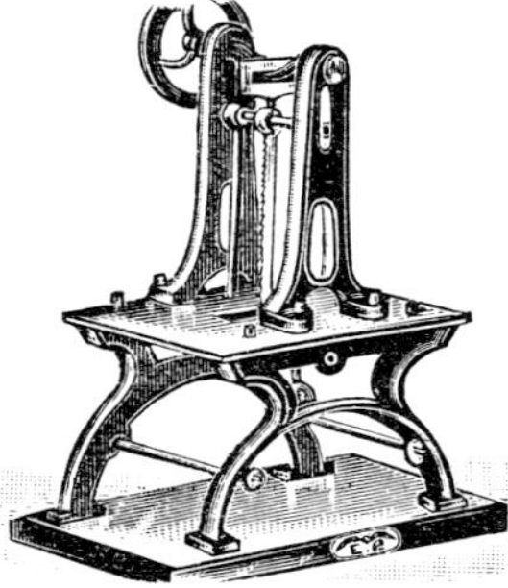

No. 19.

Model Upright Saw

Price ... **2/-**

Postage 3d.

No. 62.

Model Sorting Machine

With 3 pint sorter and 2 tubs.

10 in. long $6\frac{1}{2}$ in. high.

Price ... **7/11**

Postage 4d.

No. 102 as No 101

Model Sorting Machine

8 in. long 7 in high

Price ... **2/6**

Postage 3d.

Model Punching Machine

Price ... **1/9** Postage 3d.

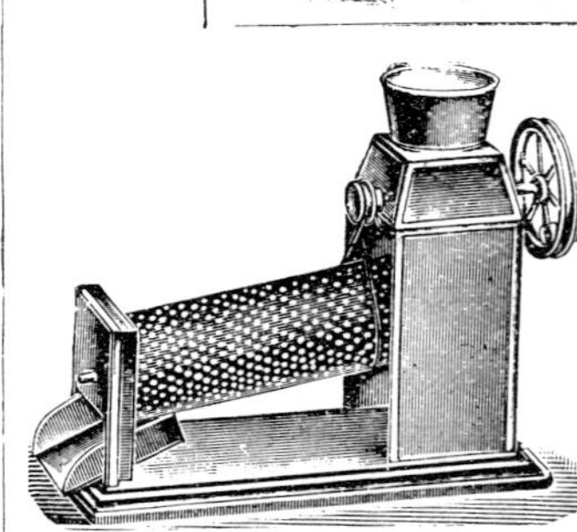

No. 101.

Model Sorting Machine

Sand is poured into the funnel and passes through the turning cylinder where it is sorted into 3 degrees of fineness.

6 in. long, 5 in. high.

Price ... **1/3** Postage 3d.

No. 109.

Model Thrashing Machine on Wheels

With moving sieve and corn elevator.

10 in. long, 6 in. wide $8\frac{1}{4}$ in. high.

Price ... **11/6**

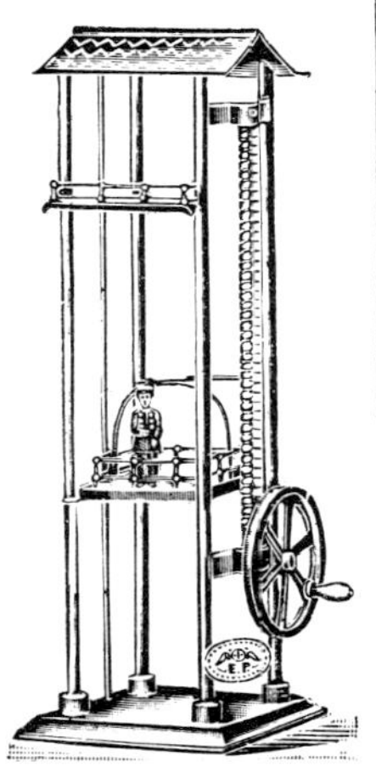

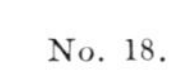

No. 18.

Model Dredger

Price **4/6**

No. 30.

Model Elevator

Price ... **4/6**

Postage 3d.

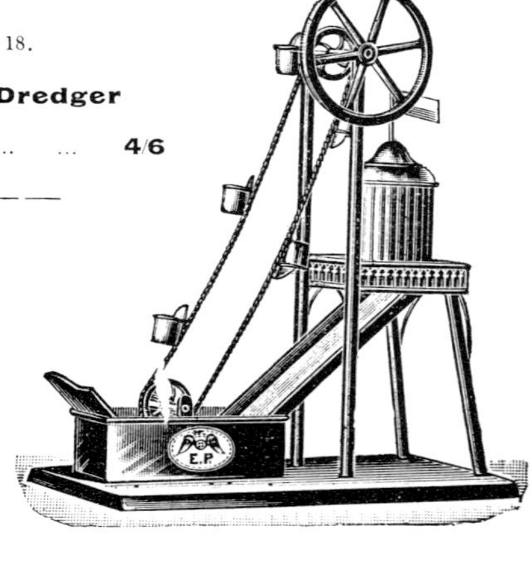

Gamage's Working Models, with and without Engines.

Model Butter Machine.

With glass inside,
6 in. diameter. $5\frac{1}{2}$ in. high.
Price 2/9
Postage 3d.

No. 17.

Model Wheel of Life.

Price 3/9

Postage 4d.

Model Chaff Cutter.

With 2 knives. 6 in. long.

Price 3/6

Postage 3d.

Model Chromotrope.

With changeable discs. $7\frac{1}{2}$ in. high.

Price 2/6

Postage 3d.

Model Grinding Mill.

$5\frac{1}{4}$ in. long. $6\frac{1}{2}$ in. high.
Price 5/6
Postage 3d.

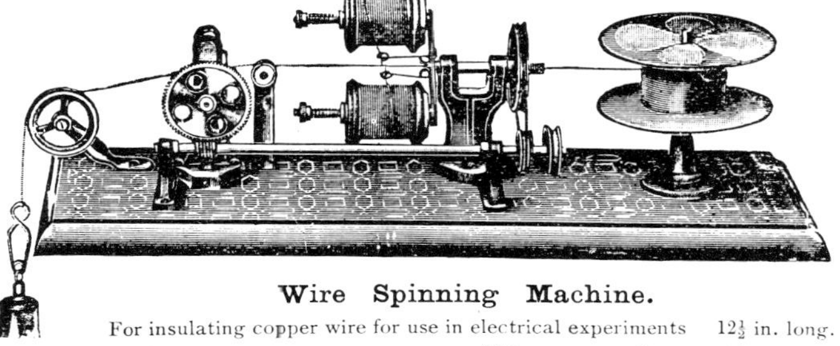

Wire Spinning Machine.

For insulating copper wire for use in electrical experiments $12\frac{1}{2}$ in. long.
Price ... ... 7/6 Postage 3d.

Model House and Fountain.

As illustration. Price 4/6 Postage 4d.

Model Fountains.

Quite new. No. 40 2/6 No. 41 4/6 No. 42 6/11
Postage 3d.

Model Dredger with Steam Engine.

Model Circular Saw.

No. 113. Fitted with best Steam Engine.
As illustration, Price 8/11 Postage 6d.

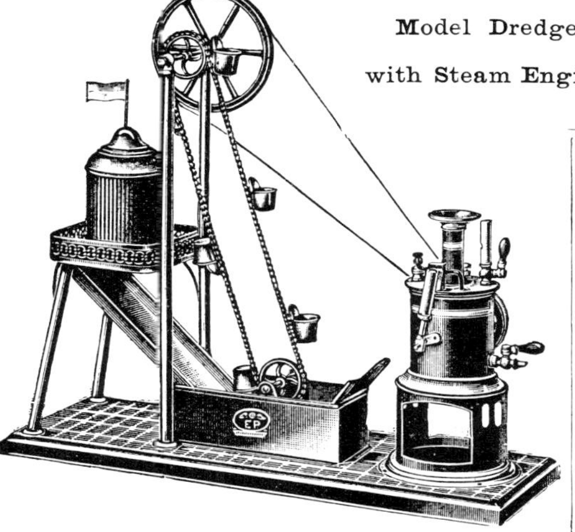

No. 121 As illustration, fitted with best Steam Engine.
Price 13/6

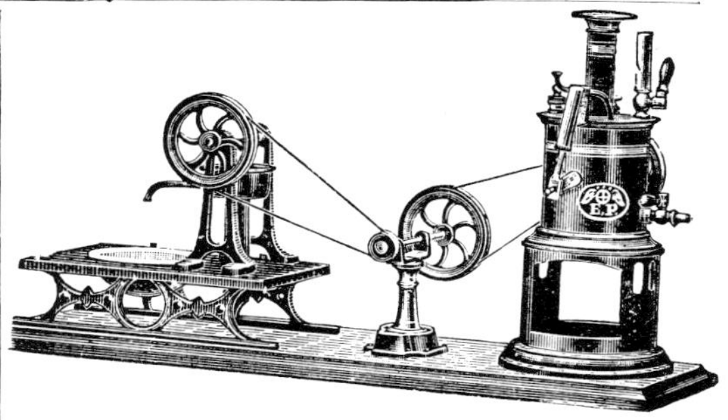

Model Pump.

No. 119. Fitted with best Steam Engine, as illustrated
Price 13/6

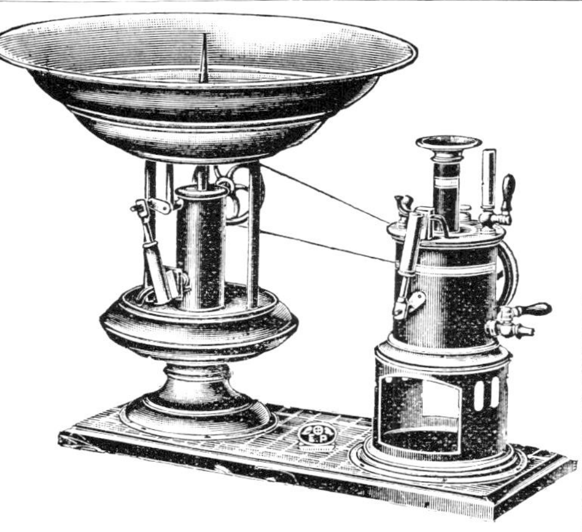

Superior Quality Fountain.

No. 201 Fitted with good Steam Engine.

Price ... 13/6

Model Windmill.

No. 16.

Price ... 2/6

Postage 3d.

Model Brewery with Steam Engine.

No. 121A.

Similar to illustration, fitted with best Steam Engine

Price 21/-

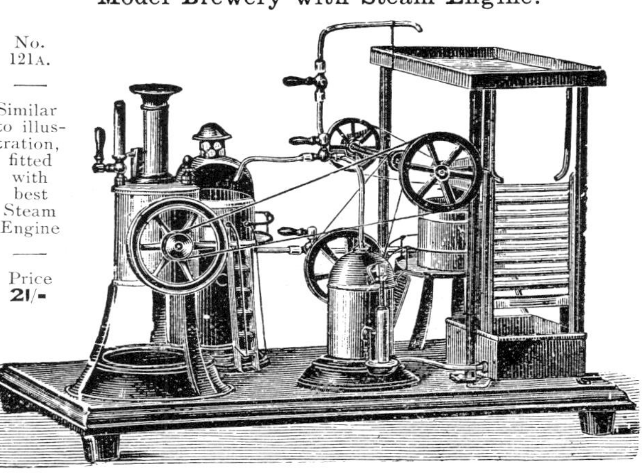

Gamage's Steam & Clockwork Boats.

No. 27.
Clockwork Torpedo Boat.

Price .. **2/6** .. Postage 3d.

No. 28.
Clockwork .. Torpedo Boat.
Price **4/11**
Postage 3d.

No. 205.
Clockwork Gun Boat.
Price .. .. **6/6** .. Postage 3d.

Special Purchase

250 STEAM MODEL SCREW BOATS

(As illustration.) **TO BE CLEARED** (As illustration.)

AT LESS THAN COST PRICE!!!

Best Make and Workmanship, and Guaranteed to Work.

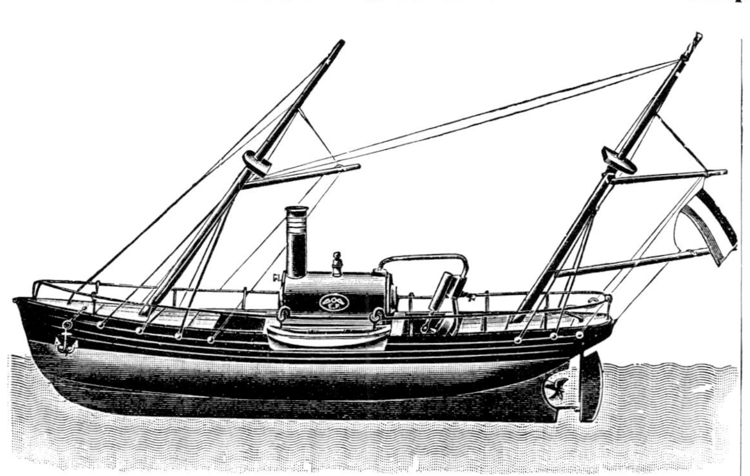

No. 230.

No. 234.

No. 228, 12 in. long,
3/6

No. 230, 18 in. long, two Masts and two Lifeboats
8/6

No. 233, 24 in. long, two Masts and two Lifeboats
35/-

No. 234, 27½ in. long, two Masts, two Lifeboats, and two funnels,
63/-

Gamage's Submarine Boats, Diving Fish, &c.

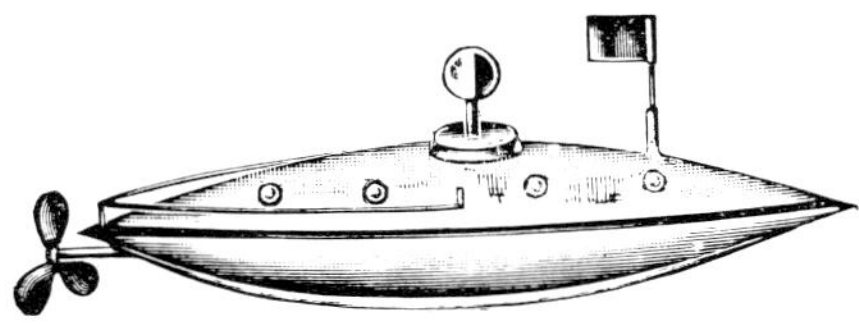

Clockwork Submarine Boats.

10½d. Postage 3d.

Ditto, larger .. .. **1/4½** Postage 3d.

Ditto, ... **2/6** Postage 3d.

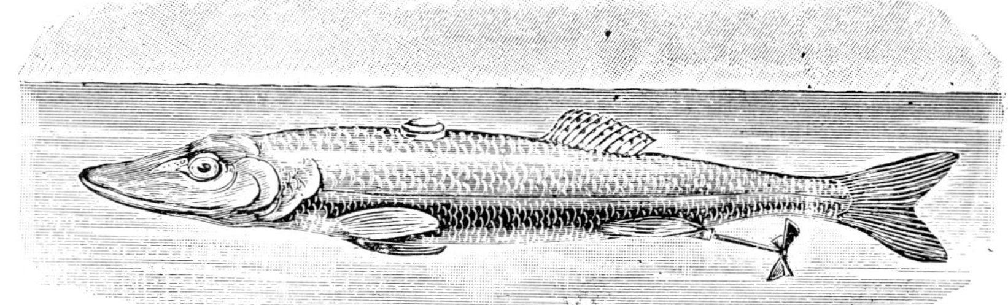

The Plunging Pike.

Alternately diving and rising to the surface of the water, cannot sink. Well japanned fitted with strong clockwork movement. Price **6/6** Postage 3d.

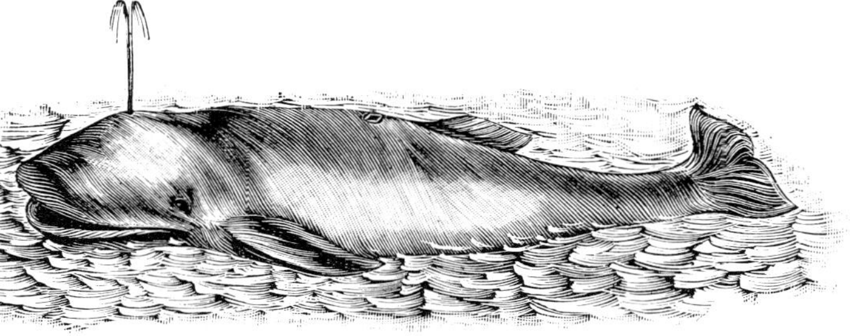

The Whale.

Fitted with strong clockwork movement. A great novelty. **6/6** Postage 3d.

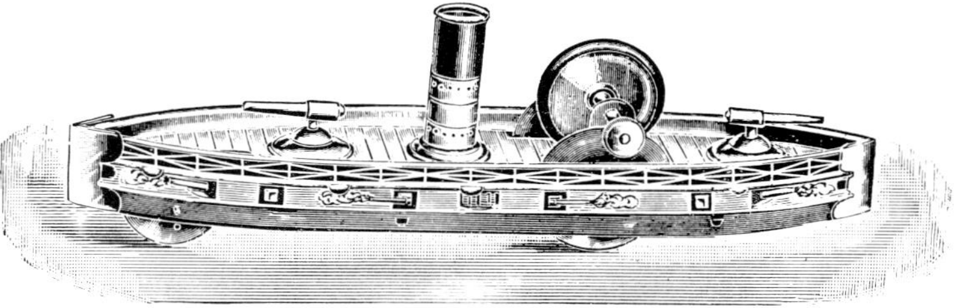

Mechanical Gun Boat.

Price .. .. **10½d.** Postage 3d.

Model Submarine Boat.

Alternately diving and rising to the surface of the water, cannot sink. Finely japanned and fitted with powerful clockwork movement.

No. 1.	13½ in. long	..	**6/6**	Postage 3d
No. 2.	18 ,,	..	**12/9**	
No. 3.	27 ,,	..	**37/6**	

Ocean Liner "Britannia."

Propelled by steam.

Handsomely enamelled, fitted with 2 lifeboats and figures 22 in. long.

Price **25/-**

Gamage's Clockwork and Steam Torpedo Boats, &c.

Gun Boat.

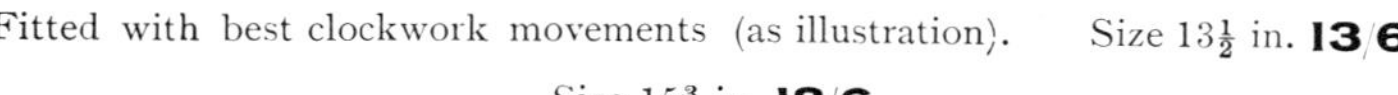

Fitted with best clockwork movements (as illustration). Size 13½ in. **13/6**

Size 15¾ in. **18/6**

Steam Torpedo Boat.

Fitted with powerful Engine beautifully japanned	**17/6**
Ditto, ...	**27/6**
Ditto, larger, a handsome boat	**47/6**

Gun Boat.

Fitted with best clockwork movements.

Size 17½ in. **22/6**

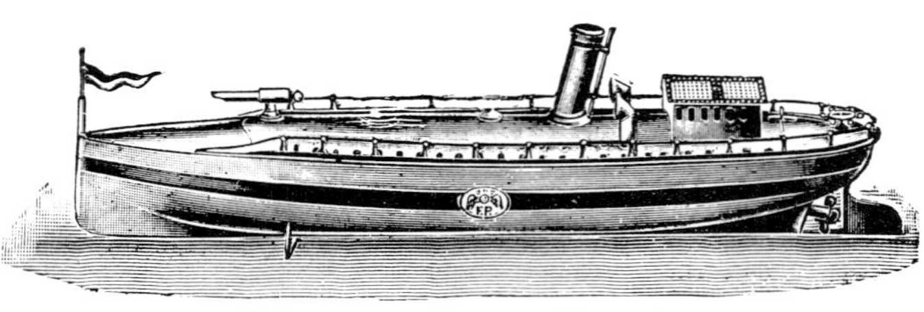

Steam Gun Boat.

Fitted with best quality Engine 12 in. long, best white japanned, with 1 quick firing cannon, armoured turret and ventilator.

6/6 Postage 3d.

Steam Despatch Boat.

20 in. long, best white japanned, with mast, 9 ventilators, 6 cannons, 4 life-boats compass, 2 anchors, with 3 funnels. Complete .. **18/6**

24 in. long, best white japanned with 2 signal masts with arc lamps and look out, 13 ventilators, 8 cannons, 6 life-boats, compass, 2 anchors, life-belt, with 3 funnels. Complete **25/6**

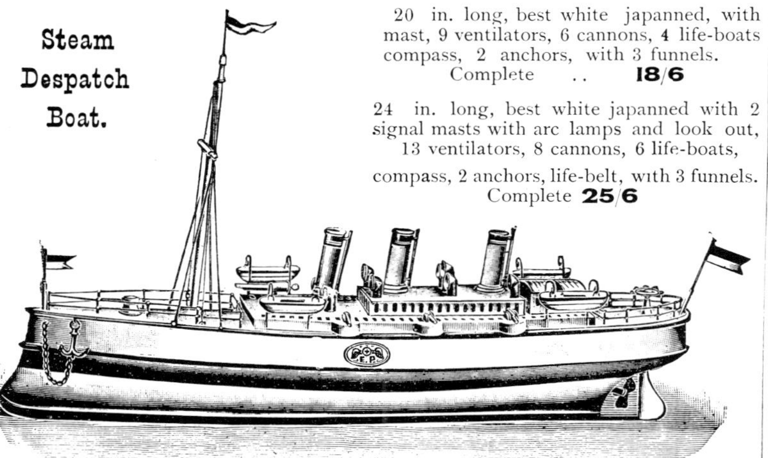

Steam Despatch Boat.

Best white japanned, with mast, 8 ventilators, 4 cannons, 2 life-boats, 2 anchors, fitted with best quality engine, **11/6** 16 in. long.

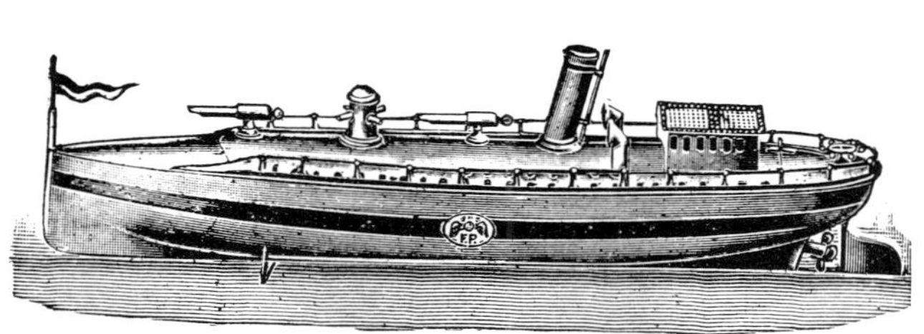

Steam Torpedo Boats.

No. 127. Steam Torpedo Boat, fitted with good Engine. Length 11½ in. Price **7/6** Postage 4d.

No. 127A.	Do., do., (as illustration) length 15¾ in.	**10/6**
No. 127B.	Do., do., length 19½ in	**15/6**

Torpedo Catcher.

Fitted with best clockwork movements, beautifully japanned. 13½ in.	**15/-**
Ditto, large size ..	**25/-**
Ditto, larger size ..	**45/-**

Gamage's Steam, Clockwork and Electric Boats, etc.

No. G. **Clockwork River Paddle Boat,** Finely Japanned, 20 in. long, **21/-**

Screw Ship.

No. 60. Screw Clockwork Ship, best movements, beautifully Japanned. Length 13½ in. Price **10/6**

Clockwork Paddle Boat.

No. E ... ... **3/6** Postage 3d.
No. F, with Canopy **6/6** ,,

No. 128A. **Screw Steam Boat.**

Fitted with Reliable Engine, 10 in. long, Well Enamelled, **3/6**

Clockwork River Boats.

No. 5. Clockwork Screw Boat ... **6/6** No. 6 As illustration ... **8/6**

No. 128. **Screw Steam Boat.**

Painted White, &c. Fitted with Reliable Engine, 13¾ in. long, **6/6**
Postage 3d.

Electric Boats.

No. 180. Small size ... **17/6** No. 181. Medium size, as illustration .. **23/6**

Screw Steam Boa

Fitted with Good, Reliable Engine, with Brass Boiler. Japanned Gold and White.

Price ... **21/-**

No. A	**Clockwork Boat**	... **1/6**	Postage 3d.
,, B	,, ,,	... **2/6**	,,
,, C	,, ,,	... **3/6**	,,
,, D	,, ,,	... **4/6**	,,

Gamage's Clockwork and Steam Boats.

H.M.S. GRIFFIN.

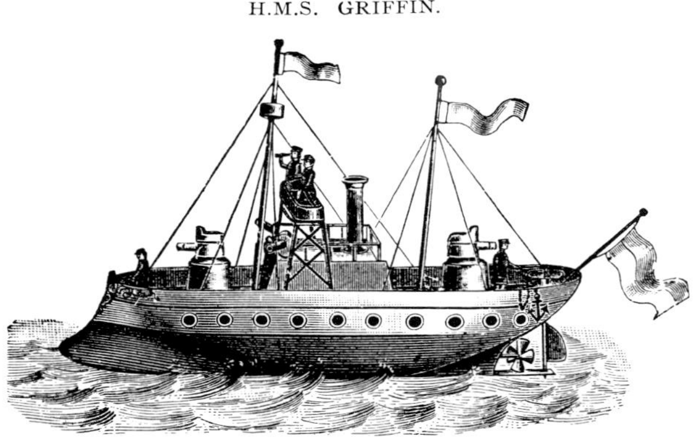

No. 1086.

Clockwork Battleship.

Fitted with 4 Guns and full equipments, $15\frac{3}{4}$ inches long.

Price .. **18/6**

Clockwork Fire Boat .. 6/6 Postage 3d.

Lighthouse.

Finely Japanned, fitted for Lighting, with Revolving Lamp and Coloured Glass Windows, (representing the flash light), light intensified through lens, very original, $17\frac{1}{2}$ inches high.

Price .. **8/6** Postage 4d.

Steam Torpedo Division Boat.

Superior make, fitted with 2 Quick Firing Guns and 2 Torpedo Tubes, 24 inches long. Price **15/-**

Man of War.

Beautifully Enamelled, fitted with very powerful Clockwork Movements,

90/-

Gamage's Steam and Clockwork Boats—*continued.*

Steam Torpedo Boat.

Beautifully Japanned with 1 Torpedo Tube. Price **7/11** Postage 6d.

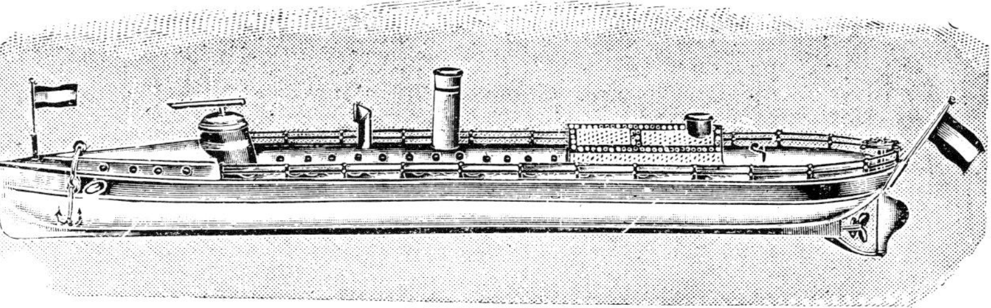

Steam Torpedo Boat.

Beautifully Japanned, fitted with Powerful Engine and 1 Torpedo Tube.

Price .. .. **9/11** Postage 6d.

Steam Battleship.

"TERRIBLE."

Extra fine finish and richly fitted up with 6 Life boats, 2 fore and aft Barbette Guns, 14 Cannon, 3 Guns in casements, 4 Quick Firing Guns with shields, and 4 imitation Search Lights.

32 inches long .. **84/-**

Special Clockwork Battleship.

Fitted with 16 Guns, Well Enamelled.

Length

Price .. **50/-**

Ocean Liner.

"COLUMBIA"

Propelled by Steam, Beautifully Enamelled, Fitted with 4 Life Boats and 6 Guns, 26 in. long.

Price .. **42/-**

Ditto,

"OCEANIC."

As illustration.

Fitted with 6 Life Boats.

Price .. **70/-**

Gamage's Clockwo k and Steam Boats—*continued.*

Gun Boat 'Terror.'

Built from original dockyard designs.

Propelled by steam.

Beautifully Japanned and finished, fitted with 2 life boats, 4 cannons and 1 quick firing gun. 20 inches long.

Price **18/6**

Gun Boat 'Mars.'

Propelled by Steam.

Finely Japanned, with 2 life boats, 6 cannons and 2 quick firing guns, 24 in. long.

Price **25/-**

Gun Boat 'Tiger.'

Propelled by Steam. Finely Japanned, with 4 life boats, 8 cannons and 2 quick firing guns, 30 in. long.

Price **35/-**

WAR! WAR! WAR!

BUY YOUR SONS

SOLDIERS of the KING and BOER SOLDIERS,

Which will enable them to learn THE ART OF MODERN WARFARE.

A. W. GAMAGE Ltd. have the **LARGEST COLLECTION** of **TOY SOLDIERS** (English and Foreign) in Great Britain, and an **IMMENSE STOCK** of **Guns, Cannon, Forts, Swords, Tents, Ambulances, Armour Sets, Armoured Trains, &c., &c., &c.,** at **PRICES that will DEFY COMPETITION.**

SOLDIERS OF THE KING.—*MADE IN LONDON. Designed and Modelled by First-class English Artists, and produced entirely by British Labour.* **6d. Boxes, 4½d.,** postage 2d. **1/- Boxes, 10½d.,** postage 2d.

THEY are made exact to scale, that is, a foot soldier is the same size as a horse soldier, and the Horses are in proportion to the men, whilst the uniforms and colorings have been most carefully considered so as to give a correct representation of the various regiments.

No. 1B 1st Life Guards ... **4½**d.
,, 6B 2nd Dragoon (Scots Greys)... **4½**d.
,, 10B 11th Hussars ... **4½**d.
,, 12B 16th Lancers (Active Service)... **4½**d.
,, 20B Manchester Regt.... **4½**d.
,, 21B Northumberland Fusiliers (Active Service Order) ... **4½**d.

No. 13B 17th Lancers ... **4½**d.
,, 15B Mounted Infantry .. **4½**d.

All these have Movable Arms.

No. 16B Coldstream Guards **4½**d.
,, 22B Blue Jackets (H.M.'s Navy) ... **4½**d.
,, 17B Lancashire Fusiliers **4½**d.
,, 23B Cameron Highlandrs **4½**d.

Postage 2d.

OUR INDIAN ARMY.

No. 67 Madras Native Infantry **10½**d.
,, 66 Bombay Lancers ... **10½**d.
,, 46 10th Bengal Lancers... **10½**d.
,, 68 2nd Bombay Native Infy. **10½**d.
,, 19 West India Regiment **10½**d.
,, 45 3rd. Madras Light Cavly. **10½**d.

No. 47 1st Bengal Cavalry ... **10½**d.
,, 62 1st Bengal Cavalry (10 large mounted soldiers) **1 9**
,, 63 10th Bengal Lancers (10 large mounted soldiers) **1 9**

Postage 3d.

No. 43 2nd Life Guards ... **10½**d.
,, 1 1st Life Guards ... **10½**d.
,, 31 1st Dragoon Guards **10½**d.
,, 2 Royal Horse Guards **10½**d.
,, 32 2nd Dragoon Guards (R. Scots Greys) ... **10½**d.
,, 77 Gordon Highlanders and Pipers ... **10½**d.
,, 34 Grenadier Guards **10½**d.
,, 7 7th Royal Fusiliers **10½**d.
,, 99 The 13th Hussars **10½**d.
,, 13 3rd Hussars (King's Own) ... **10½**d.
,, 12 11th Hussars (Prince Albert's Own) ... **10½**d.
,, 23 5th Lancers (R. Irish) **10½**d.
,, 24 9th ,, (Queen's R.) **10½**d.
,, 18 Worcesters're Reg. **10½**d.
,, 16 The Buffs (East Kent Regiment) ... **10½**d.

No. 15. **Argyle and Sutherland Highlanders** (Princess Louise's 91st) **10½**d.

No. 11 The Black Watch (Royal Highlanders) ... ... **10½**d.
,, 91 United States Infantry ... ... **10½**d.
,, 92 Sparish Infantry ... ... **10½**d.
,, 84 Types of British Army, containing 2nd Life Guards and 7th Royal Fusiliers ... ... **10½**d.
,, 81 17th Lancers (Active Service Order) .. .. **10½**d.
,, 82 Colors and Pioneers of the Scots Guards ... ... **10½**d.
,, 77 Gordon Highlanders and Pipers ... ... **10½**d.
,, 75 The Scots Guards (Movable Arms) ... ...
,, 74 The Royal Welsh Fusiliers (23rd Regiment) ... **10½**d.
,, 33 15th Lancers (Queen's) ... ... **10½**d.
,, 17 Somersetshire Light Infantry (Prince Albert's 13th) **10½**d.
,, 36 Royal Sussex Regiment ... ... **10½**d.
,, 100 The 21st Lancers ... ... **10½**d.
,, 8 4th Hussars (Queen's Own) ... ... **10½**d.
,, 3 5th Dragoon Guards ... ... **10½**d.
,, 98 The King's Royal Rifle Corps ... ... **10½**d.
,, 49 The South Australian Lancers ... . **10½**d.

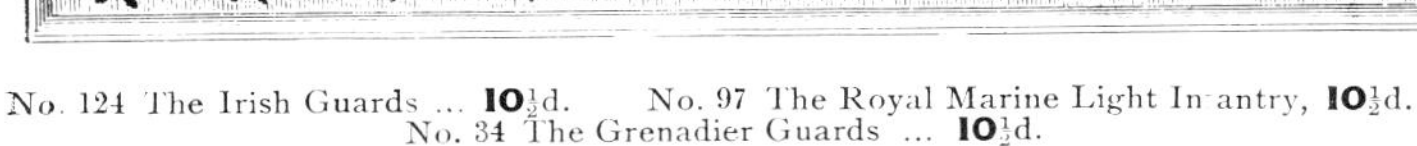

No. 124 The Irish Guards ... **10½**d. No. 97 The Royal Marine Light Infantry, **10½**d.
No. 34 The Grenadier Guards ... **10½**d.

No. 122 The Black Watch Highlanders, **10½**d. No. 121 The West Surrey Regiment, **10½**d.
Copyright models.

No. 104 City Imperial Volunteers ... ... **10½**d. box, postage 2d.

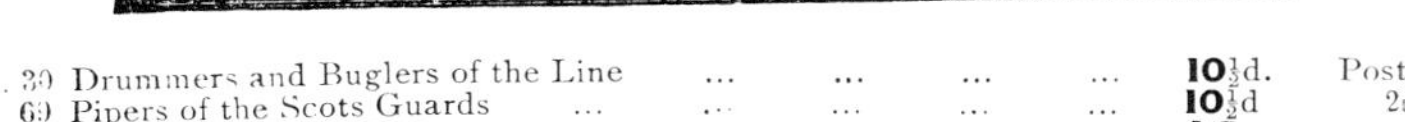

No. 39 Drummers and Buglers of the Line ... ... **10½**d. Postage
,, 69 Pipers of the Scots Guards ... ... **10½**d 2d.
,, 27 Brass Band of the Line ... ... **1/9**, postage 3d.

No. 37 Full Band of the Coldstream Guards ...

Price **3/3** Postage 3d.

(Continued on next page.)

LONDON MADE TOY SOLDIERS—*continued.*

No. 105. **Imperial Yeomanry** 10½d. box. Postage 2d,

No. 6. **Boer Cavalry,** 10½d.

No. 26. **Boer Infantry,** 10½d.

No. 44. **Dragoon Guards (Queen's Bays)** 10½d.

No. 123.
THE . . .
Bikanir Camel Corps.
10½d.
Postage 3d.

No. 48.
Egyptian Camel Corps.
Detachable Men. Price 1/9 Postage 3d.

Types of the British Army.

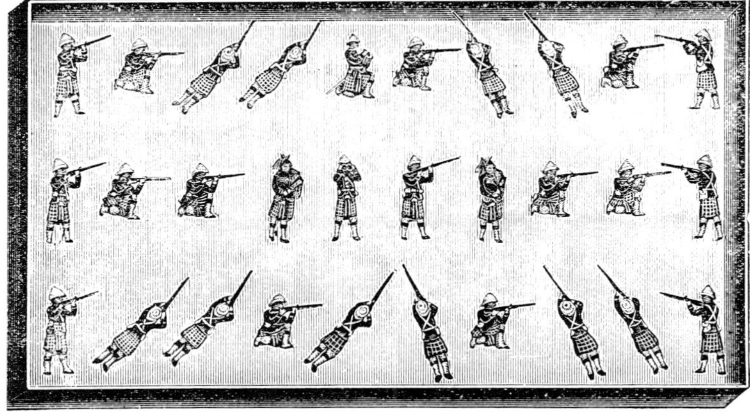

No. 89. **The Cameron Highlanders,** 2/3.
No. 90. **The Coldstream Guards** .. 2/3.
Copyright Models. Postage 3d.

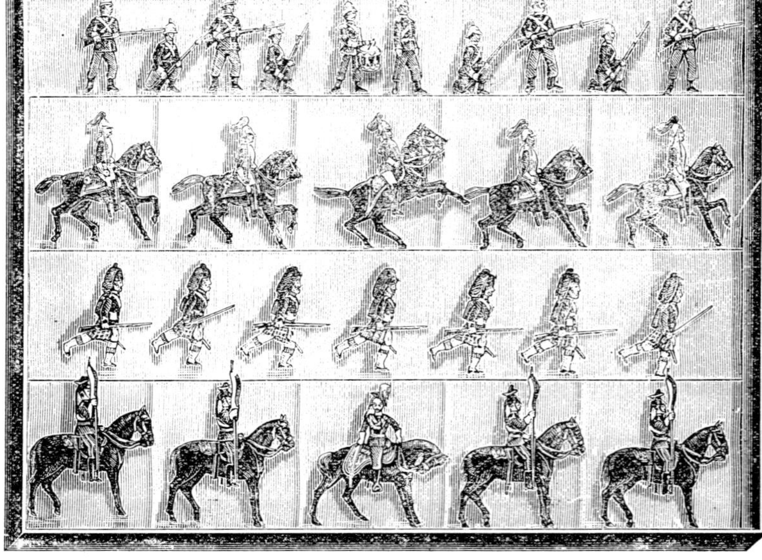

No. 22.

No. 41.	2nd Dragoon and Grenadier Guards	1/9
,, 56.	Grenadier Guards and The Buffs	1/9
,, 52.	2nd Life Guards and 5th Lancers	1/9
,, 51.	11th Hussars and 16th Lancers	1/9
,, 85.	5th Dragoon Guards, 2nd Dragoons, Scots Guards and Northumberland Fusiliers ... ... Postage 3d.	1/9
,, 21.	1st Life Guards, 11th Hussars, West India Regiment, The Buffs (E. Kent Regiment)	3/3
,, 22.	Royal Horse Guards, 5th Lancers, The Black Watch (Royal Highlanders), Worcester Regiment ...	3/3
,, 29.	Complete Mule Battery, 1st Life Guards, 3rd Hussars, 9th Lancers, and Queen's Royal West Surrey Regiment Postage 4d.	5/9
,, 93.	Contains a complete Company of Coldstream Guards, with Officers, Full Band, Colors and Pioneers, and a Squadron of Royal Horse Guards, with Trumpeters, &c., packed in a well-made wooden framed box, with tray to lift out. Size of box 2-ft. by 1-ft. 1-in. Carriage paid.	10/6

No. 73. Price 21/- Carriage paid.

No. 73. This is a very large and handsome Presentation Selection of London-made Metal Soldiers, got up in the best style and packed in a splendidly lined wooden box, with extra tray. Size of box 2-ft. 2-in. by 1-ft. 3-in. Containing the following Regiments: The Royal Horse Artillery, 2nd Life Guards, 17th Lancers, Royal Welsh Fusiliers, Band of the Line, The Gordon Highlanders, and a General Officer.

English & Continental Soldiers.

Superior quality Bavarian make Soldiers. English Infantry and Cavalry in Khaki. Also Boer Infantry and Cavalry, C.I.V's., Rough Riders, &c. KHAKI SOLDIERS, &c.

Solid Metal Soldiers, Beautifully Finished and Packed in Strong Boxes.

No. 1109. English Infantry, 12 Large Size Soldiers in box .. 6/6 Post 6d.
,, 1112. English Horse Guards 14/6
,, 1112. Assorted Cavalry 14/6

A large assortment of English & Boer Cavalry and Infantry, &c.

Boer Infantry, 4½d. & 10½d. English Infantry (Khaki) 4½d. & 10½d.
,, Cavalry, 4½d. & 10½d. ,, Cavalry ,, 4½d. & 10½d.
C.I.V. Cycle Section in Khaki, 2/6 Post 3d. Rough Riders, 2/6 Post 3d.

Soldiers to Shoot.

No. 25. Each Soldier has the barrel of his gun bored out and a spring attached complete with bullets. 10½d. Post 2d.

LATEST NOVELTY !!! GILT SOLDIERS

Small Foot 6d. doz. Colored 1/-
Large Horse & Foot, 1/- & 2/- doz.

No. 125. **The Royal Horse Artillery,** (Review Order), 2/-
,, 126. **Ditto,** (Active Service Order) 3/-
Patented. Postage 3d.

No. 28.

Complete Mountain Artillery.

With Quick-firing Gun to take on and off the mules, ammunition included in each box.

Warranted a perfect and well-working model.

Price 2/- .. Postage 3d.

No. 39.

Royal Horse Artillery.

Complete with Quick-firing Gun with Levelling Screw and Amunition.

This is a splendid Model, carefully proportioned in every particular, and is altogether very realistic. The Gunners may be removed from their seats, and the seats from the gun for firing. The ammunition is carried in the limber.

Price 4/11 .. Postage 3d.

For extra Guns, see Page 56.

No. 79. Landing Party of **British Sailors,** with breech-loading Field Gun, complete with ammunition. Price 2/- Postage 3d.

No. 78. Blue Jackets of the Royal Navy. Price 10½d. Postage 3d.

No. 80. White Jackets of the Royal Navy. Price 10½d. Postage 3d.

DRILLING GROUND.

Infantry.

No. 49. Complete with Company of Infantry, 19 Men, 2 Drummers, 1 Officer Mounted and 1 Dismounted, 3/11 Postage 3d.

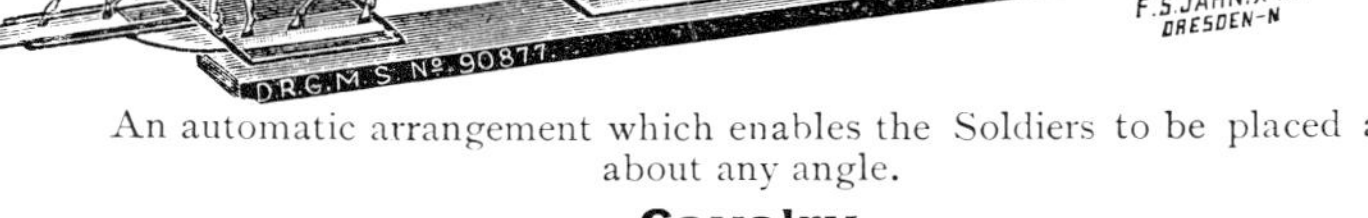

An automatic arrangement which enables the Soldiers to be placed at about any angle.

Cavalry.

No. 21. Complete with Company of English Cavalry, 9 Lancers, 1 Officer and 2 Trumpeters, 4/6. Postage 3d.

No. 1142. **Lord Roberts' Arrival in London,** including Mounted Escorts, Bands, Street Decorations, &c., 25/- Larger size 35/-

No. 1159. **English Camp,** complete with 3 Tents, Baggage Wagons, Earthwork, Trees, Cooking arrangements, Troops of Infantry and Cavalry, &c., &c., 25/-

No. 948. **A Baloon Section,** complete with Wagons, Bicycles, Trees, &c., 17/6.

No. 949. **Telegraph Section,** complete with Poles, Wires, Battery, 3 Wagons, 34 Soldiers and 2 Mounted Officers, 25/-

No. 1177. **Ambulance Station** complete with Cart, Tent, Flag, Men, Soldiers, Stretchers, &c. .. .. 10/6.

No. 831. **Cavalry Set.** 24 Large Mounted Soldiers, best quality and beautifully colored, 2 Regiments in a Box, 17/6.

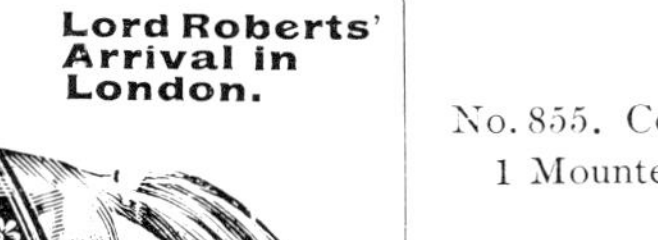

Lord Roberts' Arrival in London.

Reviews, etc.

No. 855. Containing 1 Battery, 2 Line Regmts., 1 Mounted Regiment, Band of the Line. All in Khaki.

Price.. .. ..12/6 Carriage Free.

BANDMASTER beating time, and BAND playing "SOLDIERS OF THE KING," or "BRITISH GRENADIERS."

Price.. .. ..14/6 each

Gamage's Forts, Tents, &c.—*continued.*

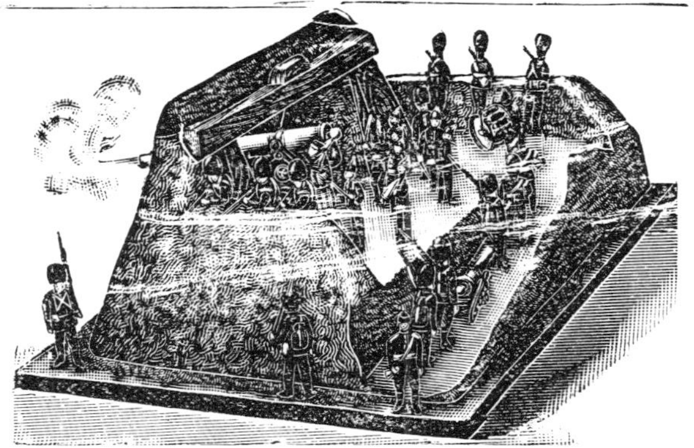

Outposts. Most realistic, with Grass Slopes, etc.
No. 11. Price **2/-** .. carriage 4d.
No. 12 (as illustration). Price **4/6** .. carriage 6d.
Soldiers and Guns Extra (see pages 51 to 56.)

New Collapsible Fort. Beautifully Enamelled Tin.
Falls to pieces on being struck with shot, etc. .. **15/-** each.

Beautifully designed, with Grass Slopes, Centre Tower, etc.
No. 13 .. .. **14/6** each. | No. 14 (Extra Large) .. **25/-** each.
Soldiers and Guns Extra, see pages 51 to 56. Carriage paid.

Tents for Toy Soldiers.

All made to fold up.

Size 6—White. **6d.** each.
Red or Blue. **9½d.** ,,
8½d. each.
Size 4—**4d.** each.
6½d. ,,
Size 3—**3d.** each.
6d. ,,
Size 2—**2½d.** each.
4d. ,,
Size 1—**2d.** each.
3d. ,,

Postage on quantities of 1 to 3 .. .. 1d. 3 to 6 .. .. 1½d. 6 to 12 .. .. 2d. Orders for 1 dozen or more Post Free.

Officer's Tents with Table and Chairs, **10½d.** each .. postage 1d.

Khaki Tents, 2d., 2½d. and 3d. each .. postage 1d. **Red and White Striped, Oblong or Circular Tents, 4d.** each .. postage 1d.

Soldiers of the King
or
Two Forage Caps Full of Soldiers.

No. 1—Cavalry.

The box itself is made out of two Forage Caps, one an Officer's and the other a Trooper's (one fitting inside the other) with chin straps, and contains a Trumpeter and a full troop of the 5th Hussars, *i.e.*, a Captain and twenty-two Non-commissioned Officers & Troopers mounted, and all carrying steel swords.

Price .. **8½d.** each.
List price 1/-
Postage .. 1½d.

Soldiers of the King
or
Two Forage Caps Full of Soldiers.

No. 2—Infantry.

The box itself is made out of two Forage Caps, one a Sergeant's and the other a Private's, with chin straps, and contains a Major mounted, and a Company of Scots Guards, *i.e.*, one Captain, two Lieutenants, five Sergeants, and fifty-six Privates, all Officers carrying steel swords.

Price .. **8½d.** each.
List Price 1/-
Postage .. 1½d.

The above Illustration shows the contents of the two **1/-** boxes of "**Soldiers of the King,**" one of the Smartest Toys ever put before the public. All the Soldiers are made to stand up, and are from designs by Richard Simkin.

The Troop and Company can be drilled and paraded in various ways. 18 R.A. 21 Scots Guards. 36 Cavalry. 21 Infantry.

FORTS, CITAD LS, OUTPOSTS, etc.

Toy Fortresses representing the Principal Fortresses and Castles of Great Britain and the Continent, naturally coloured, with Drawbridges, Moats, Embankments, &c.

Fortress can be illuminated.

No.	Size.	Price.
No. 2105	14½ X 10	2/11
,, 2106	X	4/6
,, 2107	X	7/6
,, 2108	X	13/6

Carriage extra.

Enamelled Metal Fort and Tunnel.

Mounted with Guns, which fire rubber pellets by means of Amorces (paper caps).

Price .. **45/-**

EXTRA GUNS, **4/6** and **5/6** each. Postage 3d.

Rubber Pellets, 9d. doz. Postage 1d.

Castle Fortress.

Well made. Suitable for Toy Soldiers on page 52.

No.	Size.	Price
2092	13½ x 8½	**1/6**
2093	18 x 13½	**2/3**
2094	20 x 13½	**3/3**

Carriage extra.

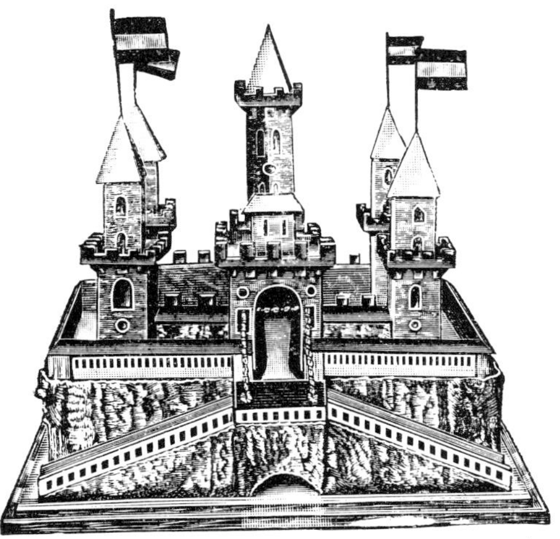

Fortress. New design.

No.	Size.	Price.
No. 1186	16½ x 14	4/3
,, 1187	20 x 17½	6/6
,, 1188	33 x 22½	9/6

Carriage extra.

Metal Mountain with Targets (all collapsible). Suitable for practice with small cannon, &c. Beautifully enamelled. Price .. **37/6**

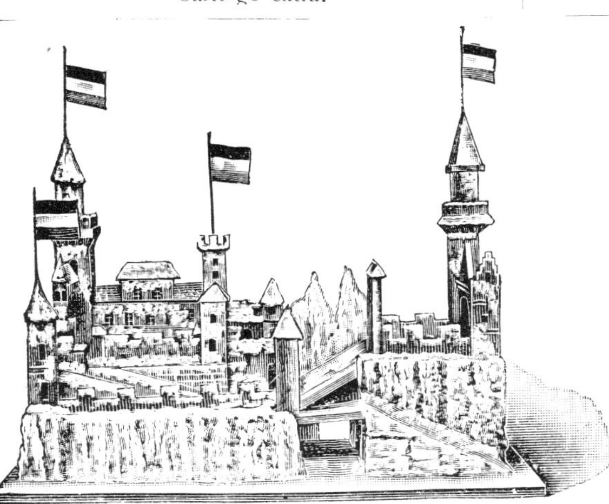

Fortress. Snow effect.

No.	Size.	Price.
No. 2119A	x	4/6
,, 2119B	19½ x 13	6/6
,, 2119C	25 x 13	9/6
,, 2119D	x	12/6

Metal Fortress. Beautifully enamelled for arranging Toy Soldiers, Battle Scenes, &c. Price **37/6**

Cannon, &c., see next page.

Toy Guns & Cannon.

The Novelties of the Season, Chinese Cracker Cannon and Amorces or Cap Cannon.

No. 1.

No. 2.

No. 3.

These Guns are made specially to fire Chinese Crackers. Very simple and quite safe. No boy should be without one.

No. 1. For Baby Chinese Crackers, Price **6½**d. Postage 2d. Crackers **6**d. per packet.

No. 1A. Medium Size Crackers, **1/-** Postage 2d. Crackers **6**d. per packet.

No. 2. For Larger Size Crackers, Price **4/6**

A very Handsome Cannon.

Crackers ... **2**d. per packet.

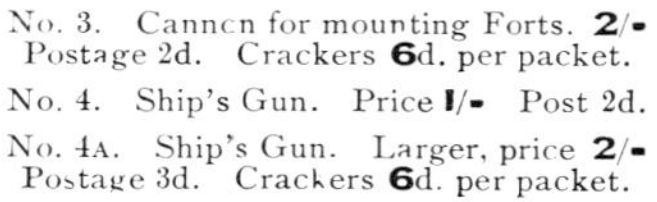

No. 3. Cannon for mounting Forts. **2/-** Postage 2d. Crackers **6**d. per packet.

No. 4. Ship's Gun. Price **1/-** Post 2d.

No. 4A. Ship's Gun. Larger, price **2/-** Postage 3d. Crackers **6**d. per packet.

Amorces or Paper Cap Cannon, giving a very loud report. Made of strong brass, breech loading complete with rubber pellet which can be fired with great precision at a distance of 12 to 20 feet. Small Size, **4/6** Large Size, **5/6** Postage 3d.

Extra Rubber Pellets ... **9**d. and **1/3** doz.
Amorces ... ... **3**d. per dozen Boxes.
Cheaper make Cap Cannon ... ... **6**d.
Larger Size ... ... **1/-** Postage 3d.

SPECIAL NOTICE.—Amorces and Chinese Crackers being explosive, are not allowed to be sent through the post, and the railway expenses being too high, A. W. Gamage, Ltd., can only supply them over the counter. They may be obtained at any Toy Shop.

Small Toy Cannon.
Suitable for mounting Forts, etc., with springs.
Price **1**d. and **2**d. each. Postage 1d.

Long Tom Cannon,
1d. each. Postage 1d.

Khaki Carriage
with Strong Springs,
2d. each.
Postage 1d.

Well Mounted **Spring Cannon.** Price **6**d.
Large Size, **1/**. Postage 1d.

Masked Cannon,
Painted KHAKI,
With Strong Springs,
3d. each.
Postage 1½d.

Best Quality
Spring Cannon,
Complete with Ammunition, as illustration.

No. 1	**1/3**
No. 2	**2/-**

Larger Cannon, with Strong Springs
4d. each. Postage 1d.
Strong Wood Cannon with Spring,
Price **1**/- Postage 3d.

Maxim Cannon,
with Strong Spring.
Price **10½**d.
Postage 1½d.

Strong Cannon,
Lead Wheels.
Fitted with strong Spring.
Price .. **10½**d.
Postage 1½d.

Gatling Gun.
The Best Novelty of the Season. With Magazine for Ammunition.

Shoots small shot with amazing rapidity.
Price .. **10½**d.
Extra shot in Handsome Souvenir Tin Boxes, 6d per box.
Postage .. 3d.

No B.
4·7 Naval Gun.
English make.
Patent, **1/6**
Postage .. 2d.

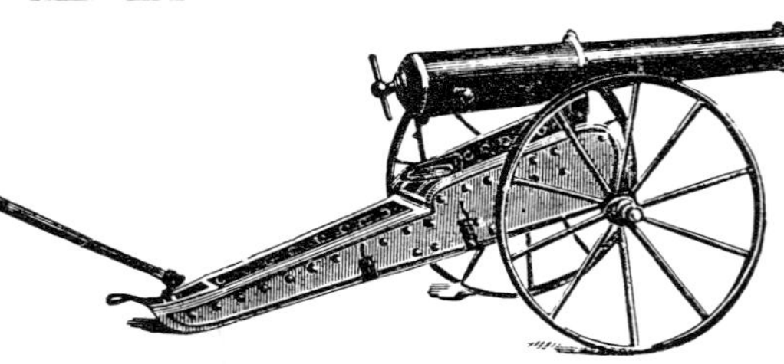

Superior Quality
Spring Cannon.
Adjustable for sighting, as illustration.

No. 3	**2/9**
,, 4	**4/9**
,, 5	**7/6**
,, 6	**10/6**

Postage 3d. under 10/-

MACHINE GUN—The Gun is well made and is capable of firing 200 shots per minute. The action is as follows: the cup on the barrel of the gun is filled with peas and the handle turned rapidly until the peas are all discharged, when it can be refilled, and the gun is ready to resume operations. Carefully packed.

Price **4/6** Postage 6d.

No. A. Gun of the
Royal Horse Artillery.
English Make. Patent.
Price .. .. **10½**d.
Postage 3d.

Brass Cannon.

No. 1.	Fitted with Solid Wheels	**6**d.
,, 2.	,, Wheels with Spokes ..	**1/-**
,, 3.	,, ,, ,, ..	**1/6**
,, 4.	,, ,, ,, ..	**2/-**

Postage 2d.

Ship's Guns.
Small Brass Cannon, mounted on wood stands with runners.
No. 51, **4**d. No. 52, **6**d.
No. 53, **1/-**
Postage .. 3d.

Air Guns, Pistols, Revolvers, etc.

Actual Size. Open.

The New Watchchain Pistol.

The Smallest Pistol made.

No. 1 Nickel-plated .. 1/6 each. Postage 2d.

No. 2 Real Silver .. 2/3 each. Postage 2d.

Daisy Air Rifle.

Shoots Shots or Darts.

Price, 2/11 Repeater, 3/11 Postage 6d.

SPECIAL OFFER.

B.B. Shot for Daisy Air Guns.

In Souvenir Boxes, 6d. Postage 3d.
The Boxes are worth the money.

Repeater Pistol.

Magazine Pistol to shoot Peas. Causing great fun. Quite Harmless. Price 10½d. Postage 2d.

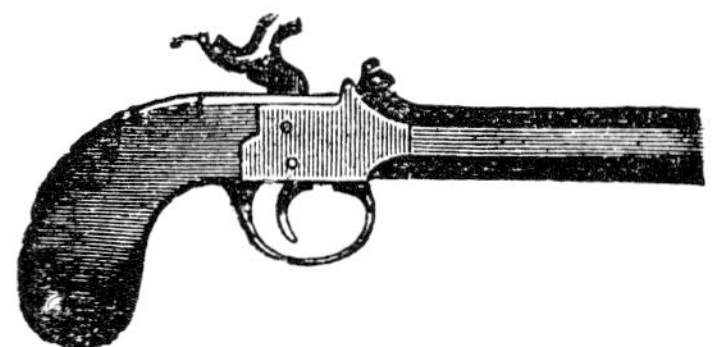

MUZZLE LOADING PISTOLS.

No. 1 .. .. 1/4½
No. 2 .. .. 2/6

Postage 4d. Percussion Caps 2d. 100

Air Pistol.

With Six Darts and Ram Rod, in box.

Price .. 1/10½
Nickelled .. 2/11

Postage 4d.

Extra Darts 6½d. per doz. Slugs 7d. per 1000.

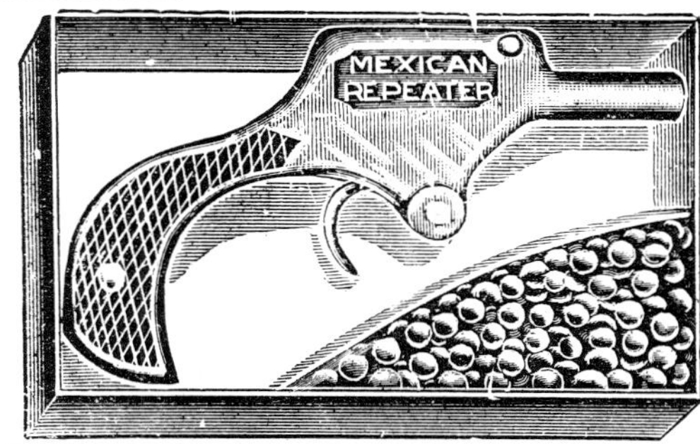

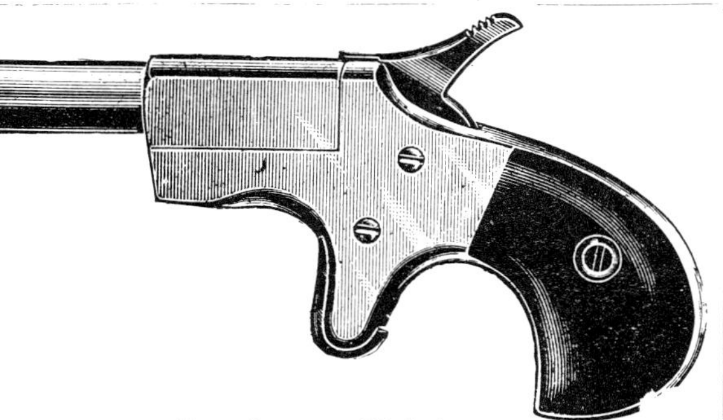

Derringer Pistol.

Nickel Plated. For No. 1 Bulleted Breech Caps, 5 in. long, 2/11
Ditto, with Patent Ejector, 4/11

B. B. Caps, 7d. per Box 100. Postage 3d.

Best Quality TOY GUNS. Quite Harmless.

No. A	Pop Gun ..	10½d.	Post 3d.
,, B	Pop Gun ..	2/4½	,, 4d.
,, C	Toy Gun to fire Paper Caps ..	10½d.	,, 3d.
,, D	Ditto ..	1/6	,, 3d.
,, E	Ditto ..	2/4½	,, 4d.
,, F	Ditto, best quality,	3/3	,, 4d.

For particulars of Air Guns, Shot Guns, Rook Rifles and Ammunition, see General List.

BRIGADE RIFLE, as illustration.

*No. 1 Brigade Rifle, with sling on stock, 3/6
,, 2 Do., with sling on stock and butt, and fitted with piling swivel 4/-
,, 3 Breechloading Rifle, fitted with piling swivel 5/6
,, 4 Do., do., with magazine and sights 5/11

*No. 1 only kept in stock. Other numbers to order.

Special Prices given for Quantities.

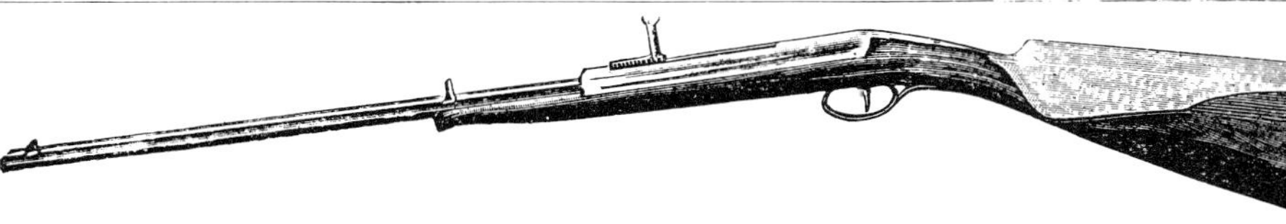

THE NEW AIR GUN. Mauser Pattern.

The sight of this Gun cannot be put out of true as in most Air Guns. Price 21/-
Slugs 8d. and 8½d. 1000.

GEM AIR GUNS.

No. 1 Bore, 13/6 No. 3, 17/6 No. 2, 20/-

THE NEW "MILLITA" AIR GUN.

Nos. 1 and 3 Bores, 35/- No. 1. Slugs, 8d. per 1000.

Darts 6½d. per doz.

LATEST NOVELTY! Handsome Model, Up-to-date Cannon.
Easily worked. Price 15/- Caps, 6d. box. Shells, 6d.

MODEL MAXIM GUN. Rene Bull's Patent. Special Price.

A Quick-firing Automatic Gun. 300 Rounds a Minute. Price 1/- Usual price 2/6
Firing Position, as illustration. Postage 3d.

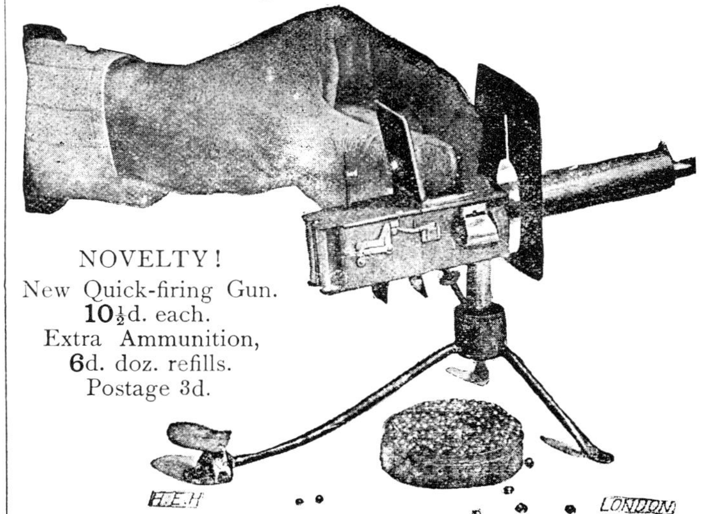

NOVELTY!
New Quick-firing Gun.
10½d. each.
Extra Ammunition,
6d. doz. refills.
Postage 3d.

For Particulars of other Guns, Revolvers and Ammunition, see General List, sent Post Free.

Gamage's Clockwork Toys, LARGEST COLLECTION IN THE WORLD. ALL THE LATEST NOVELTIES.

Clockwork Monkey.
With Jap umbrella.
Price **10½d.** Postage 3d.

Clockwork Boy on Hobby Horse.
Price **10½d.** Postage 3d.

Clockwork Clown.
Walking on hands.
Price ... **10½d.**
Postage 3d.

Clockwork Baby with Hoop.
Price ... ... **10½d.**
Postage 3d.

Clockwork Woman.
Price **2/11**
Postage 3d.

Clockwork Baby in Baby Walker.
Price ... ... **10½d.**
Postage 3d.

Clockwork Clown playing Drum and Cymbals.
Price ... **2/11** Postage 3d.

Clockwork Clown playing Cymbals.
Price ... ... **10½d.**
Postage 3d.

Clockwork Clown with Hat.
Price ... ... **10½d.**
Postage 3d.

Clockwork Clown with Pig and Ball.
Price ... ... **10½d.**
Postage 3d.

Clockwork Clown and Dog.
Price **2/6** Postage 3d.

Clockwork Man with Child
Price **1/11**
Postage 3d.

Clockwork Nigger and Drum.
Price ... **2/6**
Postage 3d.

Clockwork Handsome Cab.
10½d. Postage 3d.

Clockwork 4 Wheeler.
10½d. Postage 3d.

Clockwork Ballet Dancer.
1/11 Postage 3d.

Clockwork Fire Engine.
Price **3/6**
Postage 3d.

Clockwork Nurse with Car.
Price ... **3/6**
Postage 3d.

Clockwork Nigger and Clown on Wheels.
Price ... **1/11**
Postage 3d.

Clockwork Clown and Dog.
Price **3/6**
Postage 3d.

Clockwork Nigger on Chair.
Price ... **10½d.**
Postage 3d.

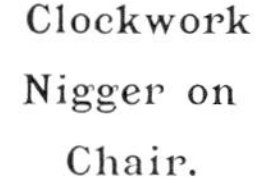

Clockwork Dog, Clown and Ball.
Price ... **10½d.**
Postage 3d.

Clockwork Tumbler.
Price ... **10½d.**
Postage 3d.

Clockwork Clown.
Price ... **10½d.**
Postage 3d.

Clockwork Musical Clowns
Price ... **3/6**
Postage 3d.

Clockwork Minstrel.
Price ... **10½d.**
Postage 3d.

Gamage's Clockwork and Mechanical Toys—*continued.*

Clockwork Performing Clown and Dogs.
Price ... **3/6** Postage 3d.

Clockwork Hen, 10½d.
Postage 3d.

Clockwork Frog, 8½d.
Postage 2d.

Clockwork Performing Dogs.
Price ... ... **10½d.** Postage 3d.

The Walking Elephant. Most Natural and Amusing.

Price **6d.** No Clockwork to get out of order. Postage 3d.

Clockwork Singing Bird in Cage, 1/-
Postage 3d.

Clockwork Duck.
Price ... **10½d.** Postage 3d.

Movable Clown and Donkey.
Very Strong Clockwork Toy.
Price ... ... **2/11** Postage 3d.

Clockwork Rabbit ... **8½d.**
,, **Skin Rabbit 10½d.**
,, **Skin Squirrel 10½d.**
Postage 3d.

Clockwork Elephant with Ball.
Price **1/4½** Postage 3d.

Clockwork Goat.
Price **10½d.** Postage 3d.

Clockwork Peacock.
Wags Head and Tail.
Price **10½d.** Postage 3d.

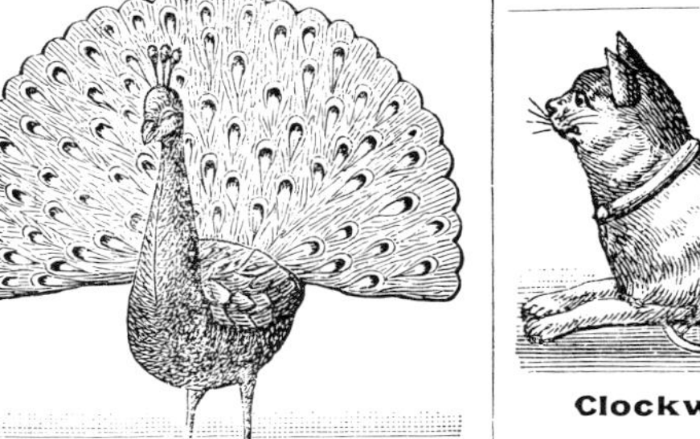

Clockwork Cat ... **10½d.**
,, **Mice** ... **10½d.**
Postage 3d.

The Jumping Kangaroo.
Jumps with life-like movements on an inclined plane.
Price **6d.** Postage 3d.

Gamage's Clockwork and Mechanical Toys—*continued.*

CLOCKWORK JOCKEY on HORSE

Price **1/11** Postage 3d Also Soldier on Horse.

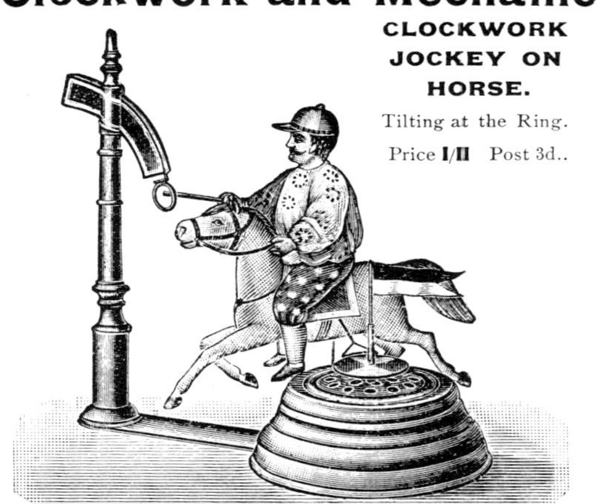

CLOCKWORK JOCKEY ON HORSE.

Tilting at the Ring.

Price **1/11** Post 3d..

CLOCKWORK MOTOR TRICYCLE.

Price ... ... **10½d.**

Postage 3d.

The "THREE FUNNY CLOWNS" THE LATEST NOVELTY OF THE SEASON! R. S. Mechanical Toy with Excellent Spring

The Three Funny Clowns. The Latest Novelty in Mechanical Toys, **10½d.** Postage 3d.

THE PRETORIA BOMB.

The two Presidents can be made to jump into the air. Quite harmless.

Price **6**d. Post 2d.

CLOCKWORK SEA LION.

DER ZAHME SEEHUND D·R G·M MARKE THE PERFORMING SEA-LION

ENGL. PATENT MADE IN GERMANY PAT. U.S.A. APPL. FOR

One of the cleverest Toys of the Century. Price **10½**d. Postage 3d.

The Two Horse Race consists of a stand supporting two jockeys on horses who, when the race is started, race round and round, passing and re-passing one another in such a manner that it is positively impossible to tell which will win until the race is over. With this game children can be kept amused for hours. It is strongly made and not likely to get out of order.

Price **10½**d. Larger Size, with four horses, **2/3** Postage 3d.

ANGSTLICHE BRAUT · ANXIOUS BRIDE

БОЯЗЛИВАЯ НЕВѢСТА SPOSA ANSIOSA

FIANCÉE INQUIÈTE · NOVIA INQUIETA

ELOPEMENT OR ANXIOUS BRIDE.

The Bridegroom cannot pedal quick enough and the Bride urges him to greater speed by throwing up her arms and waving her handkerchief.

Price **10½**d. Postage 3d.

The Equestrienne.

The Equestrienne.—This, as the name implies, consists of horse galloping round a ring, as at a circus. Standing upon the back of the horse is a fairy, who, as the horse passes under the bar, stoops and then jumps, clearing the bar in a most clever manner, alighting upon the horse's back and stands balancing herself until the horse reaches the bar, when she again jumps, continuing to ride and jump until the horse stops, **10½d.** Post 3d.

CLIMBING MONKEY.

As illustration, **10½d.** Post 3d.

D·R·PATENT ENGL·PATENT

TANZENDE PUPPE · WALTZING DOLL · POUPÉE DANSANTE · ТАНЦУЮЩАЯ КУКЛА

LEHMANN·S MADE IN GERMANY

BAMBOLA DANZANTE · DANSANDE POJKAR · MUÑECA BAILANTE · DANZENDE POP

D·R·G·M

NOVELTY! THE WALTZING GIRL.

Most Natural Movements. Price **2/6** Postage 3d.

CLOCKWORK WALKING CROCODILE

Price **6**d. Postage 3d.

CLOCKWORK BEETLE

Price **6**d. Postage 3d.

Gamage's Clockwork Toys—*continued.*

The Naughty Boy

New Clockwork Novelty, (as illustration).
Price **6d.** Postage 2d.

Magic Boxes.

Superior quality, complete with large assortment of Figures and fittings.
Price **1/4½** .. Postage 3d.

Jumping Animals.

Very amusing (clockwork).

Jumping Dog	**3/11**
,, ,, with Voice ..	**7/6**
Cat	**3/11**

Postage 3d.

The above are all of superior make and finish and do not easily get out of order.

Augustus the Tumbler.

The Novelty of the Season.

By an ingenious arrangement this funny man turns head over heels down the sloping board.

Price **10½d.**

Postage 3d.

Complete with board.

Clockwork NOVELTY.

Mr. Chamberlain making a speech.
Price **10½d.**
Postage 3d.

The Little Pianist.

1902 Novelty. Wind him up and he will play well for quite a long time Price **1/10½** Postage 3d.

Magic Boxes.

Novel and amusing Toy, complete with large assortment of Figures and fittings. Price **10½d.** Postage 3d.

Clockwork Airship.

1902 Novelty. Price **10½d.** Postage 3d.

Eifel Tower

(Clockwork) Price **1/4½** Postage 3d.

Tut Tut.

1902 Novelty. Clockwork Toy.
Price **1/4½** Postage 3d.

The Flying Bird.

Price **10½d.** Postage 3d.

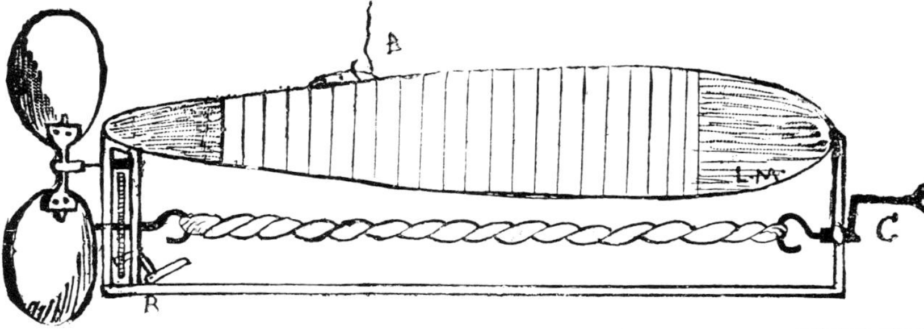

The Spencer Air Ship.

F 3419.

This Toy is suspended from the ceiling by means of a piece of string. The model is then wound up and the Air Ship flies round and round.

Price **1/6** Postage 3d.

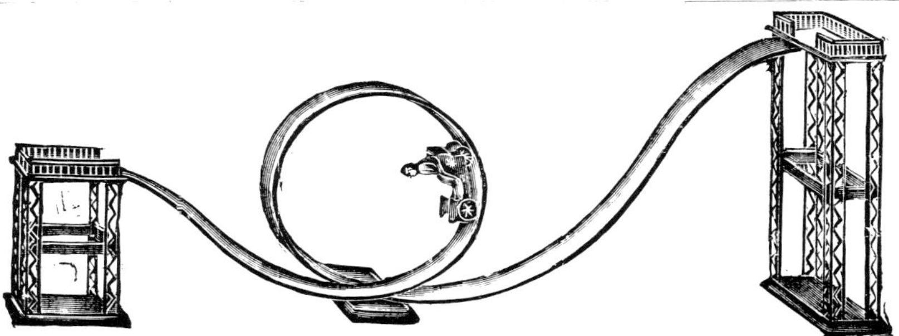

Up-to-date Novelty!

Looping the Loop,

Price .. **3/6**

Postage 3d.

Gamage's Model Automobiles and Motor Cars.

CLOCKWORK AND STEAM.

Clockwork Automobile.

10½d. Postage 2d.

Clockwork Motor Car.

Finely japanned, with strong clockwork, axle to adjust for straight or circular run, with india-rubber tyres and 1 nickelled lamp. 7¼ in. long, 4 in. wide, 4¾ in. high.

Price **4/3** Postage 3d.

Clockwork Automobile.

Price **1/11** Postage 3d.
2nd size **2/6** Postage 3d.
3rd ,, **3/6** ,, 4d.
Large ,, **6/6** ,, 6d.

Steam Motor Car. Price **1/-** Postage 3d.

The Spider Motor Car.

Driven by steam, axle to adjust ior circular and straight run, rubber tyred wheels with double spokes, 2 lamps and cushioned seat, nickelled fittings.

9½ in. long, 5 in. wide, 6½ in. high.

Price **12/6**

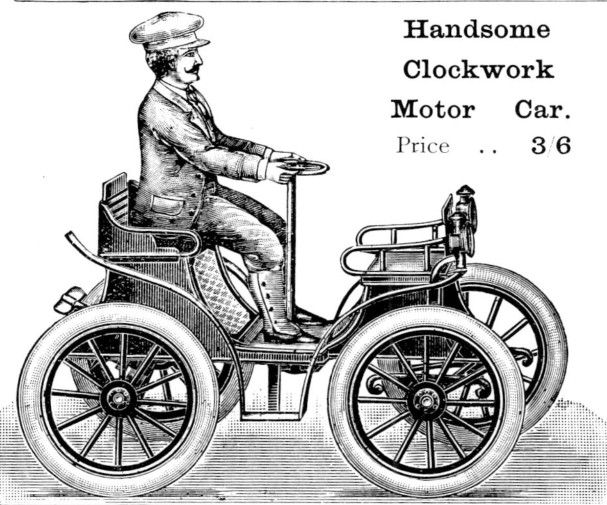

Handsome Clockwork Motor Car.

Price .. **3/6**

Motor Omnibus.

Elegantly japanned with 4 india-rubber tyred wheels, stearing gear, 1 nickelled lantern with mirror lense (not for lighting), 1 signal lantern with red lense, with figures and 2 direction boards 8½ in. long.

Driven by steam.

Price .. **15/-** each.

Victoria Motor Car.

Driven by steam, finely japanned, axle to adjust for straight or circular run, with nickelled patent wheels, pneumatic india-rubber tyred and 1 nickelled lantern.

9½ in. long, 5½ in. wide, 7 in. high.

Price **12/6**

Clockwork Motor Van.

Price .. .. .. **10½d.**

Postage 3d.

Motor Car.

Driven by steam, fiinely japanned, axle to adjust for straight and circular run, with patent nickelled wheels with india-rubber tyres, 2 nickelled lanterns and cushioned leather seats, fittings finely nickelled, very latest type. 9½ in. long, 5 in. wide, 7 in. high.

Price **14/6**

Clockwork & Mechanical Engines, &c.

No. 1202. **Clockwork Road Sweeper,** 10½d. Post 3d.

No. 1135. **Clockwork Street Roller.** 10½d. Post 3d.

No. 1024.

Mechanical Engine,

Price 10½d.

Postage .. 3d.

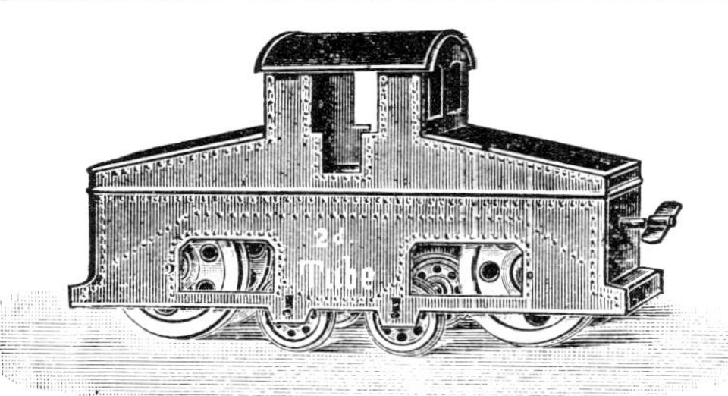

No. 1216.

Clockwork 2d. Tube Engine.

Price 10½d. Postage 3d.

No. 1000. **Patent Clockwork Engine,** 6d. Postage 2d.

No. 974. **Clockwork 4-wheel Motor Cab,** 10½d. Post 3d.

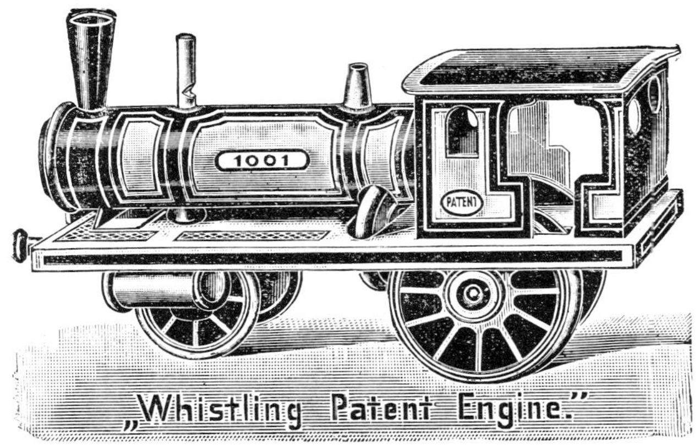

No. 1001

Patent Clockwork Engine,

10½d. Postage 2d.

No. 116.

Reversing Clockwork Engine.

10½d. Postage 3d.

No. 130.

Reversing Clockwork Engine with Bell.

Price 1/4½ .. Postage 3d.

Clockwork Engines.

French Make.

Price .. 1/- Larger Size, .. 1/9.

Postage 3d.

Gamage's Choral Tops, Best Quality Only.

No. 1. **Choral Top.**
Nicely japanned.
Price **6d.** Postage 3d.

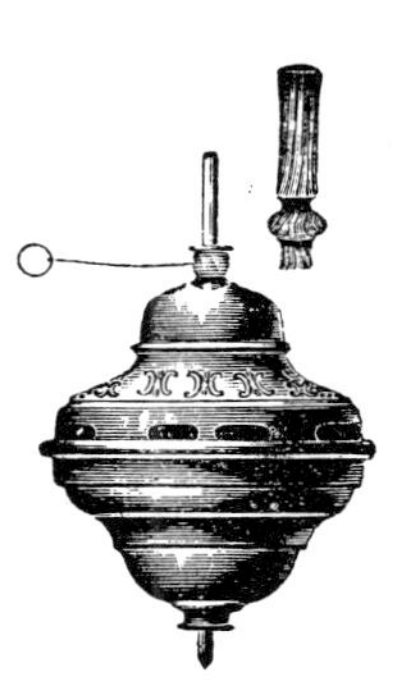

No. 2. as illustration.
Price **10½d.**
Postage 3d.

No. 9.
Nickel Plated Rack Top.
Price 1/-
Postage 3d.

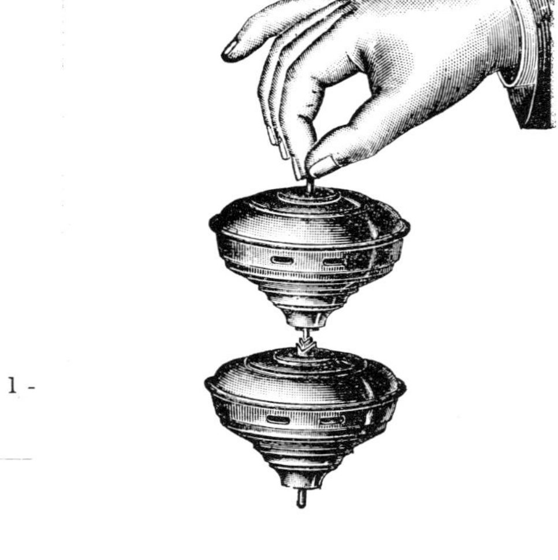

Containing boxwood peg top, whip top, humming top and bandalore.

No. 1 in cardboard box .. **6d.**
No. 2 better quality **10½d.**
No. 3 best quality **2/3**
Postage 3d.

No. 3. **Choral Top.**
Price 1/6
Postage 3d.

Novelty Top.
Plays God Save the King.
Price .. 2/11
Postage 3d.

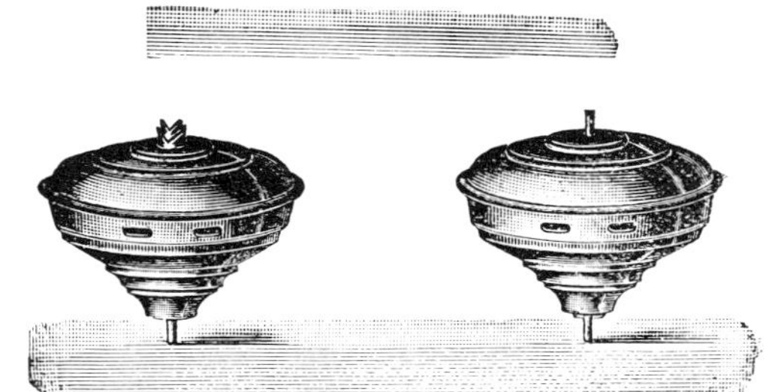

Musical Twin Tops
(As illustration).
Price .. .. **10½d.** Postage 3d.

Novelty in Skittles, complete in box with 2 balls.

Animals or Soldiers	**5/11**	Postage 6d.
Dogs	**7/6**	,, 6d.
Hussars, Frogs or Punch and Judy Figures	**8/11**	,, 6d.

Fancy Unbreakable Skittles.

Wooden Skittles.

Colored Skittles, as illustration, complete with Two Balls.

No. 1, **10½d.**	2, **1/2**	3, **1/6**	4, **1/10½d.**	5, **2/4½d.** set.
Carriage 3d.	4d.	5d.	6d.	7d.

No. 6, **3/6** .. Carriage 8d.

Cup and Ball.

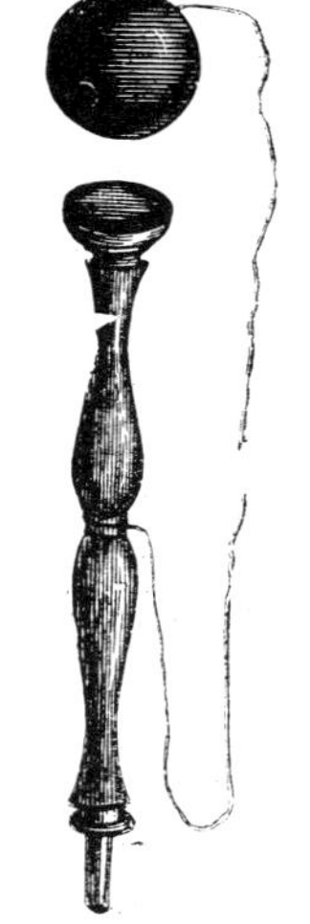

Cup and Ball, boxwood or rosewood.
Price .. .. **11d.**
Postage 2d.

Polished Ash Skittles.

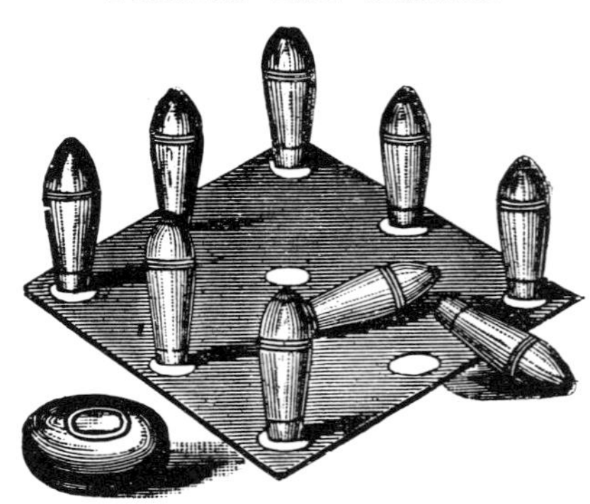

With square cloth for setting them out on. In box complete.

No. 1	.. .. ..	**2/3**
,, 2	.. .. ..	**2/6**
,, 3	.. .. ..	**3/3**
,, 4	.. .. ..	**3/9**

Ditto., without square.

No. 1	Plain	each	**1/4**
,, 2	Polished	,,	**1/6**
,, 3	,, large size	,,	**2/3**
,, 4	,, extra size	,,	**2/9**

Postage 4d. and 6d.

Gamage's Magnetic Toys.

Magnetic Duck Families.

Price .. 6d. Postage 2d.

For Magnetic Toys without Water, see next page.

Magnetic Toys.

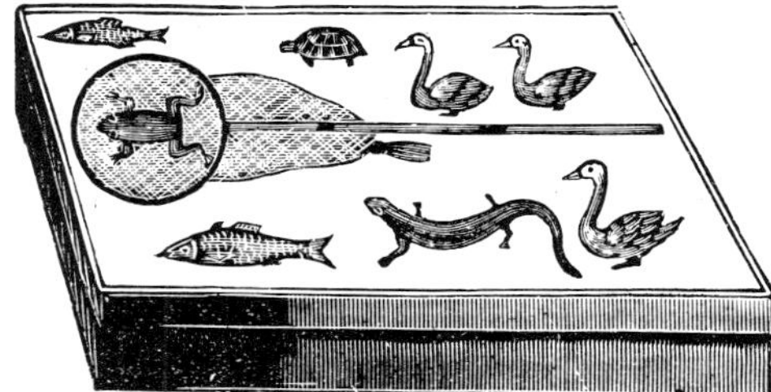

With Net complete, 10½d. and 1/10½ Postage 3d.

Magnetic Sets.

Complete Sets in Glass Top Boxes.

No. 881	.. ..	1/-	Postage 3d.
No. 884	As illustration	2/-	,, 3d.
No. 885	.. ..	2/6	,, 4d.

Magnetic Sets.

In Square Box, complete with Tank.
Prices, 1/6 2/6 Large size, 4/6 Postage 3d. and 4d.
Extra Large, a very Handsome Set, 15/- and 25/- Post Free

Magnetic Sets.

In Box, complete with Tank.

Prices .. 10½d. 1/10½ Large size, 3/6
Postage 3d. and 4d.

Magnetic Navy. Complete in box, with Tank.
No. 1 contains 3 boats, 2/3 No. 2 contains 4 boats, 3/3 No. 4 contains 6 boats, 5/-
No. 6 contains 7 boats, 8/6 No 7 contains 9 boats, 10/6

Gamage's Doll Department. The Best and Largest Assortment in London

Dressed Dolls.

Compo and Wax Heads, Arms and Legs, dressed in up-to-date style, complete with Shoes and Stockings.

		each
No. 0	9in. **Special Line**	**8½d.**
,, 1	11in. do.	**10½d.**
,, 2	10½in. and 11in...	**1/4½**
,, 3	13 in.	**1/11**
,, 4	Assorted sizes ..	**2/11**

Postage 3d.

Full Jointed Dolls.

Made to undress, with Movable Eyes.

1[illegible]½in. **1/4½** 13in. **2/6** & **2/11**
15in. **3/6** 15½in. **4/6** 17½in. **5/11**

English Dressed Dolls.

Clothes made to take off.

Sizes 12½ in. to 27 in.

2/6	**3/11**	**5/11**	**7/6**
9/11	**10/6**	**12/6**	**15/-**
17/6	**30/-**	**35/-**	**40/-**

Postage 3d. under 10/-

Dressed Dolls.

Specially Cheap, Large Size.

Washable Faces.
Dressed in Good Style.

14½in., **1/4½**	16in., **1/11**
18in., **2/11**	21½in., **3/11**
23½in., **4/11**	25½in., **5/11**

Postage 3d.

A Large Selection of **Best Dressed Dolls** in various sizes up to 26 in.

6/11 7/6 8/11 10/6 12/6 13/6 15/- 21/- 22/6 25/- 27/6 30/- 37/6 40/-

All Full Jointed Dolls are made to undress.

Soft Body Dolls

Pretty Face, Curly Hair, Jointed, Movable Eyes.

Price .. **2/11**

Postage 3d.

Tiny Dressed Dolls.

7¾ in. high	**1/6 1/9 2/-**
9¾ in. high	**2/6**
12½ in. high	**5/11**

Postage 2d.

Superior Quality Tiny Dolls.

Made to dress & undress. Moving Eyes, Jointed, and best quality dresses, up-to-date styles.

Prices:

8/6 **15/6**
25/- **28/6**

Baby Dolls.

Novelty—Dressed Baby Dolls in Cot. Packed in box complete.

1/6 and **2/6** Postage 3d.

With Moving Eyes,

2/11 and **3/6**

Baby Dolls dressed in Long White Clothes, **2/11**

Superior Quality, **5/11 10/6**

Short Clothes,

Price **4/11** Postage 3d.

Best Quality Dressed Baby Doll in Long Clothes, White Silk, &c., &c.

13/6 21/- 22/6 28/6 35/- 50/-

A very Handsome Present.

Jumeau Dolls.

Jumeau's Undressed Dolls.

Beautifully made China Faces, real hair, shoes, socks, and chemise, moving eyes and joints.

Prices:

1	12 in. ..	**4/11**
2	14 in. ..	**6/11**
	Postage 3d.	
3	16 in. ..	**9/6**
	Postage 4d.	
4	20 in. ..	**12/6**
5	24 in. ..	**17/6**
6	28 in. ..	**25/-**

Postage Free.

Jumeau's Celebrated French Dolls.

DIRECT FROM THE FACTORY.

Jumeau's Dressed Dolls.

Beautifully Dressed, Stylish Hat and good Underclothing, Shoes and Stockings.

No. 4	high, **15/**	No. 8	high, **27/6**
,, 6	high, **17/6**	,, 10	high, **37/6**

DITTO, SUPERIOR QUALITY.

No. 5	high	**30/-**
No. 7	high	**42/-**

Jumeau's Walking and Talking Dolls.

Talking Doll, Fixed Eyes. Says "Mamma" and "Papa" quite naturally.

No. 6T .. **15/-** No. 8T .. **22/6**
No. 10T .. **20/-**

Walking and Talking Dolls.

Walking Doll, Undressed, Natural Movements .. **25/-**
Walking and Talking, Dressed in latest Styles **50/-** & **63/-**

VERY HANDSOME PRESENT FOR GIRLS.

Carriage Free on all above.

Gamages Doll Department, *continued.*

THE BEST AND LARGEST ASSORTMENT IN LONDON.

RAG DOLLS

No. 1, Neatly dressed **6d** each.

No. 2, do. larger, **10½d**, **1/-**, **1/4½** ea.

No. 3, Well Dressed Rag Dolls, **1/10½** & **2/4½**

Postage 3d.

Superior Quality London Make,

2/11 3/6 3/11

Postage 3d.

WOODEN DOLLS

Unbreakable, Jointed.

Pretty Dolls made entirely of Wood.

This doll will save you pounds, as it can be dropped or thrown to the ground without being broken, at the same time it has the appearance of a china or composition doll.

NO MORE BROKEN HEADS.

No. 1 in. .. **4/11** Postage 3d.

No. 2 in .. **6/6** Postage 3d.

No. 3 in. .. **7/11** Postage 4d.

No. 4 in. .. **9/11** Postage 5d.

Golliwog Dolls.

Small .. 6d.

Large .. 1/-

Postage 2d.

Ugly Dolls.

Novelty Ugly Doll as illustration.

6d. each.

Postage 2d.

RUBBER DOLLS.

Best quality rubber only.

No. 2,	3	4	5	6
6d.	10½d.	1/4½	1/10½	2/4½

Large Size Superior Quality Rubber Dolls **2/11** & **3/6** Postage 3d.

Sailor Rubber Dolls 10½d. **1/4½** **2/6**

Clowns, 10½d. 1/4½

Solid Rubber Boy Doll **10½d.** each. Postage extra.

FANCY FELT DOLLS

JUST the DOLL for BABY.

Assorted Fancy Felt Dolls, Dressed. No. 1, Doll. 2, Child. 3, Baby. 4, Sailor Girl. 5, Swiss Peasant. 6, Tyrolean Peasant, **2/11** each. Postage 3d.

UNDRESSED DOLLS.

Jointed Leather Bodies, very Strong.

No. X—Special Line, with Shoes and Stockings.

Jointed Knees and Thighs.

Price **1/-** each. Postage 3d.

A Quality—Jointed Leather Bodies and Legs, with Shoes and Stockings, Moving Eyes, very Strongly made, Flaxen Hair and Pretty Faces. Packed in box, complete.

No. 1	12 inches.	Price ...	**1/10½**
,, 2	14 ,,	,, ...	**2/4½**
,, 3	17 ,,	,, ...	**2/9**
,, 4	19 ,,	,, ...	**3/11**
,, 5	22 ,,	,, ...	**5/11**
,, 6	25½ ,,	,, ...	**8/11**

Postage 3d. and 4d.

B Quality—Ditto, ditto, Pink Leather Bodies, with imitation Pearl Necklace. Packed in box, complete, as illustration.

No. 1	13 inches.	Price ...	**3/11**
,, 2	15½ ,,	,, ...	**4/11**
,, 3	17½ ,,	,, ...	**5/11**
,, 4	20½ ,,	,, ...	**7/11**

Postage 3d. and 4d.

C Quality—Jointed Leather Arms and Legs, Shoes and Stockings, Moving Eyes, Superior Quality Kid.

No. 1	12½ inches.	Price ...	**2/11**
,, 2	15 ,,	,, ...	**3/11**
,, 3	18 ,,	,, ...	**4/11**
,, 4	20 ,,	,, ...	**6/11**
,, 5	24 ,,	,, ...	**8/11**

Postage 3d., 4d. and 6d.

THE LATEST NOVELTY IN UNDRESSED DOLLS.

Jointed Kid Body, CELLULOID Heads, Pretty Faces UNBREAKABLE, Shoes and Stockings.

GIRLS.

Size	Price
Size 12½ inches	**3/6**
,, 14 ,,	**4/3**
,, 16½ ,,	**5/3**
,, 20 ,,	**5/11**
,, 22 ,,	**7/11**

Postage 3d.

BOYS.

Size	Price
Size 14 inches	**2/6**
,, 15½ ,,	**2/11**
,, 18½ ,,	**3/11**

Postage 3d.

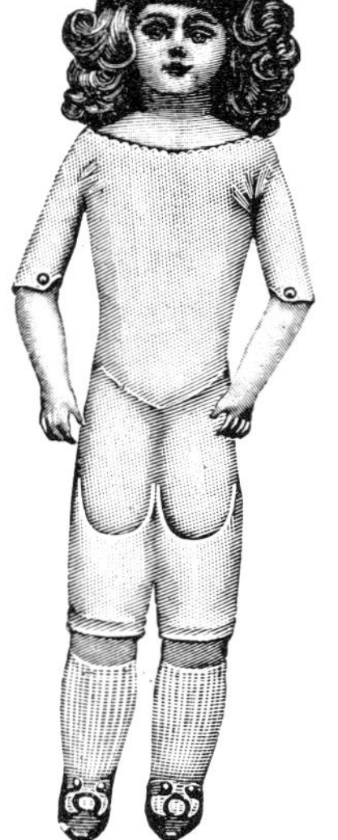

UNDRESSED DOLLS (with voice).

(Mamma and Papa).

As Quality A. No. 4v, 19 inches, **4/11** No. 5v, 22 inches, **6/11**

Postage 3d.

D Quality—Best Quality Kid, Jointed Bodies, Arms and Legs, with Superior Shoes and Silk Stockings, Flaxen Hair, Very Pretty Faces, Moving Eyes. Packed in strong box.

No. 1	12 inches.	Price ...	**4/6**
,, 2	13½ ,,	,, ...	**5/3**
,, 3	16 ,,	,, ...	**5/11**
,, 4	18½ ,,	,, ...	**7/11**
,, 5	22½ ,,	,, ...	**9/11**

Postage 3d., 4d. and 6d.

NEW UNBREAKABLE DOLL

Undressed.

Head Arms and Legs made of a **Special Unbreakable Composition.**

Moving Eyes.

No. 1016 & 1017.	No. 1063.	No. 1021.
8 in. **10½d.**	10½ in. **1/3**	14 in. **2/-**

Postage 3d. and 4d.

BOY DOLLS

Jointed Kid Bodies, with Shoes and Stockings, quite new.

No. 1	13½ inches.	Price ...	**3/6**
,, 2	15 ,,	,, ...	**3/11**
,, 3	18 ,,	,, ...	**4/6**

Postage 3d.

NIGGER DOLLS

Undressed, Brown Kid, Jointed Bodies, with Shoes and Stockings, Black Curly Hair. Quite new. Size 13 inches.

Price **2/11**

Dressed Nigger Dolls.

Size 10 inches ... ... **10½d.**

Postage 3d.

Gamage's Doll Department—*continued.*

Walking Dolls.

Well dressed Dolls, with specially constructed Joints, which enable then to walk quite naturally when held on table, etc. Price **10/6**, **12/6** and **15/6** Carriage Free.

Clockwork Revolving Dolls

1/9 and **2/-** Postage 3d.

Musical Dolls,

Revolving on Sticks, handsomely dressed.

A very amusing Toy for Baby.

No. 1, Squeakers, **10½**d.
,, 2, Musical, **1/3, 1/11**
,, 3, ,, **2/3, 2/6**
,, 4, ,, **3/6**
,, 5, ,, **4/6**
,, 6, ,, **6/6**
Squeaking Clowns, **10½**d.

Jack in Box Doll,

on Stick.

Price .. **10½**d. Postage 3d.

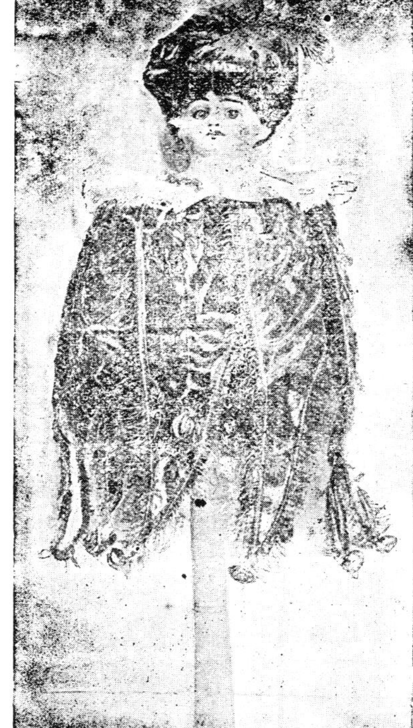

No. 2. LATEST NOVELTY.

Walking Doll.

Nicely Dressed, fitted with best Clockwork movement, so arranged that the doll walks quite naturally, as illustrated, price **25/-**

Dolls' Trunks, fitted and unfitted, Bedsteads, Furniture, etc.

Doll's Boots & Shoes.

432

Brown Leather Dolls' Shoes, as illustration, Price **3**d. pair.
Assorted Coloured Satin ditto, **6**d. and **10½**d. pair.
Bronzed Red do., **1/-**
Postage 1d.

DOLL'S TRUNKS.

Doll's Boots & Shoes.

Brown Leather Laced Boots, as illustration.

Price .. **1/-** pair.
Cheaper do. **6**d. ,,
Postage 1d.

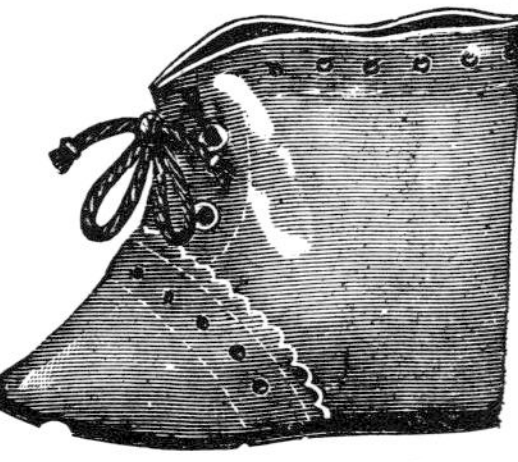

577

Dolls' Trunks, about 10 in. long, containing best quality Dressed Doll, complete with satin dresses, &c. **10/6**

No. 1. Black Trunk, 10½ in. long, containing best quality Dressed Doll, long hair, moving eyes, extra dresses, night dress, complete set of underclothing, 2 hats, handkerchiefs and scent **12/6**

No. 2. Do., 11½ in., **16/6** No. 3. Do., 12½ in., **21/-**

No. 4. Do., 11½ in. containing 1 Boy and Girl Doll with movable eyes and joints, both dressed in Sailor Clothes, with complete change for each, hand glass, &c. **22/6**

No. 5. Brown Trunk, 11½ in. long, studded with brass nails, 1 tray with fully-dressed Doll, movable eyes and joints, 1 extra silk and 1 stuff dress, night dress, chemise, skirt, &c., 2 hats, 1 pinafore, socks, handkerchiefs, &c. **22/6**

No. 6. Black Trunk, 14½ in., Doll fully-dressed, &c., &c., 3 extra dresses, 3 handkerchiefs, underclothing, trimmed lace, &c., &c. **30/-**

No. 7. Do., 15 in. Baby Doll, movable eyes and joints, bibs, rattle, bottle, binders, &c. .. **30/-**

No. 8. Brown Trunk, 18 in., with lock, dressed Doll, 2 extra dresses and skirts, &c., also music case, eye glasses, clothes brush, &c. **35/-**

No. 9. Trunk 17½ in. by 11 in., with 2 trays **55/-**

No. 10. ,, ,, ,, ,, 3 ,, **70/-**

No. 11. ,, ,, ,, ,, **90/-**

No. 12. 21 in. by 14 in., 3 trays, very handsome set **£5 5 0**

Dolls' Trouseaus, in cardboard box, containing Doll, Dresses, &c., &c. **3/11**
Larger Size .. .. **4/6** Post 4d.

Empty Doll Trunks.

No. A. Imitation Brown Leather, with fastening, Price **1/3**
No. B. Do. Larger, **2/6**
Postage 3d.

No. C. GreyGlazed Cloth CoveredTrunkwith strong fastening. Price **3/3**
No. D. Larger, **4/6**
Postage 3d.

DOLLS' SQUARE SHAPE EMPTY TRUNKS, Best quality.
1, length 12½ in., **5/11** 2, length 14 in., **7/6** 3, length 15½ in., **8/6**

DOLLS' ROUND SHAPE EMPTY TRUNKS, Best quality.
1A, length 12¾ in., **7/6** 2A, length 14 in., **8/6** 3A, length 15½ in., **10/6**

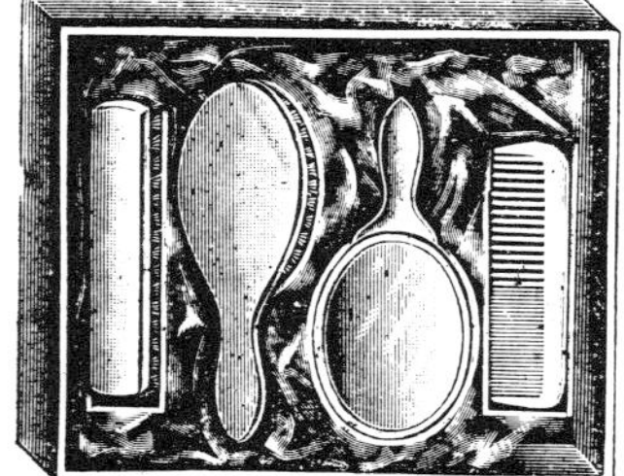

No. 1303. **Doll's Toilet Set.**
Celluloid Backs, in Silk Lined Box.
Price **1/11** Postage 3d.

No. 1304.

Doll's Toilet Set.

Celluloid Backs.

Price .. **1/-**
Postage 3d.

Do., Stronger, **1/6**
Postage 3d.

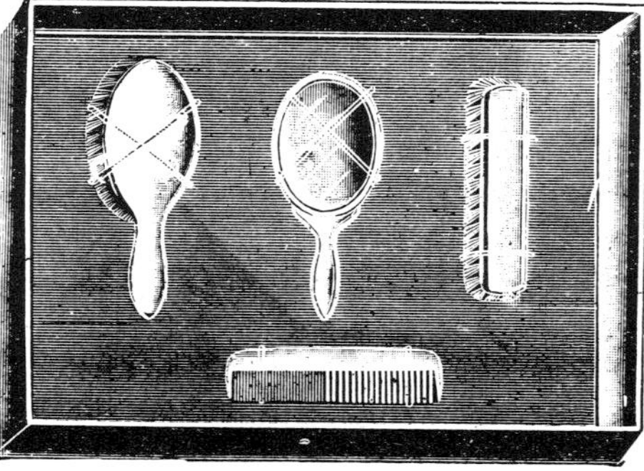

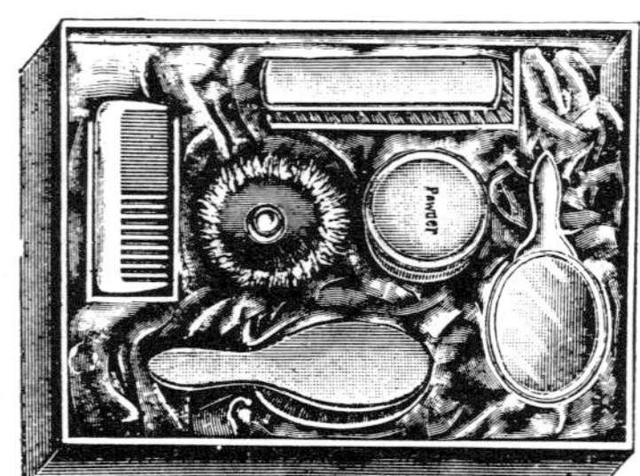

No. 1303A. **Doll's Toilet Set.**
Celluloid Backs, &c., as illustration, in Silk Lined Box. Price **2/6** Postage 3d.

Gamage's Doll Houses and Mansions.

Dolls House, (as illustr. t.on), Well F.nishe l.

No. 1358A,	4 windows.	Size 16 x 12 x 9	..	6/6
,, 1358B,	,,	,, 19 x 13 x 10½	..	8/11
,, 1358C	..	..	..	12/6
,, 1358D,	11 windows.	Size 23 x 17 x 14	..	15/-

Strong Wooden Doll House,

Covered with Paper representing Bricks.

S.raignt Front.

No. 100	Size 13 x 7½ x 5	1/6
,, 101	,, 16 x 11 x 6½	2/11
,, 102	,, ..	3/11
No. 103 Do, varnished		2/11
,, 104	,, 17½ x 11 x 8	4/6

Superior Quality Doll's House, new and up-to-date style, as illustration. Size 22 inches long, 18½ inches deep, 17½ inches high. Price **37/6**

STRONG DOLL HOUSES Best make and finish.

No. 3186,	7 Windows, ..	Size 28 x 16 x 13	Price ..	13/6
,, 2704,	7 ,, ..	,, 27½ x 17½ x 14	,, ..	16/6
,, 2705,	7 ,, ..	,, 28 x 19 x 15	,, ..	18/6
,, 2706,	,, with Staircase	..	,, ..	27/6
,, 3188,	11 ,, ,,	,, 34 x 28 x 20	,, ..	55/-

FURNISHED DOLL HOUSE

Furnished in best style.

Size **25/-**

,, **45/-**

DOLLS' MANSION

Large and beatifully finished, a very handsome present.

Size, 27½ in. x 32½ in.

Price **63/-**

Do, as illus'tn. 45½ x 30½ x 39½

Price

£6 6 0

HANDSOME DOLL'S HOUSE

Beautifully finished.

Size				Price
Size, 22 in. x	12½ in. x	21½ in.	Price ..	33/6
,, 29	,, 20	,, 29 ,,	,, ..	57/6

Carriage extra. For Particulars, see page 1.

ENGLISH MADE GABLE ROOF DOLL'S HOUSE

No. 14, as illustration, Special New Design. Best finish and made of well-seasoned wood. Price **21/-**

No. 15, do., larger size. Price **35/-**

The Improved Doll's House,

(PATENT.)

Front of House with sides open.

Back of House with sides shut.

Sides are made collapsible, so that no door is left swinging. Two children can play with the same House at the same time.

The side of House open, showing half of interior.

No.	Length	Depth	Height	Price
No. 1.	Length 23 inches.	Depth 22 inches.	Height 25 inches.	Price 47/6
No. 2.	,, 25 ,,	,, 24 ,,	,, 28 ,,	Price 60/-

Carriage and Packing extra on all Houses in this page.

Gamages Miniature Cooking Stoves, Useful and Instructive Presents for Girls.

Nos. 1 & 2.

Strongly made and japanned **Spirit Cooking Stove** as illustration No. 1, complete with lamp, No. 1, **1 4½** No. 2, **1/9** No. 3, **3/6** Carriage 3d.

No. 4 Highly finished nickel and japanned **Spirit Cooking Stove** as illustration, complete with all utensils and lamp. Price **4/6** Postage 6d.

No. 7, Superior quality nickel & japanned **Spirit Cooking Stove** as illustration. 11 in. long, **7/6** Postage 6d.

No. 7A, 14½ in. long, larger utensils, 8 in. long. Price **12/6**

No. 7B, 17 in. long **20/-**

No. 8, 11 in. long, similiar to No. 7, but fitted with new and up to date utensils. Price **14 6**

No. 4.

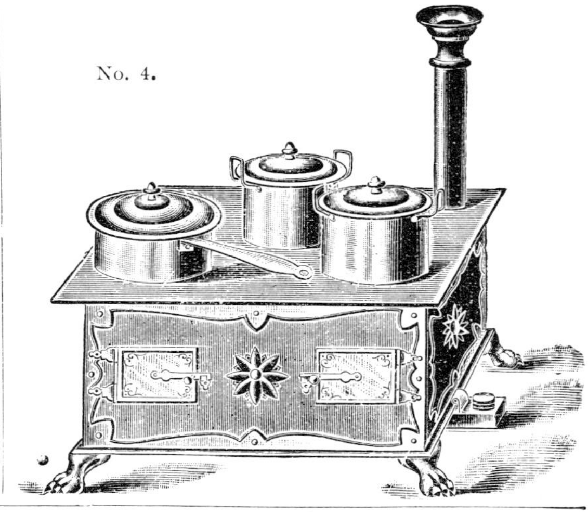

No. 4A.

No. 8A, as No. 7A but copper utensils.

Price **22/6**

EMAMELLED TILE COOKING STOVES.

Superior finish.

No. 1221 with 2 utensils	**2/11**
,, 1222 ,, ,,	**4/11**
,, 1224 with 3 utensils	**7/6**
,, 1225 ,, 4 ,,	**9/6**
,, 1226 ,, ,, ,,	**17/6**

New style **Cooking Stove** as illustration, with latest improved heaters,

No. 73 **27/6** No. 674 **37/6** No. 675 **42/-**

No. 4A. Large size **Cooking Stove**, complete as illustration.

Price .. **5/11** Postage 6d.

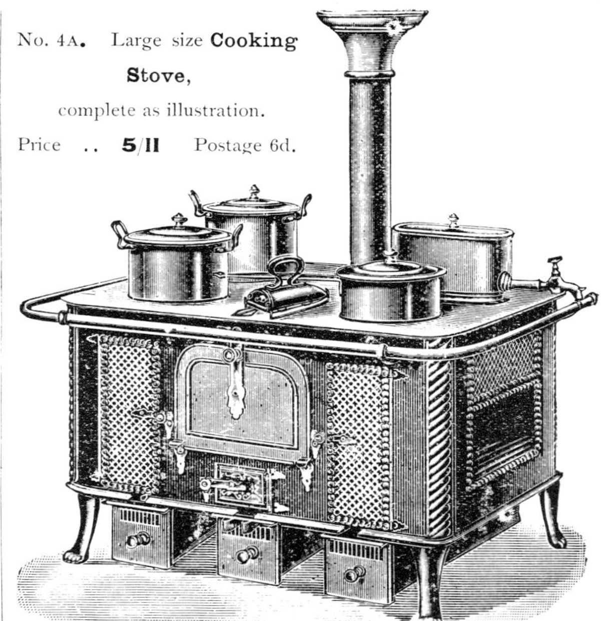

No. 9.

No. 7.

Very handsome **Gas Cooking Stove** with copper pots and pans, as illustration, length 14½ inches. Price **40/-**

Carriage extra on all Stoves under 10/-

Gamage's Shops, Stores, Warehouses, &c.

COMPLETE WITH STOC AND FITTINGS.

WAREHOUSE.

Warehouse and Granaries, complete as illustration.

No. 1	2	3
5/11	10/6	18/6
Post, 4d.	Free.	Free.

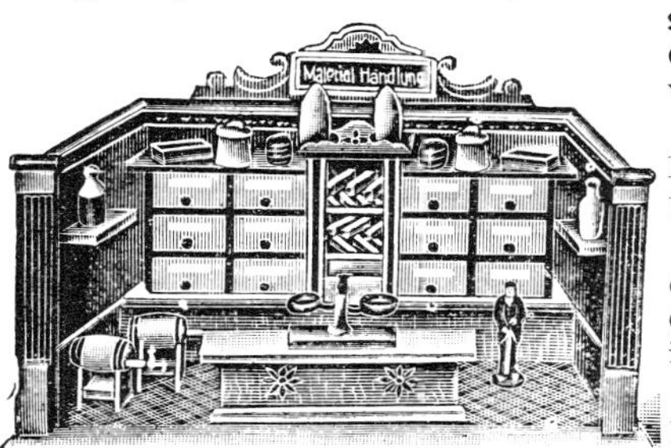

SHOPS.

Grocery Shop made of hard wood, well finished, as illustration.

No.	1	2	3	4	5
Price	1/6	2/6	3/6	6/6	10/6
Post ..	3d.	4d.	4d.	6d.	

GROCERS' SHOPS.

Complete, well-made, and finished in good styles.

No.	18	19	17
Price	2/11	5/6	7/11

Grocery Stores,

Fitted with Scales and all sorts of miniature articles for sale, drawers made to open and labelled in English.

Complete with Telephone .. .. .. Price 21/-

WAREHOUSE.

Warehouse and Granary, Varnished, with Truck, Weighbridge, and Horse .. 21/-

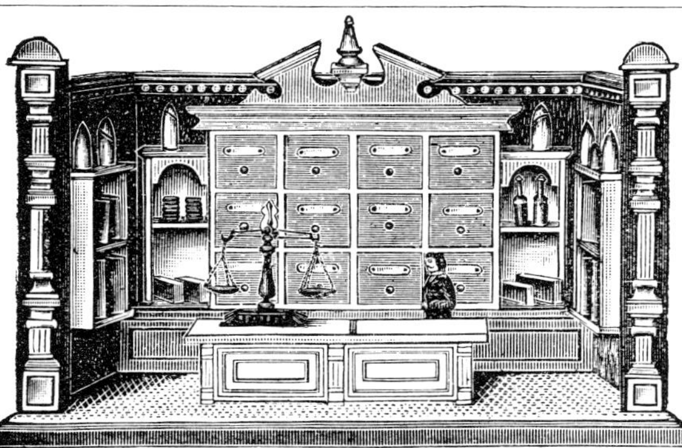

Blue & White Varnished GROCERY STORE.

As illustration, 12/6.

Strong Oak GROCERY STORES,

Complete as illustration, 15/6

Large size, 27/6

Butcher's Shop.

An instructive and amusing Toy.

4/6	8/11	11/6
Postage 6d.	8d.	Free.

NOVELTY.

Bonnet Shop.

Complete with stock of Bonnets, etc., for display. An instructive Present for a Girl

Price 25/-

Creamery

Beautifully Finished.

Price 22/6

Confectioner's Shops.

Complete with Stock, finished in good style, 5/11 & 8/11

Ditto, Best Quality, 11/6 16/6 17/6 20/- 25/- 28/6 40/- Carriage and Packing extra.

China Shops.

Shops stocked with China, 2/11 Postage 6d.

Large Size, as illustration, 5/6 Postage 8d.

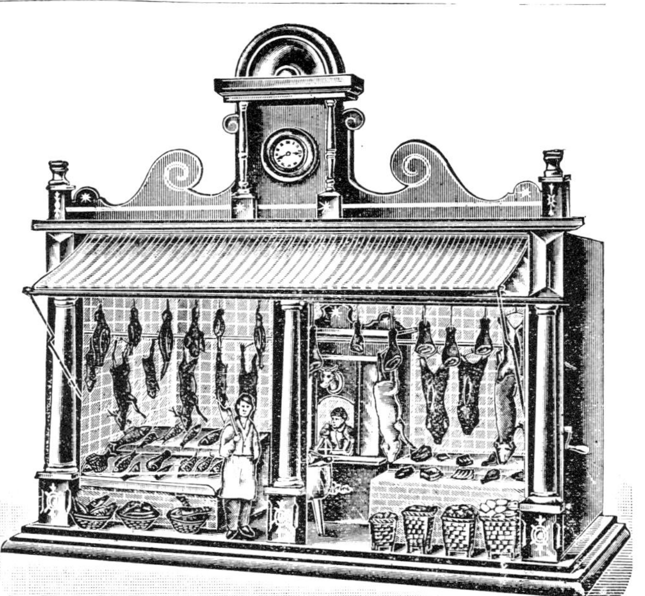

Large Size Butcher's Shop.

Very Strong. Made and finished in best Style. Complete.

Size 27½ in. by 25 in. Price 47/6

Gamage's Rocking Horses, Pole and Push Horses, &c. *(Best English Make)*

Strong Wood Hobby Horse.

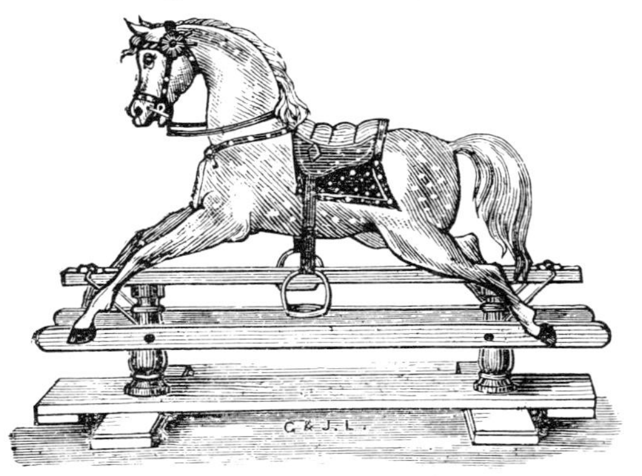

No.	About Height to Saddle.	Length of Stand.	Price.	Best quality in Brown or Cream beautifully finished.
1A	2ft. 2in.	2ft. 8½in.	19/6	25/9
2B	2ft. 7in.	3ft. 1½in.	26/6	34/6
3C	2ft. 11in.	4ft. 0in.	38/6	47/6
4D	3ft. 4in.	4ft. 7½in.	46/-	63/-

English-made Real Skin-covered Hobby Horses. Sizes as above.

No. 1 AS, 33/6 No. 2 BS 42/- No. 3 CA 63/-

Novelty of the Season!

GAMAGE'S AUTOSTEDE.

Propelled by working hand backwards and forwards, simply pulling the reins. Very natural. Steered by the feet.

No. 1	30/-
No. 2	40/-
No. 3 Rubber Tyres ..	50/-

Pole Horse. Push Horse.

POLE HORSES—Good Shape. No.	Height to Saddle.	Wood Wheels.	Iron Wheels.	PUSH HORSES. No.	Height to Saddle.	Wood Wheels.	Iron Wheels.
1	13½in.	3/6	4/6	1	13½in.	4/6	5/11
2	16 ,,	4/11	5/11	2	16 ,,	5/11	6/11
3	18 ,,	6/6	7/6	3	18 ,,	7/11	9/6
4	20 ,,	7/11	9/6	4	20 ,,	9/6	11/6
5	22½,,	9/6	—				

Strong Wood Rocking Horse.

No.	Height to Saddle.	Length of Rocker.	Price.	Extra carved, Best Finished.
0	2 ft. 2 in.	4 ft. 4 in.	13/9	17/6*
1	2 ft. 6 in.	5 ft. 0 in.	18/6	24/6*
2	2 ft. 11 in.	6 ft. 3 in.	25/6	34/6*
3	3 ft. 2 in.	6 ft. 6 in.	35/-*	

*To order in two days.

Stool Horses.

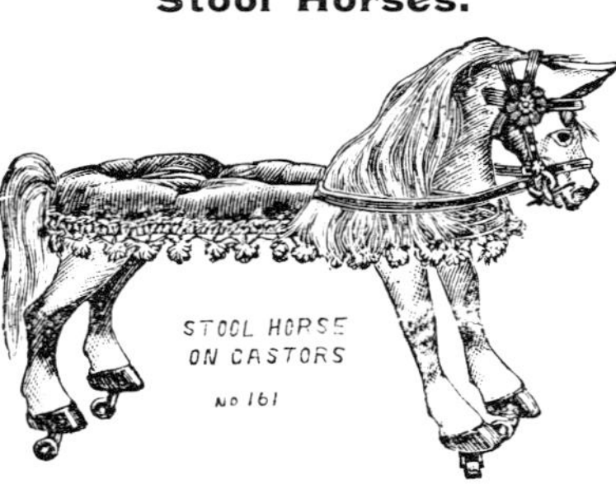

No. 161B 4/9 No. 161C 6/3
Best Carved ditto with Velvet Binks.
No. 1 5/6 No. 2 6/6

Best Quality Carved Push Horses.
Superior finish, No. 2, 10/6 No. 3, 13/9

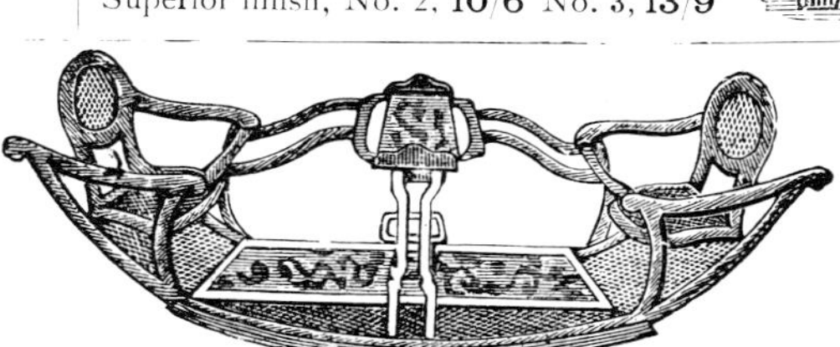

Jubilee Safety Hobby Horse.

(Royal Letters Patent, No. 2938)

	About height to Saddle.	Length of Stand.	Best Finish.
No. 2	2 ft. 5 in	3 ft. 6 in.	42/6
No. 3	2 ft. 10 in.	3 ft. 11 in.	56/-

Adjustable Saddles and Bridles can be fitted to No. 3, 19/6 extra.

Strong Wood Rocking Horse.

	Height to Saddle.	Length of Rocker.	Price.
No. 2	2 ft. 11 in.	6 ft. 3 in.	37/6
No. 3	3 ft. 2 in.	6 ft. 6 in.	47/6

Saddle Paniers and Straps. No. 2, 10/6 No. 3, 12/6 extra.

Nursery Yacht.

Perforated Seats.
To seat three.
Height 2ft. 6in.
Length 5ft. 6in.
Price, 45/6
Other sizes to order.

Carriage and Packing extra on all above.
For Particulars see page 1.

Improved Hobby Horse.

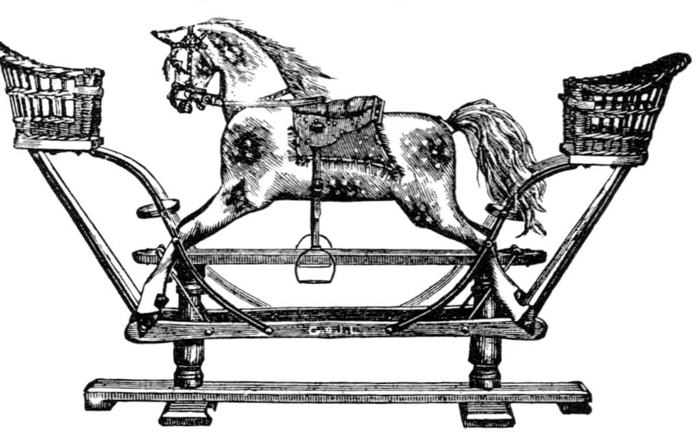

With two end Chair Seats. For three children. Very strongly made, in best quality only. Size as No. 3C Hobby Horse. Price 62/6

English-made Tradesmen's Carts, Brewers' Drays, &c.

BEST QUALITY ONLY.

Brewers' Dray

NO 116

Complete as illustration.

No. 1	No. 2	No. 3
3/3	**4/11**	**7/11**

Pair Horse Brewers' Dray

On Four Wheels.

No. 1, [illegible]/11 2, **12/9** 3, **16/6** 4, as illustration, **25/9**

Pantechnicon

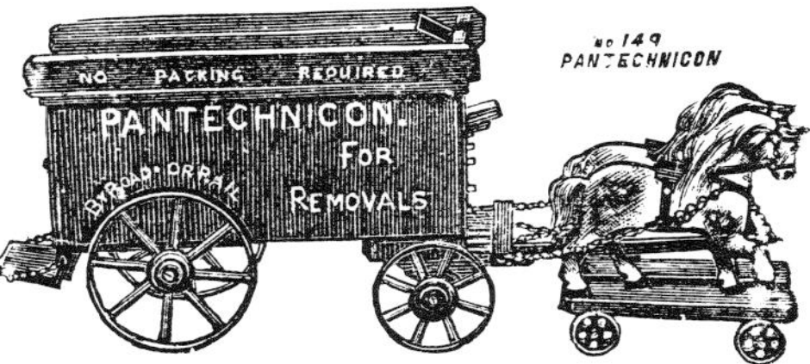

Very Strong. Complete with Two Horses.

Price .. **11/6**

Coal Trolly

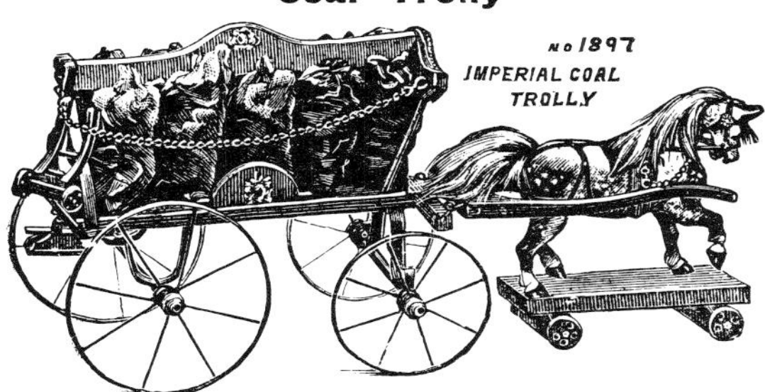

Strong Elm, Varnished, loaded with Sacks of Black Wood Blocks, on four Strong Spider Wheels.

Price .. **14/3**

If fitted with Truck, as illustration, 1/6 extra.

Parcel Cart

NO 114

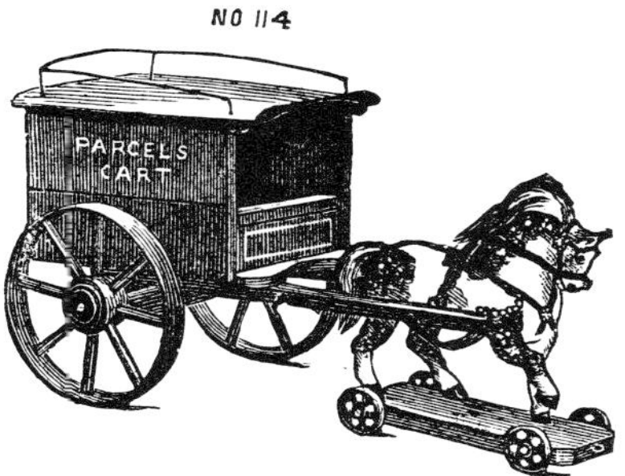

Strong Wood Parcel Cart and Horse complete

No. 1, **4/11** No. 2, **5/11**

Railway Van

Very Strong, loaded, as illustration.

Size 1 .. **8/6** Size 2 .. **10/9**

Wicker Waggonette

With Two Horses, on Light Spider Wheels.

Price **15/9**

Dairy Cart

Strong Hard Wood, on two Spider Wheels, complete with Churn and Filler

Price, Varnished .. **13/6** Painted .. **15/9**

Gipsy Van

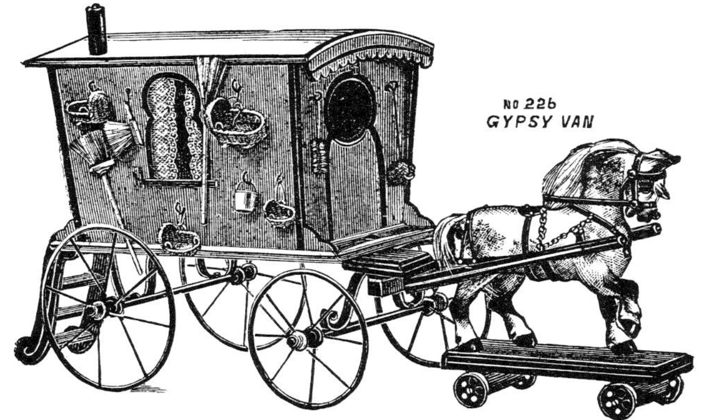

Latest Novelty. Strongly made Gipsy Van, with Brushes, Brooms, &c., complete, on Spider Wheels. Length of body 21 in. Price **17/9**

New Milk Van

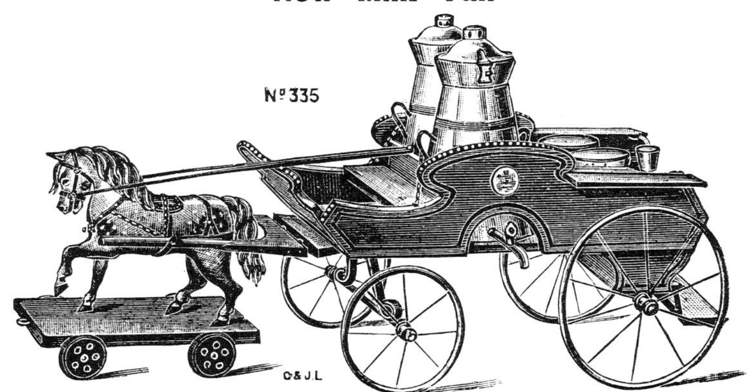

Varnished, on Strong Spider Wheels **25/6**

Painted, on 4 Strong Rubber Tyred Wheels, as illustration, with 2 Horses, **32/6**

—1906—
CATALOGUE

RAILWAYS.

A. W. GAMAGE LTD. have a larger collection of Steam and Clockwork Trains than ever from 10½d. to 10 guineas in all leading English systems. Separate Locomotives and Tenders, Carriages, Trucks, Automatic Mail Coaches, Automatic Shunting Trains, and all Acccessories to form a Complete Railway. Tram Systems propelled by Clockwork or Electricity.

Best Quality Clockwork Trains and Sets.

ALL GAUGES.

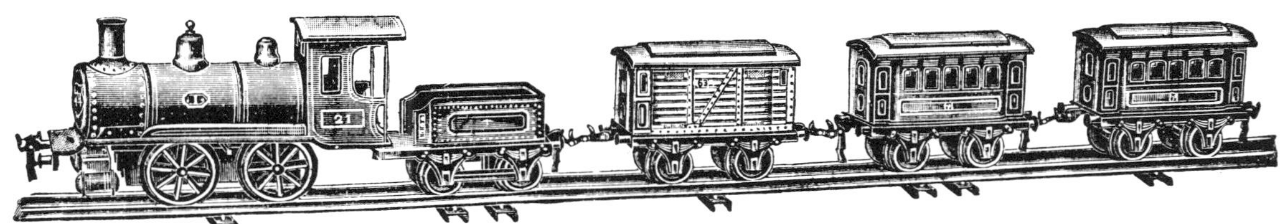

All Trains on this page have heavy engines fitted with best clockwork movement with long wind.

Special Value.

No. 1. **Gauge 0.** G.N.R. Clockwork Train, complete with Locomotive, 2 Carriages, 1 Truck and Circular Track .. .. **7/6** Postage **6d.**

No. 5. **Gauge 1.** G.N.R, Clockwork Train, as illustration, complete with Oval Track **13/6**

Clockwork Trains fitted with Brake.

Complete, as illustration, with rails in box.

No. 20. **Gauge 0.** G.N.R. or L.N.W.R. Train, complete in box with Circular Rails .. .. **12/6** Postage **6d.**

No. 2A. **Gauge 0.** Express Clockwork Train in 4 English railways (M.R., G.N.R., L.N.W.R. and L.S.W.R.). Loco. with brake on 4 axles, Tender, 2 Passenger Cars, Guard's Van; complete in box with 6 curved and 4 straight rails. Length of train, 29 in. **17/6**

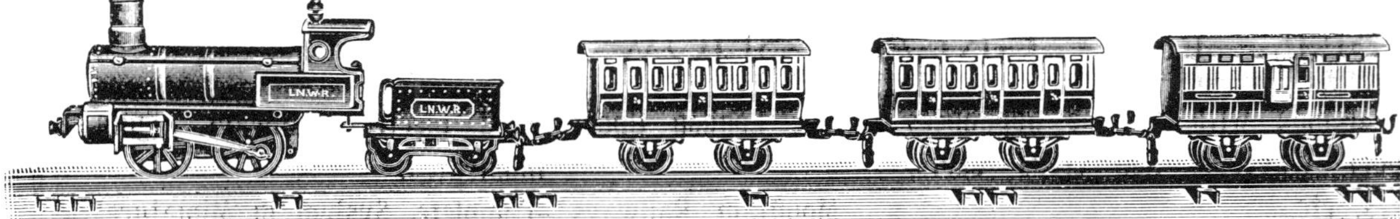

No. 2B. **Gauge 0.** Clockwork Express to run forwards and backwards, in 4 railways as 2A, 2 Carriages and Guard's Van, in box complete with oval lines. Length of train, 31 in.

Price **20/-**

No. 3. **Gauge 0.** L.N.W.R. Corridor Train, Loco. fitted with reversing gear and brake, Tender, and 2 Corridor Carriages, on Oval Track; length of train, 28 in. Price **30/-**

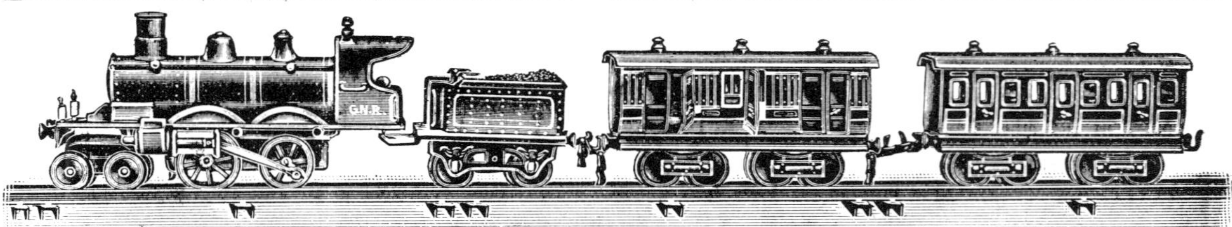

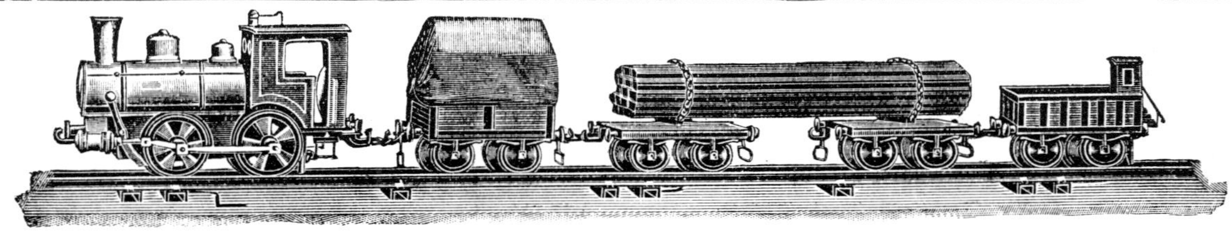

Clockwork Goods Trains.

No. H. **Gauge 0.** G.N.R. Engine and Tender, best clockwork movements, with Luggage Waggons, complete with lines Price **15/-** Postage 6d.

No. J. **Gauge 1.** L.N.W. ditto Price **25/-**

All Gauges. **BEST QUALITY CLOCKWORK TRAINS**—*contd.* **All Gauges.**

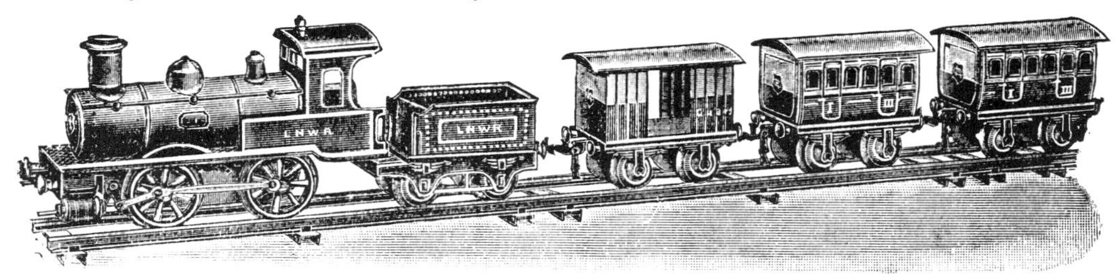

No. 23. Clockwork Train, made in 4 styles M.R., G.N.R., L.N.W.R. and L.S.W.R. Loco. fitted with brake and tender, 2 carriages and 1 luggage van, on oblong track.
Length of train 33 in. .. .. Price **25/-**

No. 23a. Ditto, Loco. fitted with reversing gear, brake, etc. .. .. .. Price **30/-**

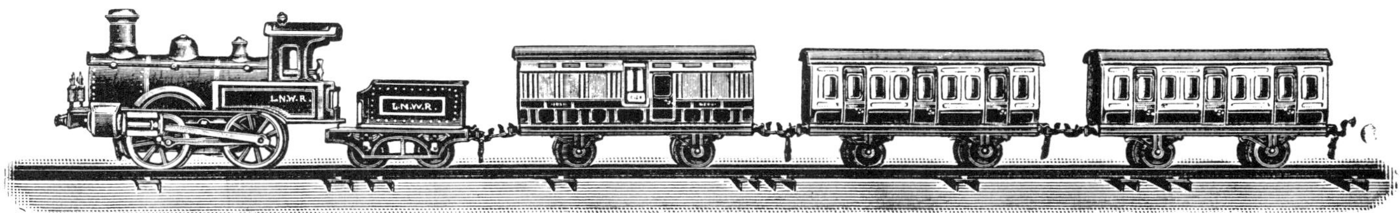

Gauge I.

No. 24a. Clockwork Train, L. & N.W. and M.Ry., Loco. fitted with brake, tender, 2 cars and 1 guard's van. Complete in box with 8 curved and 4 straight rails. Length of train 45 in. Price **32/6**

No. 24b. Ditto, **Gauge 2** Price **47/6**

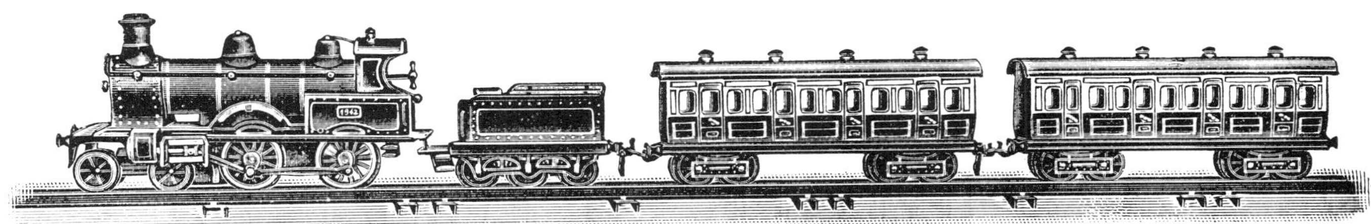

Gauge I.

No. 24c. Clockwork Express Train, L.N.W.R. Loco. fitted with very strong spring, brake and reversing gear; also fast and slow movement, 2 passenger cars and 1 guard's van on bogie wheels. Complete in box with 8 curved and 4 straight rails. Length of train 62 in. Price **63/-**

No. 24d. Ditto, **Gauge 2** Price **90/-**

No. 62a. Ditto, **Gauge 3** , ... **£7 10 0**

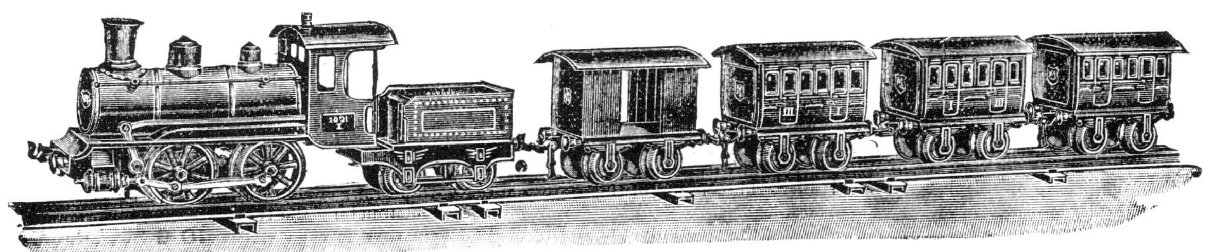

No. 26a. Clockwork Railways, L.S.W., **No. 2 Gauge,** Engine fitted with extra strong spring, automatic brake, rails and carriages, complete (as illust.), packed in strong box. Price **40/-**

No. 56. Clockwork Express Train, **No. 2 Gauge,** very powerful engine fitted with best clockwork movements, tender and 3 corridor carriages, oval lines, etc. Complete in strong wooden box. Price **70/-**

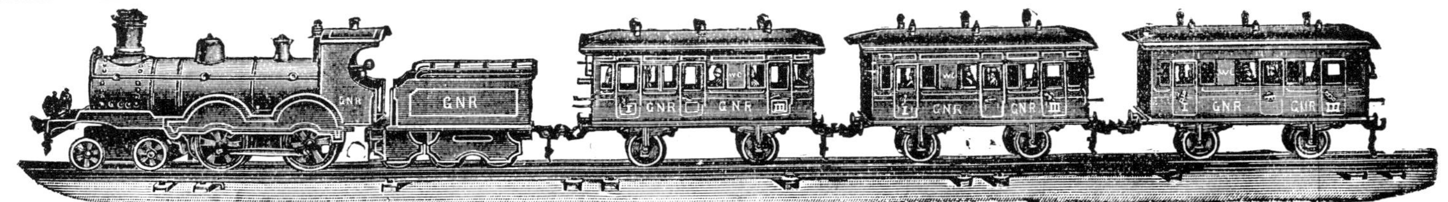

Large Powerful Engines, fitted with best Clockwork Movements and finished in up-to-date style.

No. 62. Gauge 3. Clockwork Express Train, with very powerful Engine, fitted with superior clockwork movements, fast and slow, 2 passenger carriages and goods trucks, oval track. Packed in wooden case. G.N.R. **84/-**

Gamage's New G.N.R. & L.&N.W.R. Railway Systems.

0 GAUGE.
SPECIAL VALUE

0 Gauge. **L. & N.W. and G.N.R. Clockwork Train,** comprising Engine and Tender, 1 Carriage and complete Circular Track (23 in. diameter), length of Train 14 in. Price **$1/10\frac{1}{2}$** Postage 4d.

0 Gauge. **L. & N.W. and G.N.R. Clockwork Train,** as illustration, comprising Engine and Tender, Carriage and Guard's Van, with oblong Track ($33\frac{1}{2}$ in. long, 23 in. wide), length of train 20 in. Price **2/6** Postage 4d.

0 Gauge. **L. & N.W. and G.N.R. Clockwork Train,** as illustration, complete with Carriage and Guard's Van, 7 curved and 2 straight Rails (including Stop Rail), and 2 Switches. The Locomotive of this train is fitted with a brake which allows of the train being stopped by means of the brake rail and without touching the engine. Price **4/6** Postage 6d.

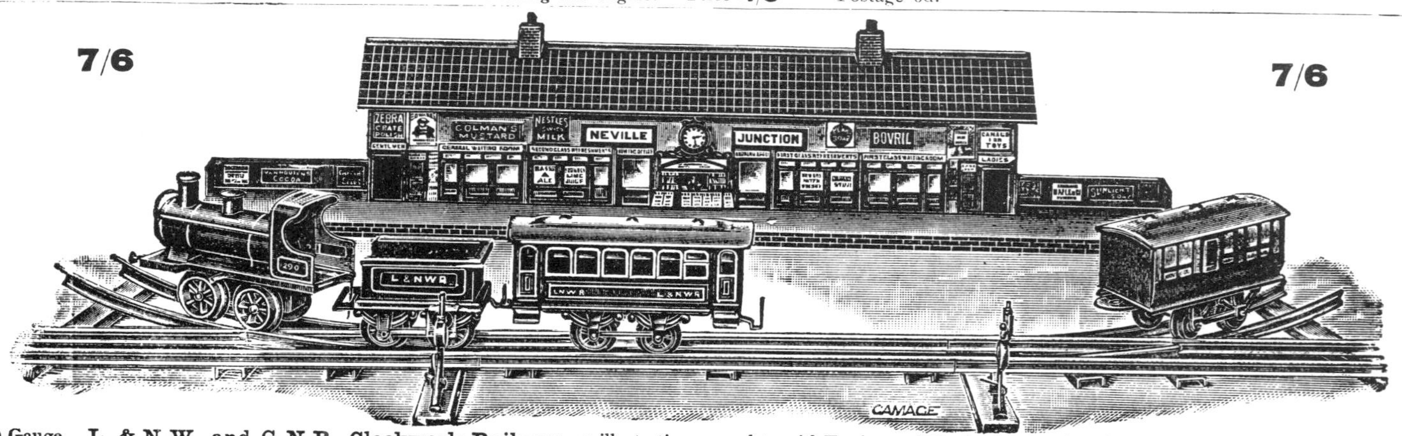

0 Gauge. **L. & N.W. and G.N.R. Clockwork Railway,** as illustration, complete with Engine and Tender, 7 curved Rails (including Stop Rail), 2 straight Rails, 2 Switches, and Station. The engine of this train is fitted with a brake enabling the train to be stopped by use of the brake rail and without touching the engine. Price complete in strong Cardboard Box .. .. **7/6** Postage 9d.

0 Gauge. **L. & N.W. and G.N.R. System,** as illustration, comprising Engine and Tender, Carriage and Guard's Van, Signal with lever, Signal Box with signal, and large Station, 7 curved Rails (including Stop Rail) and 2 straight Rails. The engine of this train is fitted with a brake enabling the train to be stopped by use of the brake rail without touching the train.
Price complete in strong cardboard box .. .. **10/6** Postage 9d.

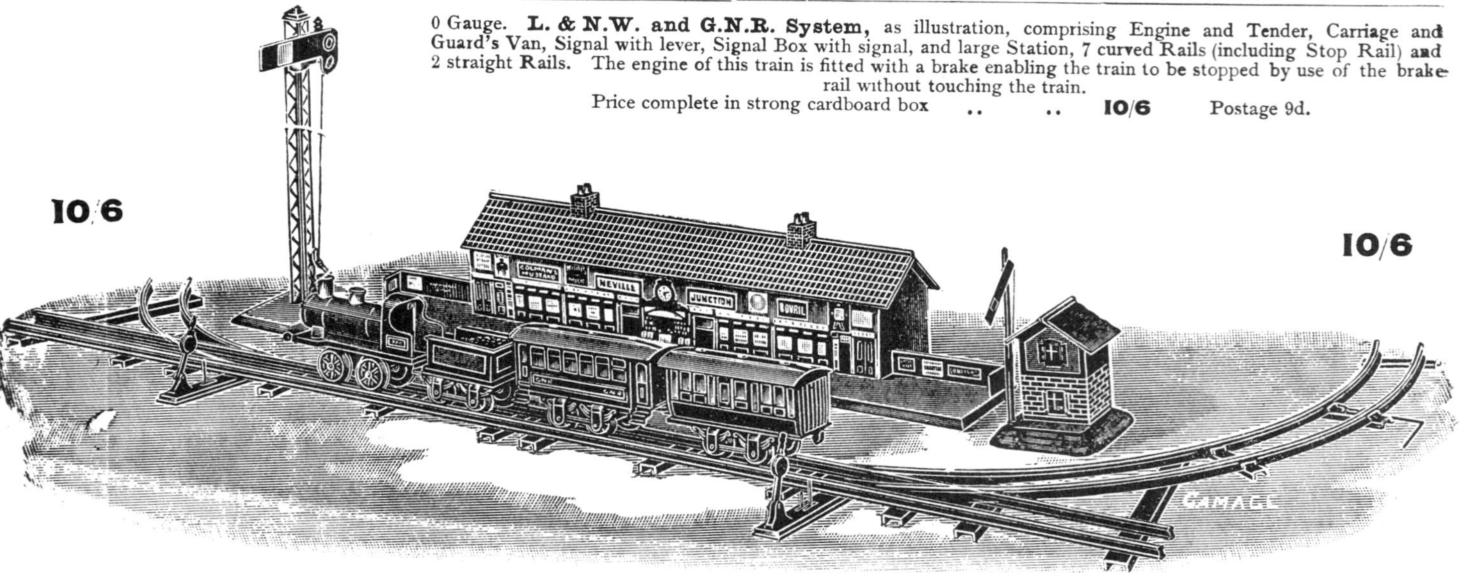

Gamage's Popular Clockwork and Tin Trains.

No. 4. **Clockwork Train** (as Illustration), packed in box.
Price **10½**d. Postage 3d.

No. 4A. **Clockwork Train,** complete, packed in box.
Price **1/6** Postage 3d.

No. 1. **Tin Train** (as Illustration), enamelled, strong, packed in box .. .. .. Price **10½d.** Postage 3d.

No. 2. **Tin Train,** with 3 Carriages and 7 Trucks, enamelled, packed in box .. .. Price **1/4½** Postage 3d.

No. 3. **Enamelled Tin Train,** 4 Corridor Carriages and 1 Ordinary Carriage, packed in box .. .. Price **1/9** Postage 3d.

No. 1459/0.

Clockwork Train.

As Illustration .. .. .. Price **5½**d.
Postage 3d.

Larger size .. .. .. Price **10½**d.
Postage 3d.

Tin Clockwork Trains, Special make.
As Illustration .. Price **1/9** Postage 3d.

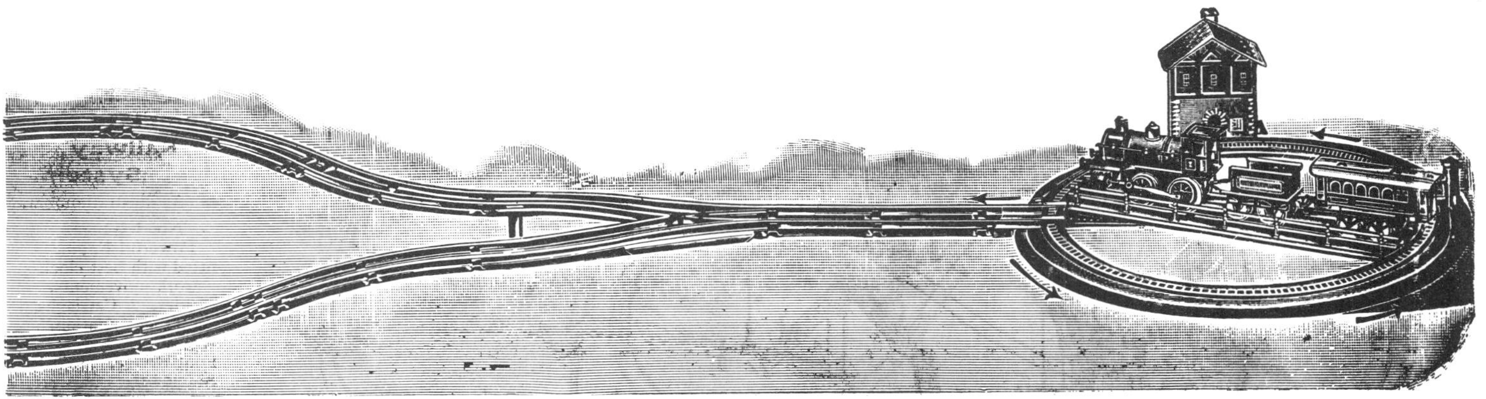

0 Gauge. 1338 **Clockwork Train, with Automatic Turntable** (as Illustration).
One of the most ingenious and interesting Novelties in Model Railways.
Price **16/6**

Complete Clockwork Railway Systems. All Gauges.

ALL MADE AS UP-TO-DATE ENGLISH RAILWAYS.

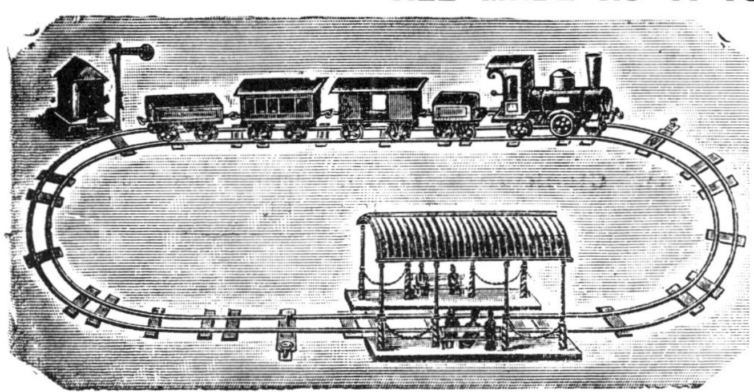

G.N. Railway Set.

No. 50 0 Gauge. Complete (as illustration), with best quality Engine, Tender, 2 Carriages, etc. and finished in English style.
Price **21/-**

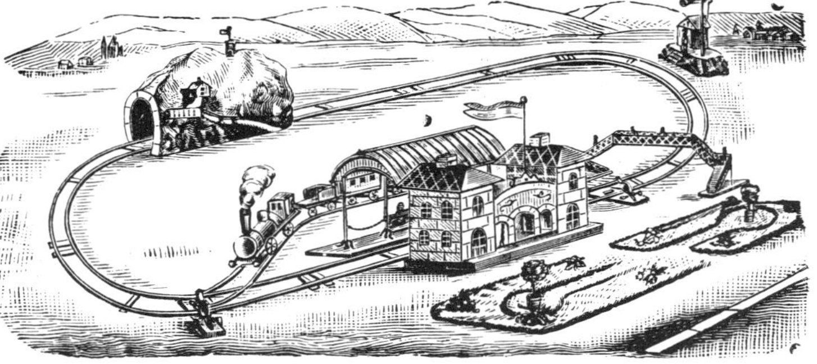

Railway System.

No. 70. Gauge 0. A Complete System (as illustration), beautifully enamelled and very realistic.
Packed in strong wooden box .. **50/-**

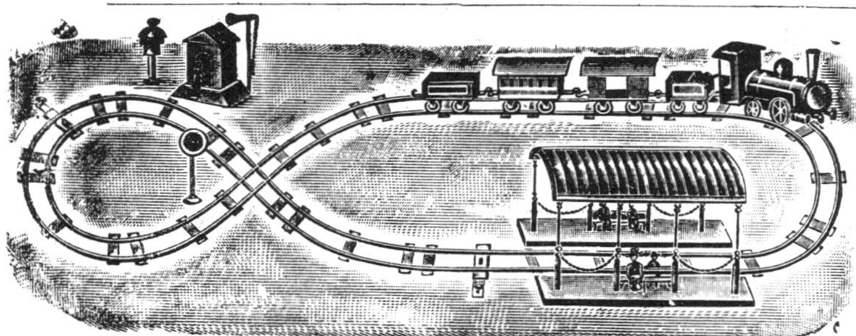

No. 55. G.N. Railway System. No. 0 Gauge (as illustration). Strong Engine fitted with best Clockwork movements, Tender, Carriage, 1 each covered and open Truck, Station, etc.
Complete in strong wooden box .. **25/-**

L.N.W. Railway System. No. 54. Gauge 1. Powerful Engine with best Clockwork Movements, Tender, Carriages, Truck, Station, Signals, Crossing, &c. In strong wooden box **45/-**

L.N.W. or M. Railway System
No. 72. No. 1 Gauge.

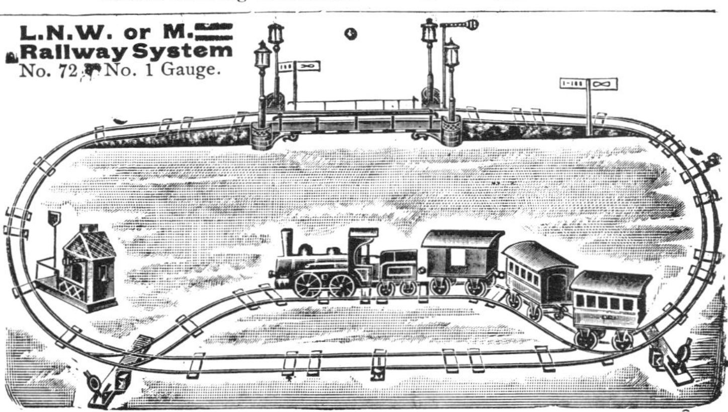

Powerful Engine with best Clockwork Movements. Carriages and Truck, as illustration, Bridge, Crossings, Signals, &c. Complete in wooden box, **58/6**

Railway System.

No. 80. Gauge 2.

Powerful G.N.R. Engine, fitted with strong brake, &c.

Carriages, Bridge, Crossing, Signals, Lines, Switches, etc.

Packed in strong box, **90/-**

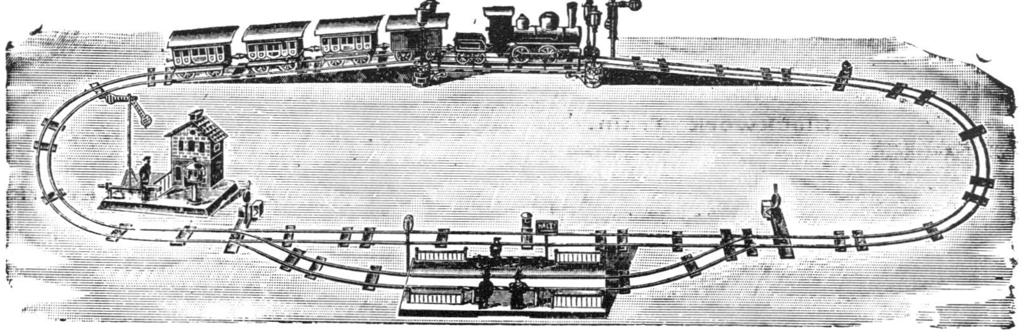

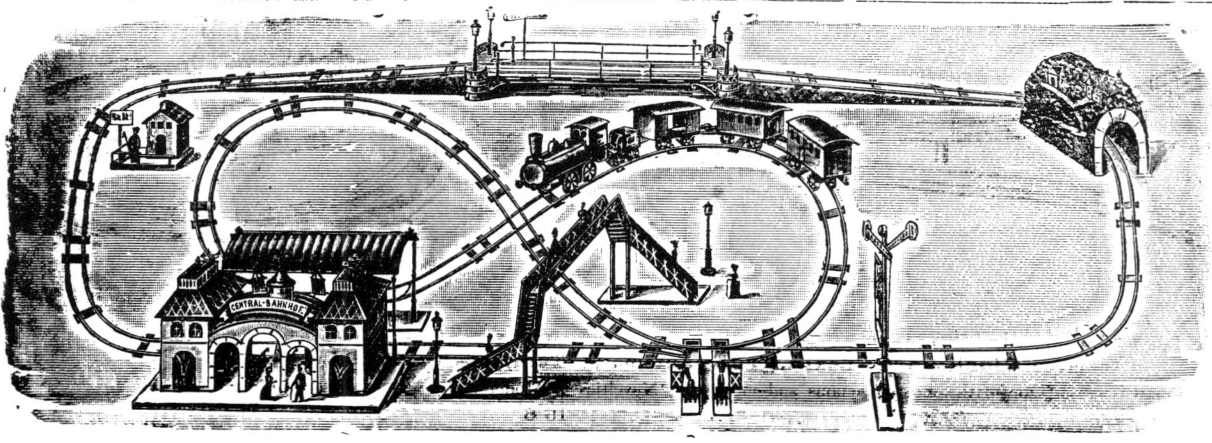

No. 66.

Complete Railway System.

As illustration.

No. 1 Gauge.
Powerful Engine fitted with best clock-work movements, Tender, 2 Carriages, 1 Truck, Station, Railway Bridge, Foot Bridge, Tunnel, Signals, Crossings, &c

Packed in strong wooden box.

Price .. **£5 19 6**
Carriage paid.

Shunting Trains, Pneumatic Signals, etc.

Gauge 0. **Clockwork Shunting Trains.**

3/- 6/11

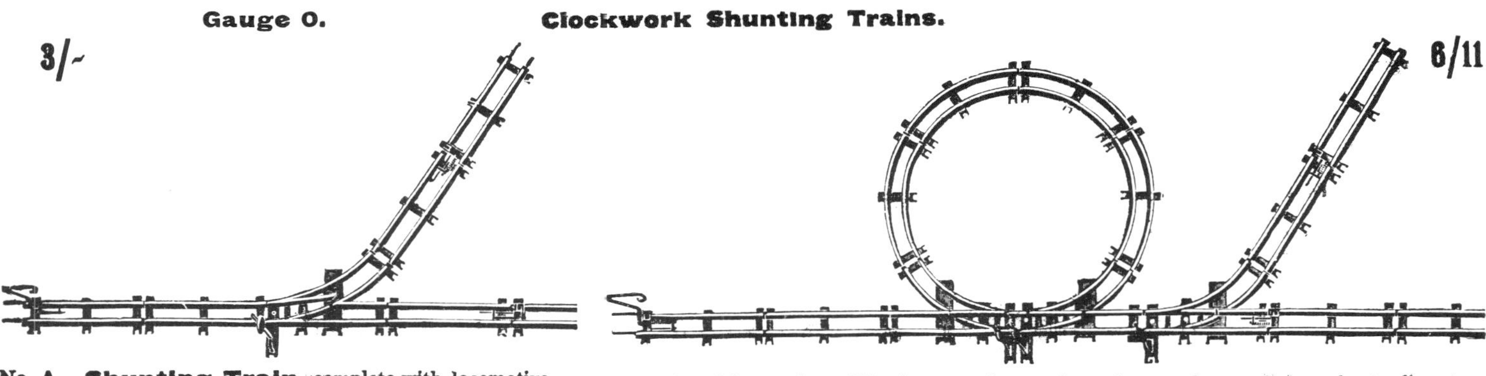

No. A. **Shunting Train,** complete with locomotive, tender and lines, with shunting attachments, **3/-** Post 3d.
No. B. Ditto, ditto, lines with 2 arms, Price **5/6** Postage 4d.

No. C. **Shunting Train,** complete with engine, tender, carriage and extra lines to form circle, as illustration, fitted with shunting attachments.
Price **6/11** Postage 4d.

No. D. **Shunting Train.**

Complete with engine and tender, 2 carriages, 18 rails and 4 switches, all fitted with shunting attachments.

Price **11/6**

No. 37092/0. **Shunting Train.** To attach and detach cars automatically. Complete with locomotive and 1 carriage, 6 curved rails and 2 straight rails, to form oval.
Price **4/11** Postage 4d.
For extra Trucks, see p. 22.

No. 37092/0½. **Shunting Train,** as illustration. Consisting of locomotive, 2 cars, 5 curved rails, 4 straight rails (including 3 slip-off rails), 1 point and 1 stop end. Price **15/9**

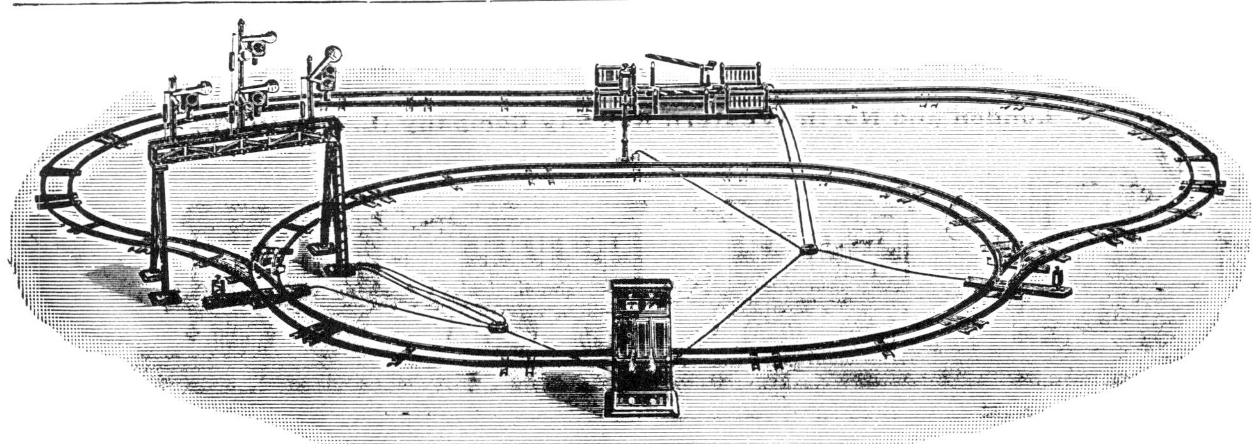

No. 2690.

Pneumatic Signals.

Complete Set, as illustration, all the signals and points being worked by pneumatic apparatus.

Gauge 0	..	**28/6**
,, 1	..	**35/-**

Smaller set.

Gauge 0	..	**16/6**
,, 1	..	**18/6**

Pneumatic Signals. Switch and Signal worked by Compressed Air. Easily fitted and worked.

Superior Steam Trains on Rails. In Strong Cardboard Boxes.

Gauge 0=1¼ in.

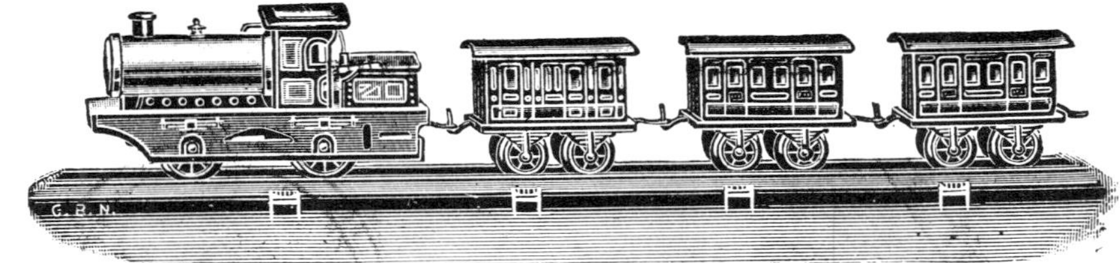

No. 30092/0. **M.R. Train,** consisting of looomotive, 2 passenger cars and 1 guard's van and oval rail formation=8 rails, complete length ot train 20 in. .. .. Price 3/3 Postage 4d.
No. 30093/0. **L. & N. W. R. Train,** same as above .. .. „ 4/11 „ 4d.

Gauge 0=1¼ in.

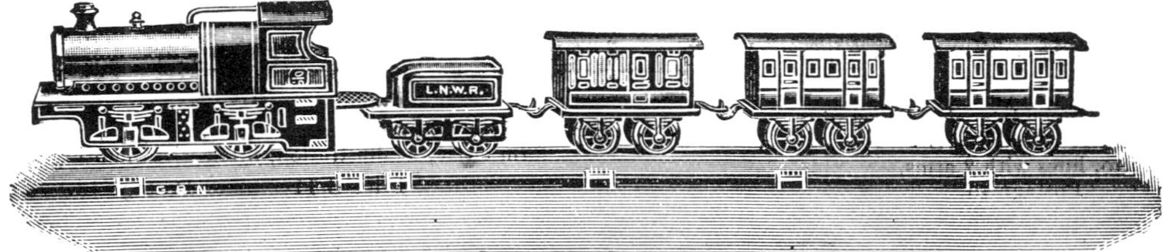

No. 31092/0. **M. R. Steam Train,** consisting of locomotive (finely japanned, with stamped frame, polished brass boiler and safety valve, including tender 10¾ in. long), 2 passenger cars and 1 guard's van and oval rail formation=8 rails, complete length of train 23½ in. .. .. Price 6/6 Postage 6d.
No. 31093/0. **L.& N. W. R. Steam Train,** same as above .. .. „ 6/6 „ 6d.
No. 38092/0. **M. R. Steam Train,** as illustration, consisting of locomotive (finely japanned, with stamped frame, polished brass boiler, oscillating brass cylinder and safety valve, including tender 11½ in. long), 2 passenger cars and 1 guard's van and oval rail formation=10 rails, complete length of train 24½ in. .. .. „ 7/11 „ 6d.
No. 38093/0. **L. & N. W. R. Steam Train,** same as above .. .. „ 7/11 „ 6d.

Gauge 0=1¼ in.

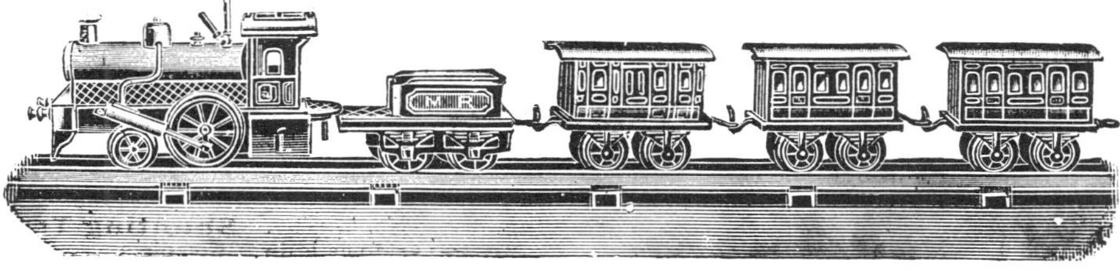

No. 32092/0. **M. R. Steam Train,** consisting of locomotive (frame nicely japanned, oxydized brass boiler, 2 oscillating brass cylinders, japanned flanged wheels, brass dome, steam whistle, flame guard and safety valve, including tender 12 in. long), 2 passenger cars and 1 guard's van and oval rail formation=10 rails, complete length of train 25 in. .. .. Price 11/6
No. 32093/0. **L. & N. W. R. Steam Train,** same as above .. .. „ 11/6

Gauge 0=1¼ in.

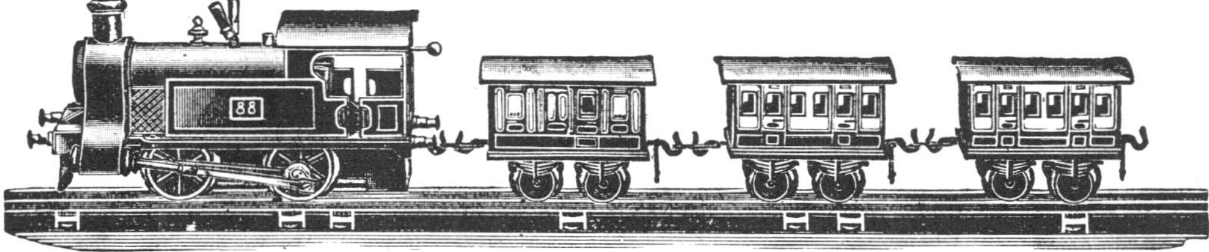

No. 29093/0. **Superior Steam Train on rails, with reversing gear,** consisting of highly finished tender locomotive, with blue oxydised brass boiler, oscillating brass cylinder, steam whistle, safety valve, steam dome and nickelled flanged wheels, with 2 L. & N. W. R. passenger cars and 1 L. & N. W. R. luggage van, with oval set of rails=10 rails, locomotive 8¼ in. long, cars 3½ in. long, length of train 22½ in., complete in a box .. .. Price 17/6

Gauge I=1¾ in. London and North Western Railway Company (L. & N. W. R.)

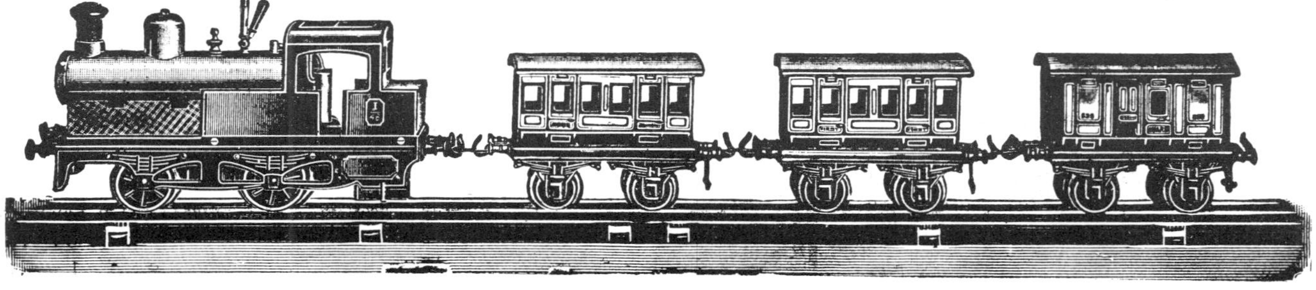

No. 24193/0. Very powerful Steam Train on rails, Gauge 1=1¾ in. Consisting of tender locomotive with brass boiler, oscillating brass cylinder, steam whistle and safety valve with 2 L. & N. W. R. passenger cars 1 L. & N. W. R. luggage van with extra large oval set of rails=12 rails, locomotive 10¼ in. long, cars 6 in. long, length of train 31½ in. Price 21/-, complete in a box.

STEAM TRAINS—*continued.*

Gauge 0=1⅜ in.

No. 33093/0. **L. & N. W. R. Steam Train,** consisting of express locomotive (2 oscillating cylinders, japanned brass boiler and best fittings, bell steam whistle, steam dome, flame guard, safety valve and starting tap, tender with imitation coal, including tender 14½ in. long), 2 passenger cars, doors to open, 1 guard's van, all cars with fittings inside highly finished, with oval rail formation=10 rails, complete length of train 25½ in. .. .. Price **21/-**

Gamage's Special Steam Railway System, Gauge 1, comprising powerful Steam Loco. with bogie wheels and 2 oscillating cylinders, with exhaust steam passing through chimney, fitted with safety valve and steam cock complete, with 3 carriages and set of rails. Supplied in G.N.R. or M.R. colour. Price **25/-**

Ditto do. Engine with **Piston Valve Cylinder,** supplied in G.N.R. or M.R. colour. Price **27/6**

Model of Stephenson's Rocket Steam Train.

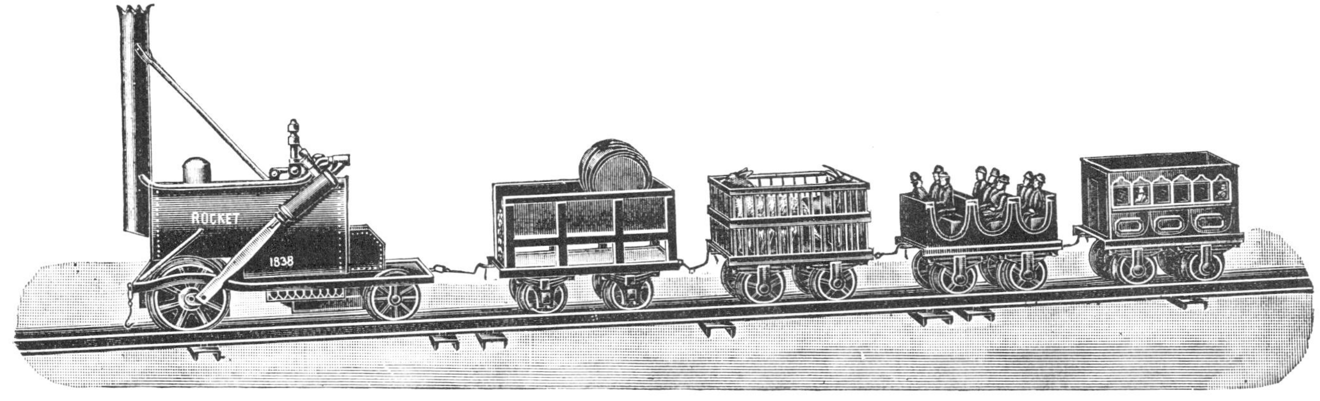

No. 4001/1838. Gauge 1. The Rocket Steam Train comprises strong steam locomotive, as illustration, fitted with 2 slide valve cylinders, **steam whistle,** safety burner, safety valve, tender with water barrel, 2 passenger cars and cattle truck, complete in box with oval track. Price **32/6**

Novelty—Model District Railway.

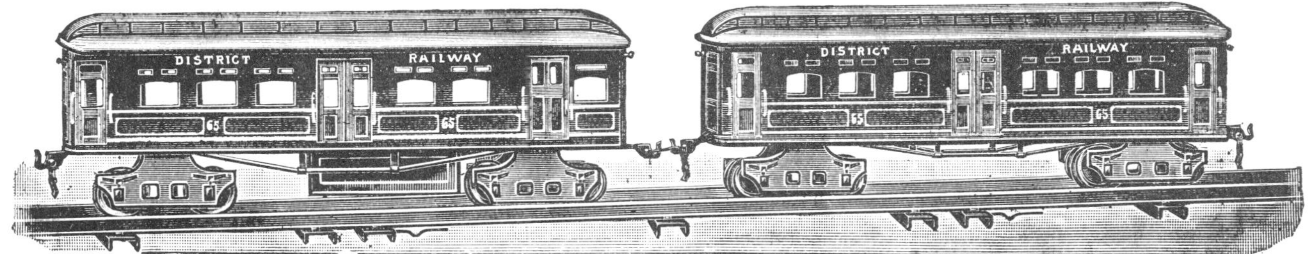

No. A. No. 0 Gauge. Clockwork "District Railway" Train, on bogie wheels, with sliding doors (opened with levers), complete in box, with set of oval lines, length of train 20 in. .. .. Price **30/-**

Car only, with best clockwork movement .. .. ,, **17/6**

No. B. Complete trains as No. A, with brake, No. 1 gauge .. .. ,, **42/-**

Car only, with best clockwork movement .. .. ,, **25/-**

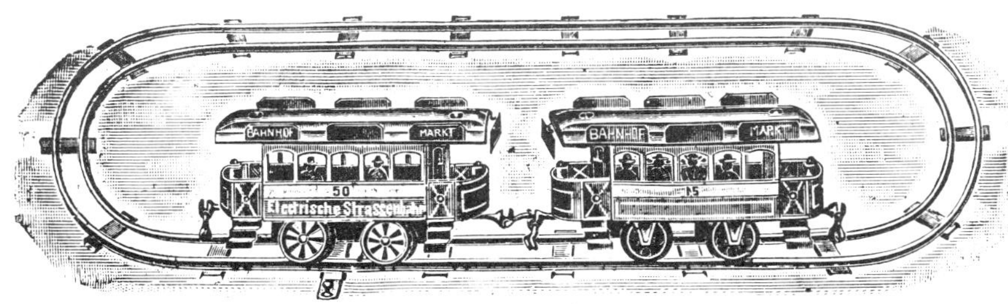

Clockwork Tram.

No. 1. Clockwork Tram Set, with 1 Tram, 0 Gauge .. **12/6**

As illustration, **17/6** Postage 6d. No. 1 Gauge, **25/-**

These Trams are fitted with Powerful Clockwork **Movements and** finished in the best style.

Extra Lines, Switches, and Crossings can be **added at will.** Particulars see pp. 17-18.

STEAM LOCOMOTIVES.

A. W. GAMAGE, Ltd., have an exceptionally fine selection of Locomotives of all types, comprising the latest improvements in Slide Valve, Piston Valve and Oscillating Cylinder Engines, with internally and externally fired Boilers.

1 Gauge, Internally Fired Steam Locomotive, with slide valve cylinders, and automatic stop and reverse gear, safety valve and steam whistle, total length 13 in. .. .. Price **25/-** Post 6d.

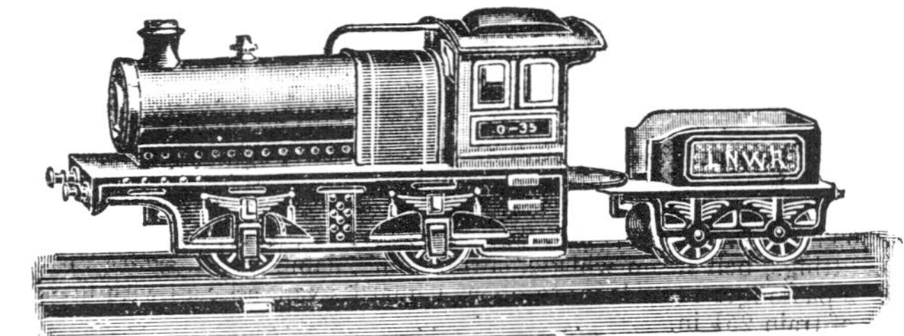

0 Gauge, Steam Locomotive and Tender, polished brass boiler, oscillating cylinder and safety valve, total length 11½ in. .. Price **3/11** Post 3d. Supplied in Midland and L. & N. W. colours.

No. 1 Gauge, Locomotive with Tender, 17 in. long (including tender), with nickelled brass flanged wheels, oscillating nickelled brass cylinders and buffers, enamelled boiler, steam whistle and safety valve **13/6**
Ditto with reversing gear .. .. .. **16/6** Postage 4d.

0 Gauge, Steam Locomotive, constructed from **ENGLISH** models. $1\frac{3}{8}$ gauge, 14 in. long (including tender), L.&S.W., L.&N.W., M., and G.N. Rys., highly japanned in the original colours of the different Railway Companies, with 2 oscillating brass cylinders, starting tap, oxydized brass boiler, steam whistle, steam dome and safety valve, 4 wheel leading bogie and 4 driving wheels, very elegant finish, with japanned tender and imitation coals .. **12/3** Postage 4d.

1 **Gauge,** with slide valve cylinders, enamelled brass boiler, nickelled flanged wheels and brass buffers, dome, safety valve, whistle, hand rails and flame guard, exhaust steam passes through chimney, tender with imitation coals, 15½ in. long .. **21/-** Do., 0 Gauge, not reversing .. **12/6**

0 Gauge, Steam Locomotive and Tender, 2 oscillating cylinders, safety valve, steam whistle, reversing gear to work from cab, 12 in. long, 4½ in. high .. .. **8/6** Postage 4d.

0 Gauge, Steam Locomotive, enamelled boiler, nickel flanged wheels, slide valve cylinders with reversing gear, steam dome, bell whistle, safety valve and steam jet oiler, steam passes through funnel, tender with imitation coal length 13½ in., **15/-** Post 4d.
1 **Gauge,** ditto .. .. **21/-** Post free.
Supplied in Midland, L.&N.W., G.N., and L.&S.W. colours.

0 Gauge, Steam Locomotive with oscillating cylinder, safety valve and cog wheel gearing to increase power, polished brass boiler, length 7 in.
Price **1/11**
Postage 3d.
Supplied in Midland and L.&N.W. colours.

2 Gauge, Steam Locomotive.
Fitted with reversing gear, worked from lever in cab, slide valve cylinders, exhaust up funnel, steam regulator, whistle and safety valve.
Price **29/6**
Enamelled in correct colours.

STEAM LOCOMOTIVES—*continued.*

Gauge 0 **L.N.W. Express Steam Locomotive,** with slide valve cylinder, guide bars, reversing gear, automatic stop, steam whistle, safety valve, geared and coupled wheels, internal flue to boiler with patent vapour lamp.
Total length 16 in. Price **30**/- Post free.

No. 117SR. **Steam Locomotive** with Tender. Gauge 1. 2 slide valve cylinders fitted with lubricator cocks, safety valve, steam whistle, water gauge, reversing gear operated from cab, exhausts up funnel, 14½ in. long, 6 in. high. Price **22/6**
No. 120SR. Gauge 3. Ditto, ditto, 23 in. long, 8 in. high, „ **50**/-
Ditto, ditto, with oscillating cylinders and without reversing gear **40**/-

Gauge 0 Internally Fired **Steam Tank Locomotive,** with slide valve cylinders with guide bars, reversing gear, safety valve, steam whistle, geared and coupled wheels, trailing bogie, central flue to boiler with patent vapour lamp. Length 10 in.

Gauge 1. Length 13 in., **35**/- Gauge 0. Length 10 in., **25**/-

G.N.R. Steam Express Loco., with 2 double action slide valve cylinders with guide bars and patent valve gear, automatic stop, fast and slow movement, steam whistle, safety valve, water gauge, internal firing with vapour lamp, exhaust steam passes up chimney to imitate smoke, 6-wheeled tender with imitation coal. Also supplied in L.N.W. colours.
Gauge 1, 21 in. long, **40**/- Gauge 2, 23 in. long, **47/6** Gauge 3, 28 in. long, **75**/-

Midland Steam Express Locomotive, with 2 patent double acting slide valve cylinders, patent valve gear, automatic stop, reverse and fast and slow movement, steam whistle, safety valve, water gauge, internally fired by patent vapour lamp, exhaust steam passes up chimney in imitation of smoke, 6-wheeled tender with imitation coal.
Gauge 1, 22 in. long, **40**/- Gauge 2, 24 in. long, **47/6** Gauge 3, 28 in. long, **75**/-

Steam Tank Locomotive, with reversing gear, oscillating brass cylinder, cog wheel gearing to increase power, oxydised brass boiler, enamelled cab, steam whistle, safety valve and steam dome.
Gauge 0, 8¼ in. long, **9/9** Post 4d.
1, 11 in. long, **14/9** Post 6d.

The Decapod.

Our 1906 model, with atmospheric burner, central flue through boiler, reversing gear.
Runs on standard gauge rails: 0, **25**/- 1, **55**/- 2, **63**/-
No bogie wheels are fitted to the 0 gauge engine, which has only 4 wheels.

This engine represents the latest strides in Model Steam Locomotives, and has been specially designed to give practical results without altering the general appearance of the engine as compared with the original. Hitherto models of the Decapod have been unsatisfactory, and would only travel on rails of a specially wide radius. This has been obviated and our 1906 model will run on standard gauge rails.

Its working parts have been entirely reconstructed to our own designs, and we very strongly recommend this locomotive to those requiring a good and powerful engine, and we guarantee it to give satisfaction.

STEAM LOCOMOTIVES—*continued.*

Bavarian State Express Locomotive (Gauge I.) Correct model and one of the latest productions in Model Engines. Slide valve cylinders with crossheads and guide bars and lubricators. Exhaust through funnel. Fitted with a feed pump, fixed under footplate, and worked from rear axle, being fed from water carried in tender. Complete with all fittings, as illustration. Also steam and water gauges fitted in cab, and 3-way cock for pump. Length over all 23 in. Height to funnel 7 in. Price .. **66/-**

Fine Steam Locomotive (Gauge I., ⅝ in.), constructed from original English models, 14 in. long (including tender), L. & S.W., L. & N.W., M. and G.N. Railways, highly japanned in the original colours of the different Railway Companies, with 2 oscillating brass cylinders, enamelled brass boiler, steam whistle, steam dome and safety valve. On 4 axles—8 wheels. Very elegant finish, with highly japanned tender and imitation coals as illust. .. **18/6** Postage 4d.

Midland Railway Express Locomotive on 4 axles, slide valve cylinders, combination oilers, japanned brass boiler, steam whistle, safety valve, 2 domes, brass hand rails and buffers, tender with imitation coal, 16½ in. long.

Gauge I. **21/**

Steam Express Locomotive (Gauge I.) with reversing gear, 2 double-acting slide valve cylinders, enamelled boiler, bell-whistle, steam dome, flame guard, safety valve, steam jet, oiler and starting tap, exhaust steam passing through funnel in imitation of smoke, tender with imitation coal, 16 in. long.

Price **39/6**

Great Northern Bogie Express Locomotive (Gauge II.),

With slide valve cylinders and guide bars fitted with reversing gear, bell-whistle, water gauge, safety valve, starting tap, and steam jet oiler, brass spring buffers, tender with imitation coal.

22 in. long. Price **50/-**

Also supplied in Midland, London & North Western and London & South Western Colours.

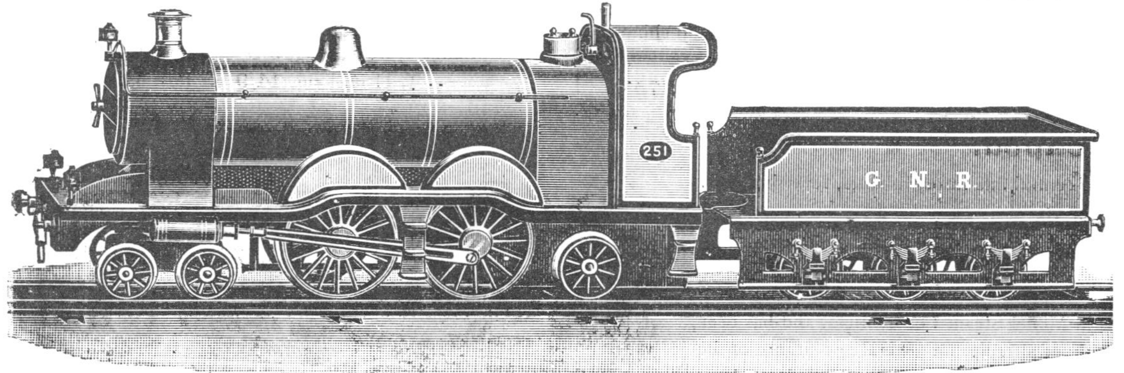

Scale Model of G.N.R. Express Locomotive.

"ATLANTIC" TYPE.

☞ Note! Gauge III. (3 in.)

4 coupled driving wheels, 2 trailers, 2 powerful slide valve cylinders which exhaust up funnel, reversing gear, spring buffers, 3 head lights, safety valve, water gauge, whistle and regulator

Fitted up with "Ever Ready" spirit lamp and reserve tank.

Boiler fitted with 4 water tubes.

Length over all 30 in.

Price **£4 2 6**

Scale Model L.N.W.R. Tank Locomotive. Gauge III (3 in.) ENGLISH MAKE.

4-cpld. driving wheels, 4 bogie wheels and 2 trailers, 2 powerful slide valve cylinders, connecting rods and reversing eccentrics, spring buffers, 2 safety valves, water gauge, whistle and regulator worked from front of smoke box where it is cool and readily accessible. The firing is by means of our Special "EVER-READY" Spirit Lamp, with gauge glass and tank for reserve spirit, with special arrangements for supplying lamp as required.

Length over all 18 in. Price **75/-**

STEAM LOCOMOTIVES—*continued.*

Magnificent New Model of Great Eastern Company's Steam Express Locomotive No. 1870. Built entirely of Castings. Two powerful Slide Valve Cylinders with lubricators, patent Link Reversing Gear, Starting Lever in front of smokebox, Safety Valve, Whistle worked from cab, Reversing Lever fitted in cab, Boiler fitted with Water Tube and Central Flue, Tender fitted as fuel tank. Length over all 23 in. Gauge 1. Price **£5 5 0**

No. 511. **Steam Tank Locomotive.**

Gauge 0, with 2 oscillating cylinders, safety valve, whistle, brass boiler, length $7\frac{1}{2}$ in., height $4\frac{1}{4}$ in.

Price **7/6** Post 4d.

Gauge $2\frac{1}{2}$.

Scale Model of **G. N. R. 8 ft. Single Express Locomotive No. 776.**

Built entirely of Castings, Boiler 11 in. long, with circulating tubes, double action slide valve cylinders fitted with lubricators, link reversing gear operated from cab, 4 in. driving wheels, steam dome, safety valve, whistle, water gauge, hand rails, 3 headlights, 4 wheel leading bogie, vacuum tubes, spring buffers, total length engine and tender $26\frac{1}{2}$ in., height $7\frac{1}{2}$ in., finely enamelled and lined in correct colours, weight 10 lb., very powerful engine.

£4 17 6

Steam gauge and syphon fitted, 6/6 extra.

North Eastern Bogie Express Locomotive No. 1619. Gauge 1.

This is a particularly fine model of very solid construction, being built entirely of castings, fitted with latest type slide valve cylinders and link reversing gear operated from cab. To facilitate the easy starting and stopping of engine a starting cock is fitted in the front of smokebox and is more readily accessible than when placed in the cab. Fitted with N.E.R. pattern safety valve and whistle. The boiler has a centre flue and also a water tube to ensure a good steam pressure.

Tender fitted as Liquid Fuel Tank. Total length 23 in. Price **£5 5 0**

L.N.W.R. Co.'s

Latest Type

Bogie Express Locomotive.

Accurately finished, with 2 fixed slide valve cylinders, flame guard, japanned brass boiler, bell steam whistle, safety valve, guide bars, water gauge, dome, brass hand rails, connecting rod, starting tap and steam jet oiler, steam passes through funnel imitating smoke, brass spring buffers and lantern.

Tender on strong axle bearings with imitation coal.

Gauge $2\frac{1}{2}$, $24\frac{1}{2}$ in. long, **60/-**

Gauge 3, 27 in. long, **79/6**

BEST QUALITY CLOCKWORK LOCOMOTIVES,

Fitted with extra powerful and long running Motors.

2020 G.N.R.

Gauge 0 Locomotive and Tender with Brake. Total length, 10½ in. Price **4/6** Postage 3d.

Do. do., with reversing gear. Price **5/11** Postage 3d.

B 1020.

0 gauge Locomotive and Tender. Powerful motor. Total length, 11 in. Price **7/11** Postage 4d.

B 1020 L.N.W.R.

0 gauge Locomotive and Tender with brake. **Extra** powerful motor. Total length, 11 in. Price **10/6** Postage 4d.

Do. do., fitted with reversing gear, **12/6** Postage 4d.

17594/0.

0 gauge G.N.R. Bogie Express Locomotive, fitted with regulator, brake, and fast and slow gearing, 13 in. long. Price **13/6** Postage 4d. Can also be obtained in L.N.W., Midland and L.S.W. colours.

E 1020. 0 gauge G.N.R. Bogie Express Locomotive, fitted with specially powerful motor for drawing heavy loads. Reversing gear and brake. Length, 12½ in. Price **15/-** Can also be obtained in L.N.W., Midland, and L.S.W. colours.

Tenders.—0 gauge, **8**d. each. Ditto, with imitation coal, **1/-** 1 gauge do. **1/-** Postage 2d.

0 gauge with 6 wheels, **2/6** 1 gauge ditto, **3/11** 1 gauge with 8 wheels, **4/6** Postage 3d.

B 1021 L.N.W.R.

1 gauge Clockwork Locomotive, fitted with outside cylinders. Extra strong pulling motor, with brake and fast and slow gearing. Length, 15½ in. Price **17/6** Postage 4d. Can also be obtained in G.N.R., Midland and L.S.W. colours.

35592/6.

0 gauge Clockwork Tank or Pilot Locomotive, with brake and reversing gear. Price **4/6** Postage 3d.

B 1021 L.N.W.

1 gauge Clockwork Locomotive, fitted with long running motor and brake. Length, 15½ in. Price **12/6** Postage 4d. Can also be obtained in L.S.W., Midland and G.N.R. colours.

0 gauge Clockwork Locomotive with Tender. This is a particularly sturdy little engine, very suitable for pulling heavy goods trains, fitted with brake. Length, 13 in.; height, 4 in. Price **7/6** Post 3d.

Do. do,, fitted with brake and reversing gear. 10 in. long, 4 in. high. Price **9/6** Post 4d.

Special Line! Locomotives.

No.		Price	
0A.	Clockwork Locomotive,	**7/6**	Postage 2d.
,, 0R.	,,	**12/6**	,,
,, 1R.	,,	**14/6**	,,

17592/1. **29/6**

1 gauge Midland Clockwork Bogie Express Locomotive (inside cylinder type), with powerful motor, brake and fast and slow mechanism.

Can also be obtained in L.N.W., G.N. and L.S.W.R. colours. Post free.

All these Locomotives are of a particularly solid construction and not easily put out of order; they can, however, be repaired by us at reasonable cost when necessary.

Best Quality Clockwork Locomotives—*continued.*

N.B. All our Locomotives are noted for their capacity to draw heavy loads on small tracks with sharp curves.

Gauge I. **Clockwork Locomotive and Tender,** fitted with Brake and Reversing Gear, 13 in. long, 5 in. high

Price **14/6** Postage 6d.

Gauge 2. Ditto, 16½ in. long, 6 in. high.

Price **17/6** Postage 6d.

Gauge I. **Latest Model G.W.R. Bogie Express Locomotive** ("Atlantic" **type**), fitted with powerful clockwork motor with Brake and Fast and Slow movement. Total length 23½ in. Price **35/-**

Gauge I. Ditto, fitted with DOUBLE SPRING. Price **59/-**

Gauge I. **G.N.R. Bogie Express Locomotive,** with imitation Slide Valve Cylinders and Guide Bars, very powerful mechanism with Brake and Fast and Slow Speeds. Length 21 in. Price **35/-**

The Celebrated "Charles Dickens." Clockwork Locomotive fitted with Brake and powerful motor with Reversing Gear and Fast and Slow Speeds.
Gauge 0, **16/6** (Postage 4d.) 1, **27/6** 2, **32/6**

Latest Model Clockwork Tank Locomotive.
Exceptionally steady rnnning loco., suitable for sharp curves, fitted with powerful motor with regulator.
Gauge 0, **15/-** (Postage 4d.) Gauge 1, **29/6**
Can be supplied in Midland, L.N.W., G.N., and S.W. colours.

L.N.W.R. Bogie Express Locomotive, with Brake and Reversing Lever.

Gauge 1, 19 in. long .. **29/6**
2, 21 in. long .. **39/6**

Can also be obtained in G.N., Midland, and S.W. colours.

New Model.

Powerful Clockwork Locomotive with very strong motor, Brake and Regulator; will run forwards or backwards.

Gauge 2½ .. **55/-**
(2⅛ in.) **63/-**

Special Clockwork and Steam Locomotives,

and Rails for Home Construction.

Gauge 0.
Clockwork Locomotive and Tender, with brake and starting lever, very strong motor, length 9½ in. over all.
Price **7/6** Postage 3d.

Gauge 0.
Clockwork Locomotive and Tender, with brake, starting and reversing levers, exceptionally steady running loco., length 9½ in. over all.
Price **12/6** Post 3d.

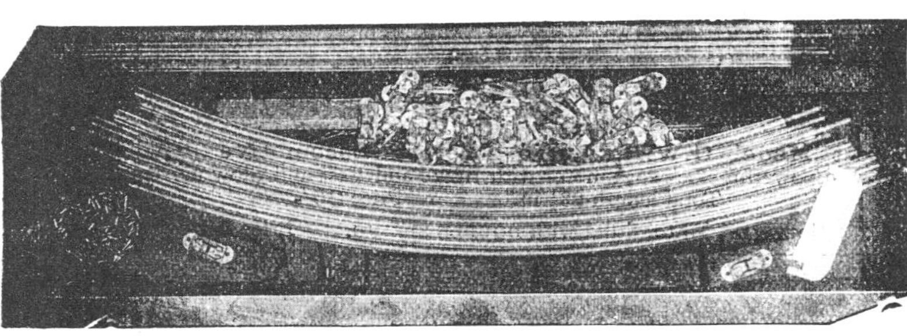

Gauge 1 Clockwork Locomotive, with starting and reversing levers, automatic brake, dummy vacuum tube, fitted with governors, very powerful loco., **14/6** Postage 6d.

Rails for customers to construct their own tracks.

THIS ILLUSTRATION SHOWS RAILS WHEN MADE UP

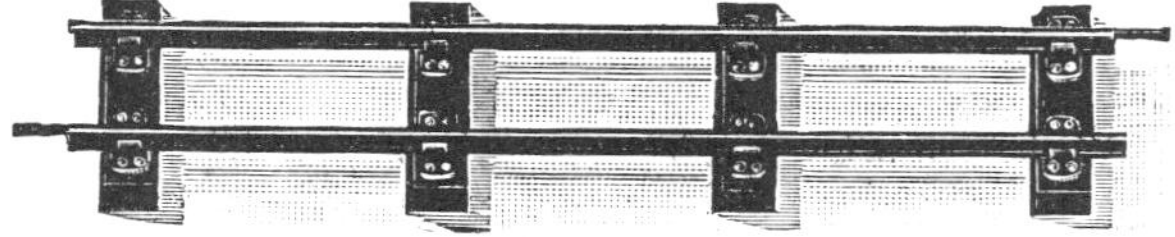

These rails are curved to the standard gauges and radius, and it is only necessary to attach them to the chairs and sleepers to make a perfect and realistic track.

Gauge 1. Consisting of 20 pieces, 14½ in. long, of curved and straight rail making a complete oval, with 54 loose chairs, 120 holding-down spikes and 30 black wood sleepers. Price **3/6** Packed in box. Post 4d.
Gauge 2 and 2½ in. 28 pieces rail, 14½ in. long, curved and straight, with 84 chairs, 168 holding-down spikes and 12 sleepers. Price **5/-** Post 4d.
Gauge 3 in. 36 pieces rail, 14½ in. long, 108 chairs, 216 holding-down spikes and 58 sleepers. Price **6/6** Post 6d.

Scale Model L.N.W.R. Tank Locomotive.

3 in. gauge. English make.

4 coupled driving wheels, 4 bogie wheels and 2 trailers, 2 powerful slide **valve cylinders**, connecting rods and reversing eccentrics, spring buffers, **2 safety valves**, water gauge, whistle, and regulator worked from front of smokebox where it is cool and readily accessible.

The Firing is by means of our special "Ever-ready" spirit lamp, with **gauge** glass and tank for reserve spirit, with special arrangement for supplying lamp as required. Length 18 in. over all.

Price **75/-**

North Eastern Railway Co's Express Locomotive.

Class 730. ATLANTIC type (4-4-2). Scale ½ in./1 ft.
Gauge 2½ in. Length over all 36 in.

Specification—2 slide valve cylinders (lagged) placed outside the frames, with eccentrics and ingenious modification of the Stephenson Link Motion reversing by lever in the cab. Steam is generated through an effective superheater, and the exhaust is carried up the funnel. It has 10 wheels, 4 leading on bogie carriage, 4 balanced coupled driving, and a pair of trailing wheels. The boiler is of the internally fired Smithies type so popular for model locos., having cast downcomer and 3 seamless water tubes braized in tube boiler and brass shell. The usual fittings include 2 safety valves pressed to blow at 25 lb., steam regulator, water and pressure gauges, and check valve. The tender has 6 wheels with dummy springs and axle-boxes, spring buffers, drawhook, etc., 2 tanks with tap for supplying methylated spirit to lamp, and the other with hand forcepump with connection to check valve to replenish boiler while under steam. The enamelling, lining, numbering, etc., is executed in first-class style giving a splendid finish to a most reliable and substantial model. Price **£10 10 0**

Complete set o Special Wide Radius Rails for above Loco., consisting of 24 in. pieces, making Circular Track 9 ft. 4 in. diam. Price **8/-** set.

Models of English Railway Carriages.

In M.R., L.N.W.R., G.N.R., L.S.W.R. companies' colours. Best enamel finish

Carriage with doors to open.
Gauge 0, 1/- 1, 2/- 2, 3/11 3, 7/6

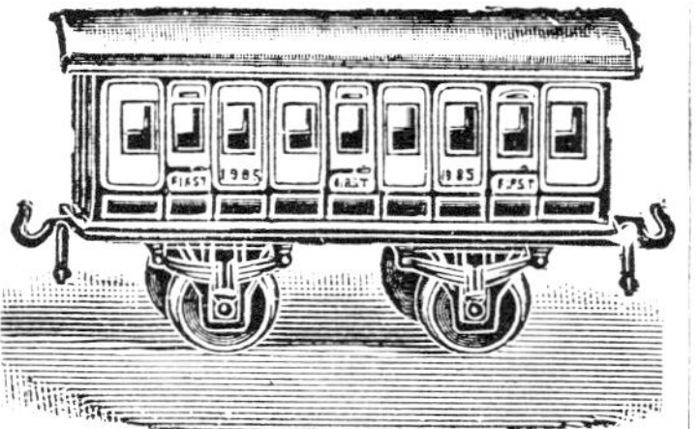
Carriage as illustration.
Gauge 0, 1/9 1, 3/6

Guard's Van.
Gauge 0, 1/9 1, 3/6

Carriage. Gauge 0, 7½d. 1, 10½d.

Express Carriage.
Gauge 2, 4/11 Gauge 3, 12 windows, 8/11

Corridor Carriage with bogie wheels. Gauge 0, 6/11 1, 10/6 2, 12/6

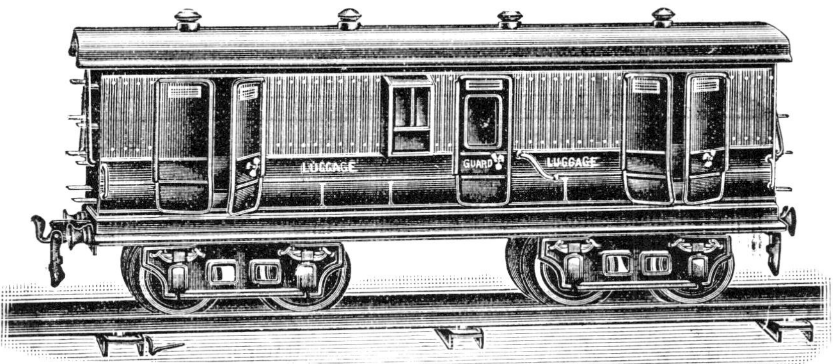

Express Luggage Van. Best finish. With bogie wheels.
Gauge 0, 2/11 1, with doors to open, 9/6 2, 13/6 3, 25/-

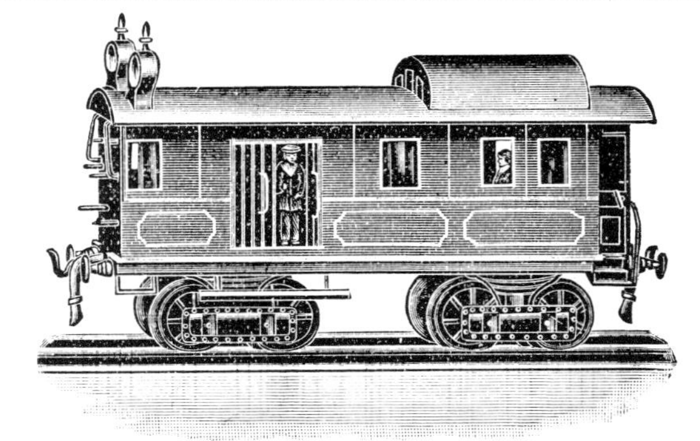
Guard's Van with bogie wheels.
Gauge 0, 6/6 1, 10/6 2, 12/6

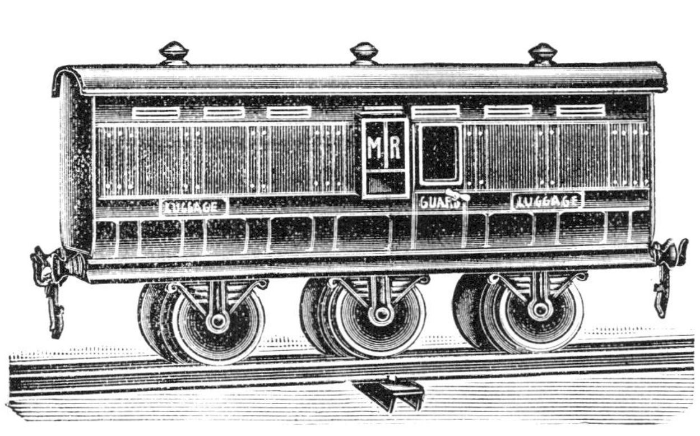

Express Luggage Van. Gauge 2, 4/11 3, 8/11

Express Carriage with bogie wheels. Very best finish.
Gauge 0, 2/11 1, with doors to open, 10/6 2, 14/6 3, 25/-

A Realistic Model of our Present Mail System.

MAIL VAN.

Automatically receives and delivers Mail Bag while Train is running at full speed. Can be attached to any 0 and 1 gauge trains.

GREAT NOVELTY.

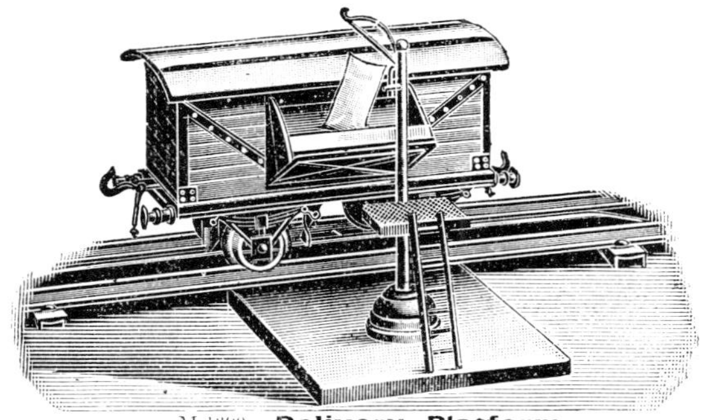

M 1390. **Delivery Platform.**

1 Gauge.—1⅞ in., Automatic Mail Bag Set, consisting of L. & N.W.R. Royal Mail Van, 6⅝ in. long, delivery platform with rail attached 14½ in. long, 6 in. high, receiving net with rail attached 14¼ in. long, 2¾ in. high, and postal bags, complete in strong cardboard box .. .. .. **13/6** set.
Same as above in M.R. model, 0 Gauge, 1⅜ in., same consisting of L. & N.W.R. Royal Mail Van, 5¼ in. long, delivery platform and rail attached 10⅝ in. long, receiving net and rail attached 10⅝ in. long, and postal bags, complete in strong carboard box .. ..
Same as above in M.R. model **10/6**

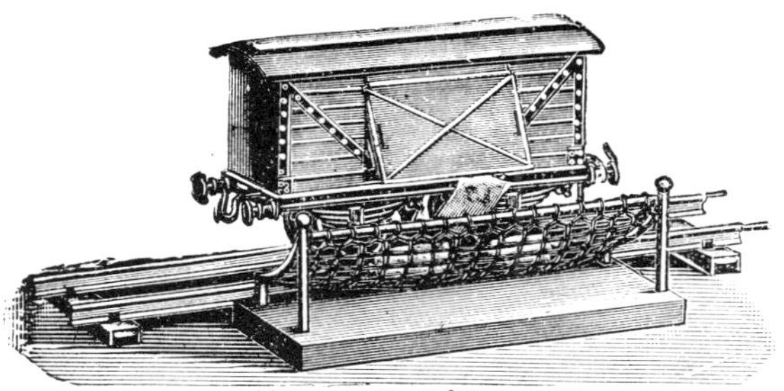

M 1390. **Receiving Net.**

Receives and delivers postal bags, everything done automatically, can be attached to any part of the rail system, made on the principle of the system employed by the Railway Companies.

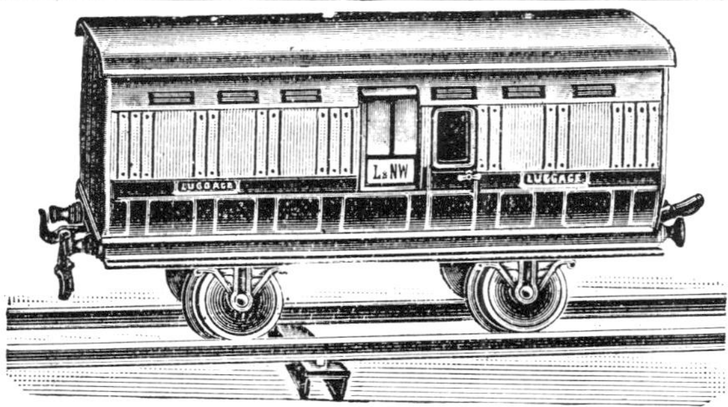

1893/1. **Guard's Van** 0 Gauge, **1/9** 1 Gauge, **3/6**

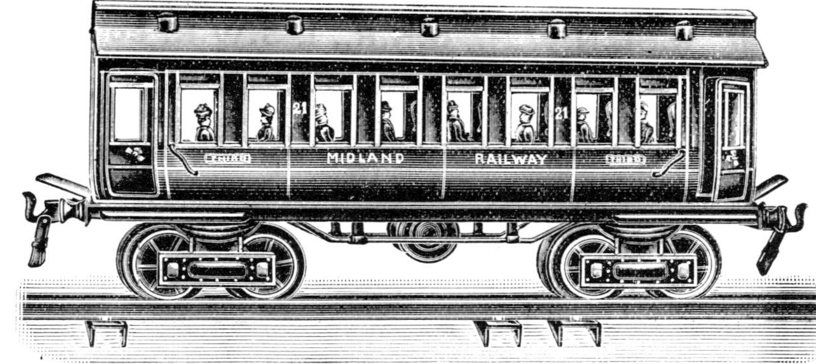

1899. New Pattern Midland **Passenger Carriage.**
0 Gauge .. .. **6/11** 1 Gauge **10/6**

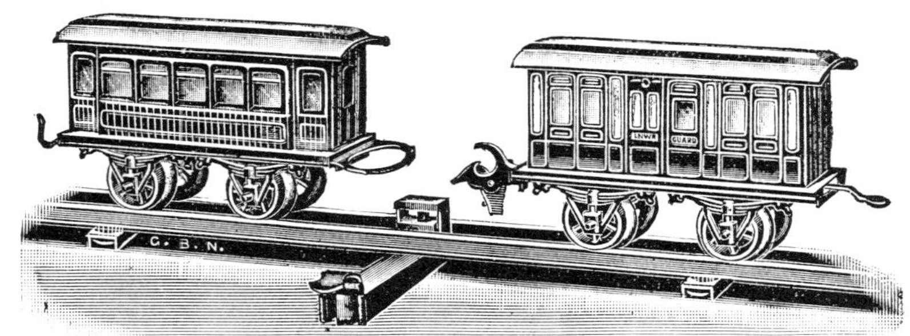

37693/0. **Slip Carriages.**

Consisting of 1 Passenger Carriage, 1 Luggage Van and Special Rail for detaching cars (length of car 5 in.), the carriages can be detached from each other without touching them whilst the train is passing, and can be attached to any 0 Gauge Railway Track. Supplied in Midland and L. & N.W.R. colours .. .. .. **4/6** set. Postage 3d.

1841. G.N.R. **Corridor Car** on Bogie Wheels.
1 Gauge **10/6**

1842. 1 Gauge, **Corridor Car** on Bogie Wheels **10/6**

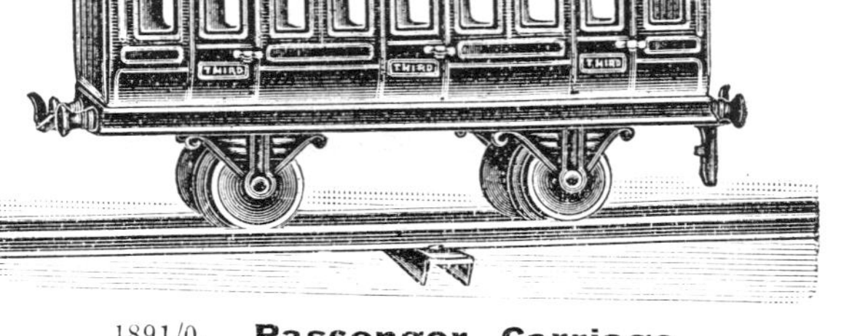

1891/0. **Passenger Carriage.**
0 Gauge **1/9**
1 Gauge **3/6**

Railway Rolling Stock. English Models.

Best enamel finish and Correct Models of those in use by the leading railway companies.

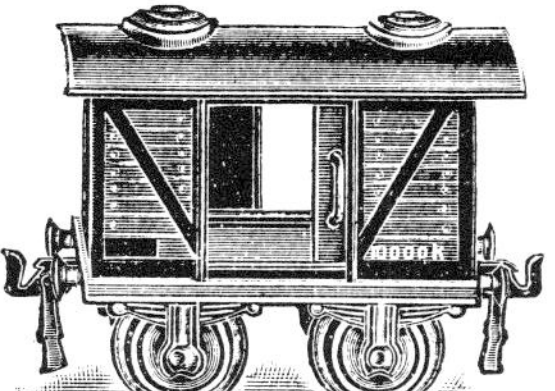

Goods Van.
With sliding doors.
Gauge 0, 1/- 1, 2/-
2, 2/6 3, 5/6

Tipping Waggon.
Gauge 0, 1/- 1, 1/11
2, 2/6 3, 3/6

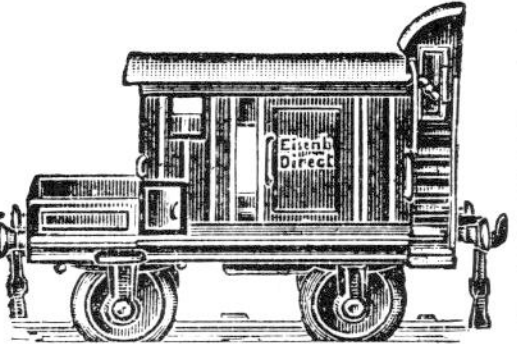

Breakdown Waggon.
With sliding doors.
Gauge 0, 2/6 1, 3/6
2, 4/6

Coal Truck.
Open, as illustration.
Gauge 0, $8\frac{1}{2}$d. 1, 1/-
2, 1/6 3, 2/6

Coal Truck.
With imitation coal.
Gauge 0, $10\frac{1}{2}$d. 1, $1/4\frac{1}{2}$

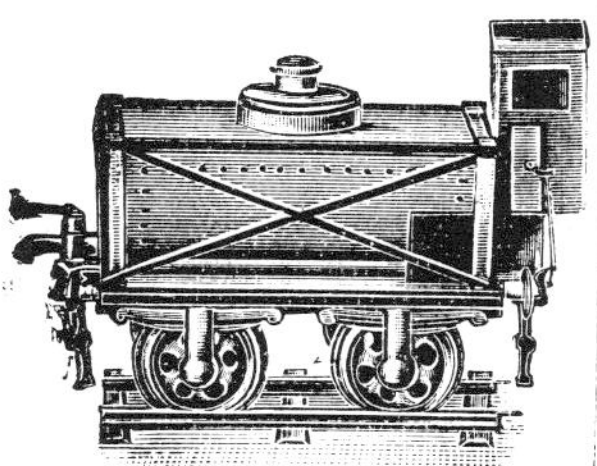

Tar Waggon.
Gauge 0, 1/3 1, 1/11

Oil Truck.
Gauge 0, 1/3 1, 1/11

Brewery Van.
With sliding doors.
Gauge 0, $8\frac{1}{2}$d. 1, 1/- 2, 1/6
3, 2/6

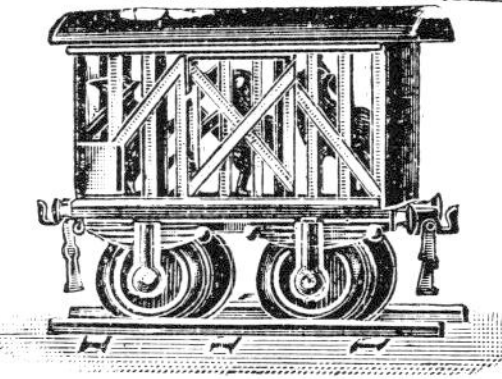

Cattle Truck
With cattle. Sliding doors.
Gauge 0, $1/4\frac{1}{2}$ 1, 2/3 2, 3/6
3, 4/6

Fruit Van with fruit.
Gauge 0, $1/4\frac{1}{2}$ 1, 3/-

Transport Waggon.
Gauge 0, $1/4\frac{1}{2}$ 1, 2/- 2, 2/9 3, 4/11

Loaded Timber Waggons.
Gauge 0, 2/- 1, 3/- 2, 3/9 3, 4/3 pair.

Covered Cement Truck.
Gauge 0, 1/3 1, 1/9
2, 2/3

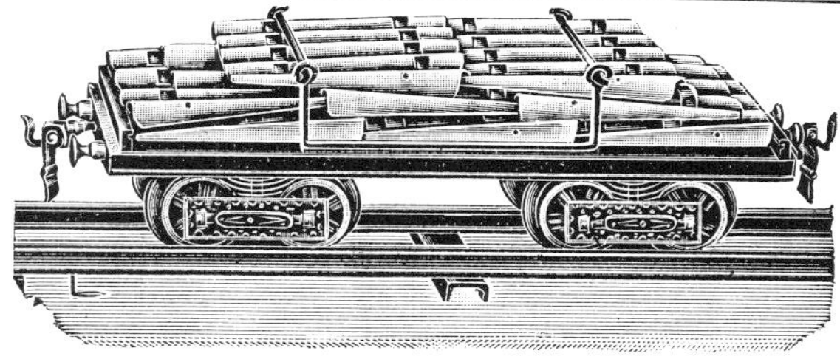

Truck loaded with Sleepers.
Gauge 0, 2/6 1, 3/6 2, 4/6

Large Goods or Coal Truck.
With bogie wheels.
Gauge 0, $9\frac{1}{2}$ in. long, 2/- 1, $11\frac{3}{4}$ in. long, 3/3
2, 14 in. long, 3/9 3, $16\frac{1}{2}$ in. long, 5/11

Gas Truck.
Gauge 0, 1/- 1, $1/4\frac{1}{2}$

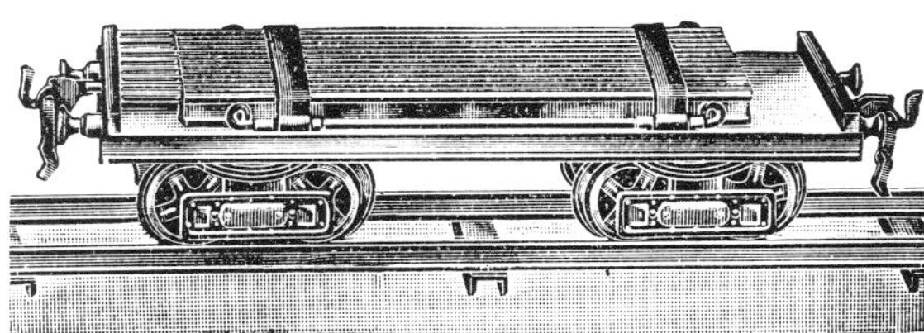

Truck loaded with Rails.
Gauge 0, 2/6 1, 3/6

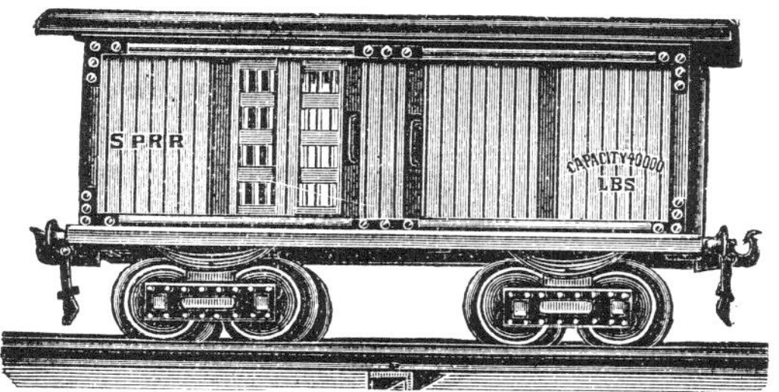

Horse Truck.
With bogie wheels and sliding doors.
Gauge 0, 4/6 1, 7/6

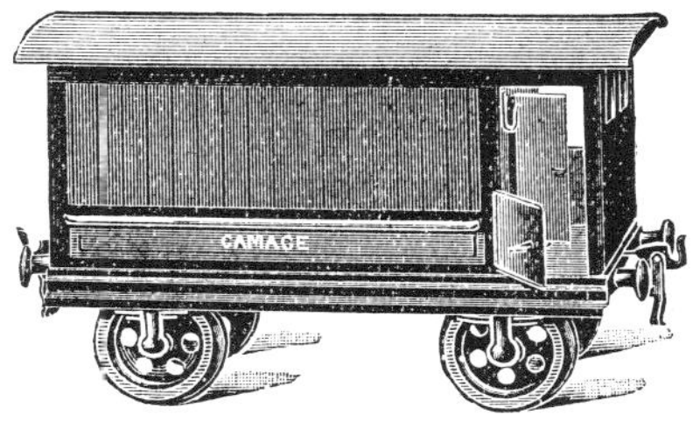

Guard's Brake Van.
Best make and finish.

Gauge	0	1	2	3
Length	4 in.	$6\frac{1}{4}$ in.	$7\frac{1}{8}$ in.	$9\frac{7}{8}$ in.
Price	1/6	2/6	3/6	5/11

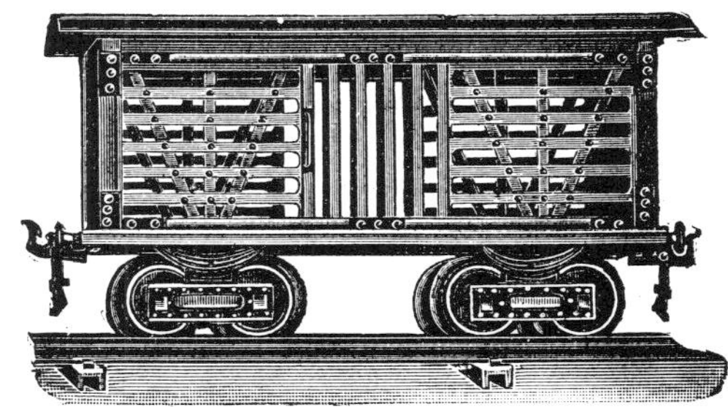

Cattle Truck.
With bogie wheels and sliding doors.
Gauge 0, 4/6 1, 5/6 2, 7/6

Postage on above, 3d. each.

Railway Rolling Stock, Travelling Cranes, etc.

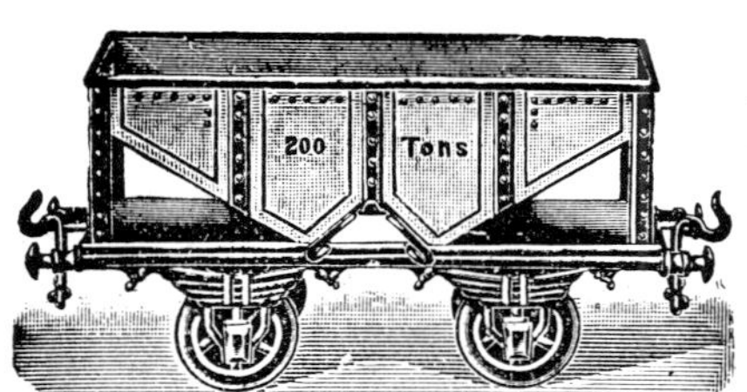

Coal or Sand Truck.
With doors to open underneath for unloading.

Gauge		Price
0	..	1/3
1	..	2/-
2	..	3/-
2½	..	3/6
3	..	3/11

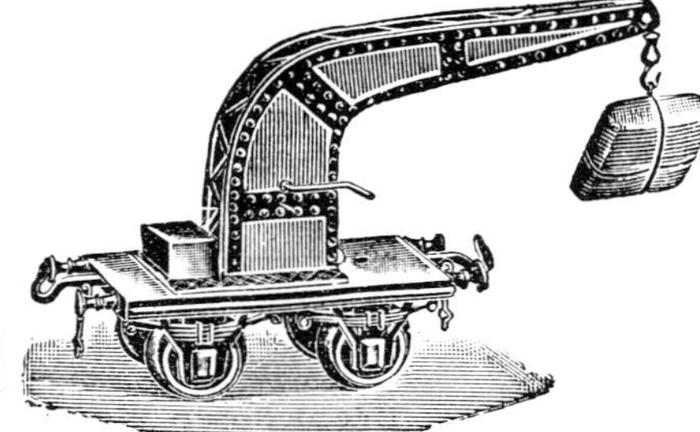

Crane Truck.
To turn in all directions.
Gauge 0, 1/8; 1, 2/3; 2, 3/-; 2½, 4/6

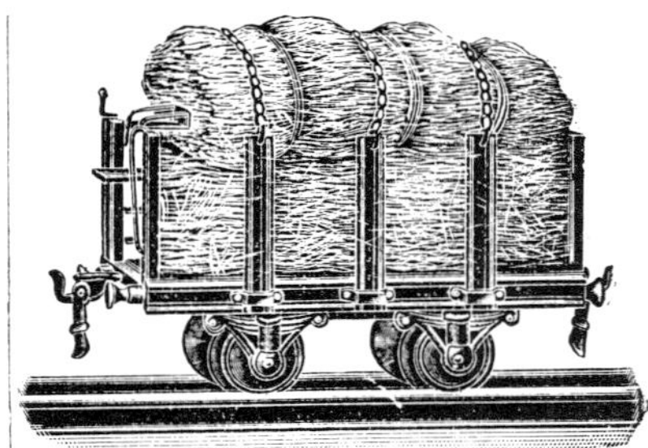

Hay Waggon.
Gauge 0, 1/9; 1, 2/9

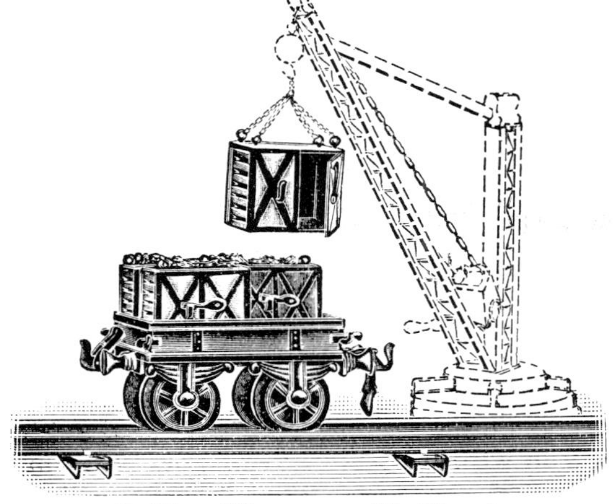

Bullion Waggon with Chests.
Gauge 1 .. 4/3 Without crane.

Crane Truck.

Gauge			Price
0	..	..	1/4½
1	..	..	2/6

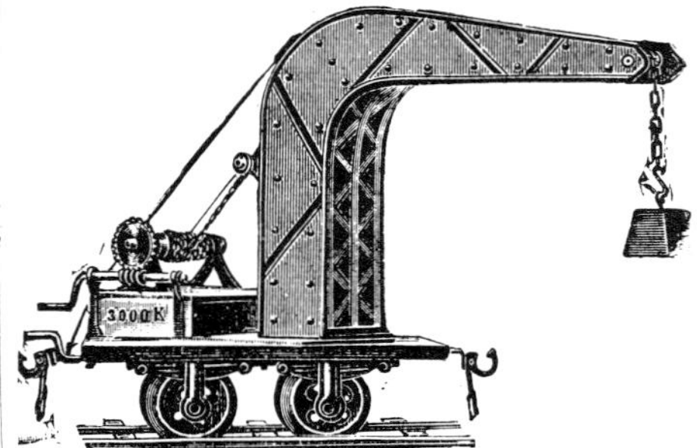

Travelling Crane.
To turn in all directions.
Gauge 0, 3/11; 1, 4/11; 2, 5/6

SPECIAL TRUCKS, etc., for use with SHUNTING TRAINS,

Fitted with Special Coupling for attaching and detaching. Supplied only in Gauge 0, 1/9 each.

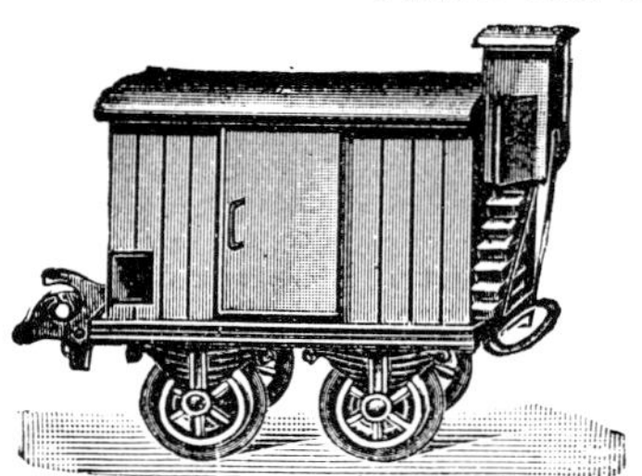

Guard's Brake Van.
1/9 each.

Tilting Truck.
1/9 each.

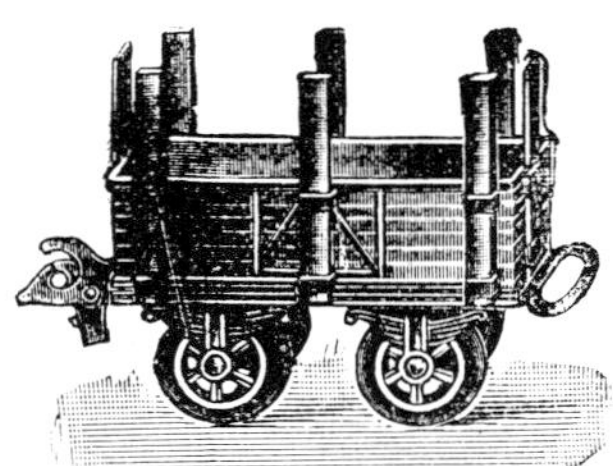

Timber Truck.
1/9 each.

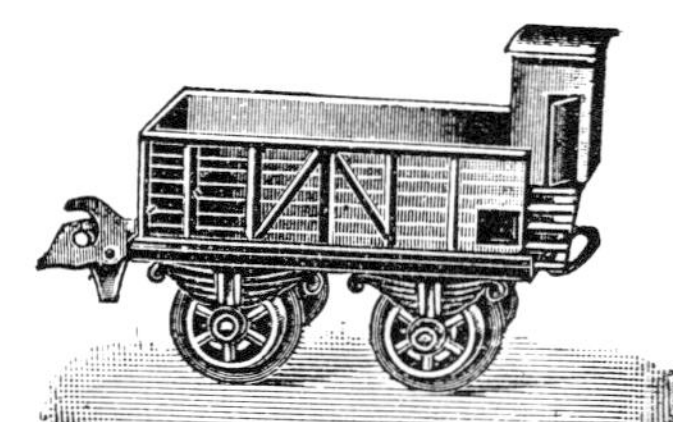

Coal Truck, with brake house.
1/9 each.

Transport Waggon.
1/9 each.

Oil Truck.
1/9 each.

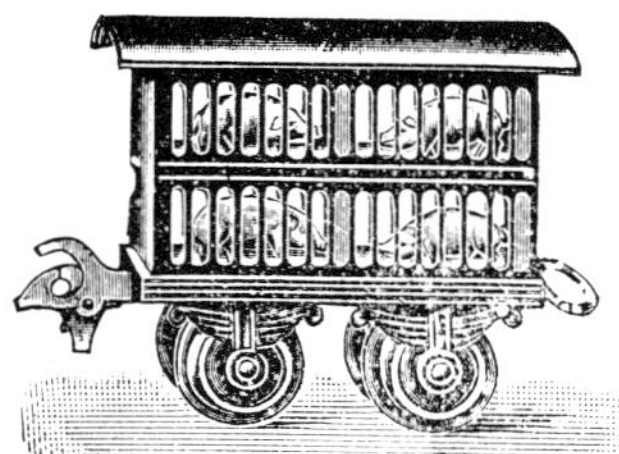

Cattle Truck.
1/9 each.

Cement Truck.
1/9 each.

The Great Railway Smash. ONE OF OUR NOVELTIES !

Consisting of two carriages and one goods van so constructed that when the train is in motion an accident occurs, one carriage being entirely smashed, the second one having two sides and top knocked out, and the goods van one side.
Set of three. Gauge 1, 7/6 Postage 4d. Gauge 2, 9/11 Post free.

Horse Transport Van.
With sliding doors.

Gauge				Price
Gauge 0,	with 2 Horses		..	1/8
,, 1,	,, 2	,,	..	2/9
,, 2,	,, 3	,,	..	3/11

Latest Types of ENGLISH MODEL RAILWAY SIGNALS.

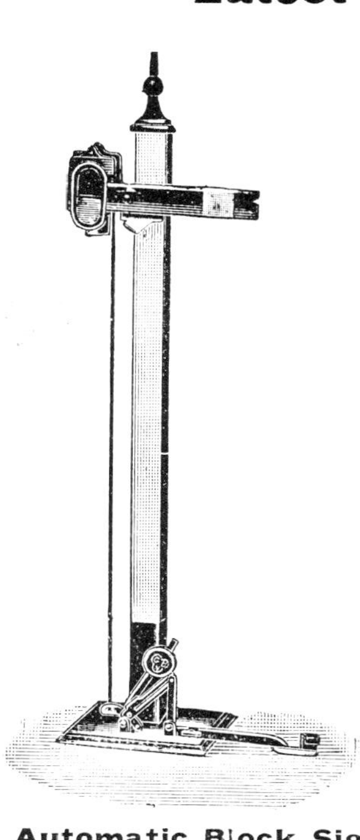

Automatic Block Signal.
As illustrated, well enamelled, with lantern to light and change colour, red and green glass, 14¼ in. high.
1/3 Postage 3d.

M.R. Signals.
Movable arm, to light up.
3/- Postage 3d.

Stop Signals.
Gauge 0, **1/6** 1, **1/9** 2, **2/-** 3, **2/6**
Postage 3d.

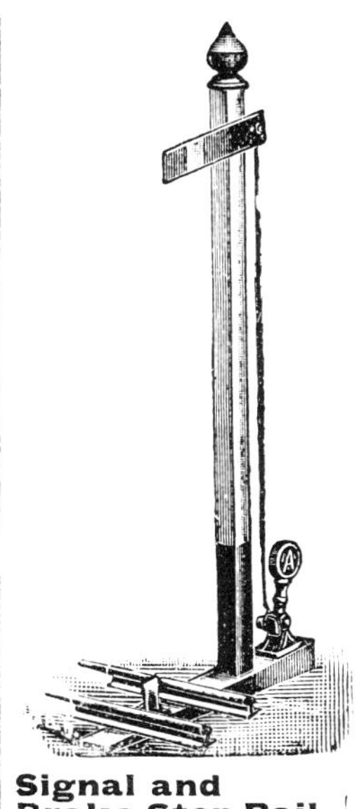

Signal and Brake Stop Rail,
Gauge 0, 11¾ in. high, **10½**d.; gauge 1, 12½ in. high, **1/4½**

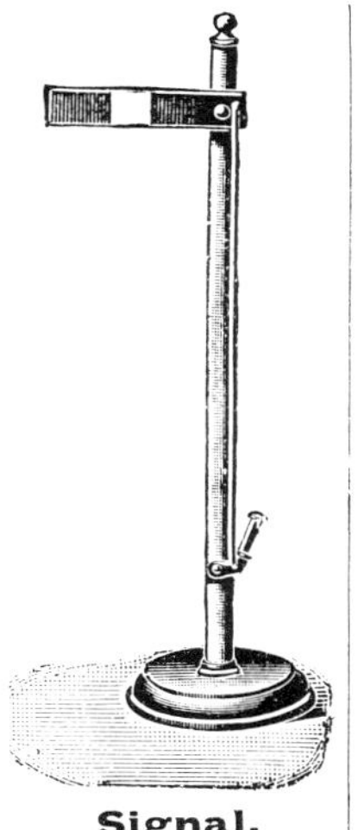

Signal.
Finely enamelled, as illustration, 11½ in. high. **5**d.

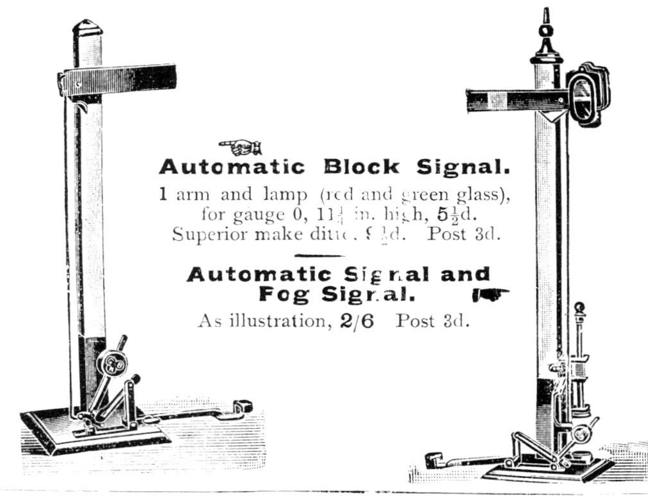

Automatic Block Signal.
1 arm and lamp (red and green glass), for gauge 0, 11¼ in. high, **5½**d.
Superior make ditto, 9½d. Post 3d.

Automatic Signal and Fog Signal.
As illustration, **2/6** Post 3d.

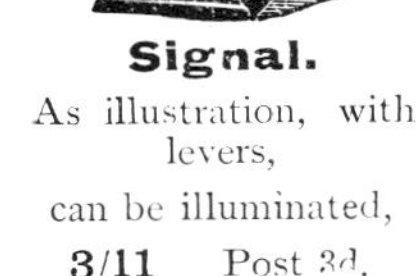

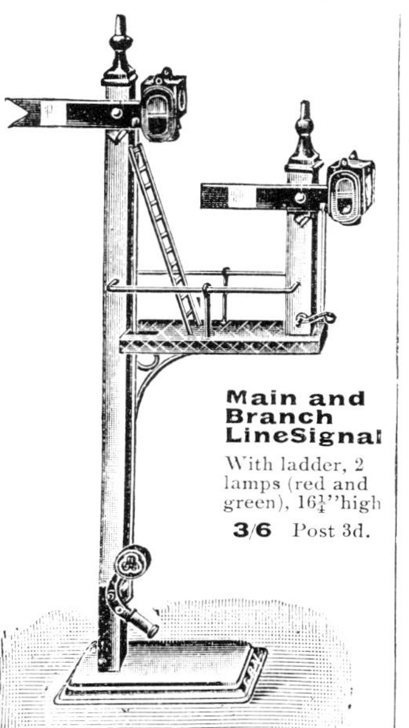

Main and Branch Line Signal
With ladder, 2 lamps (red and green), 16¼" high
3/6 Post 3d.

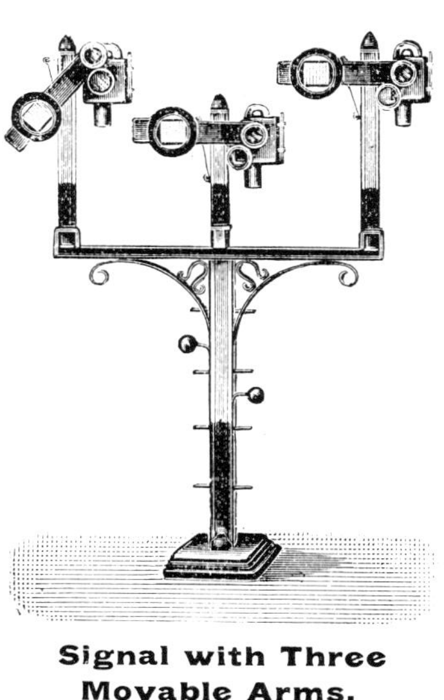

Signal with Three Movable Arms.
Can be illuminated, height 13 in.
5/6 Post 3d.

Signal.
As illustration, with levers, can be illuminated,
3/11 Post 3d.

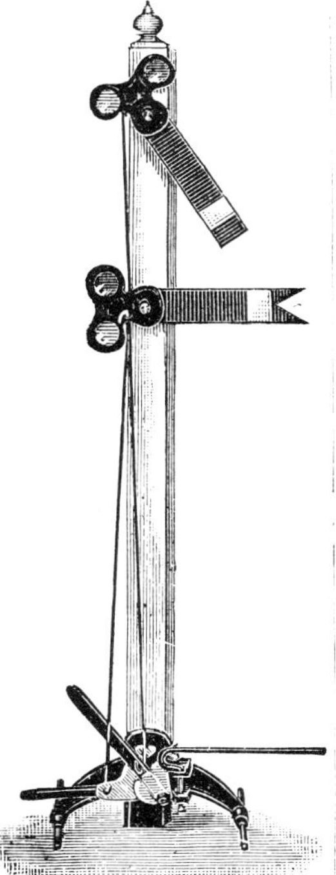

Automatic Signal.
English Make. Patent.
1 semaphore, **9½**d. Post 2d.
2 semaphores for home and distant signalling, **1/3**
Post 3d.

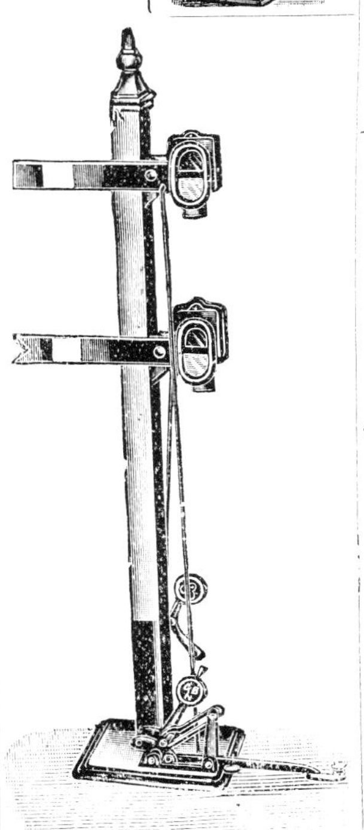

Signal, as illustration, with lamps to light, 15¾ in. high, **1/10½** Post 3d.

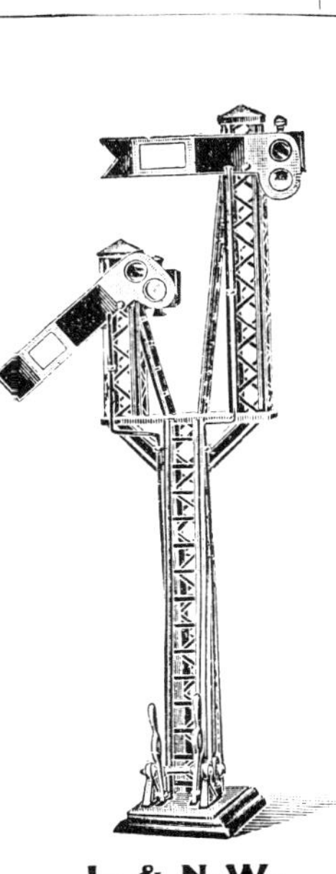

L. & N.W. Signals.
To light, **5/9** Post 3d.

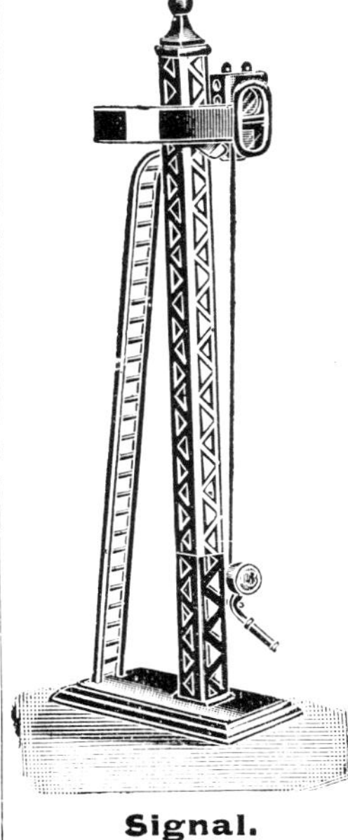

Signal.
As illustration, to light,
1/11 Post 3d.

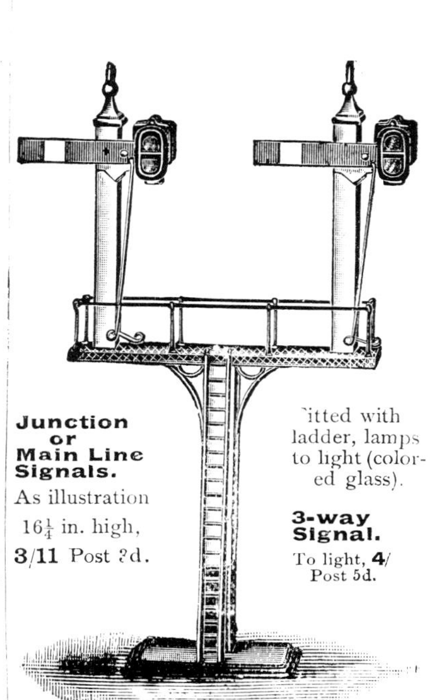

Junction or Main Line Signals.
As illustration
16¼ in. high,
3/11 Post 3d.

Fitted with ladder, lamps to light (colored glass).

3-way Signal.
To light, **4/**
Post 5d.

Signals, Footbridges, Fog Signals, etc.

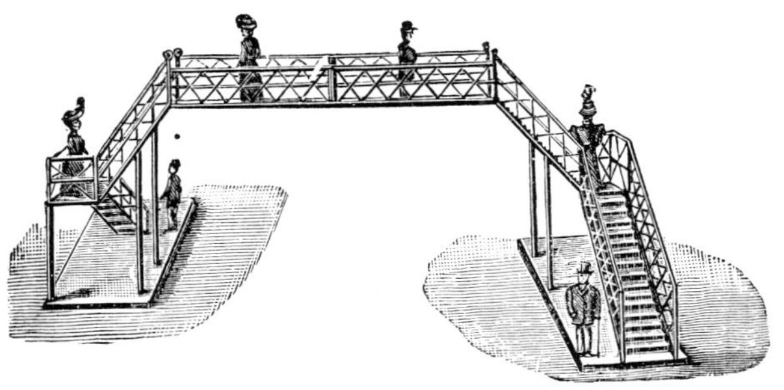

No. 2062. **Metal Footbridge,** japanned in best style, complete with passengers, **4/6**

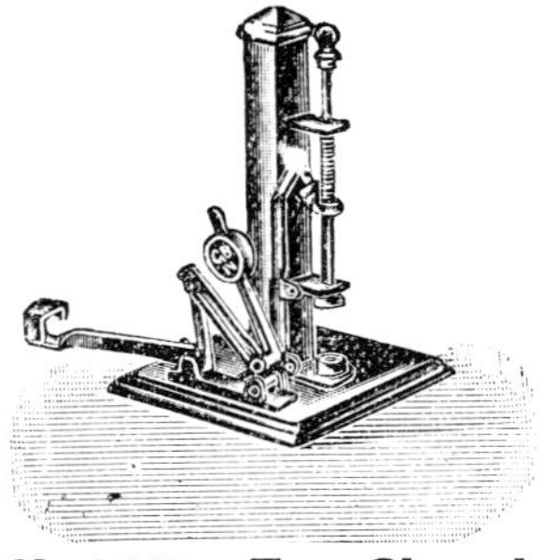

No. 14129. **Fog Signal,** made to work automatically, with good spring and lever, 6 in. high, **1/11** Post 2d.

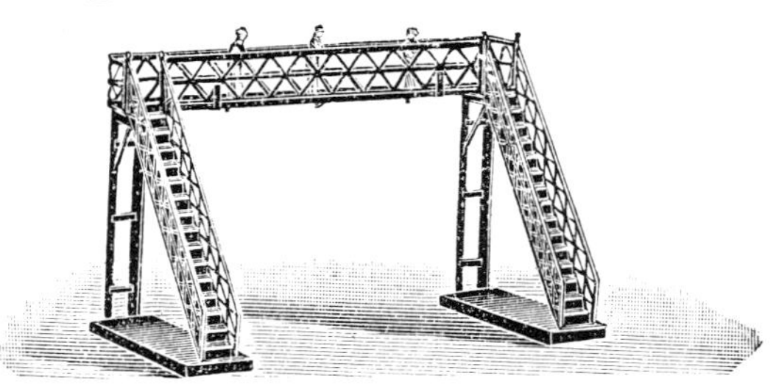

No. 2061. **Metal Footbridge,** nicely japanned, complete with passengers, can be taken to pieces,

Gauge 0, 15 in. long .. **2/6** Post 3d.
Gauge 1 or 2, 16 in. long .. **3/6** Post 3d.

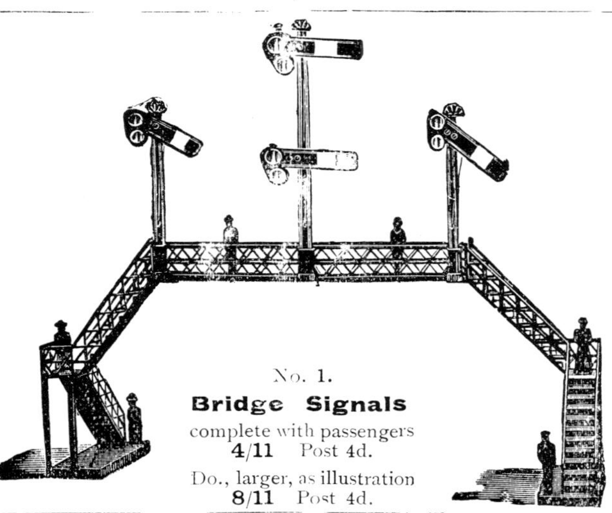

No. 1.
Bridge Signals
complete with passengers
4/11 Post 4d.
Do., larger, as illustration
8/11 Post 4d.

Notice Boards,
"Beware of the Trains,"
3½ in. high,
4½d. Post 1d.

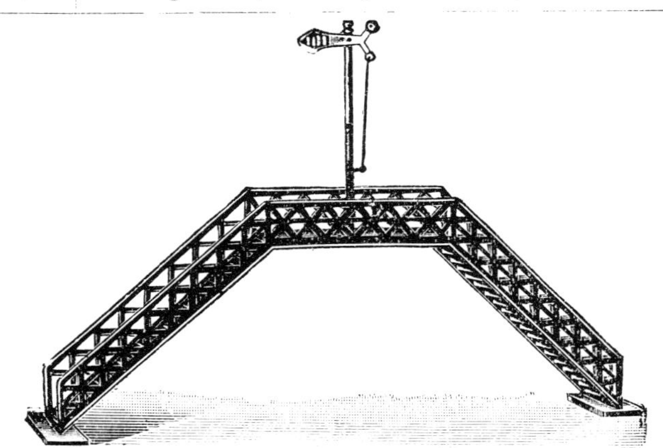

No. 569.
Metal Footbridge,
with signal, as illustration,
10½d. Post 2d.

No. 2188. **Fog Signal,** as illustration, fixed, with amorces (caps), **5½**d. Post 3d.

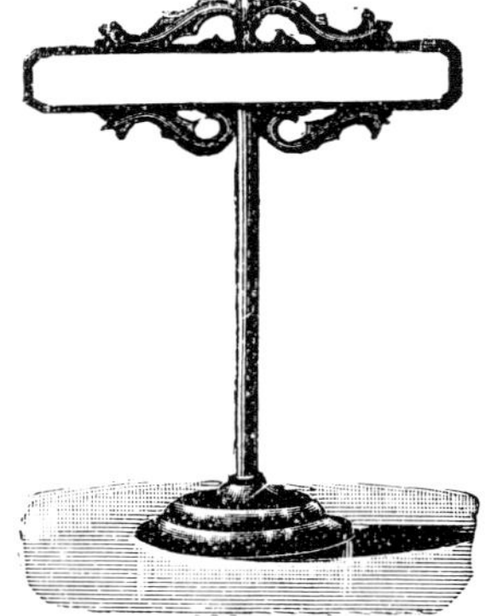

Notice Boards,
'Passengers must not cross line,' well made, 6 in. high, **6½**d. Post 1d.

Train Indicator,
with six arms which can be changed, indicating the next train to different towns,
8 in. high,
10½d. Post 2d.

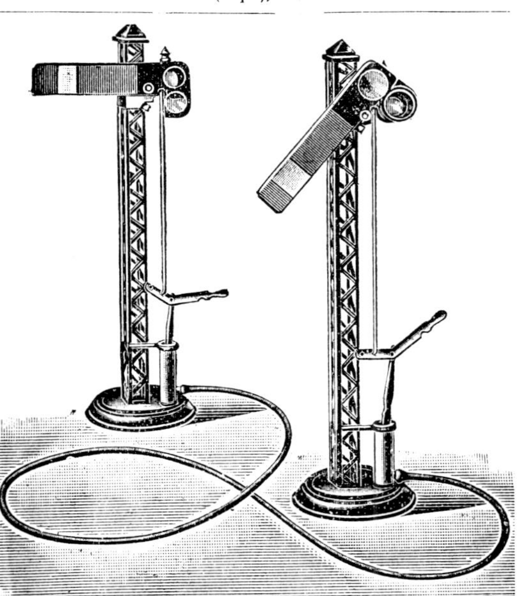

Pneumatic Signals, as illustration,
The Latest in Signals! **3/6** Post 3d.

Telegraph Poles,
finely japanned,
with 4 insulators, 9½ in. high, **4½**d.
with 8 insulators, 10¼ in. high, **6**d.
with 12 insulators, 10¾ in. high, **10½**d.

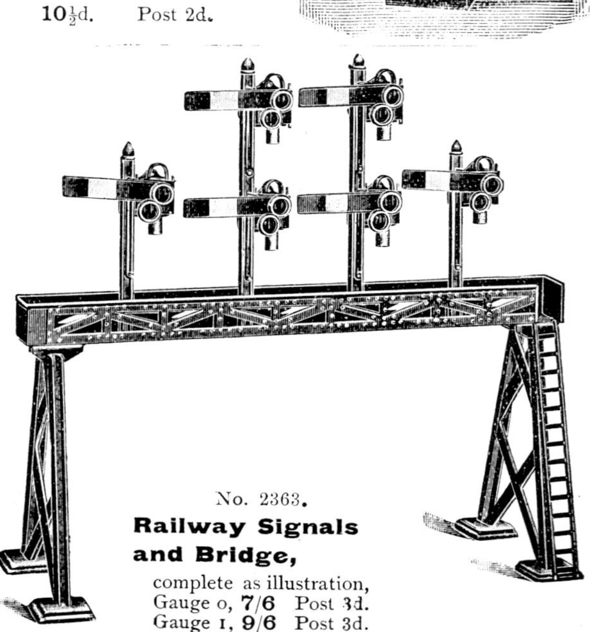

No. 2363.
Railway Signals and Bridge,
complete as illustration,
Gauge 0, **7/6** Post 3d.
Gauge 1, **9/6** Post 3d.

Railway Bridges and Crossings.

Railway Bridge with Rails.

Good model for spanning small streams, etc.
Gauge o, **2** ft. 6¾ in. long, 4¾ in. wide **2/3**

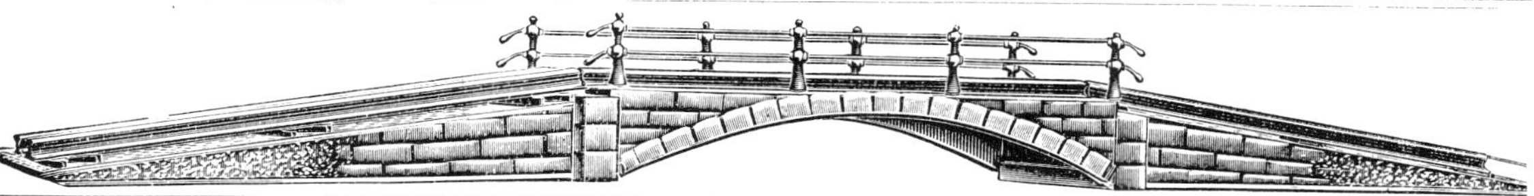

No. 75. **Bridge.**

New model. As illustration.
Gauge o **5/3**
1 .. .. **7/6**

No. 67. **Bridge.**

As illustration, with 1 span.
Gauge o **8/6**
Postage 3d.

Bridge.

No. 67A.
As illustration, 2 spans, gauge **1**, **12/6**
No. 67B.
Ditto, gauge 2, **14/6**

Swing Bridge,

Fitted with best quality clockwork movement, easily worked by lever.
Gauge o .. **23/6** 70 in. long.
Gauge 1 .. **27/6** 87 in. long.

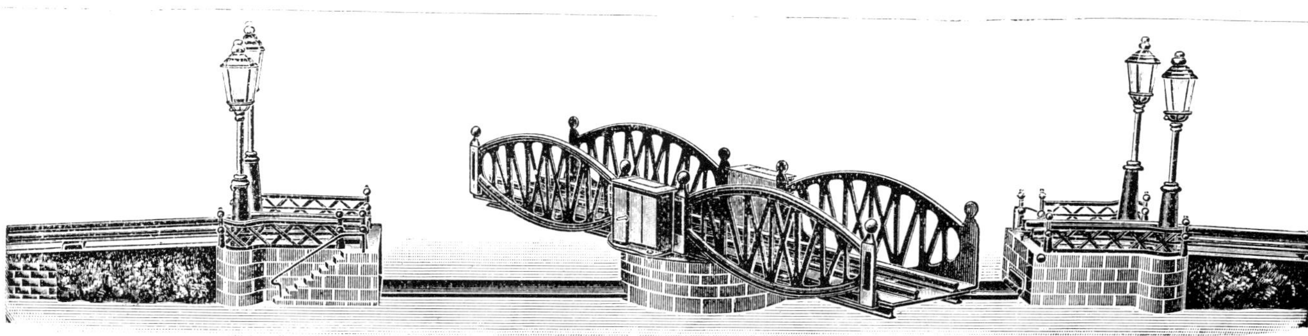

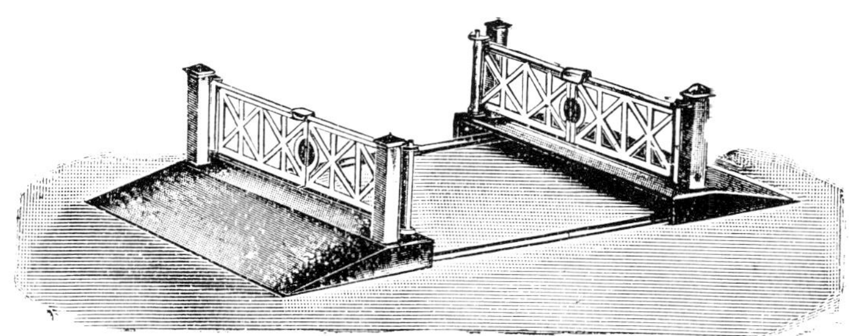

No. 14134. **Railway Crossing.**

Finely japanned, to be opened and shut, 8 in. long. Gauge o, **2/11**

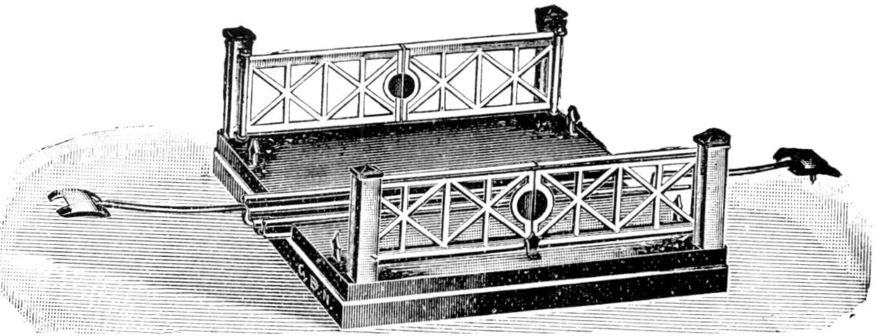

No. 14135. **Railway Crossing.**

Finely japanned, barrier opened automatically by the passing train.
Gauge o (1⅜ in.), **6/11** 1 (1⅞ in.), **7/11**

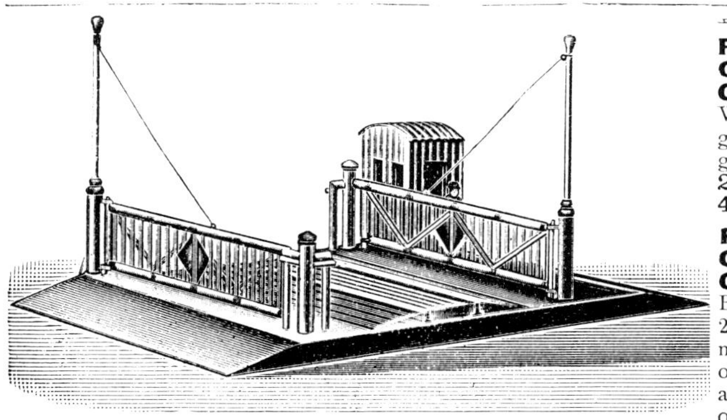

Railway Crossing Gates. No. 2386
Without guard's box, gates open and close, gauge o, 15 in. long, **2/9**; for gauge 1 or 2 **4/6** Postage 3d.

Railway Crossing Gates. No. 13759
Finely japanned, with 2 lines of rails and mechanical device for opening and closing, adjustable for gauge o to 3, **5/11** Post 4d

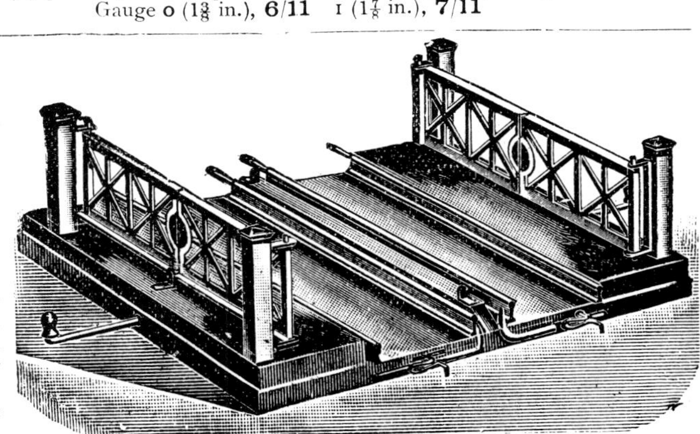

RAILWAY TUNNELS AND CUTTINGS.

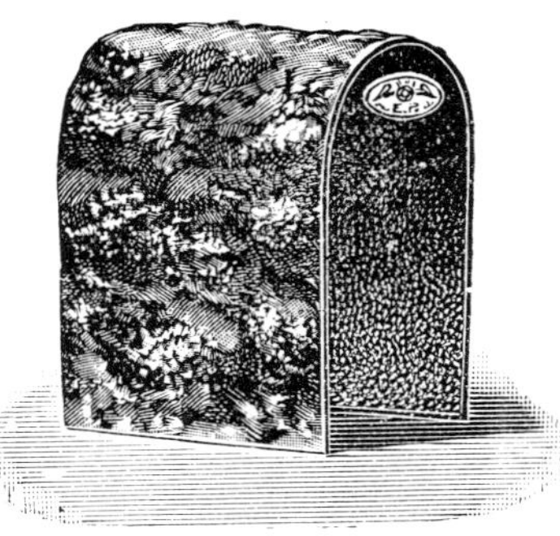

No. 20.

Metal Tunnels.

Artistically finished.

Price .. 10½d. Post 3d.

No. 8. **New Rustic Cutting.**

22 in. long. 10 in. high.

For 0 or 1 gauge trains. Finished very naturally.

Price .. 5/11 Postage 4d.

No. 10.

Handsome Metal Tunnel.

For Gauge 0. Price 2/11 Postage 4d.

No. 10A.

For Gauge 1. 4/6 Postage 4d.

No. 8A.

Railway Cutting.

With straight gauge 0 rails, and incline and decline at ends.

As illustration. Price .. 3/6

Ditto, ditto, gauge 1 rails. Price .. 4/6

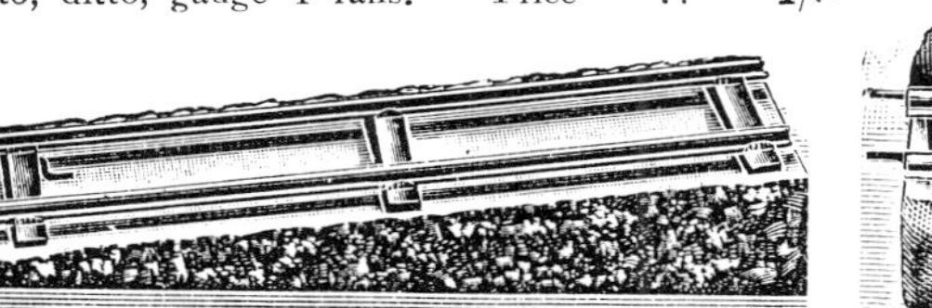

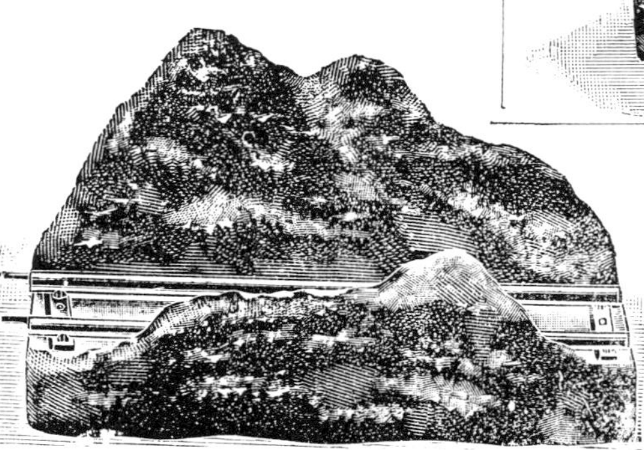

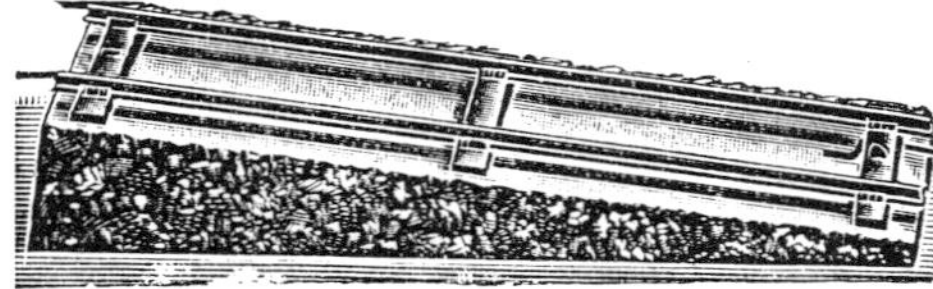

No. 21.

New Style Metal Tunnel.

Price 4/6 Postage 4d.

No. 9.

No. 9. **New Rustic Cutting,**

As illustration.

26 in. long. 11 in. high.

For 0, 1 or 2 gauge trains.

Price 9/6 Postage 6d.

No. 3. **Enamelled Tunnel.**

For 1 or 2 gauge trains.

Price 7/11 Postage 4d.

No. 3A. Do., smaller.

For 0 gauge. Price 4/11

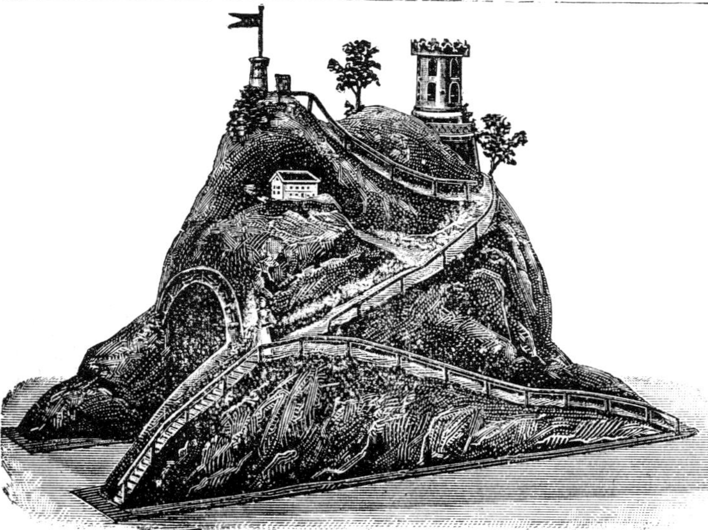

No. 7

No. 7.

Enamelled Metal Tunnel.

As illustration to take gauge 0 trains.

8/11

No. 7A.

To take gauge 1 trains, much larger.

14/6

No. 6A. **Handsome Rustic Tunnel.**

In colours. Will take gauge 0 or 1 trains.

Price 8/6 Postage 8d.

Gamage's New Model Stations.

No. 2351 **Very fine Imitation Brick-work Station,** detachable corrugated roof. Can be illuminated with candles similar to illustration.

14 in. long, 5 in. wide, 9 in. high. Price **5/6**
Do., 14 in. long, 8 in. wide, 10 in. high. Price **8/6**

No. 2646. **Very fine Imitation Brickwork Station,** with advertisements in correct colours, hinged doors, and passengers. Can be illuminated with candles. 33 in. long, 7 in. wide, 10 in. high. Price **13/6** Postage 6d.

Fine Model English Wayside Station.
23 in. long, 5 in. high. Price **2/6** Post 3d.

No. 13813/01. **Local Railway Station.**
With detachable roof, folding door, booking office, &c., well enamelled with correct advertisements.
$10\frac{5}{8}$ in. long, $3\frac{3}{8}$ in. wide.
Price .. .. **9d.**
$15\frac{1}{8}$ in. high, $4\frac{3}{8}$ in. wide, for lighting with candles.
Price **1/6**

No. 2647. **Exceptionally handsome Station,** with correctly coloured advertisements. Can be illuminated with candles. Complete with passengers. 32 in. long, $7\frac{1}{2}$ in. wide, 11 in. high. Price **16/6** Postage 6d.

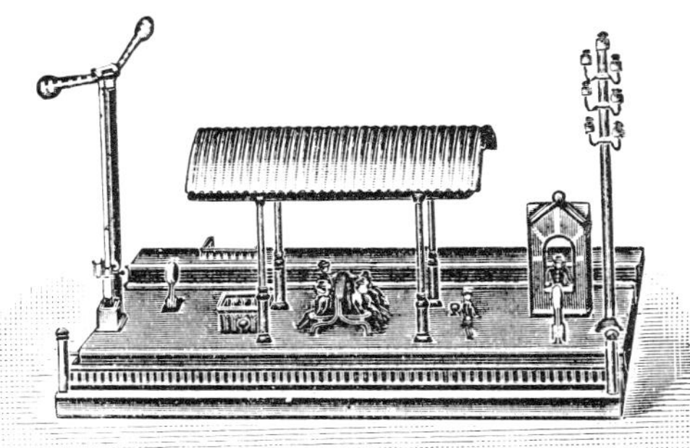

No. 2673. **Covered Platform,**
With rails, as illustration.

0 gauge	**8/11**	Post	4d.
1 gauge	**11/9**	,,	6d.

Gamage's New Model **Railway Station,** with passengers, seats, telegraph pole, lavatory, time tables, etc.
Length, 36 in.
Height, 9 in.
Price **8/6**
Postage 6d.

Cranes, Goods Sheds, Signal Boxes, etc.

Railway Crane,
easily worked,
Price **2/11** Post 3d.

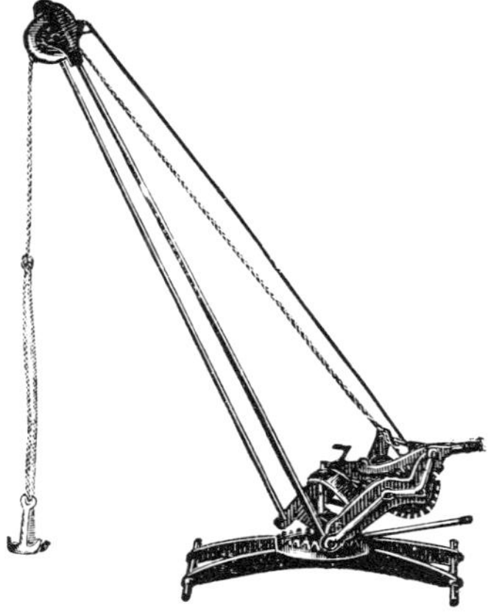

Strong Metal Crane,
English make, as illustration,
10½d. Postage 3d.

Signal Box
with Signal,
10½d.
Ditto, as illust., with detachable roof, chimney and staircase, size 7⅛ in.,
2/3 Post 3d.

No. 8296.
Signal Hut,
As illustration, size 6 by 3½ in.,
10½d. Postage 2d.

Crane.
A useful and instructive toy for boys having all movements same as the largest cranes now in use.
English make.
2/3 Postage 3d.

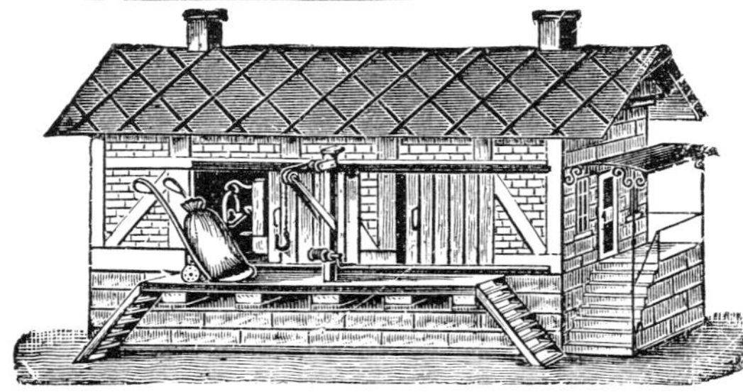

Goods Station.
Very fine model fitted with sliding doors and crane.
12½ in. long, **10/6** Post 4d.

Strong Model Crane.

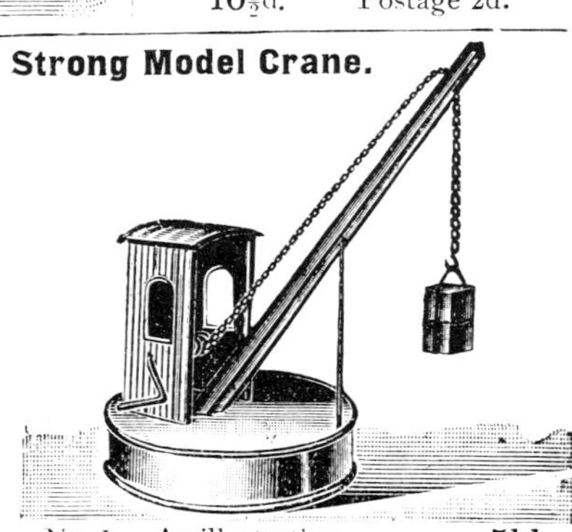

No. 1. As illustration .. **5½d.**
Postage 2d.

No. 14122. **Goods Station,**
stamped imitation brickwork, finely japanned, with sliding door and loading platform,
7 in. long, 3¾ in. high,
Price **10½**d. Post 3d.

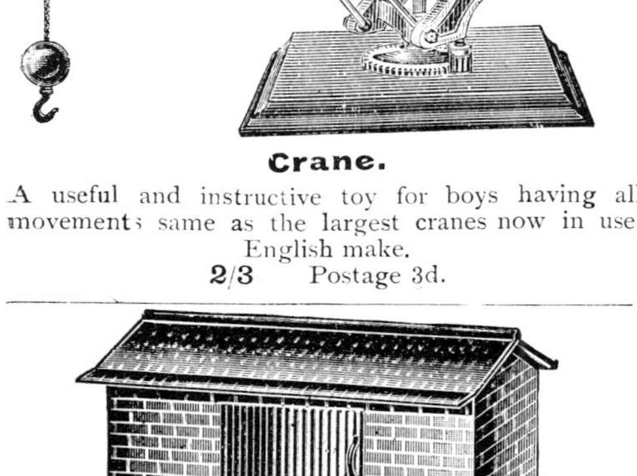

Goods Shed,
japanned, with sliding doors, steps and loading platform,
1/4½ Post 3d.

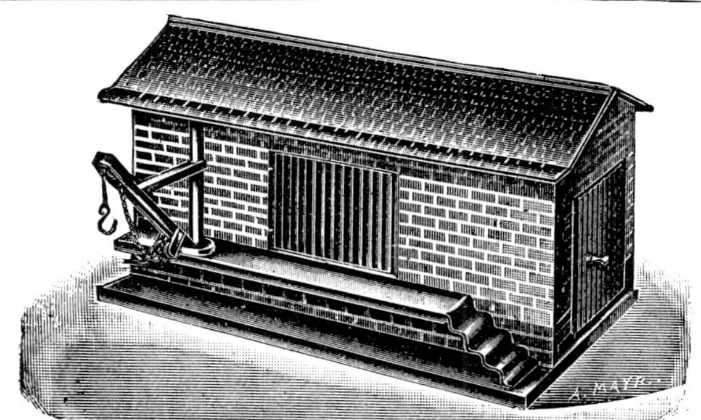

Goods Shed, nicely japanned, with sliding doors, etc.
Fitted with crane, **2/-** Postage 3d.

Travelling Crane,
folding, finely japanned, with movable trolley, and mechanism for winding up,
10½ in. long, 8 in. high,
3/11
Ditto, with ladder, superior finish,
17 in. long, 12 in. high,
12/6

RAILWAY ACCESSORIES.

Platform Barrow.
Price 6d. Postage 2d.

Railway Shunting Horn.

4½d. and 6½d.

Postage 1½d.

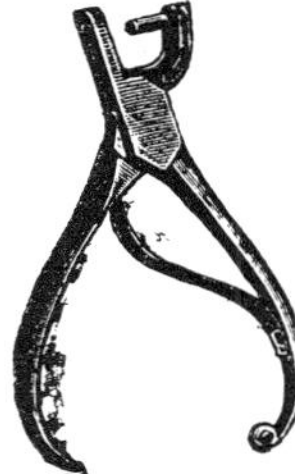

Station Lamps.

To burn Petroleum.

Elegant cast Post, with nickelled fittings, 7½ in. high.

Price 10½d.

Postage 2d.

Ticket Clippers.

Price 6½d.

Postage 2d.

Luggage Trolley.

Price .. 4½d.

Postage 2d.

No. 6099/1 E.

Railway Ticket Office.

Finely Japanned, with 12 divisions and 144 Railway Tickets for 12 different English routes. (Every ticket can be taken out separately.) 8¼ in. high, 5¼ in. wide. Price 2/11

No. 8108 E. Railway Tickets extra. One assortment consisting of 144 tickets for 12 different English routes, 9d. Postage 2d.

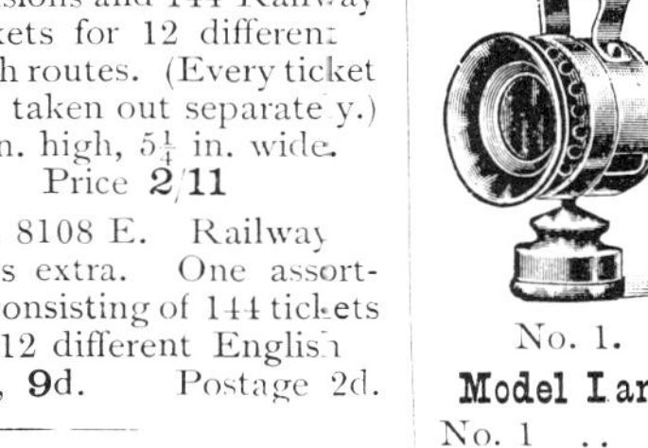

No. 1. No. 2. No. 3.

Model Lamps. For Clockwork Locomotives.

No. 1 .. Price 1/- No. 2 .. Price 1/6

No. 3 Red or Green. Price 4½d. Postage 1d.

Train Indicator. Price 2/9

Automatic Ticket Box

with 12 Tickets of English routes.

7 in. by 3⅛ in.

Price 10½d.

Postage 1d.

STATION LAMPS.

14136.

Arc Lamp.

Finely Japanned, to burn oil, with opal glass globe, lamp to wind up and down.

16½ in. high.

Price 2/3

Postage 2d.

Highest Quality.

Lowest Prices.

Advertisement Board.

1/9 Postage 1d.

Railway Ticket Stamping Apparatus.
Finely Japanned on Tin Socle, with one set of Indiarubber Types (17 numbers and 4 blocks). 4⅞ in. high. Price 2/-

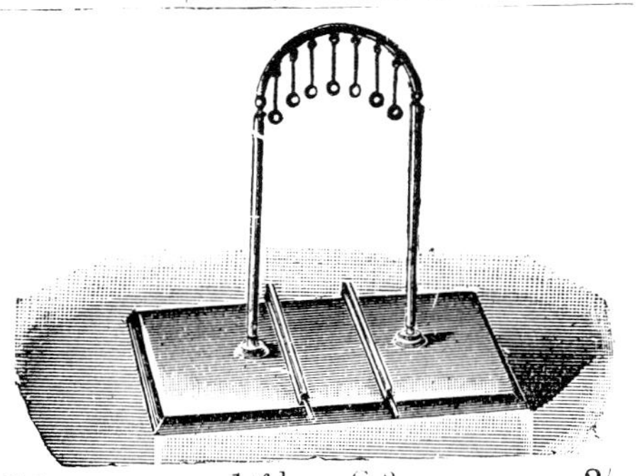

G 0.	1/4½	G 2.	2/-
G 1.	1/8	G 3.	2/11

14132 E.

Indicator

Plain finish, with English stations, finely Japanned, with 4 arms, 8 in. high.

Price 10½d.

Postage 2d.

Do., to light, 1/6

Postage 2d.

14085/2. **Booking Office.**

Stamped Imitation Brickwork and finely Japanned, with two ticket windows and ticket automat with 24 tickets, detachable roof, and fitted for lighting with candles. 6¾ in. long, 6¾ in wide, 7⅛ in. high. Price 3/- Postage 3d.

Fire Engines and Escapes, Hot Air Engines and Motors.

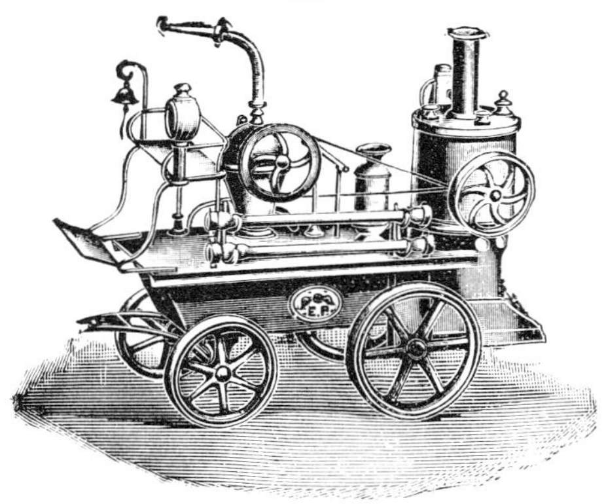

Steam Fire Engine, with hose and pipe. Size $14\frac{1}{2}$ by $4\frac{1}{4}$ by $10\frac{1}{4}$ in. .. Price **21/-**

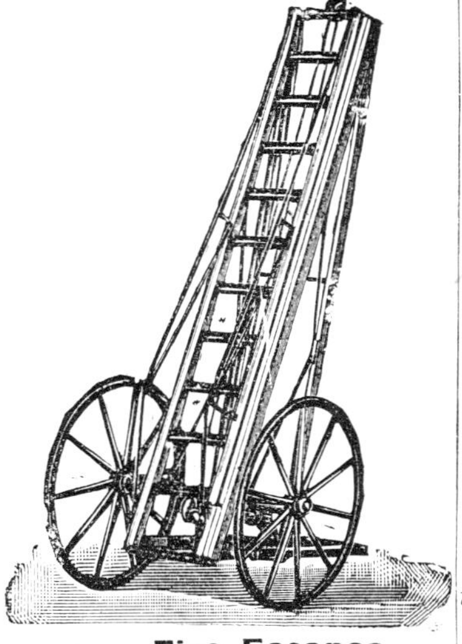

Fire Escapes. Mechanical, very strong and beautifully japanned, 23 in. high. **4/11** Postage 3d. Height, 31 in., **7/6**

Hot Air Motors. Elegant strong finish, reliable working, no cooling necessary, fittings highly nickelled, mounted on wood stand with metal plate.

No. 1, $10\frac{1}{4}$ in. long, **12/6** No. 2, $11\frac{3}{4}$ in. long, **15/-**

INSTRUCTIVE AND USEFUL PRESENTS FOR OLD AND YOUNG.

Steam Fire Engine, very strongly made, American pattern, with 1 suction and 2 force hoses, fitted with safety heating apparatus, **30/-**
Ditto, larger size, very handsome model, **50/-**

No. 336. **Horizontal Hot Air Engine.** **2/11**
No water required
Excellent Working Model.

2/11

No. 334a. $8\frac{1}{2}$ in. long, $4\frac{3}{4}$ in. wide, diameter of flywheel $2\frac{3}{8}$ in., **5/11** Post 3d.
,, 334. $9\frac{1}{2}$,, $4\frac{7}{8}$,, ,, ,, ,, 3 ,, **9/6** ,, 3d.
,, 335. $10\frac{1}{4}$,, $5\frac{1}{2}$,, diameter of flywheel, $3\frac{1}{2}$ in. **14/6**
,, 336. 13 in. long, $6\frac{1}{4}$ in. wide, diameter of flywheel, $4\frac{1}{4}$ in. **16/6**
,, 338. $14\frac{1}{2}$ in. long, 7 in. wide, diameter of flywheel, $5\frac{1}{2}$ in.

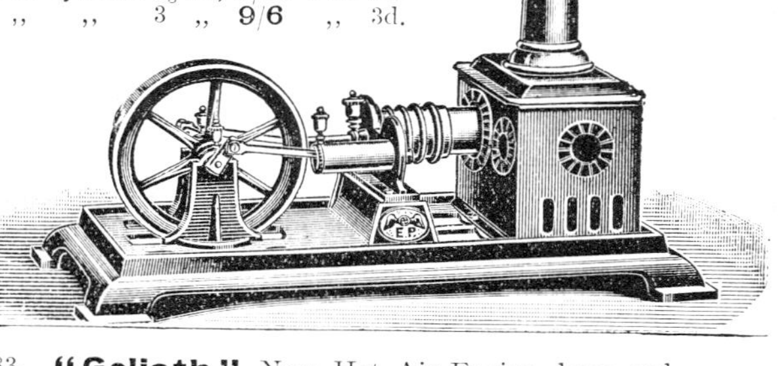

No. 583. **"Goliath"** New Hot Air Engine, large and powerful model, with 2 displacers, 2 cylinders, 2 flywheels 4 in. diameter, 3-speed pulley with cogwheel gearing, large spirit lamp to burn about 4 hours at one charge. Length of model, 17 in. Width $11\frac{1}{2}$ in. .. .. .. Price **45/-**

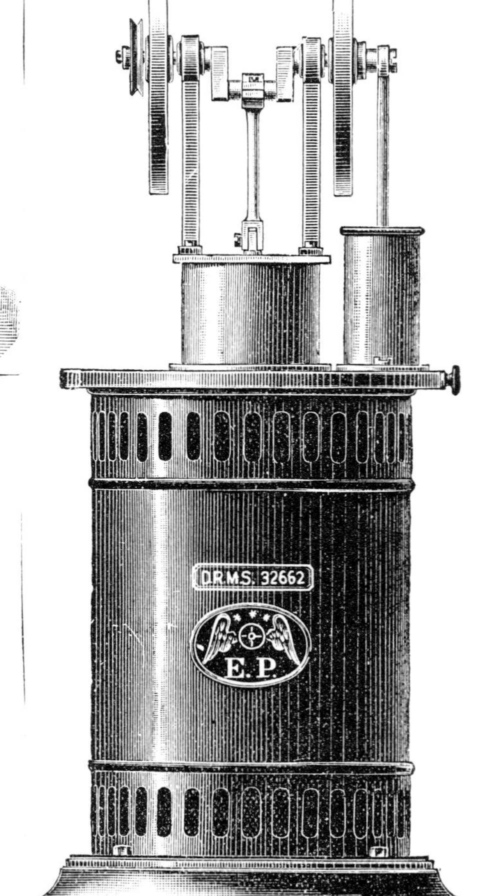

Upright Hot Air Engines.
Suitable for driving Motors, &c. No water required.
No. 331 (as illust.), **22/6** No. 332, **35/-** No. 332a, **55/-** No. 332b, **84/-**

GAMAGE'S NEW MODEL STEAM TURBINES.

No. 522, **3/6**

No. 522/2, **7/11**

No. 5221/1.

Steam Turbine, with safety valve, water outlet, screw on metal base.

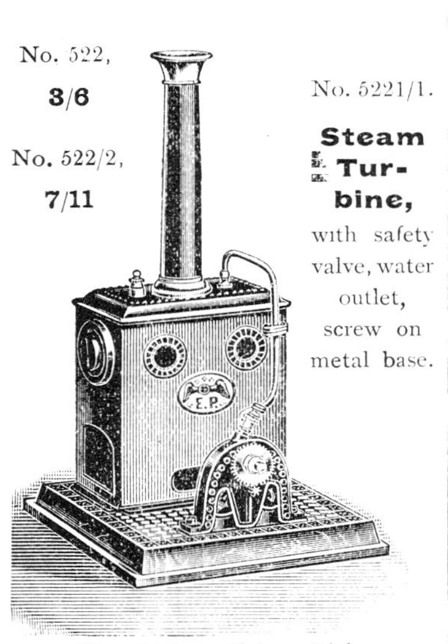

Size, 5½ in. x 5½ in. x 9½ in.
Price .. .. **3/6** Postage 3d.
No. 522A ditto. Size, 7½ in. x 7½ in. x 11½ in. Price .. **7/11** Post 3d.

"Hercules" Steam Turbine.

Vertical tubular boiler oxydised and mounted on japanned iron plate foundation, fitted with lever safety valve and water gauge. Easily handled whistle and starting cock.

No. 4121. **A highly satisfactory Model.**

No.	Length.	Width.	Height.	Price.
3	13 in.	6¼ in.	10¼ in.	**25/-**
3	15 ,,	7 ,,	12 ,,	**29/6**

The "Queen" Turbine.

No. A.

Price .. **4/11**

Postage 4d.

No. IV. Horizontal boiler, safety valve and outlet, tap, mounted on iron base, 6 ft. x 9 in. high.

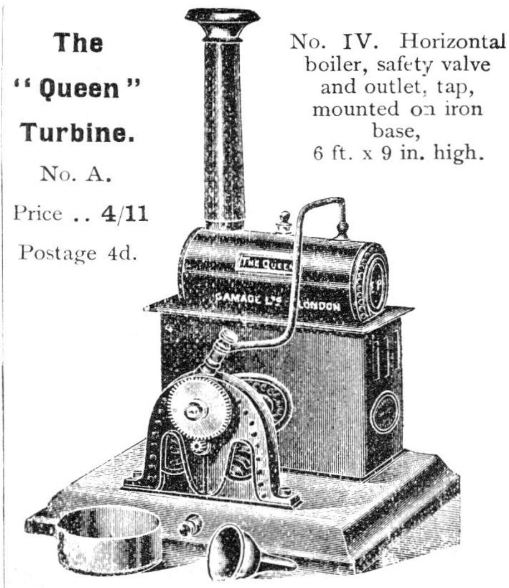

Turbine Engine.

No. 220. Similar designs to Nos. 3 and 4, polished brass boiler, safety valve, whistle and lamp. Boiler 6 x 2½ in., mounted on polished wood base, 9½ x 4¾ in. x 9½ in. high.
Price .. .. **4/6** Postage 4d.

THE "QUEEN" TURBINE.

No. B.

No. I. Vertical boiler in metal casing with whistle and safety valve, mounted on wood base, 8¾ x 4 x 11 in. high. Price .. .. **4/6** Postage 4d.

No. II. Ditto, with starting cock, mounted base, 10 x 4 x 12½ in. Price .. .. .. **7/6** Postage 4d.

No. II With 2 oxydised boilers, safety valve, 2 filling plugs and 2 lamps, mounted on metal base, 7 x 7 x 11 in. high.
Price .. .. .. **9/11** Postage 4d.

No. VI. With 2 oxydised boilers and whistle, mounted on iron base, 9½ x 8½ x 11 in. high.
Price .. .. **13/6** Post 3d.

No. VII. Ditto, with 2 mica water gauges, and 3 speed pulley wheels, mounted on iron base, 11 x 10 x 12 in. high.
Price .. .. **25/-** Post free.

No. VIII. Ditto, with pressure gauge, 2 patent outlet taps and starting cock, iron base, 11 x 10 x 15 in. high.
Price .. .. **42/-** Post free.

"AJAX" STEAM TURBINE.

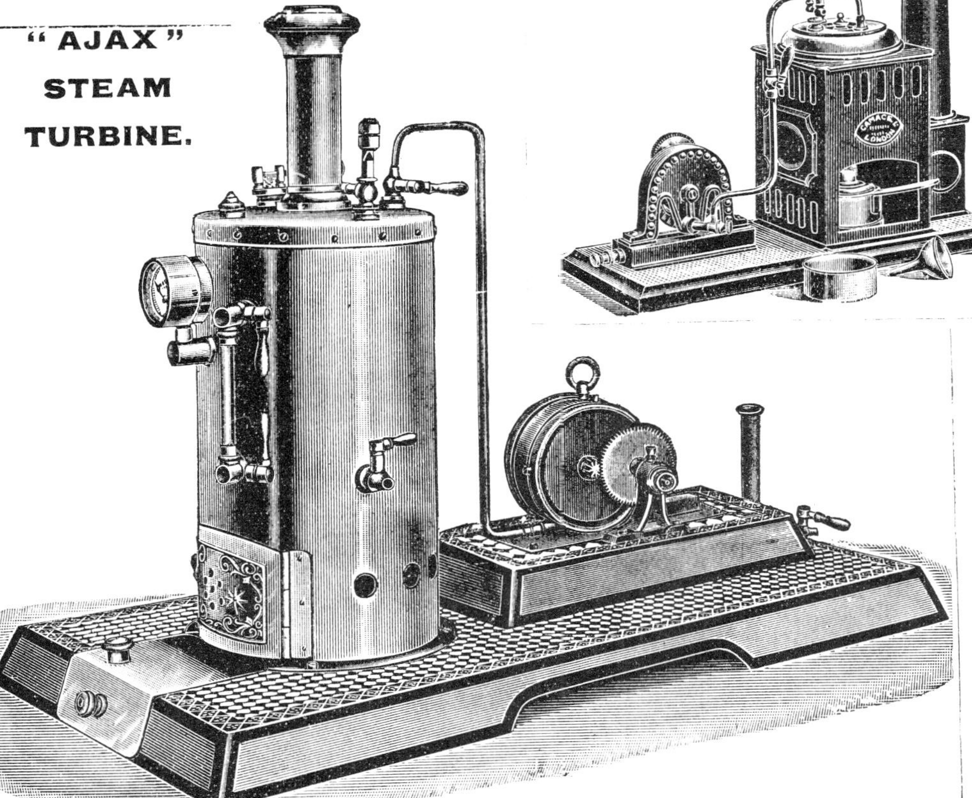

TWIN BOILER TURBINE.

1906 MODEL.

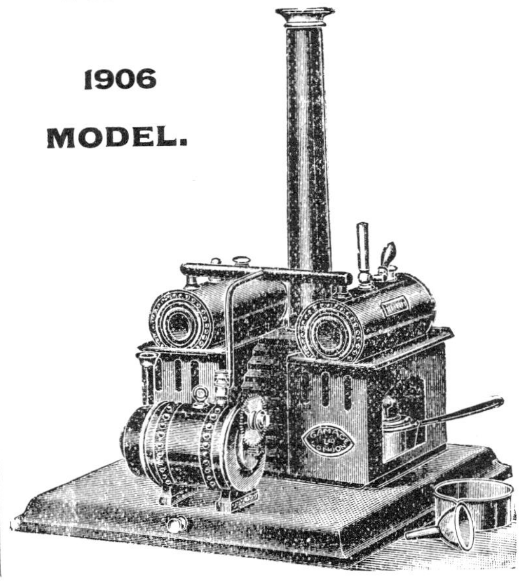

Steam Turbine, with vertical seamless 9 x 4 in. tubular boiler, oxydised and mounted on japanned iron plate foundation, fitted with lever safety valve, steam and water gauges. Easily handled whistle and starting cock, as illustration. Length over all 17½ in., width 9 in., height 15 in.
Price **50/-**

MODEL STEAM ENGINES.

All thoroughly tested before leaving Works.

Vertical Steam Engine, fitted with whistle, safety valve, oscillating brass cylinder, boiler, imitation brickwork base. Height 9 in. Price **10½d.**

No. 105.

Upright Steam Engines.

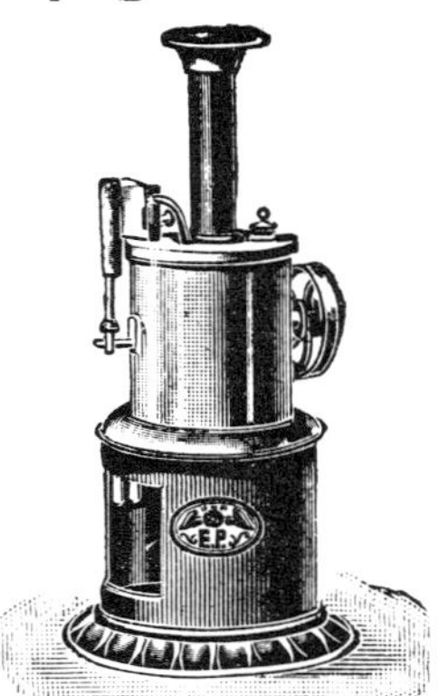

Oxydized boiler, high chimney, safety valve and whistle. Best make and finish, as illustration

No. 10, **1/9** 8 in. high

No. 11, **2/6** 9 in. high Postage 3d.

Fo. 12, **3/6** 10 in. high

No. 13, with water and pressure gauges, heavy metal base, 11½ in. high, **5/6** Postage 4d.

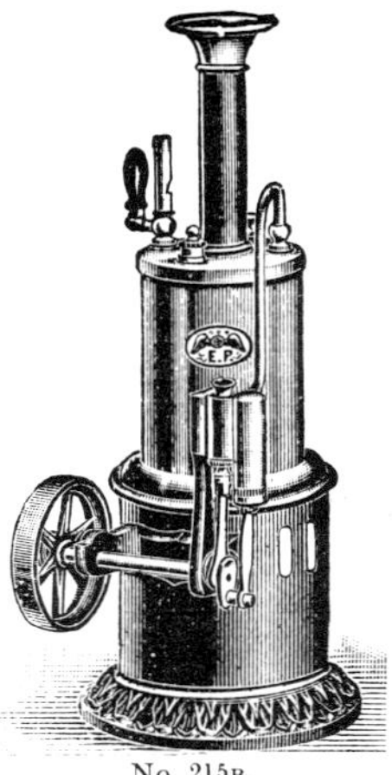

No 215B.

Steam Engine. With fixed cylinder 9¾ in. high, safety valve, steam whistle, filling and outlet screw, iron fly wheel 2 in. diameter. Price **7/6** Postage 4d.

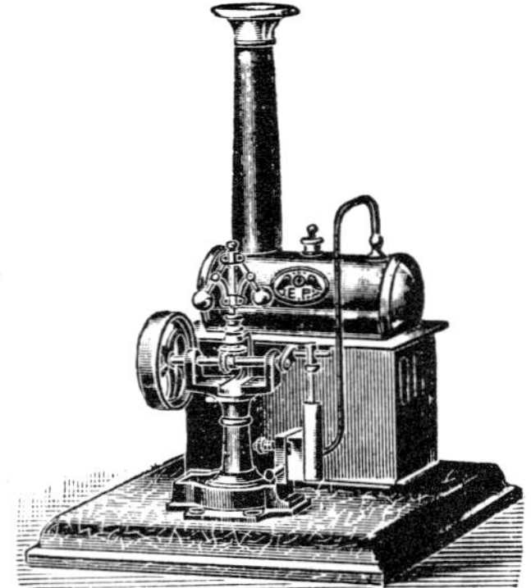

No. 420.

Horizontal Engine.

Oxydised boiler, oscillating cylinder, safety valve, governors, mounted on metal base, 5¼ in. by 5¼ in. total height 8 in., **2/11** Postage **3d.**

No. 420/2. **Steam . Engine.**

With, ,safety: valve, 'steam whistle, water outlet screw, governor on metal base. Size, 6½ in. by 6½ in. by 9¼ in. Price **4/11** Post 3d.

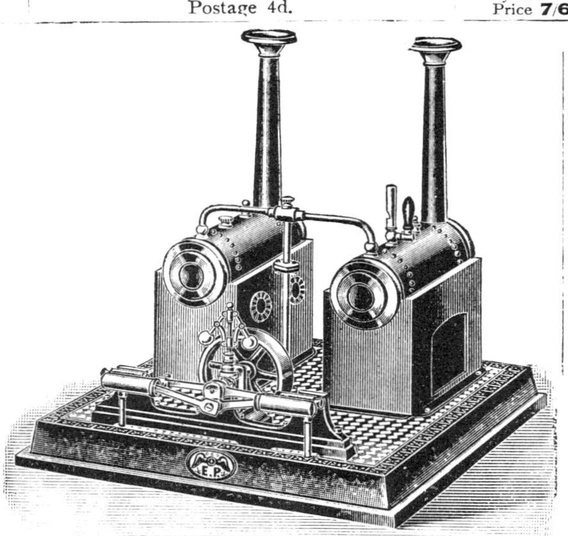

No. 530/7. **New Model Duplex Steam Engine**

With twin boilers, oscillating cylinder, 2 safety valves, steam whistle, 2 water outlet screws, governor on metal base. Size, 8 in. by 8 in. by 8¼ in. Price **21/-** Large size, **25/-**

Fine Model Vertical Steam Engine.

With inverted slide valve cylinder, mounted on iron base 5 by 5 by 2¼, total height 15 in. Fitted with exhaust pipe, starting cock, water gauge, lever safety valve, whistle, filling plug, spirit lamp and iron furnace door to open. 677/3. Price **27/6**

Vertical Engine.

oxydised brass boiler, inverted slide valve cylinder, whistle, water gauge, safety valve, &c., mounted on ebonised wood base 9½ in. by 4 in , total height 12½ in. 690/1 Price **15/-**

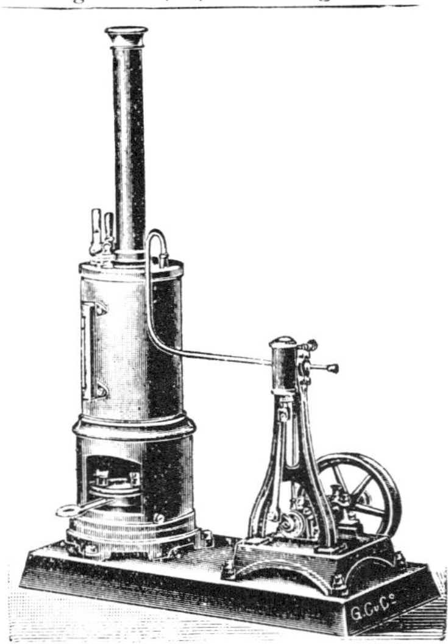

No. 165. **Vertical Steam Engines.** No. 165A.

With inverted slide valve cylinder, oxydised boiler, lever safety valve, water gauge, starting cock, force pump and governor, vapor lamp, extra heavy fly wheel mounted on heavy iron base, 4 in. by 4 in. diameter, fly wheel 3½ by ½ in., with al fittings as above except water gauge, which has no taps, 13 in. high. Price **30/-**
No. 165. Do., do., boiler 2½ in. high, fitted as above, 12 in. high. Price **25/-**

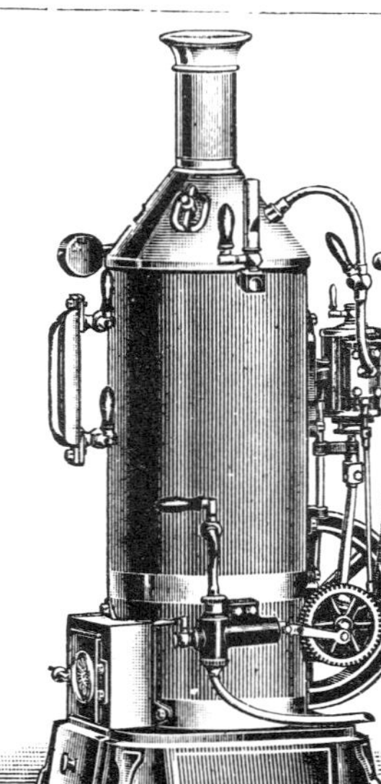

No. 165B. Magnificent **Vertical Steam Engine,** with oxydised boiler and inverted slide valve cylinder, ¾ stroke, governors, safety valve, 2-tap water gauge, whistle, starting cock, feed pump, extra heavy 4 in. fly wheel, double flame vapour lamp, and furnace door. Heavy iron base, 6 by 6 in. Total height, 16 in. Price **42/-**

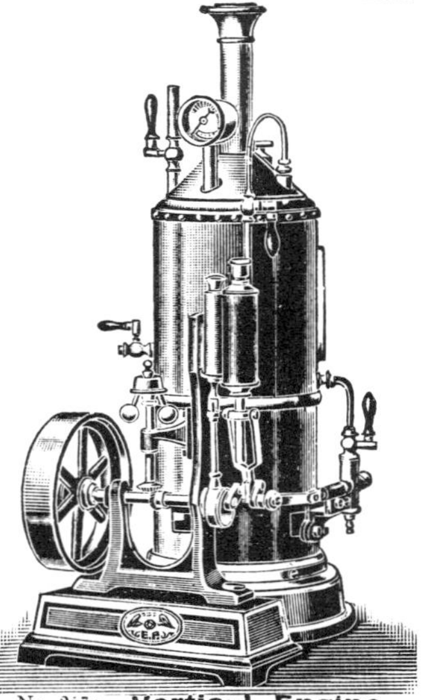

No. 257A **Vertical Engine.**

Oxydised boiler, inverted piston valve cylinders, governors, mica water gauge and shield, pressure gauge, filling plug, outlet tap, force pump, whistle, on heavy metal base, nickelled chimney, 10 in. high, **17/6** Post 3d. No, 257B. Do., do., 12 in. high, as illustration, **27/6**
No. 257C. Do., do., 13 in. high, **42/-**

Steam Engines, *continued.*

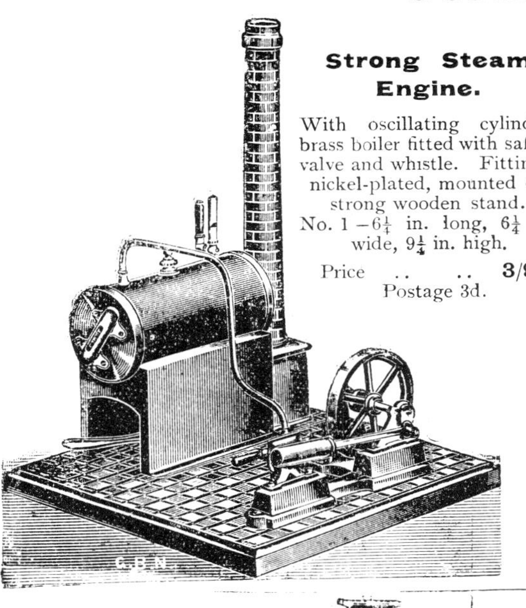

Strong Steam Engine.

With oscillating cylinder, brass boiler fitted with safety valve and whistle. Fittings, nickel-plated, mounted on strong wooden stand.
No. 1 – 6¼ in. long, 6¼ in. wide, 9¼ in. high.

Price **3/9**
Postage 3d.

Handsome Model Steam Engine.

No. 112. – Vertical Steam Engine, tubular oxydized boiler, nickel plated slide valve, cylinders and governors, lever safety valve, starting gear, water gauge with two taps, steam gauge, cup lubricators, outlet tap, spanner, fire hook, &c. 6 in. driving wheel, with 5-speed driving gear, enabling 5 models to be driven at once at 5 different speeds.

Fitted with pump and water reservoir for feeding boiler, condensing chamber for exhaust steam, atmospheric burner with large spirit tank.

Mounted on iron base.

Height of boiler, 21 in., base 12½ by 16½ in.

An entirely New and Very Handsome Model.

Price .. **£5 0 0**

Ditto, same as No. 112, smaller size to drive 3 models, and no pump
As illustration **50/-**

Small sizes .. **25/-** and **27/6**

The "Little Hercules."

As illustration. Exceptional value, enamelled boiler with Slide Valve Cylinder, and filling plug, mounted on wood base, 6 by 3¼ in. Total height 8½ in.
Price .. **10½d.** Postage 3d.

Model Steam Engine.

Price .. **59/6**
75/-

New Model Steam Engine.

With oxydized boiler, fixed cylinder, double action, steam pressure gauge with safety valve, new steam whistle, water gauge, governor, iron fly wheel, on metal base. Size 9½ by 9½ by 14½.
Price .. **30/-**

Extra Large Size, Very Fine Model,
Price .. **£6 6 0**

No. 13097.
SUPERIOR QUALITY.

Steam Stationary Engine— "SATURN."

With fixed slide valve cylinder, governors, large fly wheel (4 in. diam.) feeding pump, oxydised boiler with bell whistle, lever safety valve and water gauge, exhaust steam passing through chimney. All fittings nickelled and correctly finished.

Strongly mounted. 11in. long, 6in. wide, 10¼ in. high (with chimney).
Price .. **47/6**

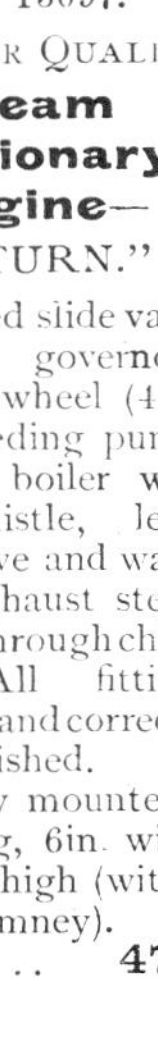

Superior Steam Engines.

With many improvements with finest fixed double action slide valve cylinder, oxydized brass boiler safety valve, bell steam whistle, steam jet oiler projecting water gauge, with two taps, outlet tap, starting tap, body of engine and chimney stamped and japanned, (imitation brickwork), steam escaping through chimney (imitating smoke). All fittings highly finished and nickelled, mounted on iron stand and fine wooden base, with stamped metal plate (imitation tiles).
Size 8¾ in. long 7 in. wide 14 in. high. Price **23/6**

CLOCKWORK and STEAM ENGINES and NOVELTIES.

No. 845/4 **10/6**

Clockwork Engine.

An excellent Model of Gas Engine.

No danger.

Length, 7 in. Width, 4[illegible] in. Height, 6 in.

Price **10/6**

No. 4112/4493.

New Pump Engine.

Price . . **32/6**

,, . . **52/6**

Engine House.

No. 845/2. **5/6**

Engine House, as illustration.

Fitted with **Clockwork** Engine.

No danger.

Length.	Width.	Height.
$9\frac{7}{8}$ in.	$4\frac{3}{4}$ in.	$12\frac{1}{2}$ in.

Price **5/6**

Postage 3d.

No. 845/1. **3/6**

Clockwork Engine.

Good Model.

Runs backwards and forwards.

Length	Width.	Height.
$6\frac{1}{2}$ in.	4 in.	$6\frac{1}{4}$ in.

Price **3/6**

Postage 3d.

No. 4118/2.

Stationary Engine.

Price **35/-**

No. 111/20s.

New Model Steam Engine, with Pump.

Price . . **30/-**

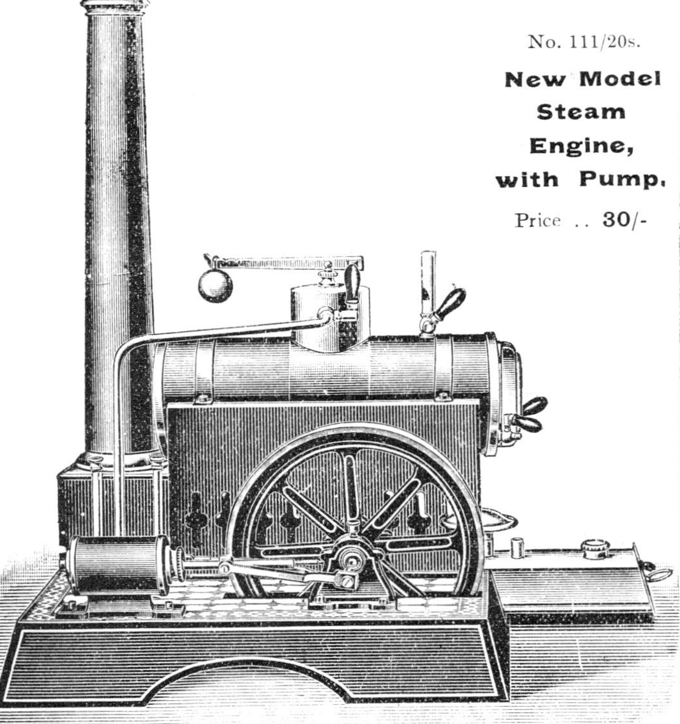

No. 4140.

Steam Engine,

As illustration.

Very fine Model. Price . . **£6 10 0**

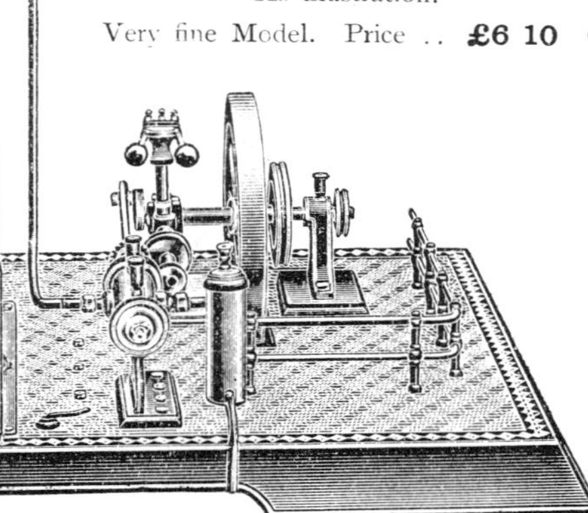

Model Steam Engines—continued.

Engine House.

Metal Engine House, with Steam Engine complete, with fly wheel outside house for connecting models. Exhaust steam passes through chimney.

Size 9¾ by 4¾ by 13½ in.

Price **5/6** Postage 4d.

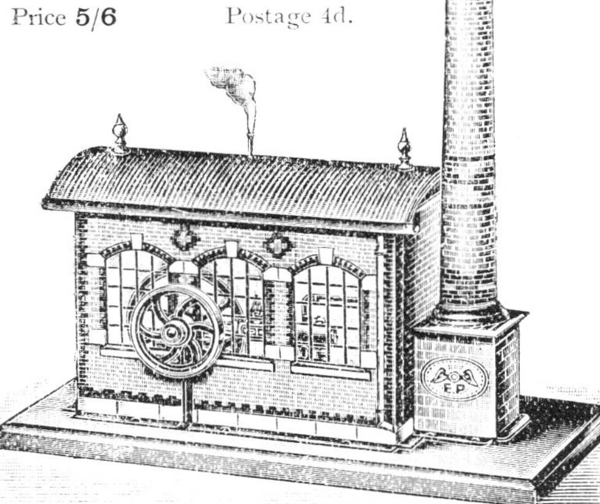

New Style Model **Steam Engine**, fitted with brass boiler, oscillating cylinder, fittings all well nickelled. Price **9/6**

No. 4158.

Engine House.

Enamelled in best style, complete with Steam Engine.

Price .. **30/-**

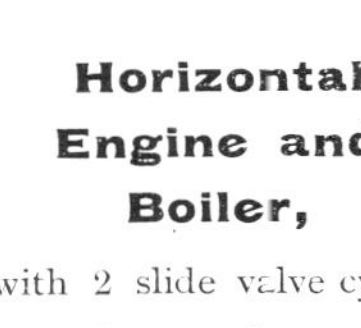

Horizontal Engine and Boiler,

with 2 slide valve cylinders, lever safety valve, bell-whistle, outlet tap, water gauge and 2-speed pulley, mounted on solid iron base,

13½ by 12 in., **47/6**

No. 4130/1.

Fine

Horizontal Engine

in Engine Shed, with oxydized boiler, slide valve cylinders, governors, bell-whistle, wafety valve, water gauge, with shafting to drive 2 models. Mounted on enamelled base, 11½ by 6¾ in., height 9½ in., **30/-**

Ditto, size 15 by 9½ in., height 12 in., **35/-**

Engine Hall

Best Make.

Length ... 16½ in.
Width ... 12½ in.
Height ... 17 in.

Price **75/-**

Do., smaller, **59/6**

The boiler is located inside of imitation masonry. The engine has horizontal compound (high and low pressure) cylinders and a regulator, whistle, lever safety valve, water gauge, water cock, working with great punctuality, the exhaust steam passes through the chimney.

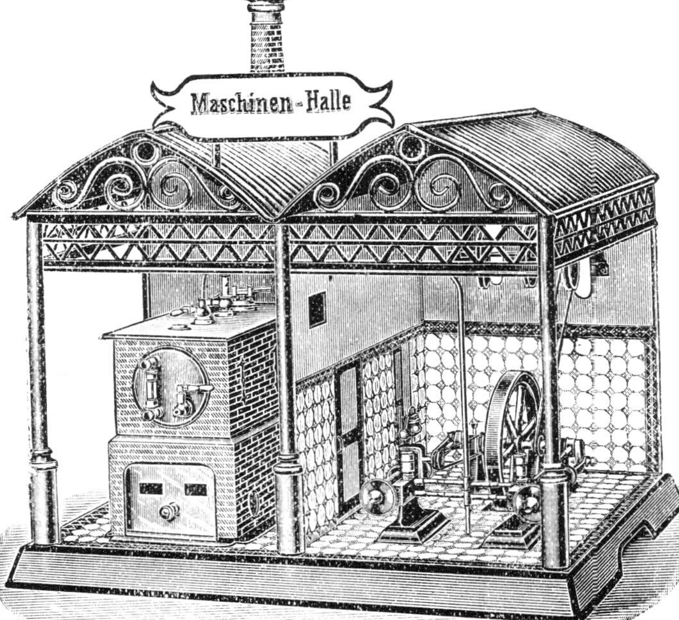

No. 258.

Model Steam Engine.

With fixed cylinder, oxydized brass boiler shed, safety valve, steam whistle, water outlet screw, governors, on metal base.

Size 8½ by 8½ by 13¼ in.

Price **12/6**

Do. No. 258A.

Size 9 by 9 by 14½ in.

Price **17/6**

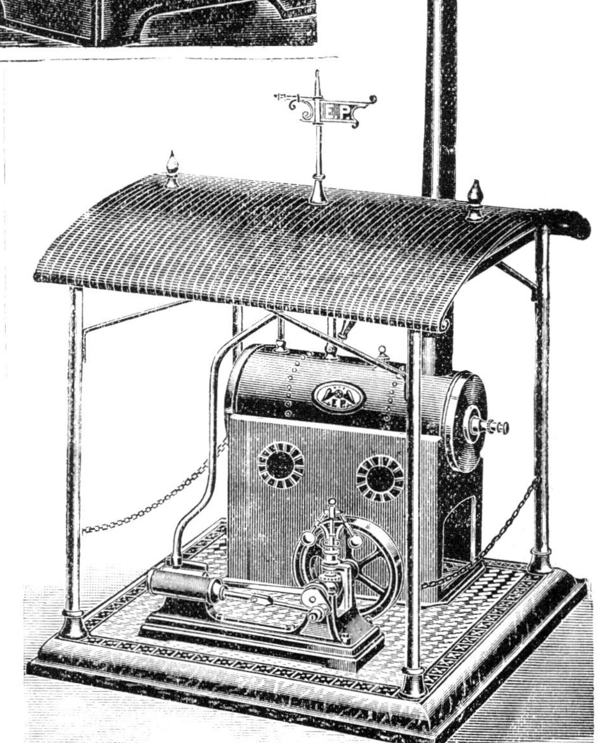

Steam Rollers, Traction Engines, etc.

SPLENDID VALUE

No. B. **Steam Roller.**

Steam Roller with reversible gear, safety valve, oscillating brass cylinder, steam whistle, flame guard, and polished brass boiler, 8 in. long, 5 in. wide, $8\frac{3}{4}$ in. high. Price **9/11** Post 4d.

Steam Traction Engine.

Fitted with powerful fixed cylinders, governors, safety valve and whistle.

Price .. **17/6** Post 4d.

No. A.

Steam Roller.

With reversible gear, safety valve, oscillating brass cylinder, steam whistle, flame guard, and oxydized brass boiler.

$10\frac{1}{4}$ in. long
$4\frac{1}{2}$ in. wide
$8\frac{3}{4}$ in. high

Price .. **13/9**

Post 4d.

Clockwork Locomobile.

As illustration. Can be used also as a stationary engine to drive models. Has all appearance and action of real steam engine. Fitted with starting lever and governors.

Price **13/6**

Ditto, Clockwork Fire Engine on stand, **12/6**

On Wheels .. **16/6**

Postage 2d.

No. 4129.

Steam Traction Engine.

Fitted with fixed cylinders, governors, safety valve, whistle, water gauge, as illustration.

Price **50/-**

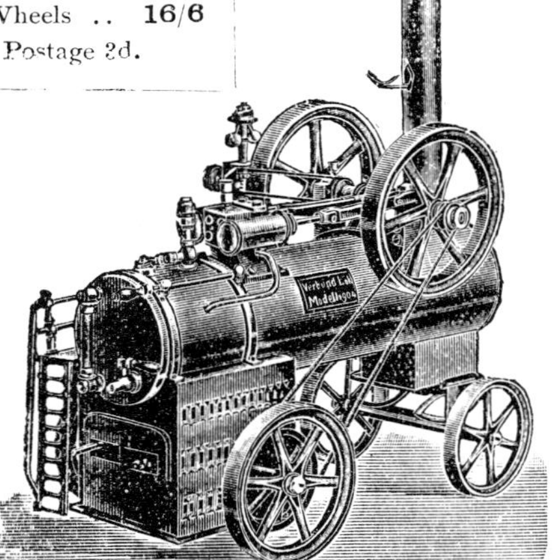

Clockwork Stationary Engine.

Very original.

Has all movements and appearance of actual steam engine fitted with governors.

Price .. **10/6**

Postage 3d.

No. 1

Traction Engine.

$8\frac{1}{2}$ in. long, 4 in. wide, 9 in. high.

Price .. **13/6**

Postage 3d.

With double action slide valve cylinder, safety valve, solid oxydized brass boiler, water gauge, bell whistle and flame guard.

Stationary Steam Engine.

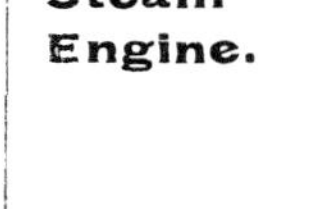

Price .. **18/6**

Post 4d.

No. 506 **Steam Roller.**

Fitted with fixed cylinders, safety valve, steam whistle, governors, gauge tap, chain gear, which is easily detached, making a useful stationary engine.

$11\frac{1}{2}$ in. high, $10\frac{1}{2}$ in. long.

Price .. **45/-**

Steam Sweeper.

$10\frac{1}{2}$ in. high, $10\frac{1}{2}$ in. long.

Price **45/-**

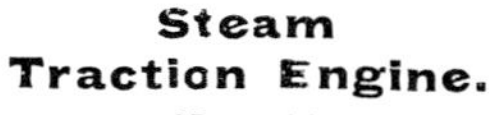

Steam Traction Engine.

No. 500.

Fitted with fixed cylinders, steam whistle, safety valve and governors, gauge taps, &c., &c.
Length 9 in., height 11 in.
As illustration.

Price **37/6**

GAMAGE'S BEST QUALITY MODELS OF ENGINEERS' TOOLS, &c.

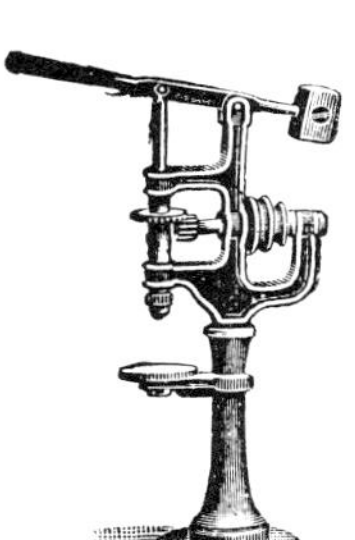

No. 4263/1.

Model Drilling Machine

Best quality material and finish

Price .. 3/11

Postage 3d.

Larger size, Price .. 8/6

Postage 3d.

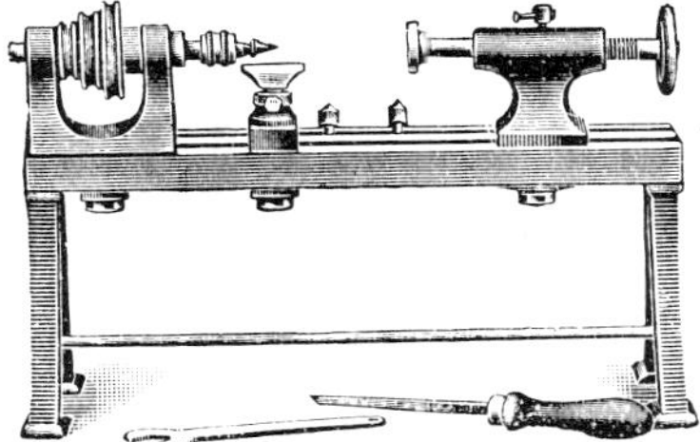

No. 4261/2. **Model Lathe.**

Large size, as illustration .. 9/6

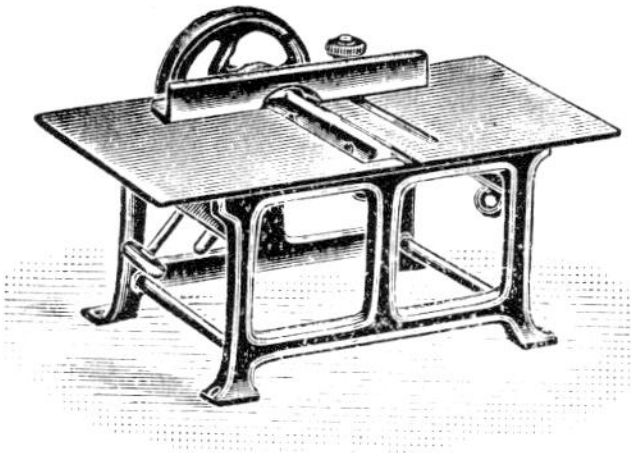

No. 4259.

Planing Machine.

Price .. 4/11 Postage 3d.

No. 4251/2.

Model Grindstone.

Superior quality, material and finish,

Price 3/- Post 3d.

Special Line, extra heavy Grindstones, 3 by 1 in. .. 1/9

Do. with hood 2/6

Postage 3d.

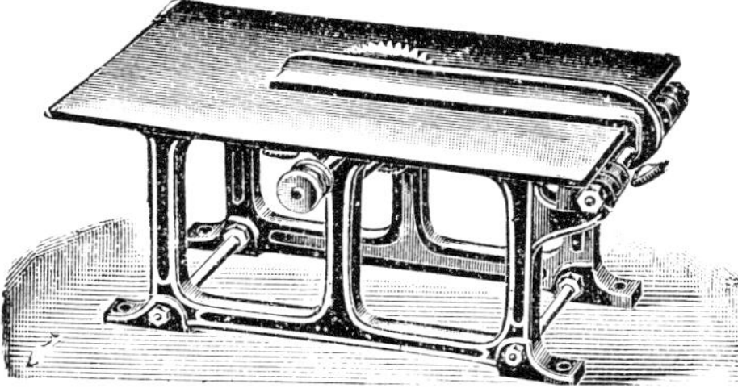

No. 9256/194. **Circular Saw,** extra fine finish, strong cast iron stand, finely japanned, with highly nickelled table to lift and adjust, guide rail, pully wheel (adaptable for small belt and string) and steel saw. 7½ in. long, 5⅛ in. wide, 6/6 Post 3d.

No. 6/254. **Model Circular Saw.**

With guide.

Best quality material and finish.

Price 2/6 Post 3d.

No. 4267.

Steam Hammer.

Price 10/6 Post 3d.

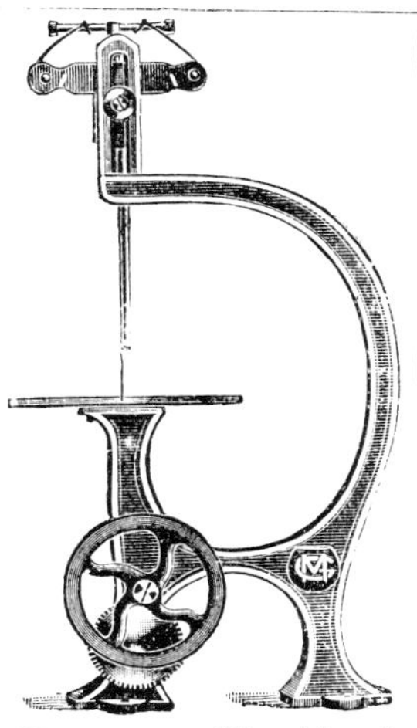

No. 4256. **Vertical Band Saw.**

Best finish. 7/11 Post 3d.

No. 4252.

Model Polisher.

Price 2/- Post 3d.

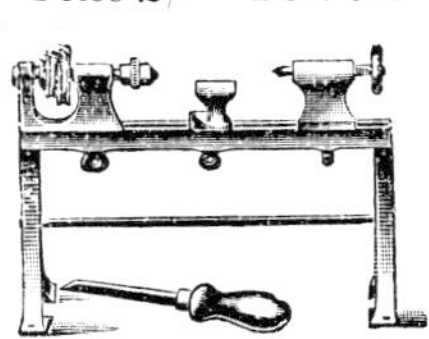

No. 4260/3.

Model Lathe.

Superior quality material and finish.

Price .. 3/6

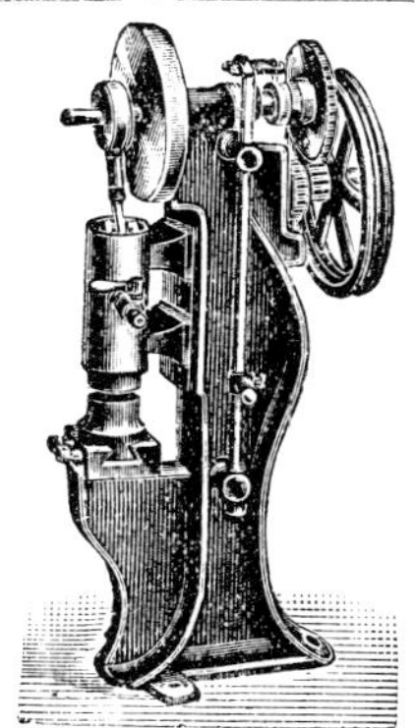

No. 504.

Punching Machine.

Price 12/6 Post 3d.

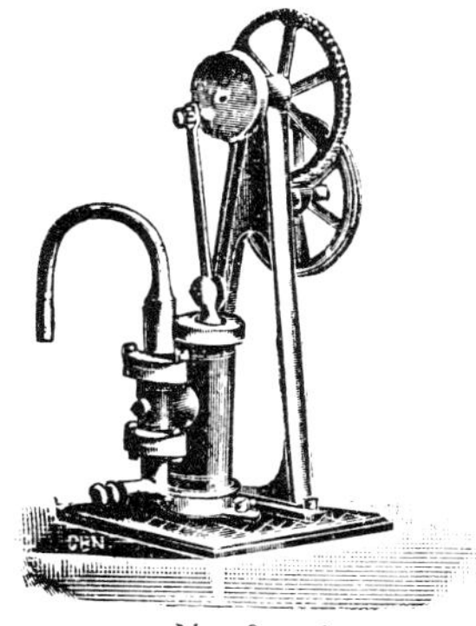

No. 9∪∪∪1.

Force Pump

(Model for Instruction), best finish, cast iron stand, brass pump, nickel finish.

Price .. 8/6 Post 3d.

Height 5 in., base 2¼ by 2¼ in.

No. 4249. **Model Forge.**

Can be used with fire. Price 10/- Post 3d.

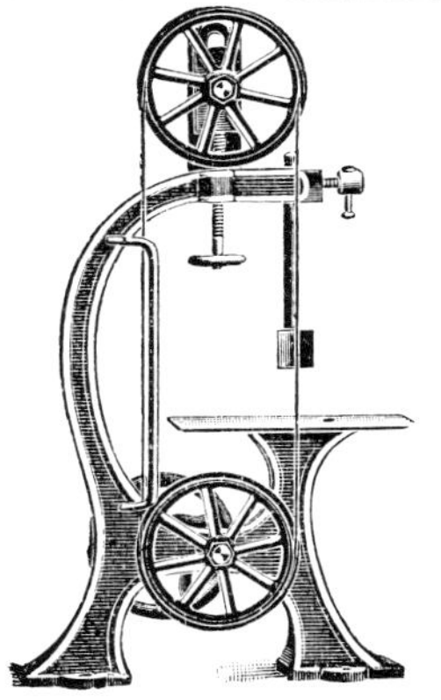

No. 4255/2.

Model Bands.

Superior quality and finish.

Price .. 8/6

Cheaper make .. 4/-

Postage 3d.

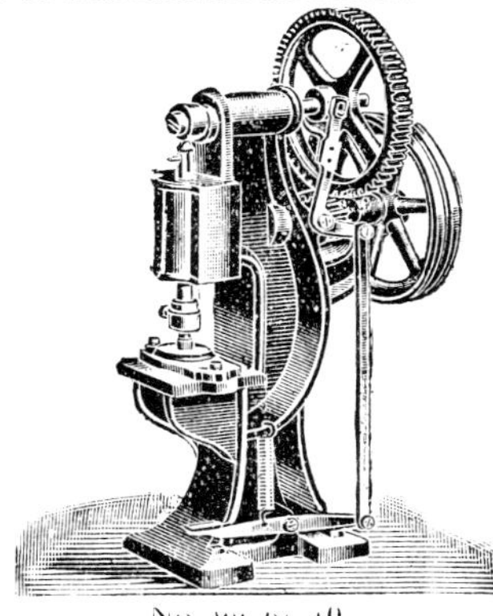

No. 9956/240.

Eccentric Press.

Extra fine, strong finish, strong cast iron stand, finely japanned, cog wheel gearing, all parts screwed. 6⅝ in. high, 4 in. wide.

Price .. 8/11 Post 3d.

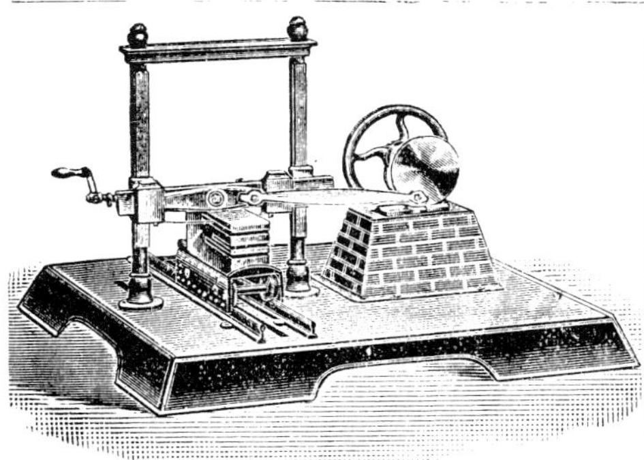

No. 4258.

New Model Travelling Saw.

Price .. 15/- Post 4d.

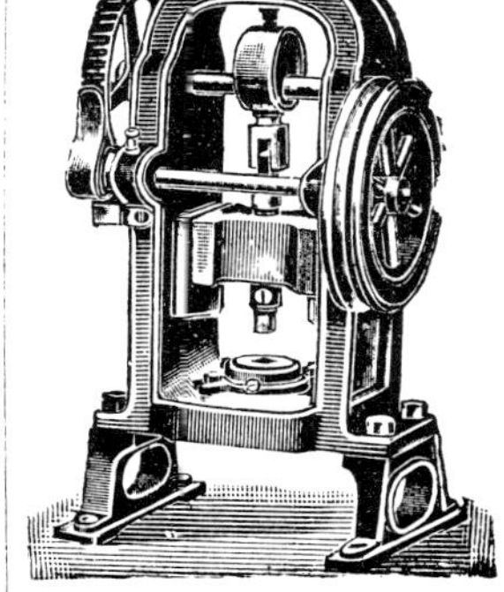

No. 4254/2/3. **Model Circular Saw,** with guide, best quality material and finish, 3/9 Larger size 5/9 Post 3d.

No. 9956/192.

Eccentric Press, extra fine finish, strong cast iron stand, finely japanned, with strong pressure pad, prismatic guiding lock, mounting for the punch and cog-wheel gear, with oilers in bearings. All parts screwed.

6⅝ in. high, 4 in. wide. Price .. 14/6 Postage 3d.

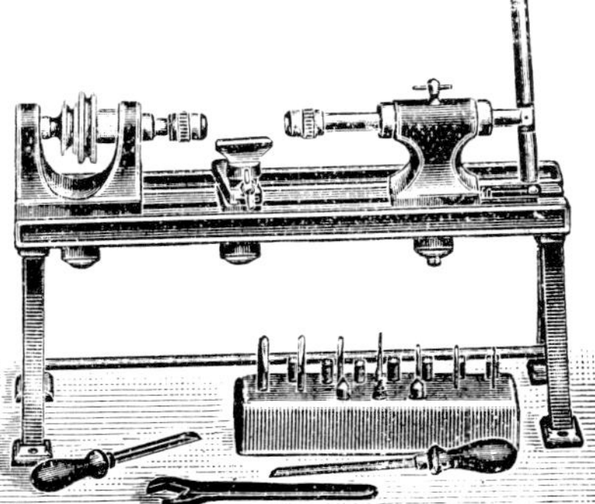

No. 4262. **Model Lathe.**

With 10 drills.

Price .. .. 12/6 Postage 3d.

Gamage's Model Engineers' Tools, Shafting, &c.

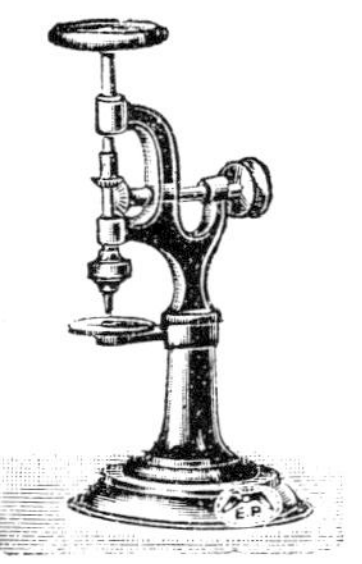

Drilling Machine.

Price 1/- Post 2d.

Circular Saw or Upright Saw.

Price 1/- Postage 2d.

Hammer.

Price 1/- Postage 2d.

Superior quality with covering, 1/11

Polishing Bobs.

Price 1/- Post 2d.

Model Grindstone.

Price .. 1/- Postage 1d.
,, .. 2/- ,, 3d.

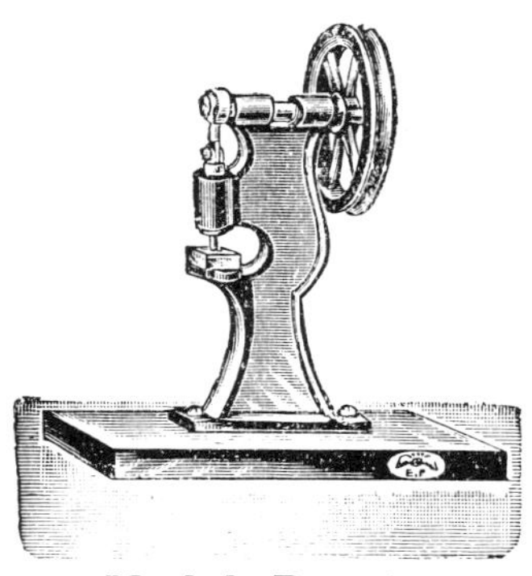

Model Punch.

Price 1/9
Postage 3d.

Model Lathe.

Price .. 2/- Postage 3d.

Special make, 10½d. ,, 3d.

Work Bench.

With Grindstone, Circular Saw and Screw Vice.

Price .. .. Postage

Model – Circular Saw.

Price .. .. 2/- Postage 3d.

Vertical Band Saw.

5½ in. high. Price 3/- Postage 3d.

Workshop Shafting.

6 in. long with 4 pulley wheels		10½d	Postage	2d.
9 in. ,, 4	,,	1/9	,,	3d.
11 in. 4	,,	2/6	,,	3d.
14 in. ,, 6	,,	3/6	,,	3d.

The 11 in and 14 in. have cast iron columns. The 6 in. and 9 in. have composition columns.

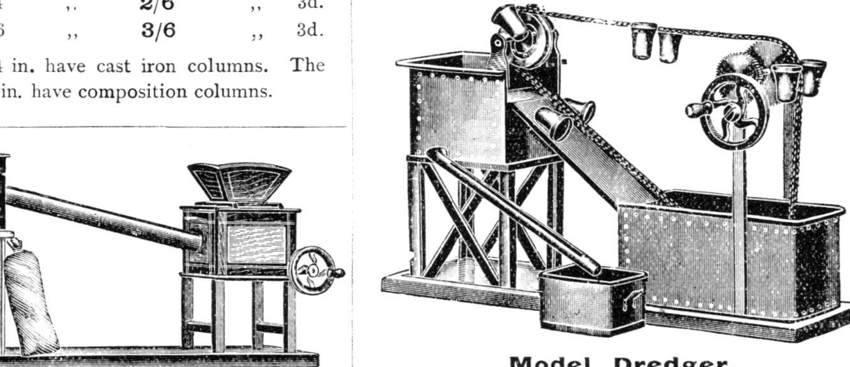

Model Grinder. Best finish.

Price .. .. 5/11 Postage 3d.

Model Fan.

Price .. .. 1/- Postage 2d.
Superior quality .. .. 1/9 ,, 2d.

Workshop Shafting.

6¼ in. long, with 5 pulleys .. 3/6 Postage 3d.
16 in. ,, ,, 6 ,, .. 8/11 ,, 3d.

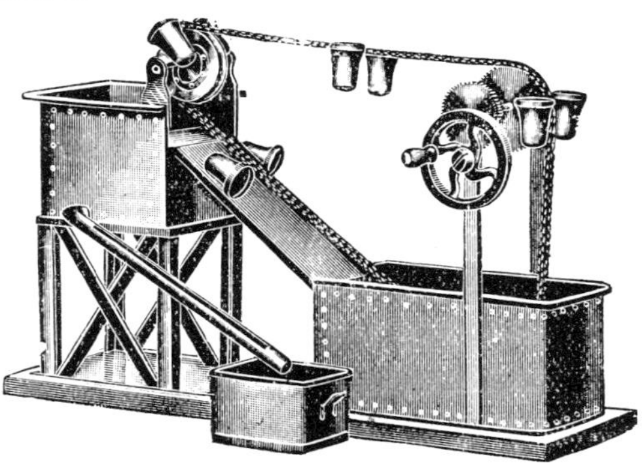

Model Dredger.

Best quality make and finish.

Price, as illustration .. .. 10/6 Postage 3d.

Model Dredger.

With 4 buckets .. .. .. Postage

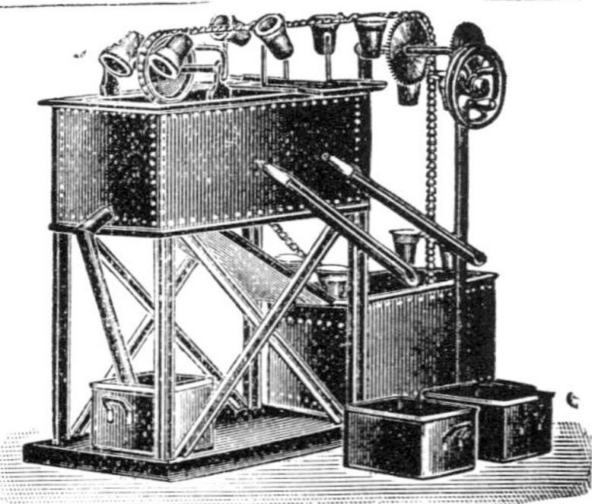

Dredger (New Model).

Price .. .. 15/- Postage 3d.

Bench, fitted with Tools complete (as illustration), 2/6 Postage 6d.

MODEL FOUNTAINS, PUMPS, DREDGERS, etc.

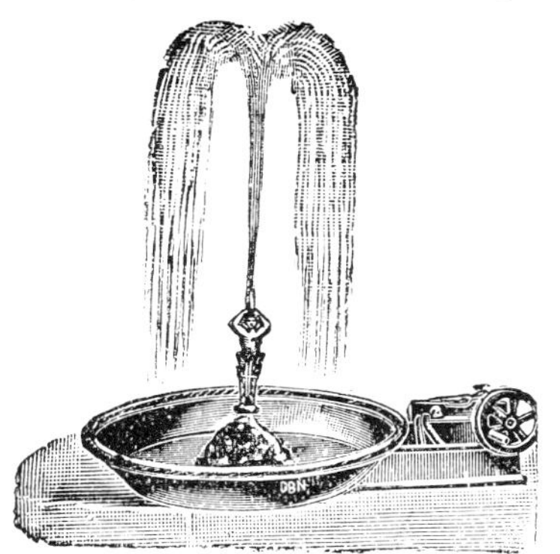

No. 9986/58. **Fountain** with Figure, finely japanned, with brass cylinder, 6½ in. diameter. Price .. **2/-** Post 3d.

Model Fountain.
As illustration.
Price **4/6**
Postage 3d.
Larger size .. .. **6/6** Post 4d.

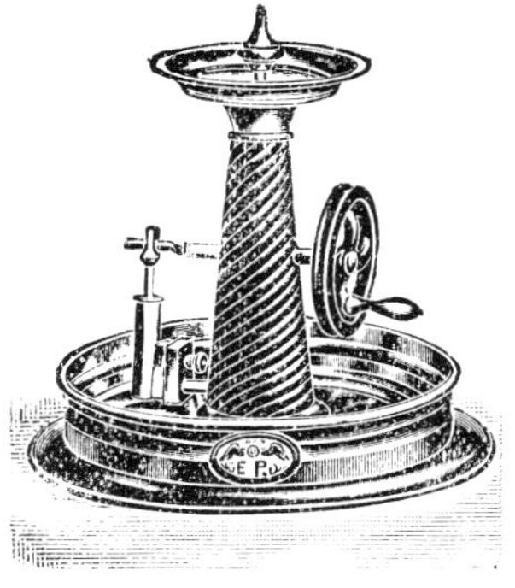

Model Fountain.
As illustration..
Price **2/6**
Postage 3d.

No. 9956/60. **Fountain,** with 3 jets and figure finely japanned, with 2 brass cylinders, 8¼ in. diameter.
Price .. .. **4/6** Postage 3d.

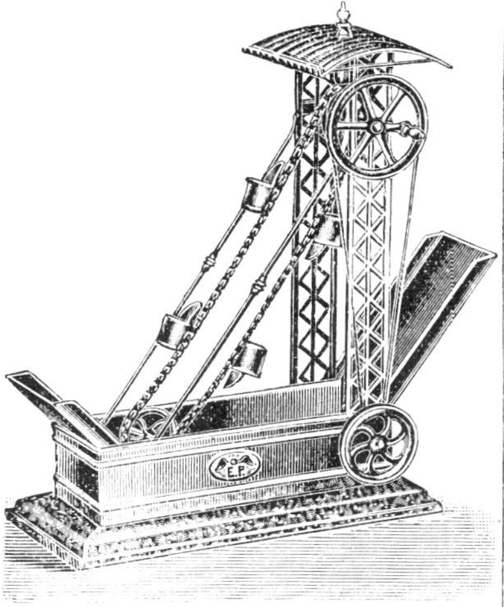

Model Dredger, with 4 buckets, 8 in. long x 4 in. x 9 in. .. **3/3** Post 4d.
6 buckets, 12 in. x 4¾ in. x 12 in. .. **6/3** Postage 4d.
7 buckets, 7½ in. x 7½ in. x 18¾ in. **8/11** Postage 6d.
8 buckets, 18¾ in. x 6 in. x 14 in. .. **10/6** Postage 6d.

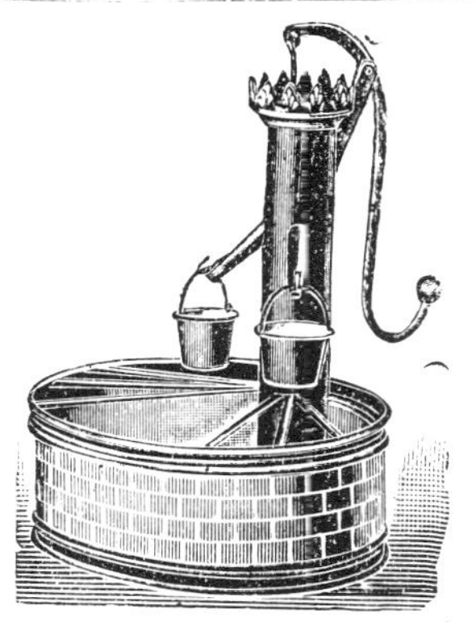

Working Model Hand Pump,
With 2 spouts and 2 buckets, 6⅞ in. high, basin 5½ in. long, **1/10.** 9½ in. high, basin 6⅛ in. long, **2/11** 10¼ in. high, basin 6⅞ in. long, **3/9** Post 4d.

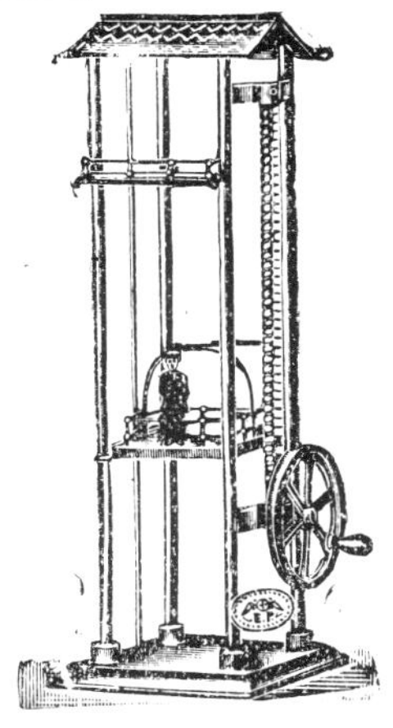

Model Elevator.
Price **3/3**
Postage 3d.

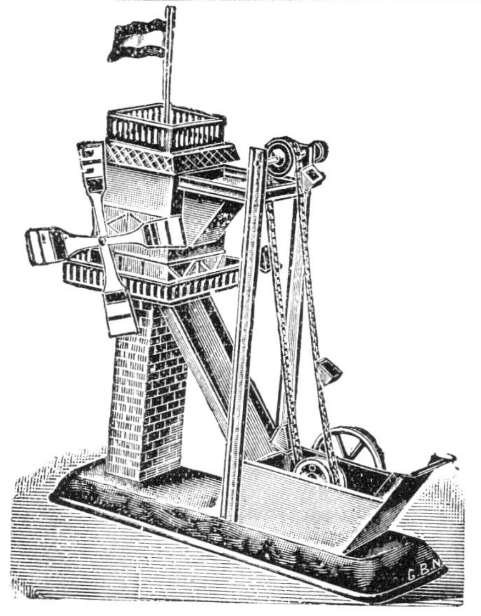

Gamage's Windmill with Dredger.
Well enamelled and very strongly finished, with four buckets and hammerwork, 10 in. long, 12⅝ in. high.
Price .. .. **3/3** Postage 3d.

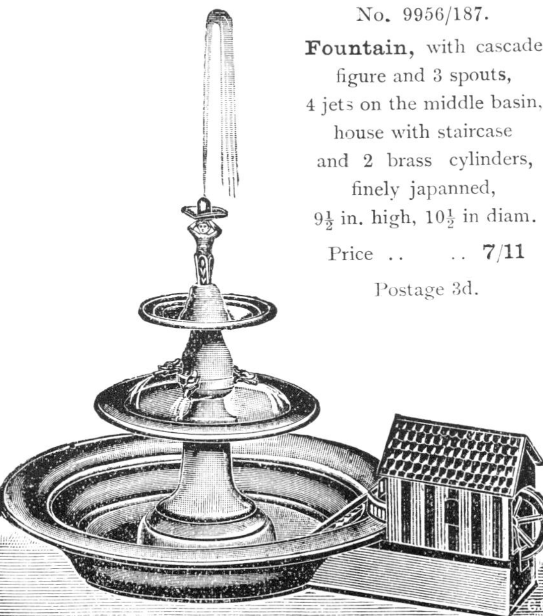

No. 9956/187.
Fountain, with cascade figure and 3 spouts, 4 jets on the middle basin, house with staircase and 2 brass cylinders, finely japanned, 9½ in. high, 10½ in diam.
Price **7/11**
Postage 3d.

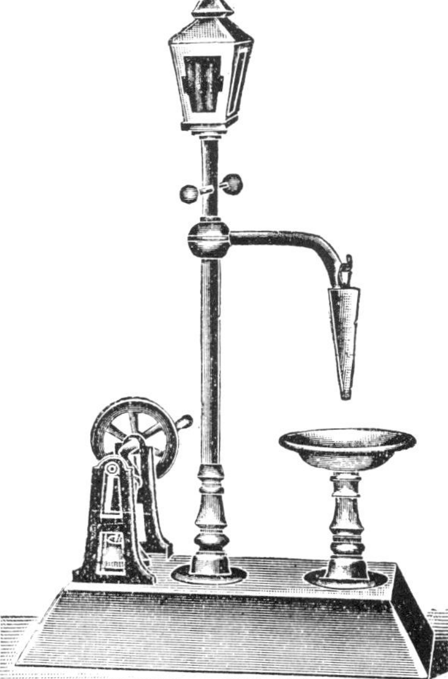

No. 604.
Model Pump. As illustration.
Price .. .. **1/10½** Postage 3d.

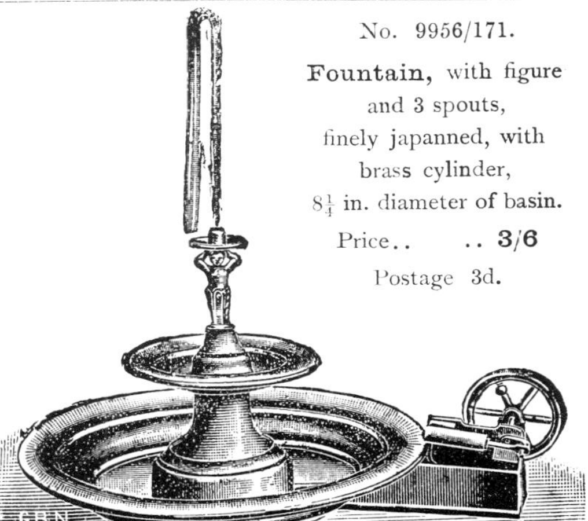

No. 9956/171.
Fountain, with figure and 3 spouts, finely japanned, with brass cylinder, 8¼ in. diameter of basin.
Price.. .. **3/6**
Postage 3d.

RAILWAY LINES, CHAIRS, SLEEPERS, &c.—*continued.*

No. 8790. **Stop Ends,** finely japanned, spring buffers, 0 gauge, 1⅜ in., **1/-** 1 gauge, 1⅞ in., **1/4** 2 gauge, 2⅛ in., **1/6**

Curved Tin Rail for Customers to Construct their own Track.

No. 1 gauge consist of 20 pieces of 14½ in. in length, of rail curved and straight making complete oval set with 54 loose chairs and 120 holding-down spikes, and 30 black wood sleepers. Price .. **3/6**

No. 2 and 2½ in. gauge, 28 pieces rail, 14½ in. long, curved and straight, with 84 chairs and 168 holding-down spikes and 42 sleepers. Price **5/-**

No. 3, 3 in. gauge with 36 pieces rail, 14 in. long, 108 chairs, 216 holding-down spikes and 58 sleepers. Price **6/6**

These rails are curved to the standard gauges and radius, and it is only necessary to attach them to the chairs and sleepers. This makes a most perfect and realistic track.

No. 14090. **Brake Rails** for inserting in track. 0 gauge, **3**d. ea. 1 gauge, **4**d. each.

Railway Lines, Chairs, Sleepers, etc. For Home Construction.

No. M. Solid Brass Rail, made to Scale of ¾ in. to 1 ft. in 36 in. length, with 10 fixed chairs to each piece. Ends of rail fitted with fish plates. Complete, **1/6** length. Brass Fish Plates with 4 bolts and nuts, **1/6** doz.

No. N. Solid Steel Rail, Scale 1 in. to 1 ft. in 16 in. lengths, drilled for fish plates and for pinning direct down to sleepers, **9**d. ft. Iron Chairs for above, **2/3** doz.

No. K. Light Brass Rail, in 16 in. length, with 3 fixed chairs. Complete, **2/6** doz. ft. Heavy Solid Steel Rail (made to order any gauge) and fitted with heavy wood sleepers and iron chairs in 3 ft. lengths, Straight, **3/6** length. Curved, **4/9** length Switches for above, any gauge, **12/6** each.

No. D. Tin Rail, in 16 in. lengths, with 3 fixed chairs, **1/6** doz ft,

Wooden Sleepers, painted dull black, **6**d. doz. Holding-down Spikes, **3**d. per 100. Any of these can be curved to order if diameter and exact gauge are given. Cost is about double the price of straight for small quantities. Rail only in 16 in. lengths, with connecting wires ready for making up. Tin, **1/2** Brass, **2/-** doz. pieces. Switches, Crossings, Buffers, &c., to suit above rails, to order.

Special Quotations upon application.

Straight and Curved Rails with Brake Stop for Stopping and Reversing Loco.
0 gauge, **6**d. 1 gauge, **7**d. 2 gauge, **9**d. 3 gauge, **9**d. ea.
Postage 2d.

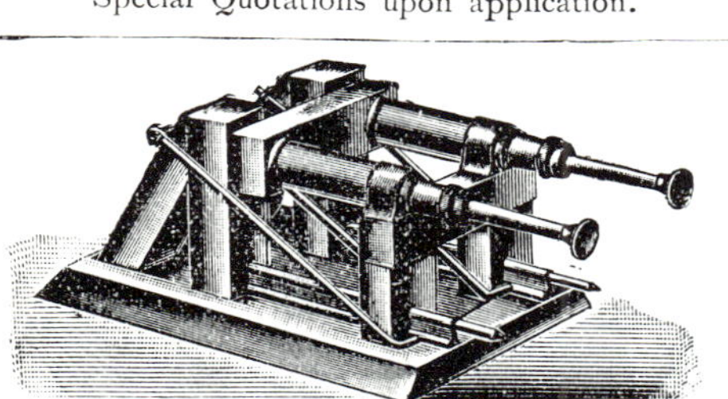

New Spring Stop Buffers.
0 gauge, **1/8** 1 gauge, **2/3** 2 gauge, **3/-** 3 gauge, **4/6** Postage 3d.

New Stop Buffers. As illustration.
0 gauge, **1/3** 1, **1/6** 2, **1/9** Postage 3d.

SPECIAL LINE.
Stop Buffers.
0 gauge, **7½**d.
Postage 3d.

Stop Buffers. As illustration. 0 gauge, **10½**d. 1 gauge, **1/-** 2 gauge, **1/3** 3 gauge, **1/6**
Postage 3d.

No. 2337. **New Turn-table.** 0 gauge, **10/6** 1 gauge, **14/6** 2 gauge, **16/6** Post 4d.

No. 13,961/0.
Engine Shed, with Switch.
0 gauge, 21¾ in. long, 7½ in. high, 9 in. wide.
Price **8/6**

No. 13,961/1.
Gauge 1, 34¼ in. long, 9½ in. high, 12 in. wide.
Price .. .. **15/9** Postage 6d.

Through a practical arrangement the locomotive can be brought to a stop entering the shed, when going at full speed.

No. 7234.
Engine Shed.
Stamped imitation brickwork, realistically japanned, with embossed windows, 4 doors to open, 2 adjustable lines inside, fitting gauge 0 and 1 (1⅜ & 1⅞ in.). 16 in. long, 13 in. wide .. **16/6**

TURN-TABLES.

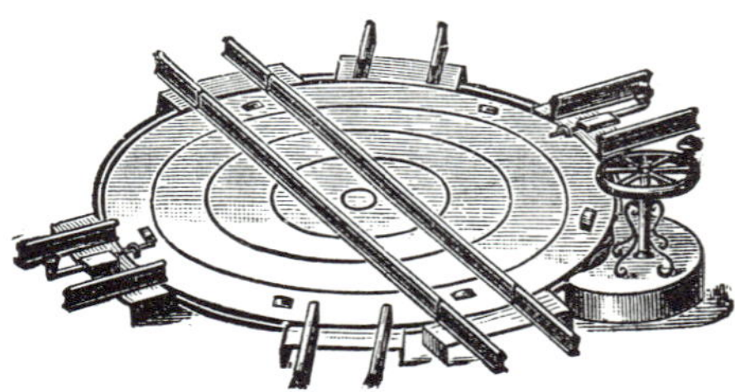

Strongly made and well japanned. A quality.
0 gauge, **3/11**; 1, **7/6**; 2, **8/-**; 3, **10/6**
Postage 3d.

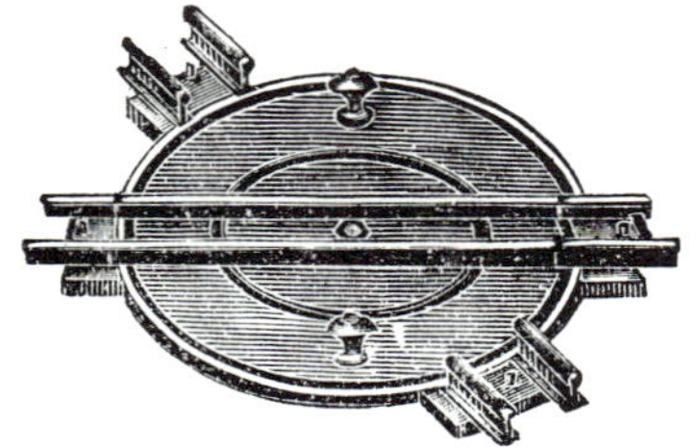

B quality, Cheap Make, 0 gauge, **1/6.**
1 gauge, **2/-** Postage 3d

Gamage's New Model Electric Trams, Signal Lamps, &c.

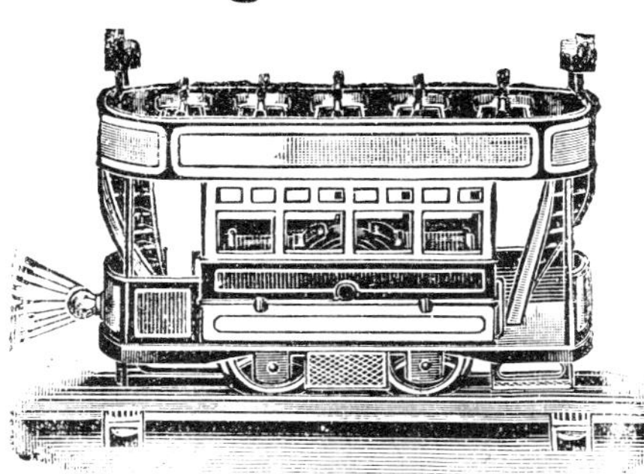

0 Gauge, Correct Model of an up-to-date Electric Tram, lighted by electricity, complete with oval track (10 rails), packed in cardboard box, can be worked by batteries or accumulators, voltage required 4 volts, $7\frac{1}{4}$ in. long.

Price **18/6** Postage 6d.

Two pint bichromate batteries will drive above Tram.

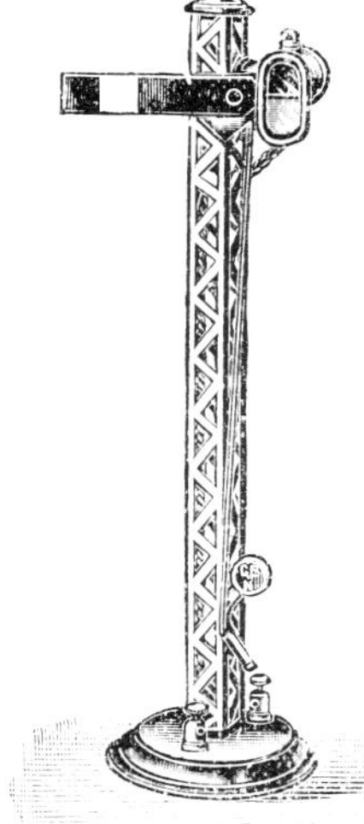

4 volt Electric Signal, to light $12\frac{1}{2}$ in. high, **2/6** Postage 3d.

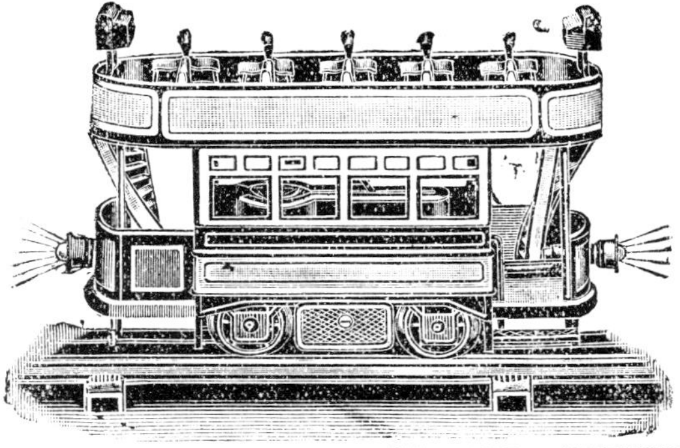

1 Gauge, Latest Model of an up-to-date Electric Tram to run with a 4 volt current (either battery or accumulator), it has an electric head light at both ends, complete with an oval track (10 rails).

Price **27/6**

Two pint bichromate batteries will drive above Tram.

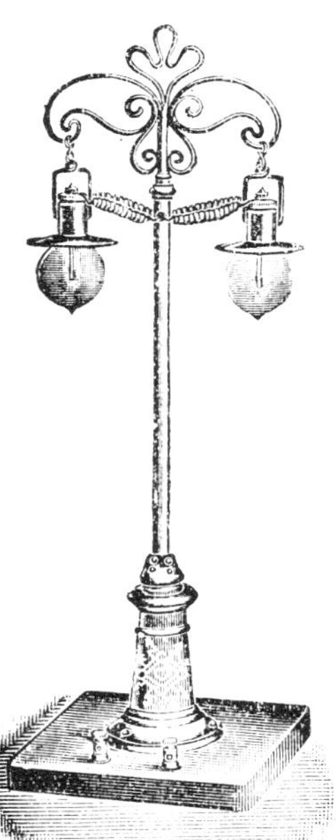

4 volt Electric Arc Lamp, $14\frac{1}{4}$ in. high.

Price **4/9**

Postage 3d.

4 volt Lamps for Electric Trams.

Price **8**d. each

Postage 1d.

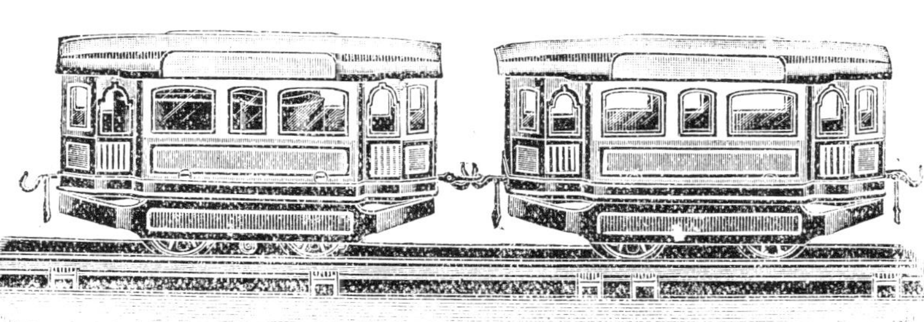

0 Gauge, Electric Tram, with *one* car only and circular track of 6 rails, packed in strong cardboard box, can be driven by two bichromate batteries or a 4 volt accumulator .. .. **10/6** Postage 6d.

Ditto, with two cars .. .. **13/6** ,, 6d.

Extra Trailing Cars .. .. **3/-** ,, 2d.

4 volt Electric Street or Station Lamp, 8 in. high.

Price .. **3/-** Post 3d.

4 volt Arc Lamp, as illustration,

Price .. **3/6**

Postage 3d.

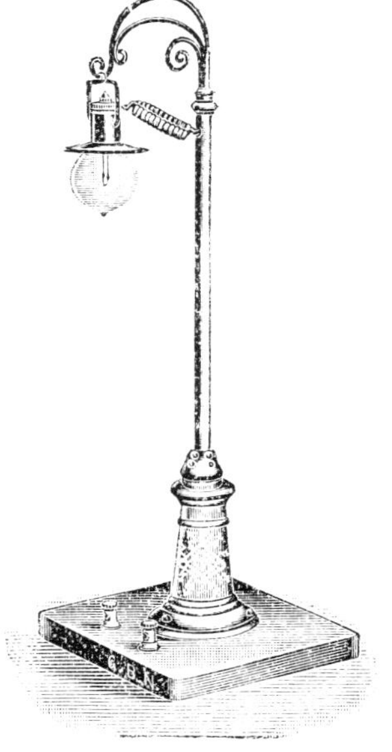

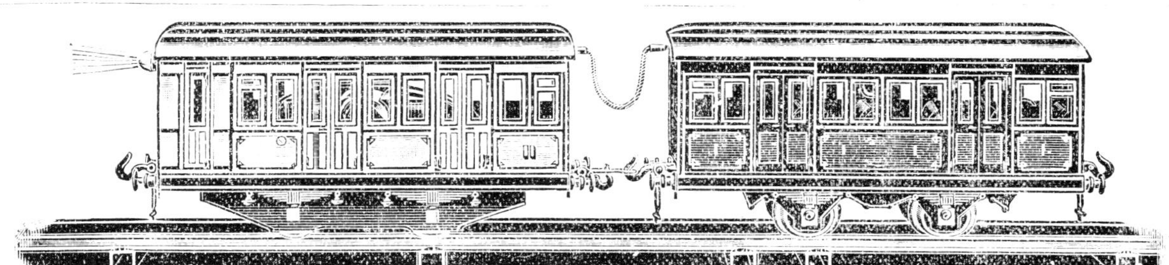

1 Gauge, Electric Tram, with *one* motor car, complete with oval track (12 rails), packed in strong wooden box, can be worked by two bichromate batteries or a 4 volt accumulator .. .. **12/6** Postage 6d.

Ditto, with two cars .. .. **15/-** ,, 6d.

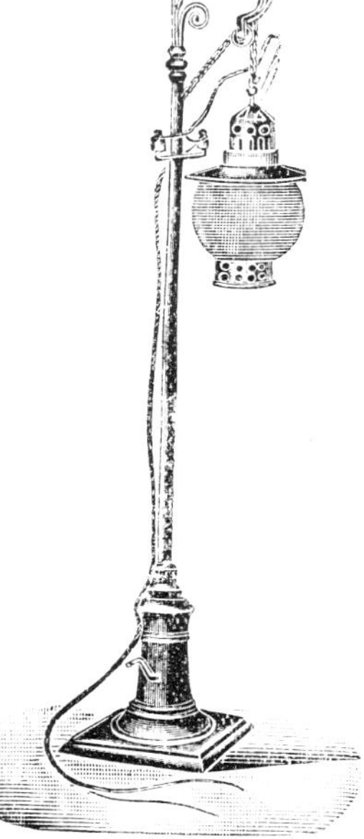

4 volt Electric Arc Lamp, to wind up and down.

Price **3/9**

Postage 3d.

0 Gauge, Electric Train, as illustration, lighted inside and out with electric light, complete with oval track (10 rails) .. **22/6**

1 Gauge, ditto, with 12 rail track **35/-**

Can be worked by two bichromate batteries or 4 volt accumulator.

Model Boats (*continued*).

A Large Stock not illustrated in this Catalogue always on show to select from.

No. 6868/4. **Torpedo Boat,** finely japanned, built after original dockyard designs, typical slender form, travelling very fast, with strong clockwork.
684 17 in. long Price **6/6** Postage 3d. .. 684A 23 in. long Price **9/11** Postage 4d.

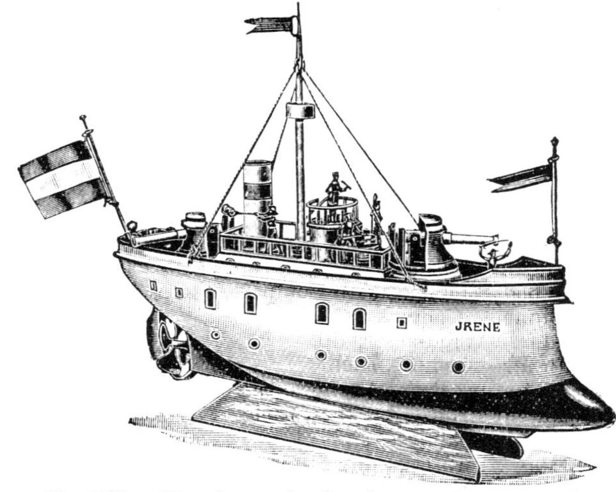

No. 1085. **Clockwork Cruiser, 'Victory.'** With clockwork movement and 2 nickelled cannon for cracker ammunition, length 12½ in. **15/-**

Cruiser. 'Alexandra.' With clockwork movement and 4 nickelled cannon for cracker ammunition, length 16 in. **22/6**

No. 13080. **Gunboat "Terror."** With 2 lifeboats, 4 cannons, and 1 quick-firing gun for crackers. Driven by very strong clockwork.
20in. long. Price .. **16/6** Postage and packi g 9d.

No. 13080A. **Gunboat "Mars."** With 2 lifeboats, 6 cannons, and 2 quick-firing guns for crackers.
24 in. long. Price **26/-**

No. 13079.

Torpedo Division Boat.

Finely japanned, with 2 quick-firing guns and 2 torpedo tubes.

Driven by very strong clockwork.

Superior make.

24 in long. Price .. **12/6**

Postage 6d.

No. 13080B.

Gunboat "Tiger."

Finely japanned, with 4 lifeboats, 8 cannons, and 2 quick-firing guns for crackers.

Driven by very strong Clockwork.

30 in. long.

Price **35/-**

CLOCKWORK AND STEAM MODEL BOATS.

Clockwork Screw Steamboat.

As illustration. Price **1/4½**

No. 13, **1/10½** No. 14, **2/11** Postage extra.

No. 39. **Clockwork Paddle Boat.**

Price .. .. .. **2/-** Postage 3d.
Larger size .. .. **4/-** ,, 3d.

No. 15.

Clockwork Screw Boat.

As illustration. Price **3/11** Postage 3d.

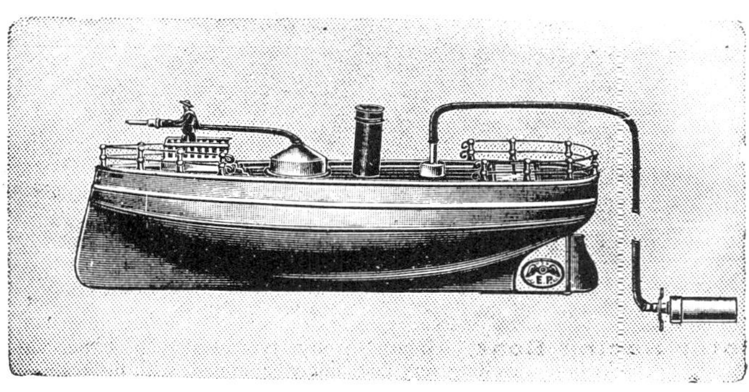

No. 471/5. **Clockwork Fire Boat.**

12 in. long, best finish Price .. **7/6** Postage 3d.

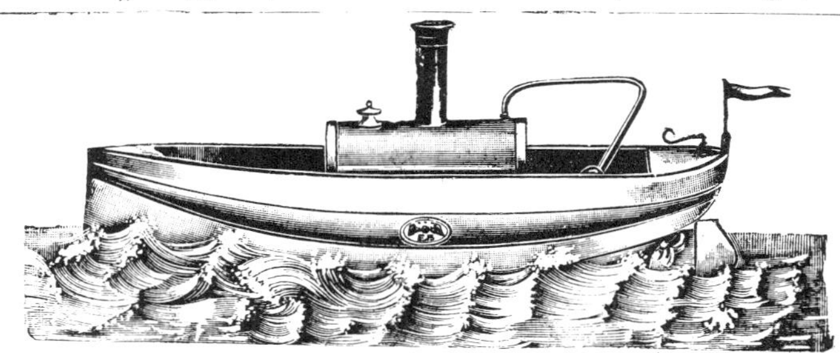

No. 128/2. **Steam Turbine Boat.**

Brass boiler, safety valve. 8¾ in. long. Price .. **3/6** Postage extra.

A Large Stock of BOATS of every description not described in this Catalogue to select from.

No. 435/2.

Clockwork River Pinnace

12 in. long with deck and rudder
Price **4/6**
Post 3d.

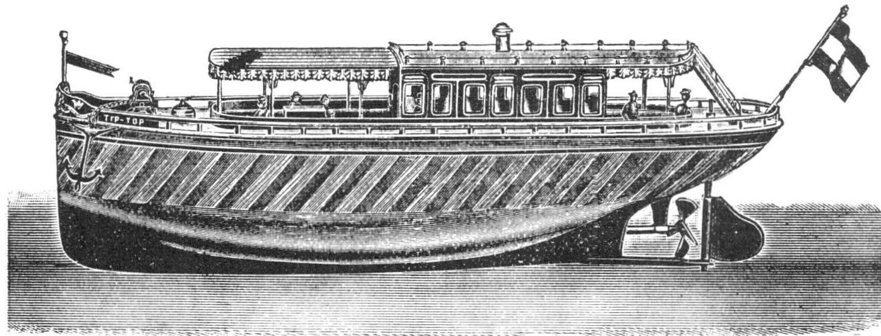

No. 1781. **New Model Clockwork Passenger Boats.**

Fitted with best movement and japanned in best style.

No. 1780 .. **9/6** No 1781 .. **15/-** No. 1782 .. **19/6** No. 1783 .. **32/6**

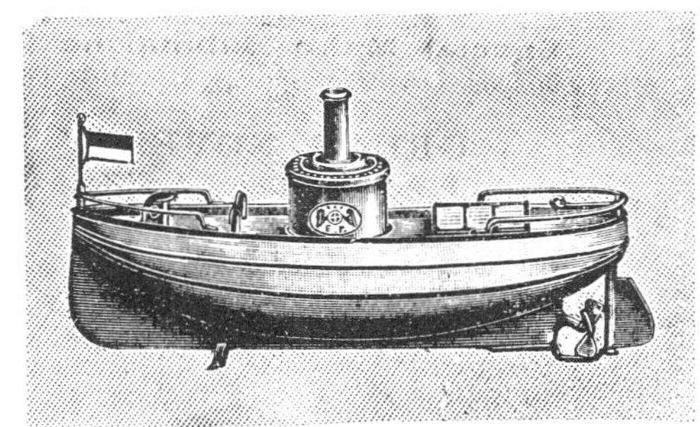

No. 435/1. **Clockwork River Pinnace.**

8¾ in. long. Price **2/6**

Postage 3d.

No. 470. **Clockwork House Boats.**

Price .. **10½d.** and **1/4½** Postage 3d.
Do. Screw. Price **1/11** and **3/-** ,, 3d.

No. 425. **Clockwork Screw Model Steamer.**

No. 25 .. .. Price **6/6** Post 3d. No. 26 .. .. Price **7/11** Post 3d.
No. 27 .. .. Price **9/11** Post 4d.

NOVELTIES.—Firing, Submarine and Motor Boats.

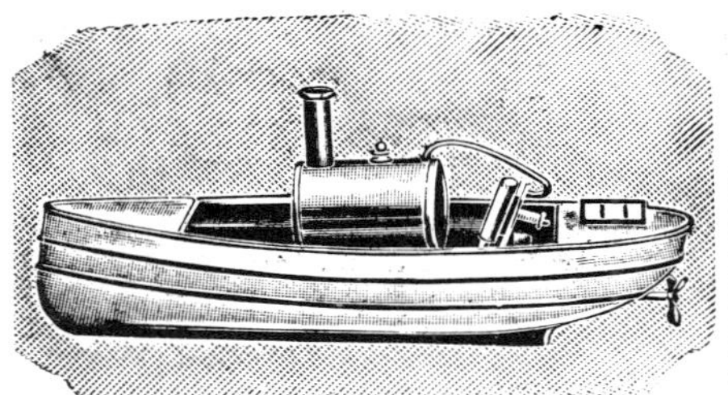

Steamboat, well japanned, fitted with brass boiler and oscillating cylinder.

11½ in. long. Price **1/9** Postage 3d.

Clockwork Auto Racing Boats.

No. 3237	..	**10½d.**	Postage 3d.
,, 3238	..	**1/4½**	,, 3d.
,, 3239	..	**2/-**	,, 3d.

No. 96. **Clockwork Motor Boats.**

No. 91	92	93	94	95	96, as illus.	Postage,
10½d.	1/4½	**1/10½**	2/9½	3/3	4/6	3d.

Clockwork Auto Racing Boat.

No. 3240 .. Price **3/-** Postage 3d.

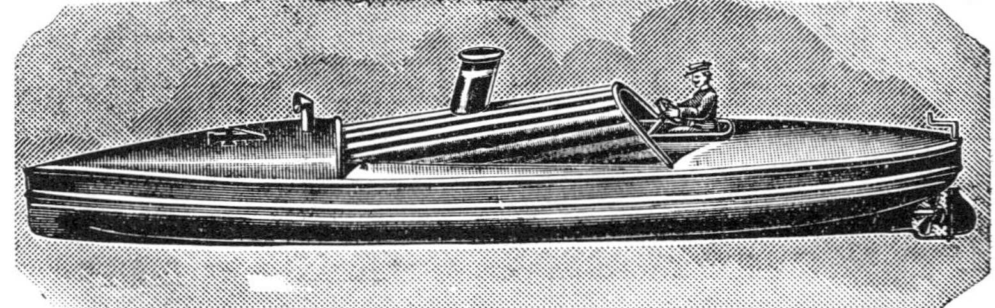

Motor Racing Boat. Great Novelty, typical slender shape, with strong clockwork, travelling very fast, finely japanned, with figures.
Size 12½ in. long, **2/11** 17 in. long, **4/11** 23 in. long, **7/6** Postage 3d.

Racing Motor Boats, fitted with best clockwork movement.
No. 38a, 8¾ in. long, **2/3** Post 3d. No. 38b, 15 in. long, **9/6** Post 4d.

Clockwork Motor Boat.

No. 438. 8 in. long.
1/9 Postage 3d.

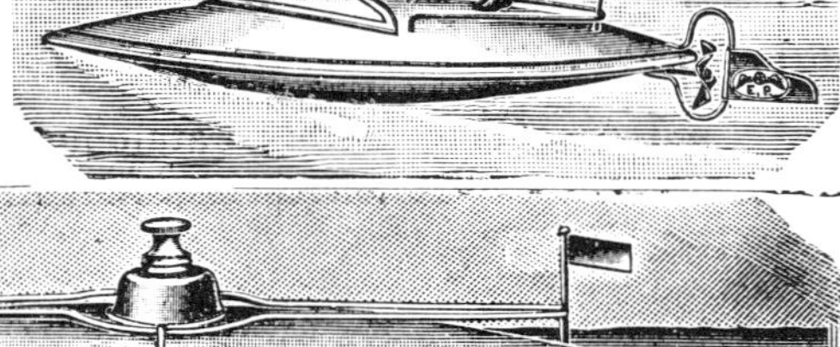

Special Make Submarine Boat.

10 in. long, very strong springs .. **2/6** Postage 3d.

Model Submarine Boats, alternately diving and rising to the surface of the water, finely japanned, with strong clockwork, working excellently, packed in strong, handsome boxes .. .. No. 13331/0, 10¼ in. long, **2/-** Post 3d.
13331/0½, 13⅜ in. long, **3/11** Post 3d. 13331/1, 13⅔ in. long, superior, **5/6** ,, 4d.

GREAT NOVELTY!

Automatically Firing Gun Boats. ☞

Finely japanned and well finished, with best quality clockwork and automatic steering gear. After winding up the clockwork, put the boat on the water. It will sail straight ahead for some distance, then, just as if it intended to attack an enemy, it will suddenly fire a shot, turn round and steer back to its original starting place, as shown in illustration.

With 1 gun, 10¼ in. long	.. ..	**4/9**
Ditto, 14¾ ,,	.. ..	**7/11**

Postage 3d.

With 2 guns, firing 2 shots at intervals, 19½ in. long **11/9**
Postage 4d.

SUBMARINE, TORPEDO and GUN BOATS.

No. 3139. **Clockwork Torpedo Boats.**

No. 3139 .. **10½**d. Postage 3d.
No. 3199 .. **2/-** „ 3d.

No. 152. **Clockwork Submarine.** 8 in. long. **2/-** Postage 3d.

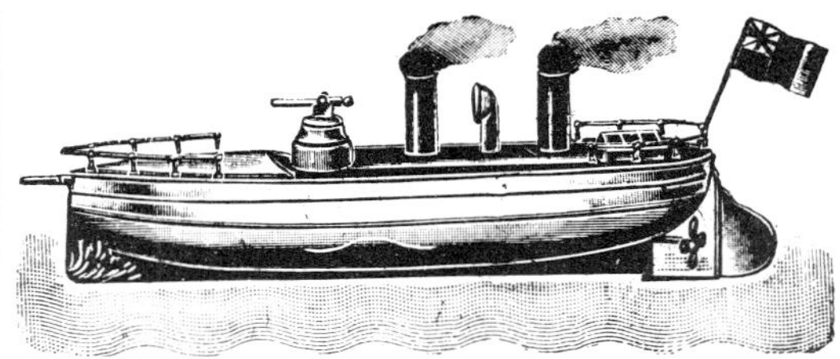

No. 3200.

Clockwork Torpedo Boats.

No. 3200, **3/6** Post 3d. No. 3202, **4/6** Post 3d.

No. 430/1. **Clockwork Gun Boats.**
8 in. long, with 2 cannons .. **3/6** Postage 3d.

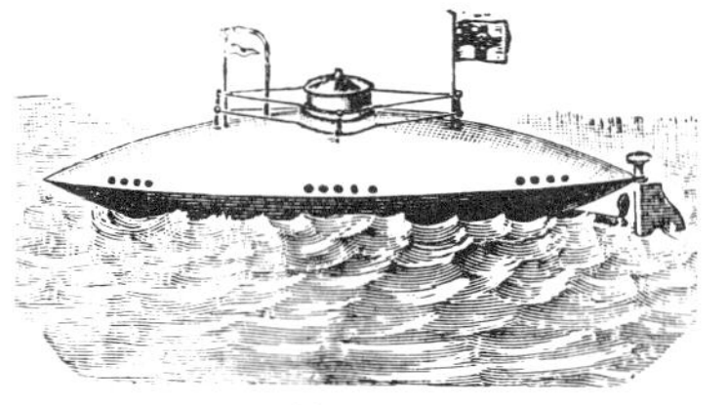

No. 150.

Clockwork Submarine.

6½ in. long .. .. Price **10½**d.
No. 151. Do., 9 in. long „ **1/4½**
Postage 3d.

No. 430/2. **Clockwork Gun Boat.**
12 in. long, with 2 quick-firing guns, 1 armoured turret with 2 cannons. Price **7/6** Postage 3d.

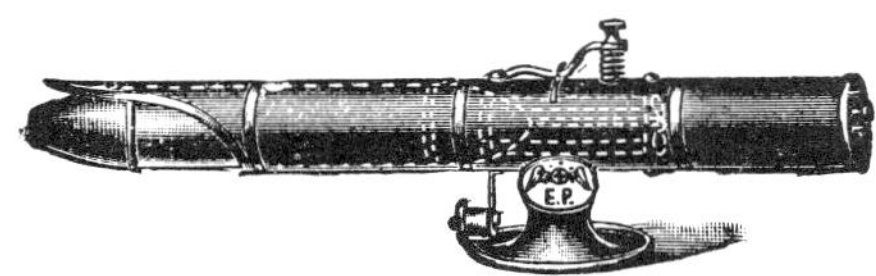

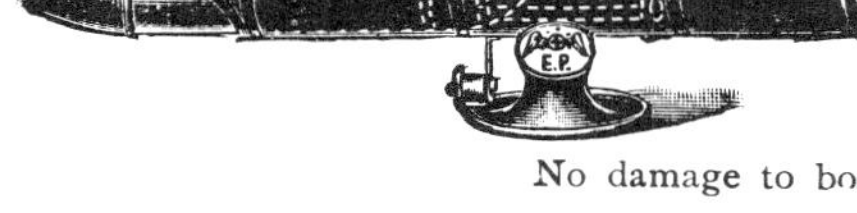

No. 461. **Firing Torpedo.**

Tube 12 in. long. Boat 8 in. long. "This is fired quite easily, and a boat, as illustration, is supplied, which, when struck, sinks.

No damage to boat, which can be refloated.

Price .. .. **6/11** complete. Postage 4d.

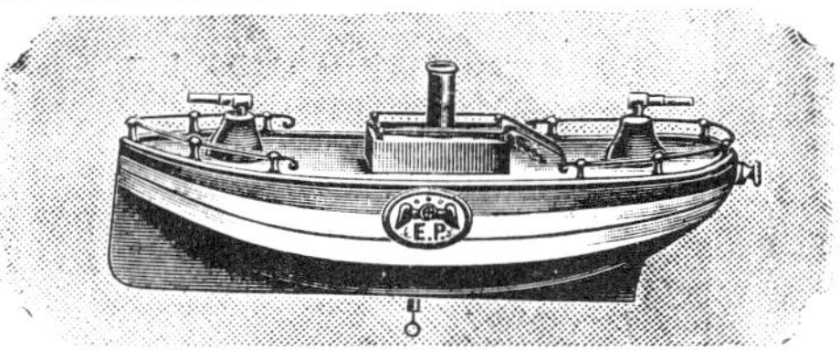

Sinking Boat.

No. 1080. **Torpedo Boat.**
Fitted with best Clockwork movement .. .. Price **13/6** Postage 6d.

CLOCKWORK GUN BOATS.
VERY STRONGLY MADE.
3/6 5/6 7/- 9/11 Post 3d. & 4d.

No. 430/3.

Clockwork Gun Boat.

16 in. long, with 3 quick-firing guns, 1 armoured turret with 2 cannons.
Price .. .. **10/6** Postage 6d.

No. 13957/1.. **Torpedo Boat.**
Finely japanned, typical slender form, with very strong clockwork, with 2 quick-firing guns for crackers, 2 torpedo tubes, 3 ventilators, 2 chimneys, mast and 2 anchors. 27½ in. long.
Price .. **16/6** Postage extra.

No. 13957/2. **Torpedo Boat.**
As illustration. Finely japanned, typical slender form, with very strong clockwork, with 1 quick-firing gun for crackers, 4 torpedo tubes, 3 ventilators, 2 chimneys, mast and 2 anchors.
39½ in. long. Price **35/-**

MAGNETIC FISH PONDS.

Magnetic Sets.

Complete Sets in Glass Top Boxes.

No. 881	1/-	Postage	3d.
No. 884 (as illustration)	2/-	,,	3d.
No. 885	2/6	,,	4d.

Special Line. Magnetic Toys.

No. 18. 14 pieces and magnet .. .. **1/4½** Postage 4d.

Magnetic Toys.

With net complete, **10½d** and **1/10½** Postage 3d.

For MAGNETIC TOYS without Water, see next page.

Magnetic Yacht Race. Complete as illustration, **5/11** Post 4d.

No. 16. **Fish Pond,** consisting of 11 pieces and magnet .. **10½d.**
Postage 3d.

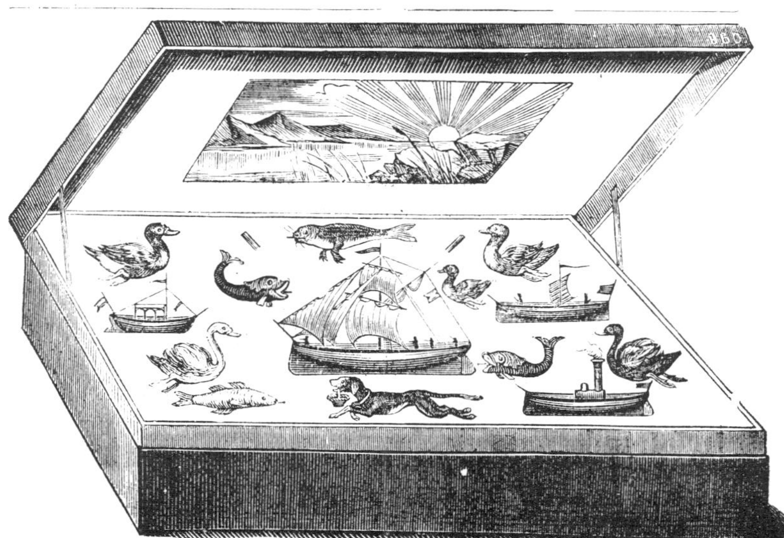

Magnetic Sets.

In square box, complete with tank. No. 1, **1/6**; No. 2, **2/6**; medium size, No. 3, **4/6**; No. 4, **7/6**; No. 4a, **9/11**; No. 5, **12/6** Post 3d. and 4d.

Einsatz

In Box complete with Tank **10½d., 1/10½**
Large size, **3/6** (as illustration). Postage 3d. and 4d.

Magnetic Toys for use with and without Water.

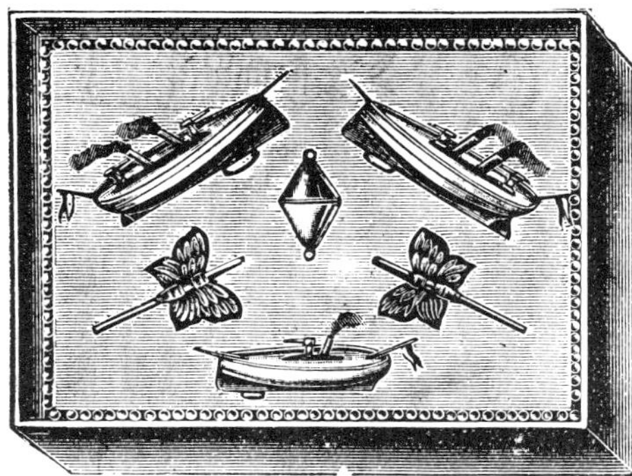

No. 4/7.
Magnetic Fleets.
As illustration.
Price .. .. 10½d. Postage 3d.
No. 48 .. 1/4½ No. 49 .. 1/10½ Postage 3d.

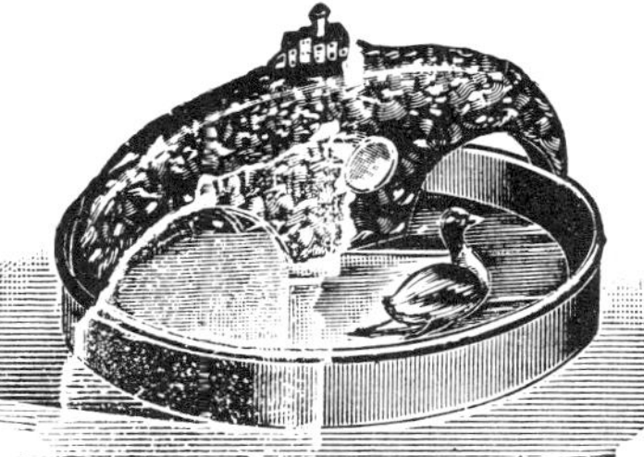

No. 125.
Clockwork Islands.
As illustration.
Price .. 1/10½d.
Postage 3d,

No. 127
Clock-work Islands.
As illustration.
Price 10½d.
Superior, 2/6
Large size, 5/11
Postage 4d.

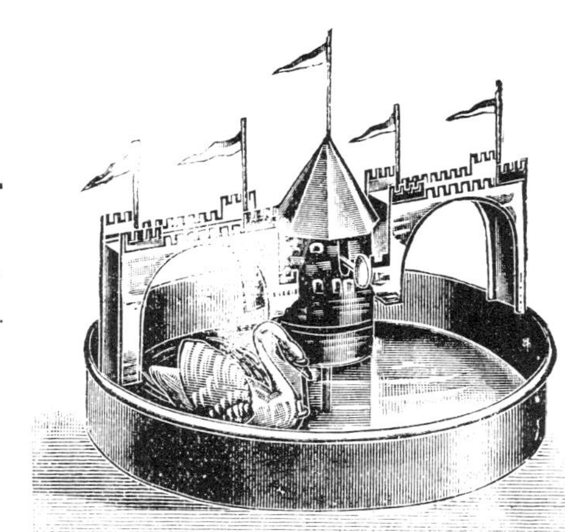

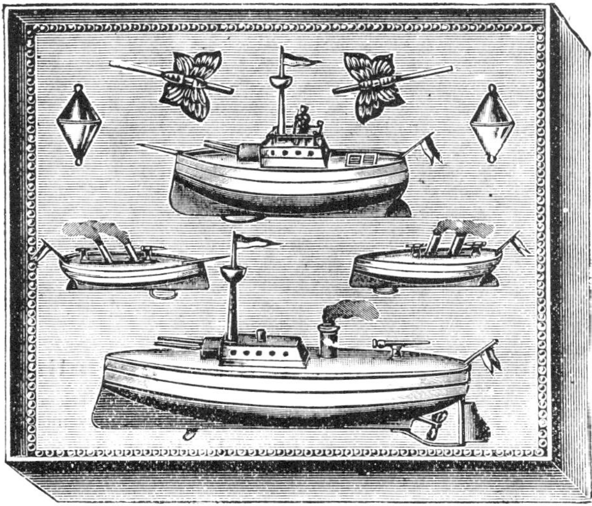

No. 4 0. **Magnetic Fleets.**
As illustration. Price .. 2 11 Postage extra.

Magnetic Fish Pond.
No water required.
Large size Magnetic Fish Fonds, complete, with Folding Tank, Rods, Fish, &c.
All beautifully coloured.
Price .. 4 3
Postage 3d.

Magnetic Fish Pond.
No water required.
Complete as illustration. With Folding Tank, Rod, Fish, Magnet, &c,

No. 1 .. 6d. | No. 3 .. 1/6
2 .. 9d. | ,, 4 .. 3/-

Postage 3d.

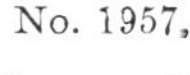

No. 1957,
Magnetic Navy.
Complete in Box.
No. 1 boats,
2/- 2/11
4/6 7/11
9/6
Postage 3d.

New Fighting Fleet.
2 boats, 10½d
3 boats, 1/4½
Postage 3d.

Swimming and Diving Novelties.

Clockwork Diver.
Metal. Dives automatically in the water, rising again to surface. 8½ in. high
Price **5/-** Postage 4d.

Gamage's Clockwork Swimmer.
Splendid idea, swims with a lifelike movement.
Price **3/11** Postage 3d.

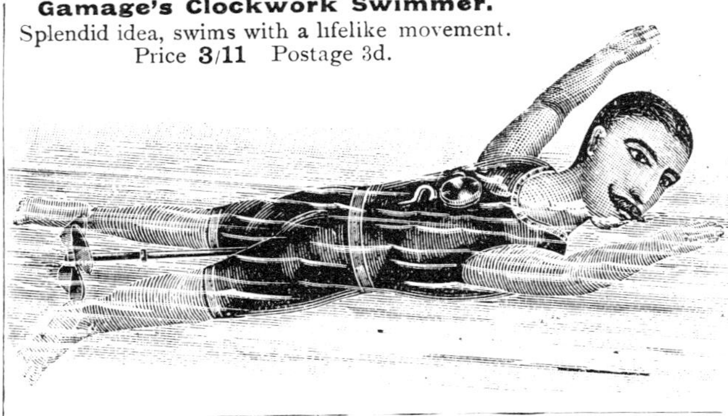

The Funny Diver "Ko-Ko."
Diving in the water and rising again to the surface, through air pressure (air is blown into the tube). Finely japanned, with rubber tube and glass mouthpiece. Packed in cardboard box, 5 in. high .. .. Price **9½**d. .. .. Postage 3d.
Ditto in celluloid, 4¾ in. high **10½**d.

No. 480c.
Model Buoy.
10½d.
Postage 6½d.

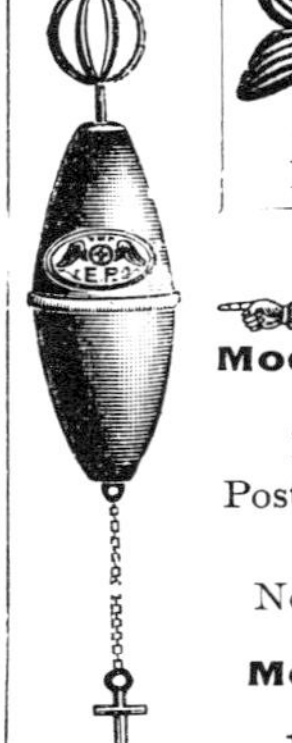

Clockwork Gold Fish.
No. 3261. **10½**d. Post 2d.

No. 480.
Model Buoy.
10½d.
Postage 1½d.

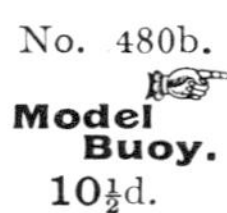

No. 480b.
Model Buoy.
10½d.
Postage 1½d.

Celluloid Diver. 7 in. high, complete with mouthpiece and rubber tube. Price **1/3** Post 3d.

Very original. Great novelty.
Clockwork Water Cycle.
As illust., **2/11** Postage 3d.

The Swimming Ducks.
Fitted with clockwork, **10½**d. Lar er size, **1/10½** Post 2d.

Gamage's Speciality.
Captain Boyton on his Water Tricycle. Fitted with best clockwork movement.
Price **5/11** Postage 3d.

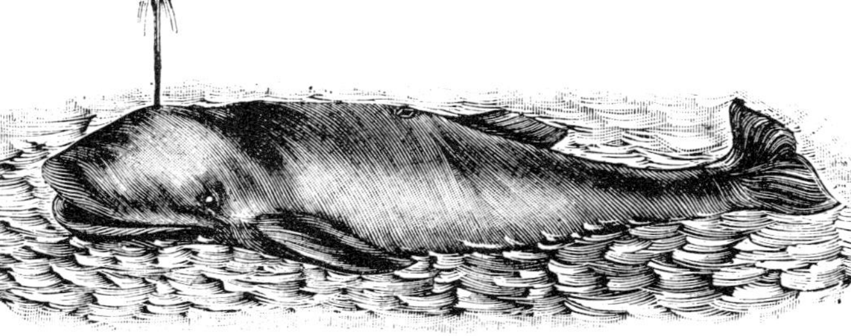

The Spouting Whale.
Fitted with good clockwork movement, which causes the whale to emit water (as illust.) when swimming .. **3/6** Postage 3d.

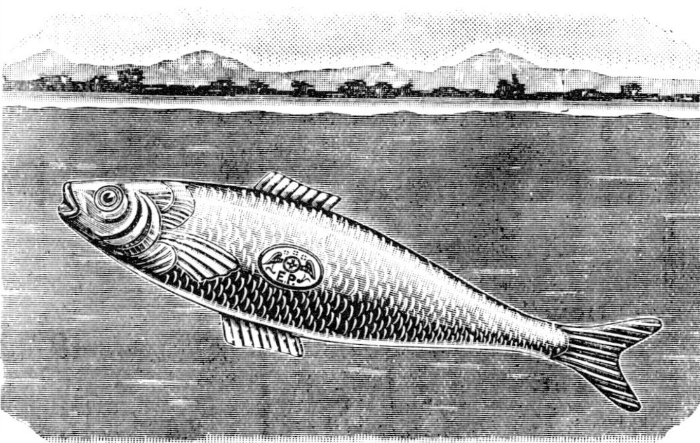

Swimming Fish, will not sink, **1/6** Postage 2d.

Diving Fish. Alternately diving and rising to the surface of the water, cannot sink. Well japanned, fitted with strong clockwork movements .. **2/9** Postage 3d.

Celluloid Fireman.
Price **10½**d. and **1/4½**
Postage 3d.

Gamage's Amateur Fireman.
(Aroused from his peaceful slumbers and attired only in his pyjamas, seeks to put out the fire.
Fitted with fire extinguishing apparatus, quite a novelty.
Price .. .. **3/6** .. Postage 3d.

English Made Metal Soldiers.

ALL OUR SOLDIERS are made exact to scale, that is a Foot Soldier is the same size as a Horse Soldier, and the Horses are in proportion to the men ; whilst the Uniforms and Colourings have been most carefully considered and will be found perfectly correct in all details.

We hold a stock of 500,000 Soldiers of all nations,

But owing to the exceptional demand at Christmas time Customers are urged to give their orders as early as possible so as to prevent any possibility of delay.

Infantry, 4½d. box.

16B Coldstream Guards
17B Lancashire Fusiliers
18B Grenadier Guards
19B Dublin Fusiliers
20B Manchester Regiment

Postage extra on all toy soldiers.

Infantry, 4½d. box.

21B Northumberland Fusiliers
22B Bluejackets
23B Cameron Highlanders
24B Whitejackets
25B Japanese Infantry
26B Russian Infantry

Cavalry, 4½d. box.

1B 1st Life Guards
6B 2nd Dragoons (Scots Greys)
10B 11th Hussars
11B 16th Lancers (Active Service)
13B 17th Lancers
15B Mounted Infantry

Infantry, 10½d. box.

34 Grenadier Guards
111 Grenadier Guards (attention)
120 Coldstream Guards (firing, kneeling)
75 Scots Guards
69 Pipers of the Scots Guards
82 Colours and Pioneers of the Scots Guards
107 Irish Guards
124 Irish Guards (firing, lying)
7 7th Royal Fusiliers
74 Welsh Fusiliers
86 Lancashire Fusiliers
109 Dublin Fusiliers
116 Soudanese Infantry
117 Egyptian Infantry
133 Russian Infantry
134 Japanese Infantry

Infantry, 10½d. box.

9 Rifle Brigade
98 King's Royal Rifles
11 The Black Watch (Royal Highlanders)
15 Argyle and Sutherland Highlanders
77 Gordon Highlanders
118 Gordon Highlanders (firing, lying)
112 Seaforth Highlanders
114 Cameron Highlanders (active service)
122 The Black Watch (firing, standing)
78 Bluejackets
80 Whitejackets
35 Royal Marine Artillery
97 Royal Marine Light Infantry
104 City Imperial Volunteers
67 1st Madras Native Infantry
68 2nd Bombay Native Infantry

Infantry, 10½d. box.

16 East Kent Regiment
17 Somerset Regiment
18 Worcester Regiment
19 West India Regiment
36 Royal Sussex Regiment
76 Middlesex Regiment
96 York and Lancaster Regiment
110 Devonshire Regiment (khaki)
113 East Yorkshire Regiment
119 Gloucester Regiment (khaki)
121 Royal West Surrey Regiment
26 Boer Infantry
91 American Infantry
92 Spanish Infantry
147 Zulus

Cavalry, 10½d. box.

6 Boer Cavalry
45 3rd Madras Cavalry
46 10th Bengal Lancers
47 1st Bengal Cavalry
66 1st Bombay Lancers
71 Turkish Cavalry
115 Egyptian Cavalry
123 Bikanir Camel Corps
135 Japanese Cavalry
136 Russian Cavalry

Cavalry, 10½d. box.

1 1st Life Guards
43 2nd Life Guards
2 Horse Guards
3 5th Dragoon Guards
106 6th Dragoon Guards
31 1st Dragoons
32 2nd Dragoons (Scots Greys)
106 6th Dragoons (Inniskilling)
13 3rd Hussars
8 4th Hussars
12 11th Hussars
99 13th Hussars
23 5th Lancers
24 9th Lancers
128 12th Lancers
33 16th Lancers
81 17th Lancers (active service)
94 21st Lancers (khaki)
100 21st Lancers (review order)

Soldiers to Shoot.

No. 25. Each soldier has the barrel of his gun bored out and a spring attached.

Complete with bullets, 10½d. Post 2d.

38 South African Mounted Infantry
49 South Australian Lancers
83 Middlesex Yeomanry
84 2nd Life Guards and 7th Royal Fusiliers
105 Imperial Yeomanry
127 7th Dragoon Guards

No. 14. Women Officers, Timbrel Band and "The War Cry." Price **10½d.**

No. 10. Officers, Band and Colours. Price **10½d.**

London Made Metal Soldiers.

No. 30. **Drummers and Buglers of the Line.**
Price .. .. 10½d. Postage 3d.

King Edward VII. on Horseback.
A Fine Model
2/- & 2/6
Postage 2d.

No. 27.

Brass Band of the Line.

Price .. .. **1/9** Postage 3d.

101 Full Band of the 1st Life Guards .. **4/9** ,, 4d.

No. 141. **Infanterie de Ligne.** (Infantry of the Line).
Price .. .. **10½d.** Postage 3d

No. 142. **Zouaves.**
Price .. .. **10½d.** Postage 3d.

40 Containing 1st Dragoons, Royal and Somersetshire Light Infantry **1/9**
41 Containing 2nd Dragoons (Scots Greys) and Grenadier Guards .. **1/9**
42 Containing 1st Life Guards, and Royal Sussex Regiment **1/9**
56 Containing Grenadier Guards, and East Kent Regiment **1/9**
59 Containing 2nd Dragoons (Scots Greys) **1/9**
Postage 4d.

88 Containing Seaforth Highlanders and Pipers **1/9**
62 The 1st Bengal Cavalry **1/9**
63 The 10th Bengal Lancers **1/9**
64 The 2nd Madras Lancers, and 7th Bengal Infantry **1/9**
Postage 4d.

No. 140. **Dragoons.**
Price 10½d. Postage 3d.

No. 123. **Bikanir Camel Corps.** Price .. **10½d.** Postage 3d.
48 Camel Corps, with 6 Camels .. .. **1/9** ,, 3d.

No. 138. **Cuirassiers.** Price .. .. .. **10½d.** Postage 3d.

No. 139. **Chasseurs a Cheval** .. .. **10½d.** Postage 3d.
57 Containing 1st Dragoon Guards .. .. .. **1/3** ,, 3d.
58 Containing Royal Horse Guards, 2nd Dragoons, and Mounted Infantry .. .. **1/3** ,, 3d.

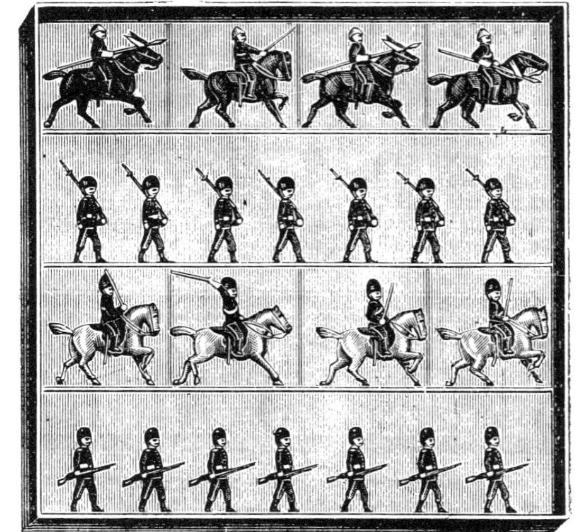

No. 85.

Types of the British Army.

Containing 5th Dragoon Guards, 2nd Dragoons (Scot Greys), and Northumberland Fusiliers.

Price .. .. **1/9** Postage 3d

Toy Soldiers—*continued.* **New Model Ambulance Waggons, Field Artillery, &c.**

No. 146. **Army Service Corps.** 1/9 Post 4d.

No. 144. **Royal Field Artillery.** Price .. .. **4/6** Postage 4d.

No. 145.

Royal Medical Corps (Red Cross).

Price .. .. **2/3** Postage 4d.

No. 39. **Royal Horse Artillery (Corrected and Enlarged).** 4/11 Post 4d.

No. 125. The Royal Horse Artillery (Review Order) **2/-**
(Patented). Copyright Models. Postage 3d

No. 126. The Royal Horse Artillery (Army Service Order) **2/-**
(Patented). Copyright Models. Postage 3d.

No.		Price	Post
52	Types of the British Army, containing 2nd Life Guards, 5th Lancers (Royal Irish)	**1/9**	3d.
50	Types of the British Army, containing 1st Life Guards, 4th Hussars (Queen's Own)	**1/9**	3d.
51	Types of the British Army, containing 11th Hussars (Prince Albert's Own), 16th Lancers (Queen's)	**1/9**	3d.
95	Japanese Cavalry and Infantry	**1/9**	3d.
62	1st Bengal Cavalry	**1/9**	3d.
65	Containing Russian Cavalry and Infantry	**1/9**	3d
59	2nd Dragoons (Royal Scots Greys)	**1/9**	3d.
64	2nd Madras Lancers and 7th Bengal Infantry	**1/9**	3d.
63	10th Bengal Lancers	**1/9**	3d.
	Indian Army.		
61	3rd Madras Cavalry	**2/3**	3d.
60	1st Bombay Lancers	**2/3**	3d.
72	Life Guards as at Waterloo and Present Time	**2/3**	3d.
53	Containing Horse Guards, 4th Hussars and Grenadier Guards	**2/3**	3d.
54	Containing 1st Life Guards, 2nd Dragoon Guards and 9th Lancers	**2/3**	3d.
55	Containing 2nd Dragoons, 3rd Hussars and 16th Lancers ..	**2/3**	3d.
21	Containing 1st Life Guards, 11th Hussars, West India Regiment and East Kent Regiment	**3/3**	4d.
22	Containing Royal Horse Guards, 5th Lancers, The Black Watch and Worcestershire Regiment	**3/3**	4d.
20	Containing Russian and Japanese Cavalry	**3/3**	4d.

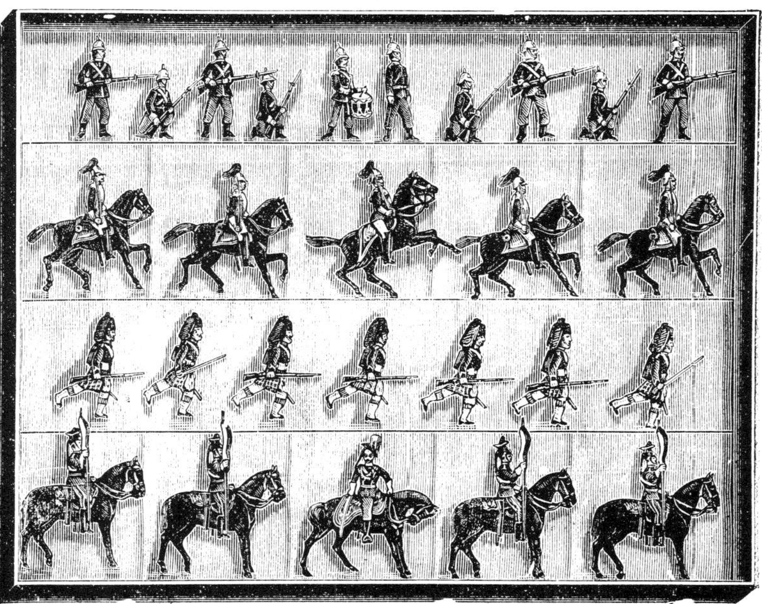

No. 79.

Landing Party of British Sailors.

With breech-loading Field Gun, complete with ammunition.

Price .. .. .. **2/-** Postage 3d.

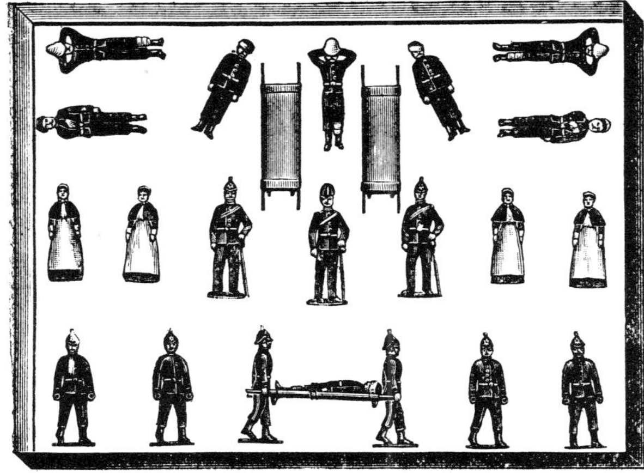

No. 137.

The Army Medical Service, with Nursing Sisters and Wounded

Price .. .. 2/- Postage 3d.

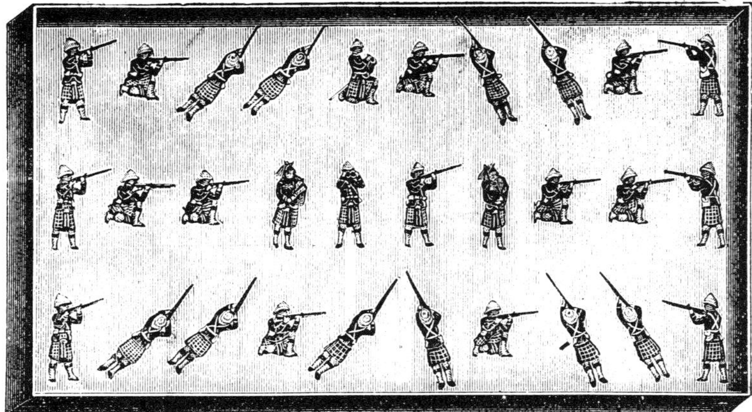

No. 89. Containing the Cameron Highlanders, in three positions (firing).
Price .. .. .. 2/3 Post 4d.

No. 90. Containing the Coldstream Guards, in three positions (firing).
Price .. .. .. 2/3 Post 4d.

No. 73. Price 21/- Carriage paid.

No. 73. This is a very large and handsome Presentation Selection of London-made Metal Soldiers, got up in the best style and packed in a splendidly lined wooden box, with extra tray. Size of box, 2 ft. 2 in. by 1 ft. 3 in. Containing the following Regiments—The Royal Horse Artillery, 2nd Life Guards, 17th Lancers, Royal Welsh Fusiliers, Band of the Line, The Gordon Highlanders, and a General Officer.

No. 28. **Complete Mountain Artillery.**

With Qu ck-firing Gun o take on and off the mules, ammunition included in each box. Warranted a perfect and well-working model. Price .. 2/- Postage 3d.

No. 93. Contains a complete Company of Coldstream Guards, with Officers, Full Band Colours and Pioneers, and a Squadron of Royal Horse Guards, with Trumpeters, &c., packed in a well-made wooden framed box, with tray to lift out. Size of box, 2 ft. by 1 ft. 1 in.
Price .. .. 10/6 Carriage paid.

No. 102. **Types of the British Army.**

Containing the Grenadiers, Coldstreams, Scots and Irish Guards.

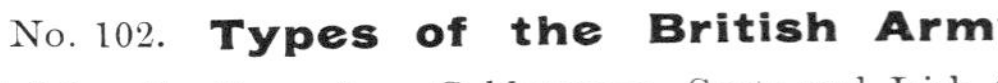

Price .. .. .. 3/3 Postage 4d.

No. 37. **Full Band of the Coldstream Guards.**

Price .. .. .. 3/3 Postage 4d

FAMOUS FOOTBALL TEAMS.

This unique set has just been introduced. It furnishes an exact representation of the various well-known Football Teams in this country. The figures are modelled in excellent style, showing the various positions assumed by the players in the field, and the club colours are faithfully reproduced according to the team represented. The Teams as opposite side are now ready.

Aston Villa.
Derby County.
Sheffield Wednesday.
Notts County.
Everton.
Sunderland.
Manchester City
Preston North End.
Tottenham Hotspur.
Corinthians.
Woolwich Arsenal.
Blackburn Rovers.

Price .. **10½d.** Postage 3d.

LONDON MADE TOY SOLDIERS.

No. 93. This Presentation Case consists of a complete company of Coldstream Guards, with officers, full band, colours and pioneers; with a squadron of Royal Horse Guards, with trumpeters, etc. Packed in well-made wooden framed box, with tray to lift out. Size of box, 2 ft. by 1 ft. 1 in.

Price, complete **10/6**

No. 129. Containing: The 12th Lancers, 2nd Dragoons (Scots Greys), 1st Dragoon Guards, 11th Hussars, and 2nd Life Guards; totalling 70 pieces of cavalry. Size of case, 2 ft. 1 in. by 1 ft. 5 in. by 3 in., with one inside tray.

Price .. .. .. **12/6** each.

No. 132. Containing. The Royal Horse Artillery, 2nd Dragoons (Scots Greys), 11th Hussars, 12th Lancers, 2nd Life Guards, Horse Guards, 7th Dragoon Guards full Band of the Line, the Seaforth Highlanders with pipers, Welsh Fusiliers with goat, the Coldstream Guards standing, lying and kneeling firing, the East Kent Regiment, Mule Battery, 4·7 Naval Gun, and a General Officer; totalling 167 pieces of infantry and cavalry. Size of case, 2 ft. 10 in. by 1 ft. 7 in. by 6 in., with two inside trays.

Price .. .. **48/6** each.

No. 130. Containing a splendid collection of the Scots Guards, marching, running, standing-at-ease, standing, lying and kneeling firing, together with pipers, drum and bugle band, colours and pioneers, mounted and unmounted officers. Size of case, 2 ft. 1 in. by 1 ft. 5 in. by 3 in., with one inside tray, totalling 118 pieces of infantry.

Price .. .. .. **12/9** each.

No. 73. Containing the following regiments: The Royal Horse Artillery, 2nd Life Guards, 17th Lancers, Royal Welsh Fusiliers, Scots Greys, Band of the Line, the Gordon Highlanders, and a General Officer. Size of case, 2 ft. 2 in. by 1 ft. 3 in.

Price .. .. .. **21/-** each.

No. 131. Containing: The Royal Horse Artillery, Mountain Battery, Camel Corps, Scots Greys, 11th Hussars, 5th Dragoon Guards, 17th Lancers, 2nd Life Guards, Horse Guards, full band of the Coldstream Guards, the Scots Guards lying, kneeling and standing firing, the Gordon Highlanders with pipers, the Worcester Regiment. Bluejackets and Whitejackets with 4·7 Naval Guns and General Officer; totalling 275 pieces of cavalry and infantry. Size of case, 3 ft. 9 in. by 1 ft. 11 in. by 6 in., with two inside trays.

Price .. .. .. **70/-** each.

No. 29. **Types of the British Army.** Containing complete Mule Battery 1st Life Guards, 3rd Hussars, 9th Lancers, Queen's Royal West Surrey Regiment (2nd). Price **5/9**. Postage 4d.

Tents for Toy Soldiers.

All made to fold up.

Size 6, White, **5½d.** Size 5, **4½d.** Size 4, **4d** Size 3, **3d.** Size 2, **2½d.** Size 1, **2d.** each. Postage on quantities of 1 to 3, 1d. 3 to 6, 1½d. 6 to 12, 2d. Orders for 1 dozen or more, post free.

Officers' Tents, with table and chairs, **1/4** each Postage 2

New Marquee Tents, 7½d. & **1/4½** Post 2d.

Big Display of Toy Cannons.

No. A. Gun of the

Royal Horse Artillery.

English Make. Patent.

Price .. .. 10½d. Postage 3d.

Rapid Firing Gun

Fires wooden projectiles.

Price 1/- Postage 3d.

Spring Cannon.

Well mounted. Price .. 4d.

? Large size, 6d. Postage 1d.

New Pattern. **Amorces or Paper Cap Cannon.** Breech-loading, with rubber bullets, which can be fired with great precision. Small size 3/11 Large size 4/11

Extra Rubber Bullets 6d. and 9d. doz. Amorces, 3d. per doz. boxes.

Cheaper make Cap Cannon, 6d. Larger size, 1/- Postage 3d.

No. 2286. **Cap Cannon.**

Fires rubber shells.

Price .. 7/6 Postage 4d.

No. B.

4·7 Naval Gun.

English make. Patent.

Price .. .. 1/6 Postage 2d.

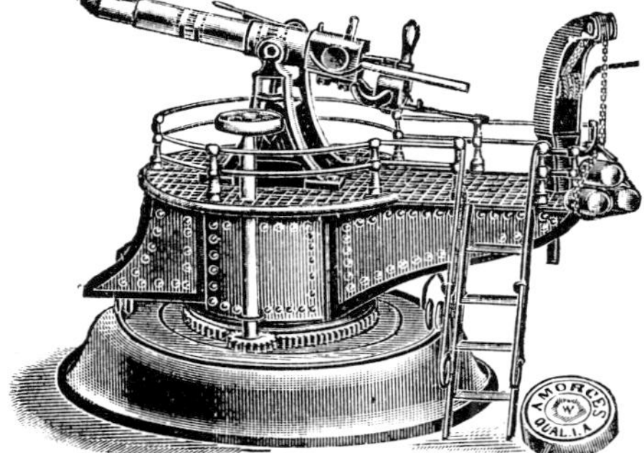

No. 1. **Breech-loading Guns.**

For Coast defence. For firing rubber bullets, with amorces; galvanised brass barrels.

No. 1 .. 9/6 No. 2 .. 13/6

Pellets, 9d. doz. Amorces, 3d. doz. boxes.

Howitzer.

Double-loading (Amorces) Gun.

Price .. .. 5/6 Postage 4d.

The Japanese Monster Cannon.

Fired by means of a spring nicely oxydised. No complicated parts to get out of order. Length 16½ in., height 5 in., wooden base. Complete as illustration, 2/9 Postage 4d.

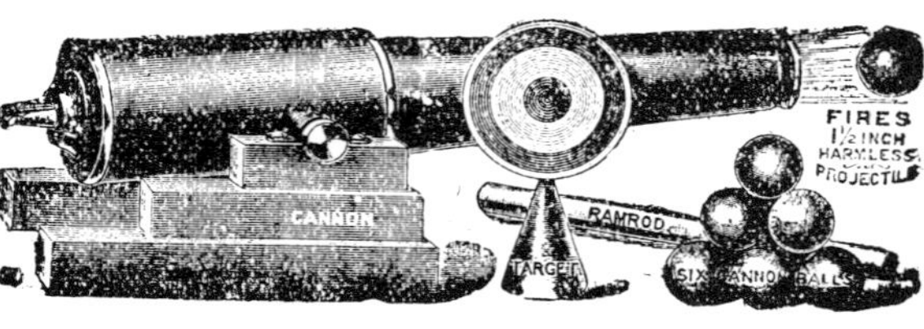

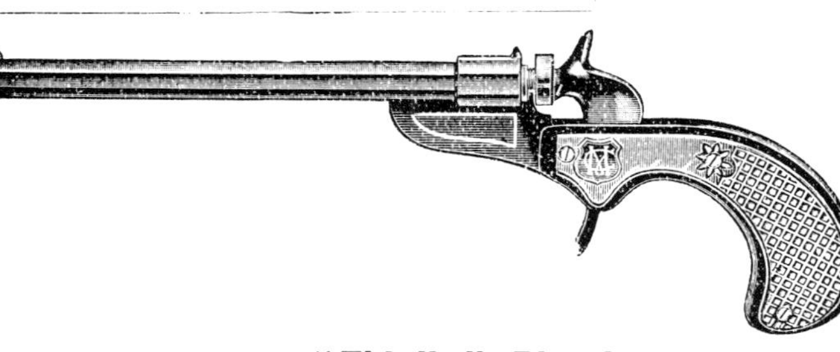

The "Fidello" Pistol.

New Pistol for amorces (paper caps) and rubber pellets. Very accurate. Distance can be increased by using two or more paper caps.

Price .. .. .. 3/6 Postage 3d.

Extra Pellets, 4½d. doz. Amorces, 3d. doz. boxes.

"Fidello." Amorces Breech-loading Gun, hickory stick, nickelled barrel, complete with 1 box of caps, 20 rubber bullets, &c.

Price 6/6

Postage 4d.

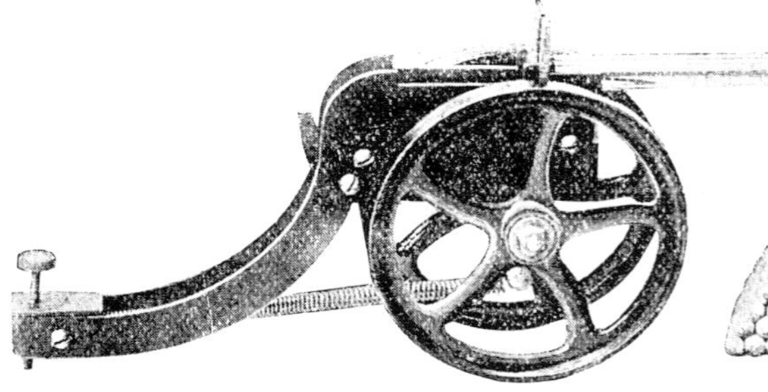

Patent applied for.

New Standard Toy Field Gun. Hits the Mark.

Perfect accuracy in aim and action. The strongest and longest range Toy Gun on the Market.

Simple in construction and of handsome appearance. All parts are easily and instantly adjustable.

11 in. long, 4¼ in. high. **Unbreakable.** Made entirely in Great Britain.

Price, complete with Ammunition, 2/6 Post free.

Double-barrel "Fidello" Guns.

For amorces caps.

Price 18/6

A really handsome and strongly made gun. Fires rubber pellets with ordinary amorces caps.

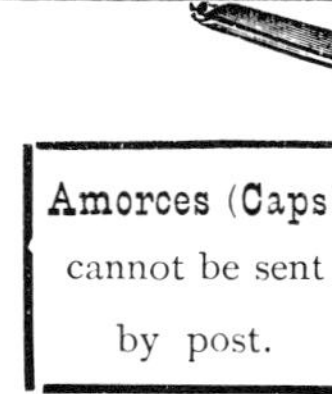

Amorces (Caps) cannot be sent by post.

Extra Rubber Bullets, 6d. and 9d. doz. Amorces, 3d. per doz. boxes. Cheaper make **Cap Cannon,** 6d. Large size, 1/- Postage 3d

GAMAGE'S CLOCKWORK AND MECHANICAL TOY DEPT.

THE LARGEST COLLECTION IN GREAT BRITAIN. ☛ 1/- TOYS for 7½d. ☚ Postage 3d. on each.

Clockwork Clown.
Price ... 7½d.
Postage 3d.

Clockwork Clown with Umbrella.
Price ... 7½d. Postage 3d.

Clockwork Girl with Dumb Bells.
Price ... 7½d. Postage 3d.

Clockwork "Buster Brown"
With Dumb Bells.
Price ... 7½d. Postage 3d.

Up-to-Date Clockwork Novelty.
Mr. Chamberlain
Expounding his Fiscal Policy.
Price ... 6d. Postage 3d.

Clockwork Clown and Star.
Price ... 7½d. Postage 3d.

Boy on Sledge (Clockwork).
Price ... 7½d. Postage 3d.

Clockwork Clown.
Price 7½d. Postage 3d.

Clockwork Elephant.
Price 7½d. Postage 3d.

Reversing Chuckling Mikado. Price 6d.
Postage 3d.

The New Blow Toy.
Very amusing. 6d. Postage 2d.

Flying Bat, 6d. Post 1½d.

Clockwork Crawling Clown. 7½d.

Heavy Swell Clockwork Toy 5½d.
Coolie ,, ,, 5½d.
Flying Birds ,, ,, 5½d.
Postage 3d.

Clockwork Toy. As illustration. 7½d.
Postage 3d.

Clockwork Clown with Ring. 7½d.
Postage 3d.

Clockwork Cock.
Price .... 7½d. Postage 3d.

Clockwork Horse 7½d.
Ditto **Rabbit** 7½d. Postage 3d.

Clockwork Butterfly. Price 7½d. Post 3d.

Clockwork Hen. Price 7½d.;
Ditto **Canary.** Price 7½d. Postage 3d.

Novelties in Clockwork Animals, Birds, etc.

Clockwork Canary .. 10½d. Ditto Hen with Voice Post 3d.

Clockwork Dog.
10½d. Postage 3d.

Clockwork Cat, 10½d. Post 3d.

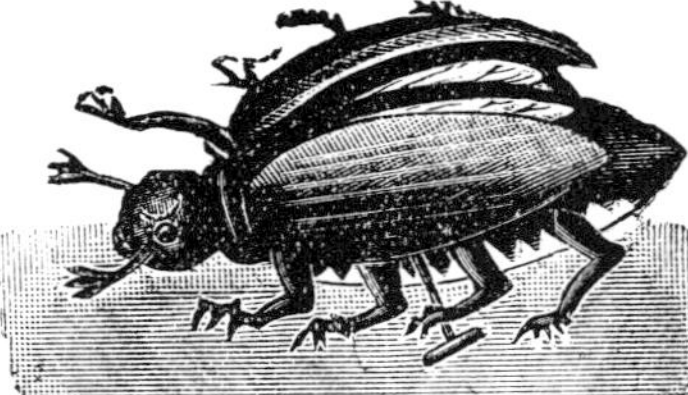

Clockwork Beetle, 10½d. Post 3d.
" Butterfly, 10½d. "

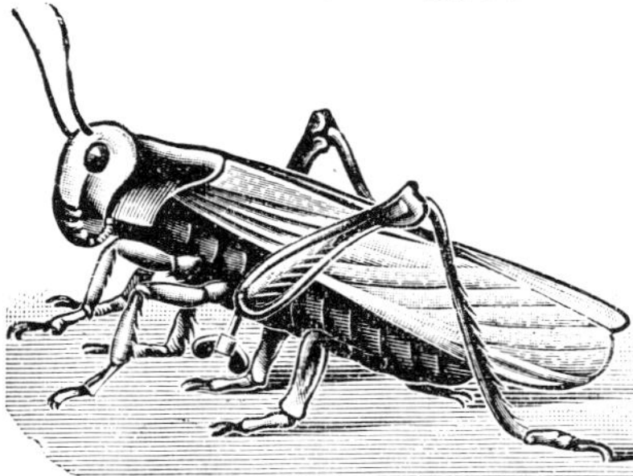

Clockwork Grasshopper.
10½d. Postage 3d.

Mechanical Swallow.
10½d. Postage 2d.

Clockwork Goat and Tailor.
10½d. Postage 3d.

Clockwork Ducks, Chickens, &c.
10½d. Postage 3d.

Clockwork Skin-covered Jumping Animals.
10½d., 1/4½ Squirrel 2/11 Post 3d.

Fur-Covered Tumbling Monkeys.
2/- 2/11 Post 3d.

Amusing and Clever Novelties Suitable for 'Xmas Presents.

Clockwork Clown Training Dog
10½d. Post 3d.

Clockwork Singing Bird in Cage.
As illust. 1/- Postage 3d.
Large size .. 1/11
Postage 3d.

The Jumping Kangaroo.

Jumps with life-like movements on an inclined plane.

Price .. 6d.

Postage 3d.

GAMAGE'S FOR 'XMAS PRESENTS

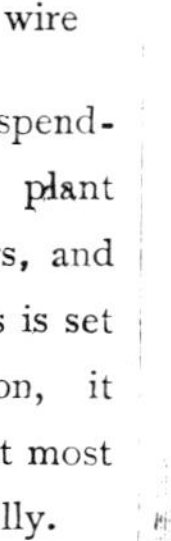

Celebrated Walking Elephant.
Price 6d.
Postage 3d.

Clockwork Butterfly.

Attached to invisible wire

When suspended over plant or flowers, and apparatus is set in motion, it flies about most naturally.

Price .. 14/6
Postage 4d.

—

Also Birds same price.

No. 880/2.

Spiral Railway.
As illustration.
Price .. 10½d. Postage 3d.

Clockwork Girl with Parrot in Cage ... 10½d. Post 3d.

Clockwork Musical Clown and Goose,
1/4½ Post 4d.

10½d. Latest Novelties in Clockwork and Mechanical Toys. 10½d. Postage 3d.

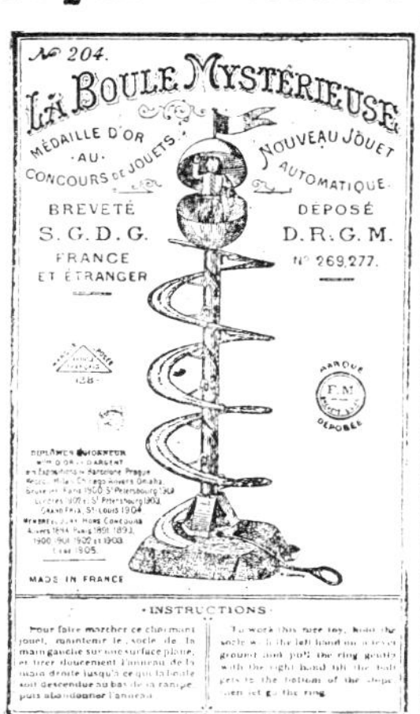

Mysterious Rolling Ball. A 1906 Novelty. Price 1 3 Postage 3d.

Clockwork Nigger Swell, 10½d. Post 3d.

Clockwork Dancing Girl, 10½d. Post 3d.

Punch. Clockwork Toy, 10½d. Post 3d.

Clockwork Skater, 10½d. Post 3d.

Clockwork Nurse, with Baby, 10½d. Post 3d.

Clockwork Clown, with ladder and monkey, **10½d.**

Clockwork Girl, feeding Parrot, 10½d.

Gymnast Walking Parallel Bars, 10½d. Post 4d.

Lancer Tilting Don Quixote, 10½d. Post 3d.

Clockwork Clown, walks backwards, 10½d.

Clockwork Clowns, 10½d. Post 3d.

Clockwork Conjuror, 10½d. Post 3d.

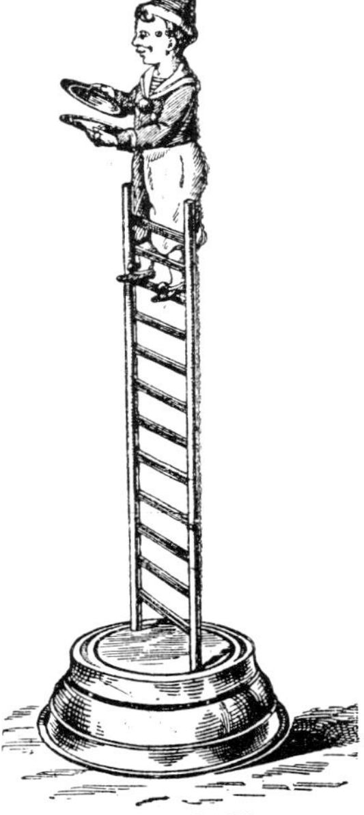

Clockwork Clown and ladder, 10½d. Post 3d.

Clockwork Ladder Climber. 10½d.

Clockwork Clown, Somersaulting, 10½d.

Clockwork Clown (Walking Rope hand over hand), **10½d.** Post 3d.

Special Novelty. Clockwork Clown, with stars, as illustration, **1/-**

Clockwork Juggler, 10½d. Post 3d.

a b

Clockwork Clowns, 10½d. each. Post 3d.

Mechanical Punch. 10½d, Post 3d.

Clockwork Clown' with Stars. **10½d.** Post 3d.

CLOCKWORK MUSICAL & MECHANICAL TOYS (contd.)

No. 69. Clockwork Musical Clowns, **2/11** Post 3d.

No. 21. Clockwork Novelty, **1/9** Post 3d.

No. 93. Clockwork Acrobatic Clowns, **1/9** Postage 3d.

No. 62. Clockwork Musical Clowns, **2/11** Postage 3d.

No. 63. Clockwork Musical Clown, **2/-** Post 3d.

No. 65F. Magic Box, (as illust.) By pushing lever B the figures dance. Complete with a lot of other amusing novelties. Price **10½**d. Best quality **1/4½** Postage 3d.

The Two-Horse Race

Consists of a stand supporting two jockeys on horses, who, when the race is started, race round and round, passing and repassing one another in such a manner that it is positively impossible to tell which will win until the race is over. With this game children can be kept amused for hours. It is strongly made and not likely to get out of order. **10½**d. Larger size with 4 horses, **2/3** Postage 3d.

No. 64.

Clockwork Musical Clowns. **2/11** Postage 3d.

No. 2500.

Mechanical Artist, quite easy, a child can use it, **10½**d. Post 3d.

AMUSING and CLEVER NOVELTIES!!

The Equestrienne.

This consists of a horse galloping round a ring, as at a circus. Standing upon the back of the horse is a fairy, who as the horse passes under the bar, stoops and then jumps, clearing the bar in a most clever manner, alights upon the horse's back and stands balancing herself until the horse reaches the the bar, when she again jumps, continuing to ride and jump until the horse stops.

Price **10½**d. Postage 3d.

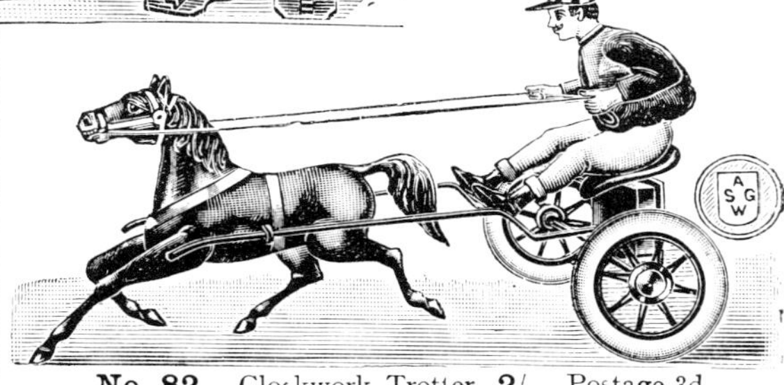

No. 82. Clockwork Trotter, **2/-** Postage 3d.

No. 31. Clockwork Dog Cart, **2/11** Postage 3d.

No. 35. Clockwork Victoria .. **3/6** Postage 3d.

CLOCKWORK AND MECHANICAL NOVELTIES—*continued.*

No. 1295.

Clockwork Nigger in Donkey Cart.

Price .. .. **10½d.** Postage 3d.
Do., Horse and Cart, **10½d.** ,,

No. 80.

Clockwork Billiard Playing with 6 Balls.
Price .. **1/3** Postage 3d.

No. 1090.

Clockwork Goat and Cart .. **10½d.** Postage 3d.
,, **Delivery Tricycle** with Boy, **10½d.** ,,

No. 1086. **Clockwork Woman** with Geese in Cage, **10½d.** Clockwork Rabbit with Wheelbarrow, **10½d.** Clockwork Woman do., **10½d.**

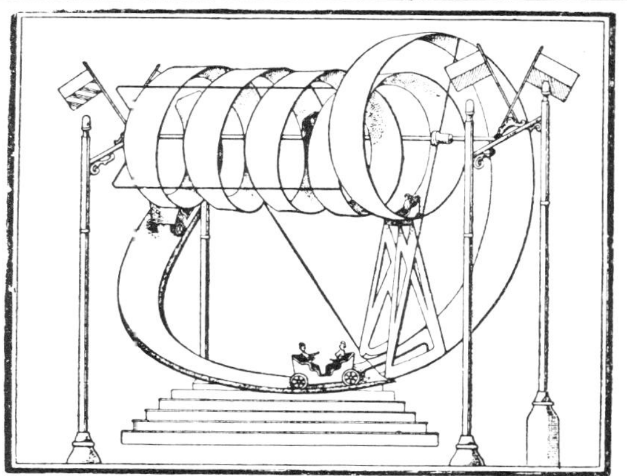

No. 120. **Aerial Whirligig** **3/6**
Extra cars 3d. each.

No. 1230. **Clockwork Toy,**
Tilting the Ring .. **2/6** Postage 3d.

No. 7390/6. **Perpetual Motor Track .. 2/6** Postage 3d.

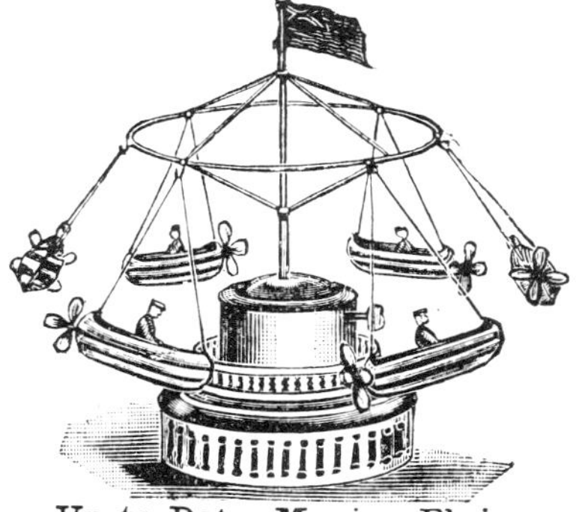

Up-to-Date Maxim Flying Machines.

No. 1 .. .. **10½d.** Postage 3d.
,, 3 .. .. **1/10½** ,, 3d.
No. 4A, with music, **2/9**
,, 5 ,, **3/6**
Postage 3d.
,, 6 ,, **4/11**
Postage 4d.

No. 7394/51.

Cyclist Looping the Loop.

Price .. **10½d.** and **1/10½** Post 3d.

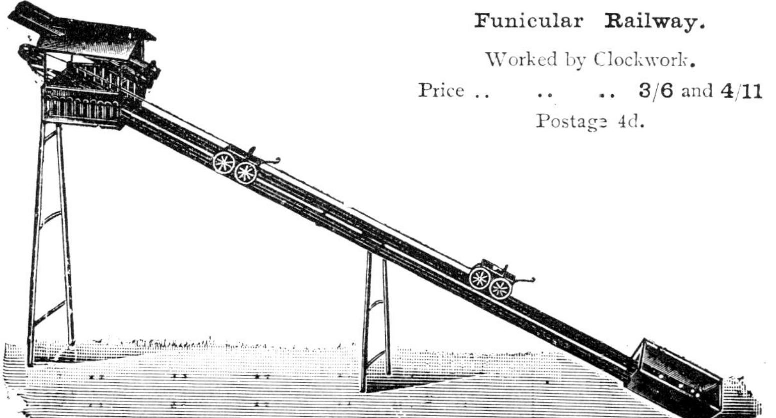

Funicular Railway.

Worked by Clockwork.

Price .. .. .. **3/6** and **4/11**
Postage 4d.

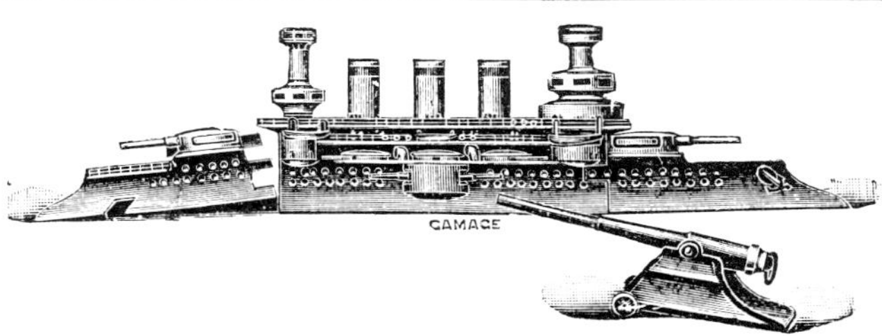

Russo-Japanese War.

Great Novelty. Battleship and Gun, complete with ammunition. The Battleship when hit by bullet flies into the air and breaks up. Price **10½d.** complete. Postage 3d. Extra Shot 2d. per doz.

CLOCKWORK MOTOR CARS, etc.

No. 9/1.
Clockwork Motor Car, with hooter. Double movement.
Price .. .. **1/10½** Postage 3d.

No. 7.
Clockwork Motor Brougham.
Price .. .. **10½d.** Postage 3d.

No. 13773. **Model Motor Cars,** with extra strong, best quality clockwork, pneumatic tyres, cooling box in fine brass finish and brake, adjustable to run various figures, 7⅛ in. long, 4 in. wide, 4⅜ in. high. Price .. **3/-** Postage 4d.

No. 488G. **Clockwork Motor Car,** as illustration.
Price .. .. **1/4½** Postage 3d.

No. 67.
Clockwork Motor Car.
Price .. .. **5½d.**
Postage 3d.

No. 13660/0. **Model Racing Car,** finest finish with extra strong, best quality clockwork, pneumatic pattern rubber tyres, and reserve tyre, with real cushions on the seats, cooling box in fine brass finish and brake, front wheel adjustable to run straight or in a circle. Size, 8¼ in. long, 4⅜ in. wide, 4 in. high.
Price **6/6**
No 13660/2. Size, 15⅜ in. long, 5⅝ in. wide, 6⅜ in. high.
Price .. .. .. **8/11** Postage 4d.

No. 14138/57. **Clockwork Motor Car,** adjustable axle, pneumatic pattern rubber tyres and brake, 9⅝ by 5⅞ in. by 5⅛ in. high. Price .. **6/6** Postage 3d.

No. 73.
Clockwork Motor Omnibus.
Price .. .. **5½d.**
Postage 3d

No. 56. **Patent Clockwork Motor Car.** Stops when lifted. Price .. .. **2/11** Postage 3d.

No. 1237. **Large Clockwork Motor Car,** powerful movement. Price .. .. **2/11** Postage 3d.

No. 78.
Clockwork Motor Brougham.
Price .. .. **5½d.**
Postage ½d.

No. 481. **Clockwork Racing Cars.**
With 1 figure .. .. **7½d.**
„ 2 „ .. .. **10½d.**
Postage 3d.

CLOCKWORK MOTOR CARS, ETC.

No. 864/7. Clockwork Touring Car with six passengers .. **1/11** Postage 3d.

No. 1489. Clockwork Motor Car with collapsible hood, **1/11** Postage 3d.

Clockwork Electric Brougham, very strong.
No. 57 .. 2/11 **No. 57a, .. 3/6** Postage 3d.

THE NOVELTY OF THE SEASON.
Realistic Motor Smash, price **2/4½** Post 3d.

No. 483. Clockwork Motor with hood .. **10½d.** Postage 3d.

No. 14126/1. Clockwork Motor Cab, finished in best style pneumatic tyres, adjustable axle, to run straight or in a circle, with 1 lantern 7⅞ in. long, 4 in. wide, 4¾ in. high **9/6** Postage 4d.

No. 14126/2. Ditto, with 2 lanterns, 8¼ in. long, 5 in. wide, 5⅛ in. high, **11/9** Postage 4d.

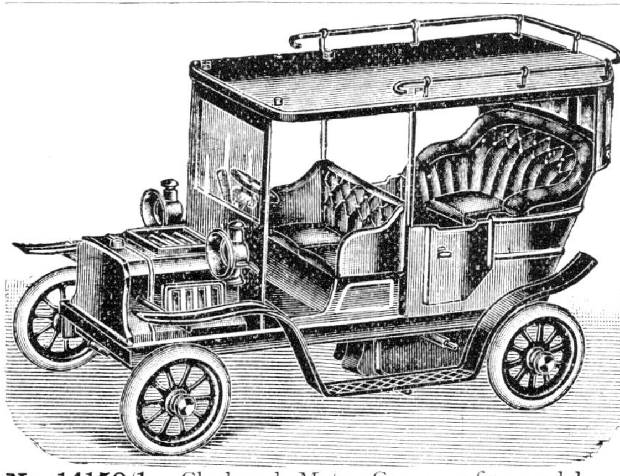

No. 14150/1. Clockwork Motor Car, very fine model, adjustable axle, to run straight or in a circle, doors to open, with 1 lantern, 8¼ in. long, 4⅛ in. wide, 5⅛ in. high, **10/6** Post 4d.

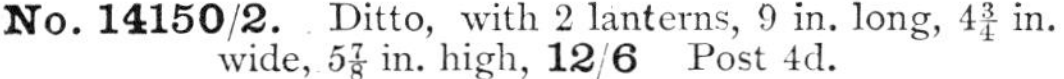

No. 14150/2. Ditto, with 2 lanterns, 9 in. long, 4¾ in. wide, 5⅞ in. high, **12/6** Post 4d.

No. 68. Clockwork Steam Roller **5½d.** Postage 3d.

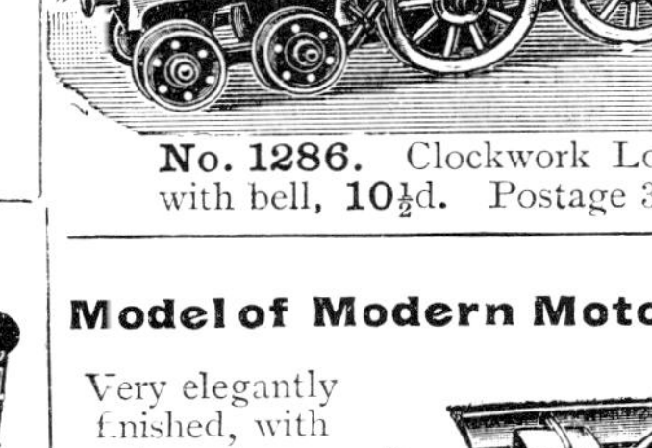

No. 1286. Clockwork Loco. with bell, **10½d.** Postage 3d.

No. 1266. Clockwork Motor Car, **5/11** Post 4d.

No. 14001/1. Clockwork Motor Car, pneumatic rubber tyres, adjustable axle, with doors to open, brake with hooter sounding "Tuff-Tuff," 8¼ in. long, 4⅛ in. wide, 4 in. high, **7/11** Post 3d.

Model of Modern Motor Car

Very elegantly finished, with extra strong, best quality clockwork, pneumatic rubber tyres, plastic seats (imitation cushions), cooling box in fine brass finish, and brake. Front axle adjustable to run straight or in a circle, with lanterns.

No. 13659. Very elegant finish, with finely nickelled head light for real burning.

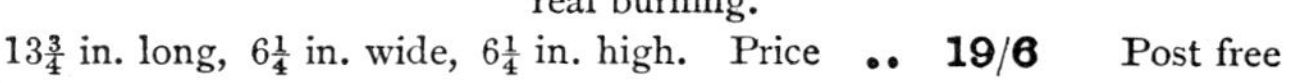

13¾ in. long, 6¼ in. wide, 6¼ in. high. Price .. **19/6** Post free

Novelty 1906. Motor Car Accident. A Clockwork Toy which travels on the ground at a good speed and suddenly smashes up, the chauffeur being thrown into the air. **2/4½** Postage 3d.

CLOCKWORK MOTOR CARS, etc.

Clockwork Racing Car.
As illustration. Price, **1/10½** Postage 3d.
Large size, **3/6** Postage 3d.

Clockwork Racing Car.
Price .. **10½d.**
Postage 3d.

Clockwork Racing Car, with Voice.
Price .. **10½d.** Postage 3d.

Clockwork Motor Mail Van.
Doors to open.
Price .. **1/4½** Postage 3d.

Special Lines—Clockwork 'Bus.'
Price **6/6** Postage 3d. Model of London Makes.

Clockwork Double Racing Cars.
Price .. **1/10½**
Postage 3d.

Clockwork Motor Brougham.
Price .. **7/11** Postage 3d.

Clockwork Motor Cycle.
Price .. **10½d.** Postage 3d.

Motor Goods Van.—With roof and curtains, finely japanned, with extra strong clockwork. Front axle adjustable for straight and circular run, with brake and rubber tyres. 7¾ by 4 by 5¼ in. Price **3/11** Postage 3d.

Clockwork Cyclist, with Bell.
Price ... **10½d.** Postage 3d.

Clockwork Omnibus (London Street Car).—With extra strong, best quality clockwork, nicely japanned, with up-to-date advertisements. With brake, front axle adjustable for straight and circular run, wheels with india rubber tyres with chauffeur.

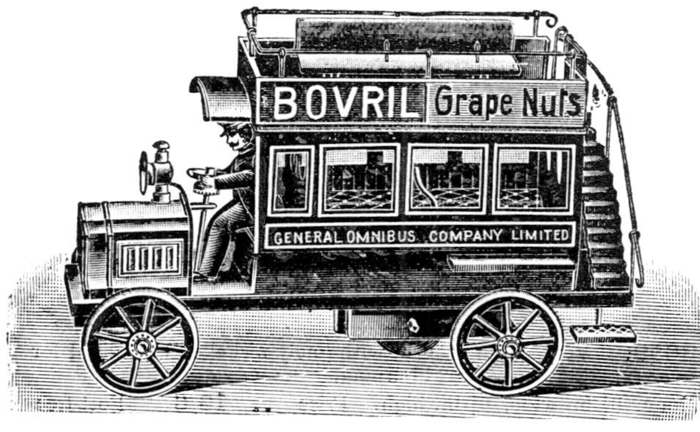

3909/0 With one Lantern, 10 by 4½ by 6½ in. high, **8/11** Postage 4d.

Small Model Clock-work Motor Bus.

10½d.

Post 3d.

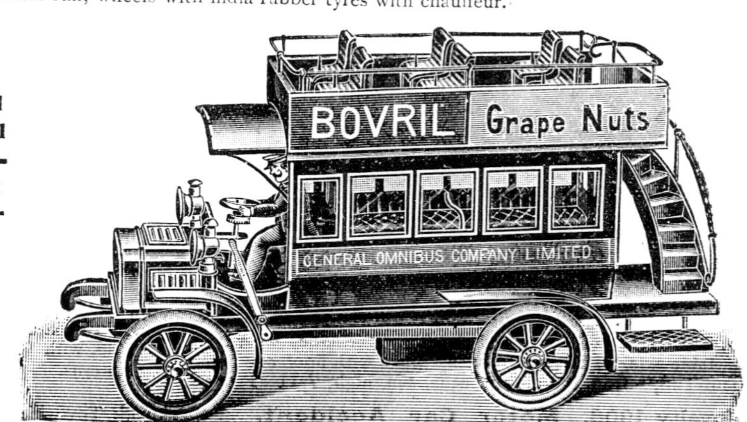

13909/1 With two Lanterns, 13 by 5 by 7½ in. high, **17/6** Postage 4d.

CLOCKWORK FIRE ENGINES.

No. 60 P

Clockwork Fire Engine.

With Galloping Horses

Price .. .. **10½d.** Postage 3d.

No. 58. **Clockwork Motor Fire Engine.**

Price .. **2/6** Postage 3d.

No. 1158 P.

Clockwork Fire Engine.

Price .. .. **1/10½** Postage 3d.

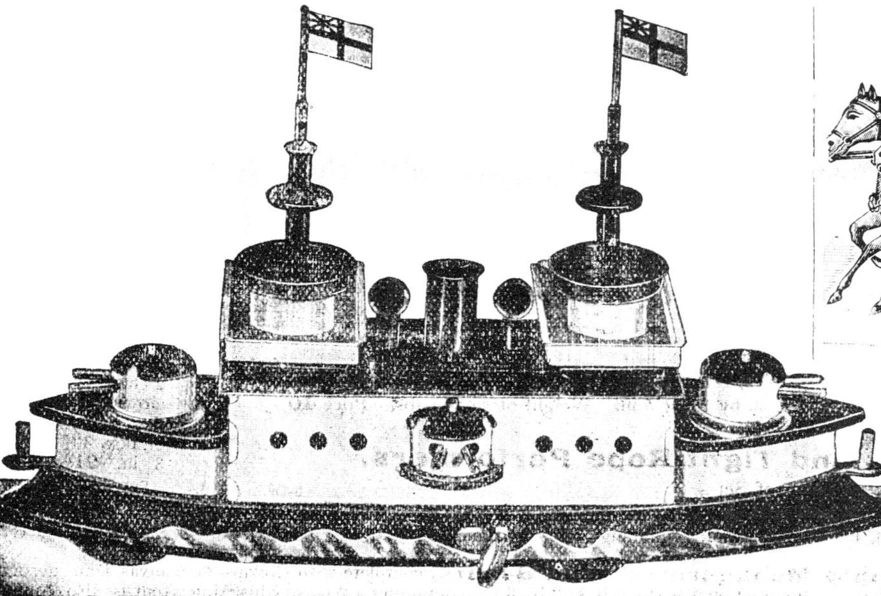

No. 1061/3. **Clockwork Battleship** .. .. .. Price **10½d.** Postage 3d.

No. 37/38.

Clockwork Fire Engine.

Best make and finish.

Price .. .. .. **5/11** & **7/6** Postage 4d.

Larger size, with felt covered horses .. Price **10/6**

Postage 3d

No. 1062/3.

Fleet of 3 Ships, leading Boat propelled by clockwork.

Price .. .. **1/9** Postage 3d.

No. 1062. **Mechanical Battleship.** Price **5½d.**

Clockwork, larger size .. .. Price **10½d.** Postage 3d.

MECHANICAL SAILING BOAT	Price **3d.** each	Postage 3d.
CLOCKWORK „ „	„ **4½d.** & **10½d.**	„ 3d.

No. 1062 ..	**Fleet of 4 Ships,** leading Boat propelled by clockwork, as illustration	Price **2 3**	Postage 3d.
„	**6** „ „ „	„ **2 9**	„ 3d.
„	**7** „ „ „	„ **3/3**	„ 4d.

HUMPTY DUMPTY CIRCUS.

These Figures are made of solid wood, leather, rubber, etc., jointed similar to a doll, but on a new principle. They are very neat and attractive in appearance, and are almost unbreakable. Their heads, arms and legs are movable, so that the figures can be set in an endless variety of positions, producing the most fascinating and grotesque results. The Donkey and Elephant can be stood on one leg, made to sit up or lie down; in fact, almost anything but talk. The Clowns can be set in the most ridiculous positions, and made to imitate any variety of tricks on the ladder, in mid-air. The numerous results attainable are most astonishing and amusing, not only to children but to grown persons as well.

N.B.—Each of the sets, except the 15/1, is accompanied with an elegant book of illustrations and rhymes, containing 150 photographic views, showing the different tricks that can be done with these toys. Set No. 15/1 is accompanied with an illustrated sheet showing 13 different tricks.

No. 15/1. Set of 4 pieces, Clown, ladder, barrel and chair. Size of box, $12\frac{1}{4}$ by $4\frac{3}{4}$ by $3\frac{1}{4}$ in. **2/-** Postage 3d.

No. 20/1. Set of 3 pieces. Clown, donkey and chair. Size of box, $13\frac{1}{2}$ by $9\frac{1}{4}$ by $3\frac{1}{4}$ in. **3/11** Postage 4d.

Carriage extra.

No. 20/3. Set of 7 pieces. 3 clowns, 2 ladders, bench and chair. Size of box, $13\frac{1}{4}$ by $9\frac{1}{4}$ by $3\frac{1}{4}$, **4/3** Postage 5d.

No. 20/7. Set of 5 pieces. Clown, ladder, elephant, chair and barrel. Size of box, $14\frac{1}{4}$ by $12\frac{1}{4}$ by $3\frac{1}{4}$ in. **5/6** Post 5d.

No. 20/16. ☞ Set of 7 pieces. 2 clowns, elephant, donkey, 2 ladders, chair and barrel. Size of box, $20\frac{3}{4}$ by $11\frac{1}{4}$ by $3\frac{1}{4}$ in. **7/11** Postage 6d.

No. 20/22. Set of 10 pieces. Clown, horse, lion, chair, ladder, barrel, whip, and 3 stands. Size of box, $20\frac{3}{4}$ by $12\frac{1}{4}$ by $3\frac{1}{4}$ in. **8/-** Post 6d.

EXTRA FINE. ☞ No. 20/26. Set of 15 pieces. 3 clowns, elephant, donkey, 2 ladders, 2 chairs, barrel, 4 stands, flag. Size of box, 24 by $18\frac{1}{4}$ by $3\frac{1}{4}$. **12/6** Postage 9d.

EXTRA FINE. No. 20/31. Set 22 pieces. Elephant, horse, donkey, dog, 2 chairs, 2 ladders, 3 clowns, tramp, hoops, flag, barrels, etc. Size of box, $30\frac{1}{4}$ by $18\frac{1}{4}$ by $3\frac{1}{4}$ in. **21/-** Weight per set 8 lbs. 7 oz.

No, 20/36. Set of 33 pieces. A very fine assortment, Size of box, 30 by 18 by 5 in. Weight of set, 17 lbs. Price **40/-**

Humpty Dumpty Acrobats and Tight Rope Performers.

No. 20/50. Contents of Set—

1 tight rope and fixtures with base (6 by $32\frac{1}{2}$), 2 lady acrobats, 2 gent acrobats, 1 poodle, 1 Chinaman, 1 hobo, 1 fancy clown, 2 ladders, 2 chairs, 1 table, 1 ball, 1 tub, 1 barrel, 1 goblet, 1 bottle, 1 pedestal (No. 12/11), 1 hoop, 1 parasol, 1 spinning plate, 1 balancing rod, 1 flag, 1 booklet .. Price **27/6**

MENAGERIE. No, 20/45. **Humpty Dumpty Menagerie of Wild Beasts,** complete with Collapsible Canvas Tent, decorated with Flags of all Nations, with movable divided curtain in the back, mounted on a wooden base 2 by 3 ft., containing a 2 ft. sawdust ring; tent is also equipped with trapeze and rings. This set contains a variety of new and lifelike animals, constructed with the same mechanical excellence that has given the Humpty-Dumpty Circus a world-wide fame. These animals are correctly painted with waterproof colours, and where hair or fur is employed it is true to nature. All of the animals balance perfectly in a great variety of positions. Attention is called to the two flexible cages, which can be formed into circles or ovals, or the two can be combined to make a single large cage for trained animal performances. This outfit may be recommended for its educational value in teaching young children the leading characteristics of wild animals. In packing, the tent folds flat on the base, and the figures and animals and accessories are packed in separate paste-board boxes, which, with the tent and fittings, are supplied in a light but strong wooden box, 39 by $26\frac{1}{4}$ by 6 in. Weight 41 lbs. Price .. **70/-**

Contents of Set No. 20/45. 1 lion, 1 giraffe, 1 buffalo, 1 tiger, 1 leopard, 1 zebra, 1 hippopotamus, 1 alligator, 1 bear, 1 ostrich, 1 monkey, 1 camel, 1 lady rider, 1 Turk lion tamer, 1 fancy clown, 3 tubs, 2 chairs, 2 ladders, 1 ball, 1 flag, 1 hoop, 1 whip, 1 goblet, 1 barrel, 2 pedestals No. 12/11, 1 pedestal No. 12/12, 2 cages, 1 tent and ring combination, 1 booklet.

Menagerie. No. 20/41. Set of 26 pieces, comprising ring master, lady rider, 2 clowns, and an assortment of animals and accessories .. .. Price **35/-**
No. 20/40. Ditto, different assortment of animals .. .. ,, **35/-**

☞ No. 20/41.

Carriage extra on all Humpty Dumpty articles.

For separate pieces, see next page.

Special Articles for HUMPTY DUMPTY TOYS (shown on previous page).

No. 10/1. Clown, cotton dress, **1/2** each. 10/3. Hobo, **1/6** 10/4. Negro Dude, **2/3** 10/5. Lady Circus Rider, **2/-** 10/6. Ring Master, **2/3** Postage 3d.

No:		
10/7.	Lion Tamer ..	**2/3**
10/8.	Lady Acrobat ..	**2/-**
10/9.	Gent ,, ..	**2/-**
10/11.	Chinaman ..	**2/-**
11/11.	Lion	**3/6**
11/12.	Tiger	**3/6**
11/13.	Leopard	**3/6**
11/14.	Hippopotamus ..	**2/9**
11/15.	Giraffe	**3/6**
11/16.	Camel	**2/9**
11/17.	Zebra	**2/9**
11/18.	Buffalo	**3/6**
11/19.	Bear	**2/-**
11/20.	Alligator ..	**2/9**
11/21.	Ostrich	**2/-**
11/22.	Monkey	**2/-**

Postage 3d.

No. 30/5. **Complete Collapsible Tent,** with ring and fitted with trapeze and rings, decorated with flags of all nations as described in No. 20/45. Size 24 by 36 by 36 in. Price **13/9**

No. 30/4.

Circus Ring.

Size $24\frac{1}{4}$ by $24\frac{1}{4}$ by $1\frac{3}{4}$ in. **4/-** /10, Tight Rope, **2/9** 12/18, Cages, **1/3** /13A, Table, **3d.** /11, Pedestal, **6d.** Chair, **3d.** Tub, **4d.** Barrel, **3d.** Ladder, **3d.** Circus Hoop, **2d.**

Elephant, **2/9** each. Donkey, **2/-** Postage 3d. extra. Horse, **2/9** Ditto, with bridle, **3/-** Poodle, **2/-** Goat, **2/-**

Postage extra on all Humpty Dumpty Toys.

FOR COMPLETE SETS SEE PREVIOUS PAGE.

Gamage's Choral Tops, Gyroscopes, etc.

Musical Twin Top.

As illustration.

Price .. .. $10\frac{1}{2}$d

Postage 3d.

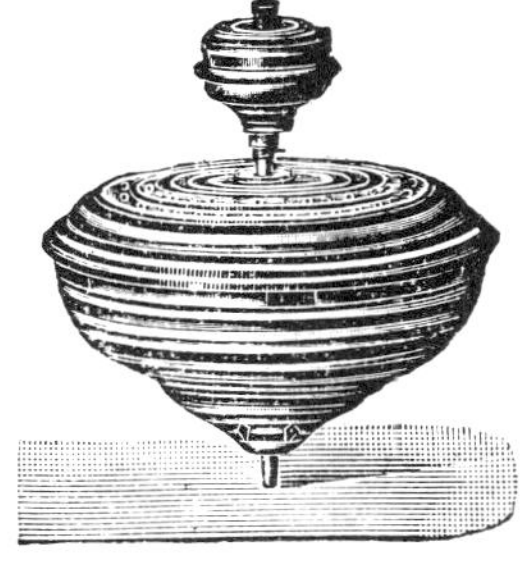

Metal Spring Top.

Very strong. No string required.

Price .. $6\frac{1}{2}$d. and $10\frac{1}{2}$d.

Postage 3d.

No. 1.

Choral Top.

Nicely japanned.

Price **6d.** Postage 3d.

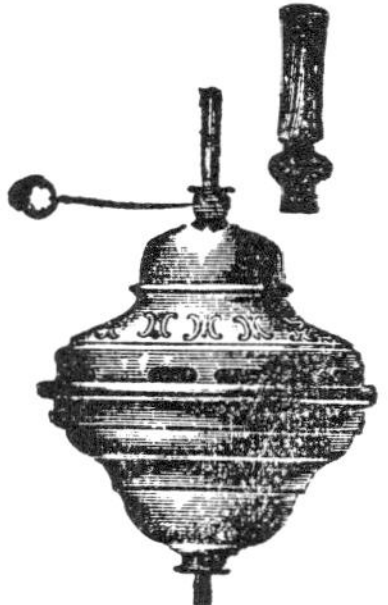

No. 2, as illustration.

Price .. $10\frac{1}{2}$d.

Postage 3d.

No. 3. **Choral Top**

Price .. **1/6**

Large size .. **2/-**

Postage 3d.

No. 9.

Nickel Plated Rack Top.

Price .. 1/-

Postage 3d.

The Gyroscope.

A truly wonderful scientific toy.

Will spin in any position.

Complete in box with stand.

No. 0. .. $6\frac{1}{2}$d.

No. 1. .. $10\frac{1}{2}$d.

No. 2 .. $1\ 4\frac{1}{2}$

Postage 3d.

Large size **Gyroscopes,** very strongly made. Prices /3 6/6 Postage 4d.

No. 24034.

Metal Spiral Top.

No string required.

Price $10\frac{1}{2}$d. Postage 3d.

The Latest Novelty! Patent Spinning Disc Tops.

A Game of Skill for Boys and Girls. No String or Whip required.

No. 9a. Disc Humming Top, with spinning stick, **10½d.** Postage 3d.

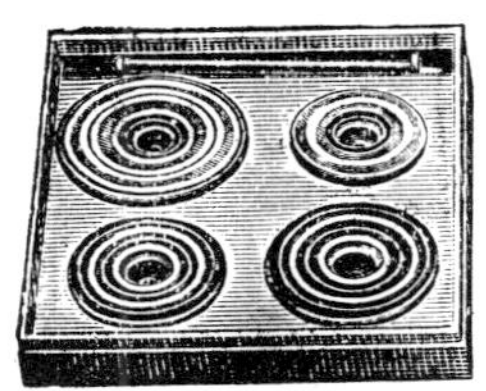

Disc Tops, with spinning stick.
No. 10. Set of 2 large tops, **10½d.**
No. 11. Set of 4 smaller do. **10½d.** Postage 3d.

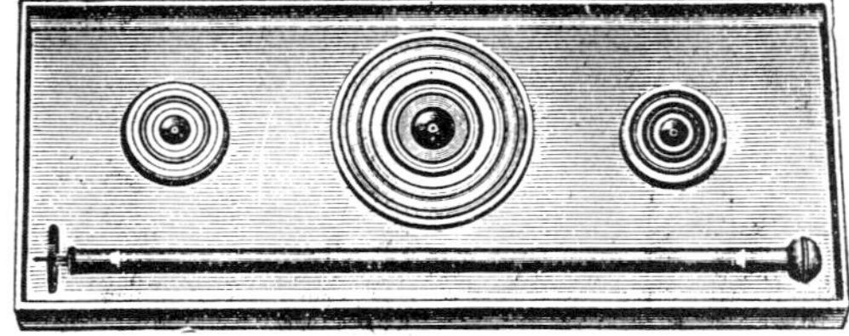

No. 12. Set of 3 Disc Tops, 1 large and 2 small, with long spinning stick .. **2/4½** Postage 4d.

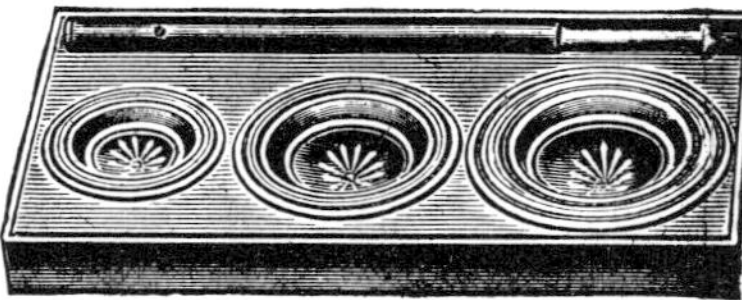

No. 14. Set of 3 Large Disc Tops, with spinning stick. **1/9** Postage 3d.

No. 17. Cameleon Disc Top. The colours change when top is spinning, giving a very pretty effect. Price **10½d.** Postage 3d.
No. 18. Larger size, **1/4½** Postage 3d.

No. 19. Set of 3 Cameleon Disc Tops, with long spinning stick, **2/11** Postage 4d.

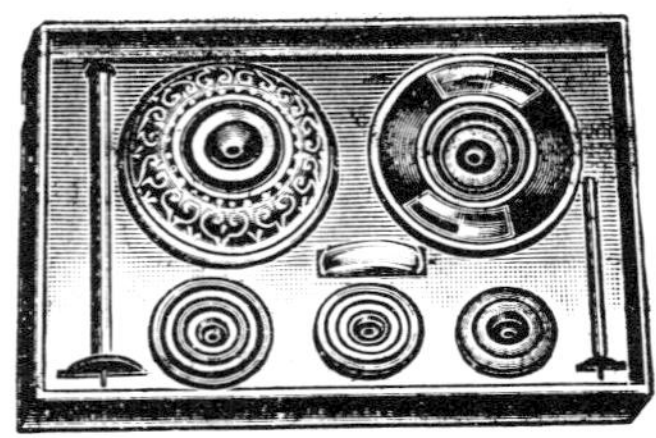

No. 21. Set of Disc Tops, as illust., with 2 spinning sticks. **2/6** Postage 3d.

Just the Sport for Boys & Girls.

No. 15. Choral Top, with spinning stick. **1/6** Postage 3d.

No. 16. Larger size ditto, as illustrated, **2/4½** Postage 4d.

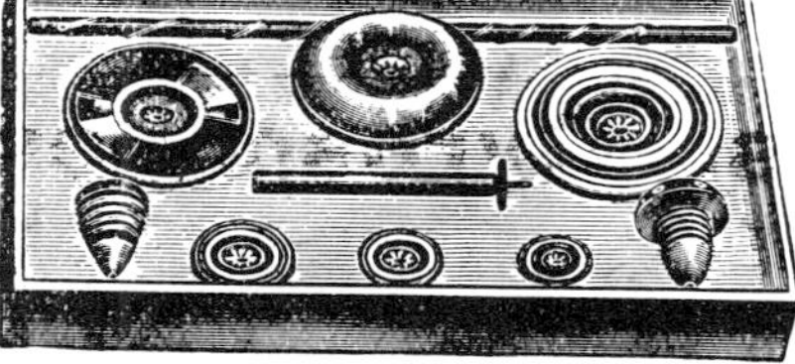

No. 7. Set of Disc Tops, as illust. **3/6** Postage 4d.

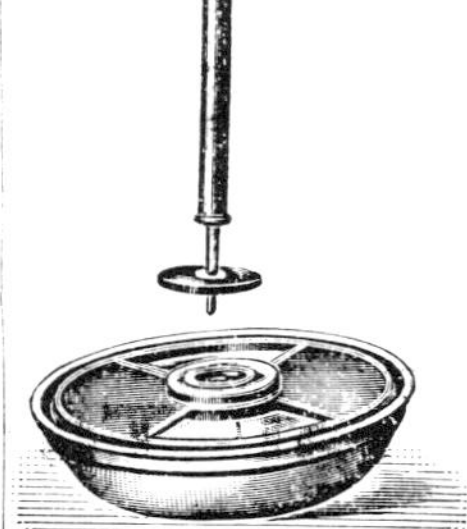

No. 20. 1 large Cameleon Disc Top, with long spinning stick, in box complete, **2/-** Postage 4d.

No. 21. Set of Disc Tops, as illustration. Complete in box, **4/3** Postage 4d.

No. 22. Set of large Disc Tops, complete in box, **4/6** Postage 4d.

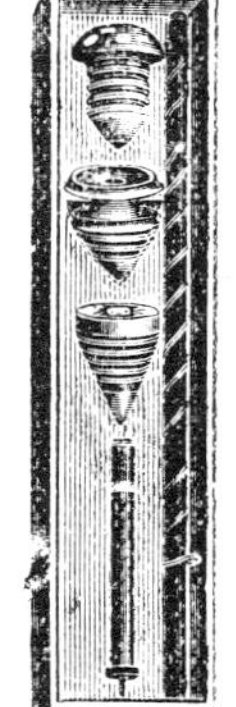

No. 23. Wooden Disc Top, with stick. **1/3** Postage 3d.

The "Never-Stop" Humming Top.

No string required.

Price .. .. .. 4½d. Postage 3d.

Set of Boxwood tops, containing boxwood peg top, whip top, humming top and bandalore.

No. 1. In cardboard box 5½d.
No. 2. Better quality .. 9½d.
No. 3. Best quality .. 2/2
Postage 3d.

Immense Variety at GAMAGE'S.

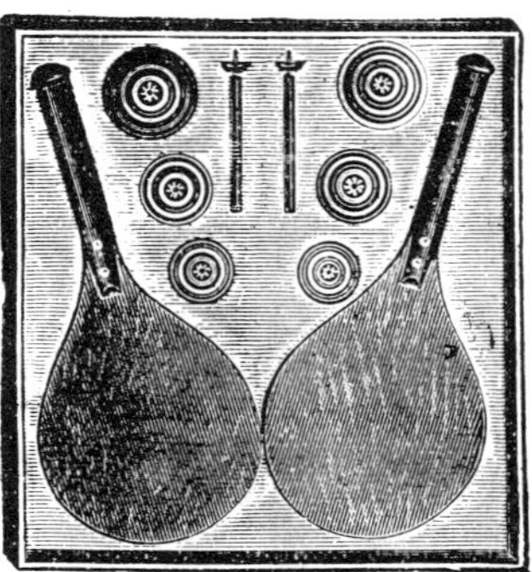

No. 8.

Set, containing 6 Tops, 2 spinning sticks, 2 bats for top throwing.

Price .. **2/9** Postage 3d.

Long Spinning Sticks

For Disc Tops.

10½d.

Post 3d.

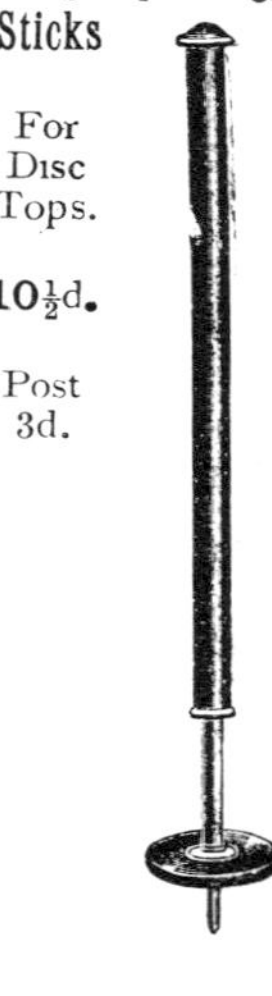

Animated Japs, Novelty Balls, Money Boxes, etc.

The very Latest

Animated Jap.

With Top Hat.
The Best Novelty of the Season.

Price .. 1/- Postage 2d.

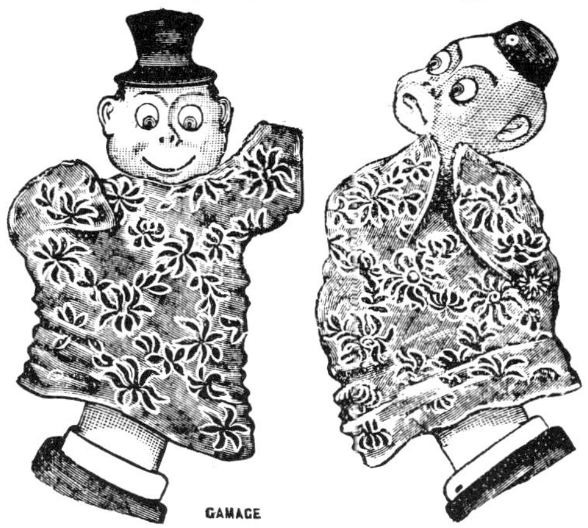

Animated Jap Clowns.

Very amusing and original. Causing plenty of fun.
Price .. 6d. each. Postage 2d.

Novelty Balls.

Various Kinds. Price .. .. 4½d.
Postage 1½d.

Novelty Pipe.

Which, when blown, produces Animal's Head.

Price .. 4½d.

Postage 3d.

The Animated Jap.

Very funny. 4½d. Post 2d.
Do. with wig, 5½d. Post 2d.

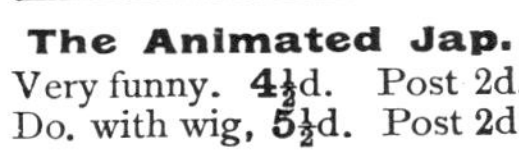

Shut

Holds 20/- Can be set to any sum up to that amount from 6d. Takes shillings and sixpences. Strongly made in oxydized silver, the works being of solid brass and steel. Cannot get out of order. Marvellous value.
Price 5½d. Postage 3d.

The World's Pocket Bank.

Open. ☛

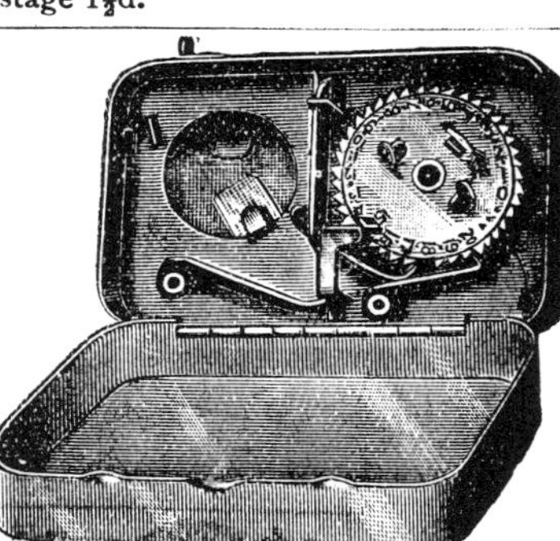

New Clock Money Box.
Price 9d. Postage 3d.

Fancy Wood Money Boxes.

Assorted oak, mahogany and walnut, polished.
Price 10½d. Postage 3d.

Polished walnut boxes, well finished.
Price 1/6 Postage 3d.

Do., Double,
2/- & 2/6 Postage 3d.

Special Cheap Line.
Price 4½d. Postage 3d.

Registered No. 479,588.

The Record Money Box.

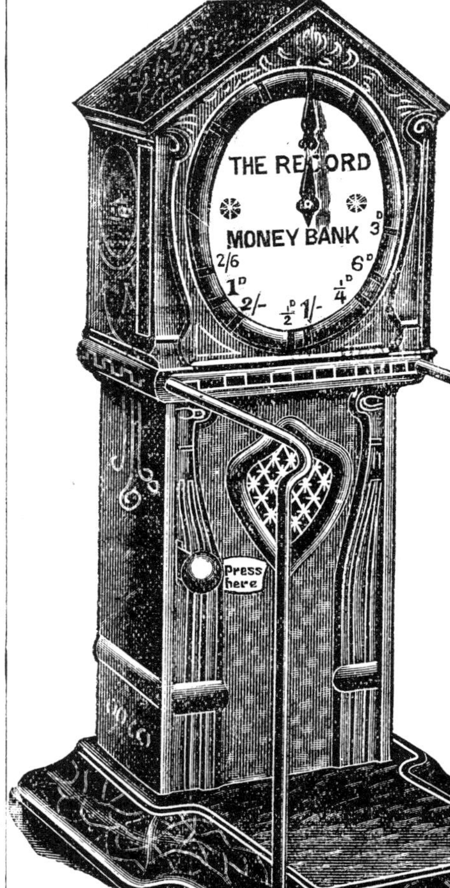

It will weigh copper and silver coins, as follows: ¼d., ½d., 1d., 3d., 6d. 1/-, 2/-, 2/6 and record them on the dial. No bad money possible. The Record is made in beautiful assorted art colours and will not tarnish, and is a splendid Model of a Weighing Machine. Each with lock and key. Price 5d. each. Postage and packing 3d

The Model Savings Bank.

CLOSED.—First turn the handle, then the bell rings and the drawer automatically opens.
Price .. 5½d. Postage 4d.

The "Daily Mail" Copper Bank.

Can be set to any amount.

Takes copper coins only.

Price 10½d. Post 2d.

The "Daily Mail" Silver Bank.

Holds £5 19s. 6d. Can be set to any sum up to that amount from 6d. Takes shillings & sixpences. Strongly made in imitation oxydised silver.
Price 10½d. Post 2d.

Our Doll Department

HAS RECENTLY BEEN ENLARGED AND WILL BE FOUND TO BE THE MOST COMPLETE IN EUROPE.

Thousands of Dolls to select from.

Baby Dolls. Boy Dolls. Sailor Dolls. Jap. Dolls. Rubber Dolls. Dressed and Undressed Dolls. Golliwogs. Baby Bunting. English Dressed Dolls. Walking Dolls. Rag Dolls. Wooden Dolls. Kid Body Dolls. Unbreakable Dolls.

Rag Dolls, unbreakable, nicely dressed, **6**d. **10½**d. **1/- 1/4½ 1/10½**

Superior **2/6 2/11** Rag Baby Dolls, **1/10½ 2/4½**
Double Rag Dolls, with 2 faces and 2 different dresses. A novelty. Price **3/6**.
Printed Rag Dolls, neatly dressed, nothing to break, Price **6**d. **10½**d. and **1/10½** Postage 3d.

Soft Body Dolls. Pretty face, curly hair, jointed, movable eyes.
11 13 15½ in.
1/- 1/6 & **1/11 2/6**
18 in. **3/6** Post 3d.
Dressed Dutch Dolls **1/-** Postage 3d.

Red Riding Hood, dressed dolls, 8½ in., **1/6** Do., jointed, 10 in., **1/11** 12 in., **2/11**
Fairy Dolls, suitable for 'Xmas Trees. **1/10½ 2/11 3/6** Post 3d.

Sailor Dolls. Girl, 10½ in. high, **1/11, 2/6** Post 3d. 13 in. sup., **3/11** 18 in., **8/11** & **9/11** Post 6d.

Special line, **6½**d. Boy, 10 in. high, **2/4½** Post 3d. 13 in., sup., **5/11** Post 3d.

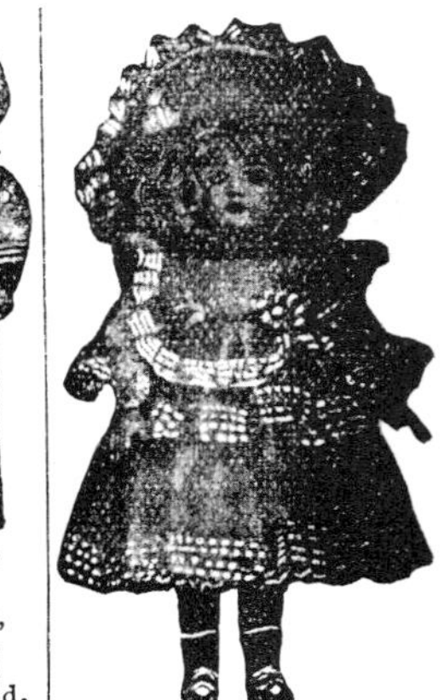

Tiny Dolls. Gamage's Special Small Size Dressed Dolls, moving eyes
6½ and 7 in., **10½**d. and **1/-** 8 and 9 in., **1/4½** and **1/6**
8 to 10 in., **1/11 2/- 2/11** 11 to 13 in., **2/6 2/11 3/6** Postage 2d.
Tiny Dolls, with silk dress and moving eyes. 11 in., **1/10½**

Dressed Dolls. Compo heads, arms and legs, dressed in up-to-date styles with shoes and stockings.

No.
0 8 to 12 in. ... **8½**d.
1 11 to 12 in., **10½**d.
2 10½ to 14 in., **1/4½**
3 10½ to 16 in., **1/11**
4 15 to 17 in., **2/6**
Postage 3d.
15 in. ... **4/6 4/11**
16 & 17 in., **5/11 7/6**

Boy Dolls, dressed. Various styles, **1/11 3/11** Superior, **12/6** and **16/6**

Jap Dolls, **2/-**

Clockwork Walking Dolls (dressed).
20 22 27 28 in.
1/6 2/3 3/6 4/3
Postage 3d.

Undressed Walking Dolls (see next page).

Baby Dolls. Special Line **6**d. and **10½**d.
Dressed Baby Dolls, with moving eyes, long dresses, **10½**d. **1/6 1/9 1/11 2/6**
Superior do., **2/11 3/6 4/11 5/11 7/11**
Assorted white linen or muslin, **8/11 10/6**
Silk Dresses, **6/11 15/- 17/6**
Best quality, beautifully dressed, **15/- 21/- 27/6 37/6 42/-**

Small Dolls, Miniature dressed dolls, suitable for small beds in doll's houses, etc., **3**d, **4**d. **6**d. **7½**d. **10½**d. Postage 1½d.

Sailor Boy and Girl.
Boy, **12/6 15/- 20/-**
Girl, **12/6 15/6 17/6 18/6 22/6 30/- 37/6**
Postage (under 20/-) 6d. extra.

Celluloid Tiny Dolls, to undress, **1/4½** and **2/6** Postage 3d.

Best Dressed Dolls. Small Sizes, in a large variety of styles. **5/11 7/11 9/11 10/6 15/- 17/6**

Superior quality Double Jointed Dolls, made to undress, with movable eyes.

12 in. ...			**2/11**
14 in. ...			**3/6**
16 in. ...	**4/11**	**5/11**	**6/11**

Postage 3d.

"Pa," "Ma," Talking Dolls. Nicely dressed.

13 in.	**2/11**	**3/6**
14 in.		**4/6**
16 in.		**6/6**
1 in.		**7/11**

Postage 3d.

N.B.—If doll ordered is out of stock, the nearest will be sent unless otherwise stated.

Japanese Dolls, superior quality, **3/11 4/11 7/11**

Japanese Doll Families. Set of 7, **10½**d. Set of 5, **6**d. Postage 3d.

Japanese Boy and Girl Dolls Imported direct from Japan.
8½ in... **6**d. 14 in. ... **1/6**
9½ ,, ...**8½**d. 16 ,, ... **1/10½**
12½,, ... **1/-** 18 ,, ... **2/3**
Postage 3d.

Best Quality Dressed Dolls. In a great variety of Up-to-date Stylish Dresses. Thousands to choose from. Various sizes, up to 26 in.
7/11 8/11 10/6 12/6 14/6 15/- 17/6 21/- 25/- 30/- 38/6 42/- 45/- 50/-

DOLLS—*continued.*

These Dolls can now be obtained all the year round

Fabrics. Printed in colours. marked for cutting out, with full instructions printed on each sheet.

Jointed Doll.. **10½**d. Baby's Ball .. **10½**d.
20 in. Doll .. **1/3** Noiseless Skittles
Life size Doll **1/10½** **1/10½**
Family of Dolls **2/3** Foxy Grandpa **10½**d.
Cat, Kittens & Ball.. **1/10½** Noah's Ark .. **1/10½**
Postage 1d.

Golliwog Dolls.
No. 1 .. **6**d.
,, 2 .. **10½**d.
,, 3 .. **1/4½**
Larger sizes,
1/10½ **2/4½** **3/6**
Postage 3d.

Wooden Dolls.

Pretty Dolls.
Unbreakable and Jointed.
Made of Wood.
This doll can be dropped or thrown to the ground without being broken, at the same time it has the appearance of a china or composition doll.

No.
1, 11 in. .. **3/11** Postage 3d.
2, 12½ in. .. **5/6** Postage 3d.
3, 14 in. .. **6/6** Postage 4d.
4, 16 in. .. **7/11** Postage 5d.

Special Line, Wooden Dolls, **10½**d. ea.
14 in., **2/6** Postage 3d.

Novelty Baby Bunting.
Dolls dressed with best white material.
Unbreakable.

No. 1	2	3	Post
10½d.	**1/4½**	**1/10½**	2d. 3d.

Rubber Dolls.
Best quality rubber only.

No. 2	3	4	5	6
6d.	**10½**d.	**1/4½**	**1/10½**	**2/4½**

Large size, superior quality rubber dolls.
1/10½, **2/11** and **3/6**
Postage 3d.

Gamage's Specialite in Strong Undressed Dolls.
Pretty Faces. Full Jointed. Beautiful Finish. F Quality. Light or Dark Hair.
No. 3, 15 in. ..**5/6** No. 6, 26 in...**10/6**
,, 4, 22 in. ..**7/6** ,, 7, 28 in.. **12/6**
,, 5, 24 in. ..**9/6** ,, 8, 30 in...**16/6**
No. 9, 32 in. .. **18/6**
Postage 3d., 4d., 5d and 6d.

G Quality do., with
Real Hair and Eyelashes.
No. 1, 15 in., **6/6** No. 2, 19 in., **8/11**
No. 3, 21 in., **12/6**
Postage 3d. and 4d. under 10/-

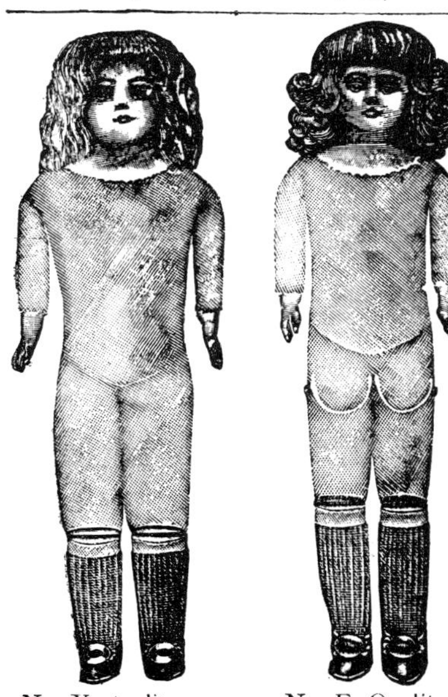

No. X Quality. No. E. Quality.

Throwdown Unbreakable Dolls.
Celluloid Head Wool Dress, **10½**d., **1/6**
Postage 3d.

Special Unbreakable "**Throwabouts.**"
Wool dressed dolls. **6**d. each. Post 3d.

Wooden Dutch Dolls.
Prices, **4½**d., **6**d., **1/-**, **2/-**, **2/9** doz.
Postage 6d. and 9d.

Gamage's Special Undressed Dolls.
Strongly made. Jointed.

12	15	16¾	18	20	24	28	32 in.	Postage
10½d.	**1/4½**	**1/10½**	**2/4½**	**2/11**	**3/11**	**5/11**	**7/11**	3d. & 4d.

Small size do., splendid value, **6½**d. each.

Undressed Compo Dolls. Full Jointed, with Eyelashes.

13	17½	20	21½	24	26 in.	Postage
1/11	**2/11**	**3/6**	**4/6**	**5/6**	**6/6**	3d. & 4d.

Undressed Dolls.

Undressed Baby Dolls. Best Quality. Wooden.
13½ in. .. **3/11** 17 in. .. **4/11** Postage 3d.

Kid Body Dolls.

No. X.—Special Line. With Shoes and Stockings.
Jointed Knees and Thighs. 12 in. high. Price **1/-** each. Postage 3d.

A Quality.—Jointed Leather Bodies and Legs, with shoes and stockings, moving eyes, very strongly made, flaxen hair and pretty faces. Packed in box, complete.
No. 1, 12 in., **1/10½** No. 2, 14 in., **2/4½** No. 3, 17 in., **2/9** No. 4 19 in., **3/11**
No. 5, 22 in., **4/11** No. 6, 25½ in., **7/6** Postage 3d. and 4d.

B Quality.—Jointed Leather Arms and Hips, moving eyes, washable limbs.
No. 1, 12 in., **3/6** No. 2, 15 in., **4/11** No. 3, 18 in., **6/6** No. 4, 20 in., **7/11**
No. 5, 24 in., **9/11** Postage 3d. and 4d.

E Quality.—Jointed Leather Body Doll, Celluloid Head and Arms, curly wig, almost unbreakable. A very fine doll.
No. 1, 12 in., **4/6** No. 2, 16 in., **7/6** No. 3, 20½ in., **10/6**
No. 4, 23 in., **13/6** Postage 3d.

Undressed Dolls with Metal Heads.
Moving Eyes and Kid Bodies. 16 in., **5/11** 19 in., **8/11** Postage 4d.
Brass Heads fitted to old dolls. Prices on application.

Walking Dolls.
Undressed Walking Dolls. No. 1, 6 in., **1/6** No. 2, 9 in., **2/-**
Best quality, pretty faces.
15½ in., **5/11** 18½ in., **6/6** 21 in., **7/6** 24½ in., **9/11**
Special Cheap Line.—Undressed Walking Doll, **1/3** Postage 3d.

Very Special Line.—**Soft Body Doll.** Celluloid Head and Limbs,
11½ in., **1/6** 14 in., **2/4½** Postage 3d.

Rubber Clowns, 10½d., **1/6**, **2/-**
Postage 3d.

Solid Rubber Boy Dolls.
10½d. Postage extra.

H Quality with
Celluloid Heads, unbreakable.
No. 1, 13 in...**4/6** No. 3, 21 in... **9/11**
,, 2, 18 in...**7/6** ,, 4, 24 in... **12/6**
Postage 3d. under 10/-

J. Quality. Superior Quality Dolls. Exceptionally Fine Models with Real Hair and Eyelashes.
No. 1, 22 in...**17/6** No. 3, 36 in...**30/-**
,, 2, 32 in...**25/-** ,, 4, 40 in...**42/-**

Undressed Dolls, with Voice.
"Mamma" and "Papa." As F Quality.
No. 1, 14 in... **4/11** No. 2, 18 in... **6/6**
,, 3, 22 in... **8/6** Postage 3d.

A Quality. B Quality.

Large Hair Stuffed Dolls.

	28	33	38	44 in.
Price ..	**5/6**	**7/6**	**12/6**	**15/-**
Postage	4d.	5d.	6d.	6d.

(English make.) DOLLS' HOUSES. (English make.)

A. W. Gamage Ltd. desire to draw particular attention to their Dolls' Houses, and beg to say that each model has been designed exclusively for them from architect's Original drawings. All of the houses are of exceptionally solid construction and will withstand rough usage.

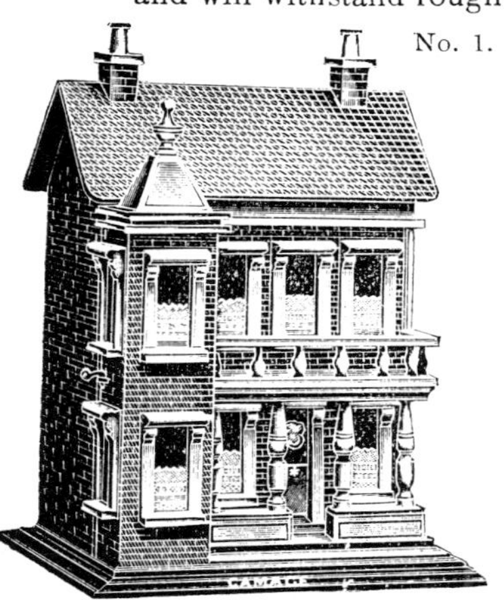

No. 1.

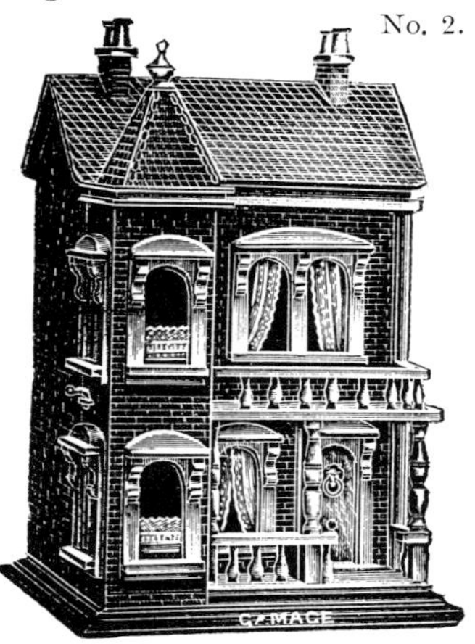

No. 2.

No. 1. Very stylish house as illustration, with 9 windows, balcony and portico, balcony supported by 4 turned pillars, gable roof and spire, 2 chimneys. The whole front of house opens on hinges. Base 18½ by 16 in., height to chimney 26 in. Price **12/6**

No. 2. Attractive Villa as illustration, with 2 rooms, 7 windows with ornamental coping, gable roof and spire, balcony and portico supported by 3 turned pillars. The whole front of house opens on hinges. Base 20 by 17 in., height to chimney 29 in. Price **15/-**

No. 3. Smart up-to-date Villa as illustrated, with 4 rooms, kitchen has dresser, dining and 2 bedrooms fitted with fireplaces, 10 windows with attic window, balcony and portico supported by 3 spiral columns richly gilded. The whole front of house opens on hinges. Base 23 by 18 in., height to chimney 33 in. Price **18/6**

No. 3.

No. 4. Fashionable Villa as illustration, with 4 rooms fitted with fireplaces, front door to open, 10 windows with attic window, 3 balconies (one with door to open into room), portico supported by 4 turned pillars, handsomely finished throughout, can be opened at both sides. Base 25 by 13½ in., height to chimney 26½ in. Price **25/-**

No. 6. Latest Design. Villa with 4 rooms and fireplaces, 10 windows with attic, glass-fronted door to open, balcony to roof, 3 steps and 2 pillars to front entrance. Can be opened both ends. Base 26½ by 18½ in. Price **37/6**

A large selection of up-to-date Model Dolls' Houses.

Special Villa,

3/6 5/6
7/11 12/6
15/- 17/6
25/- 30/-
35/- 55/-

No. 5. Handsome Dolls' House as illustration, with 4 rooms and fireplaces, 9 windows with attic window, 2 balconies with flowers in pots, attractive portico supported by 4 turned pillars, front door to open. Can be opened both ends. Base 26½ by 14 in., height to chimney 30 in. Price **30/-**

No. 7. Exceptionally Handsome Double-fronted House as illustration, 4 rooms with doors to open on landing, staircase and landing, 14 windows including 2 attic windows, 2 glass folding doors to open on balcony, glass pannelled front door to open, with porch. Opens in front in 2 sections. Base 31 by 20 in., height to chimney 34 in. Price **55/-**

Larger and Superior Houses, **£6 6 0** and **£7 7 0**

Carriage extra in all cases outside London delivery radius.

Stands.

18 in. high from floor (or to order). Can be supplied to fit all larger houses, prices from **6/9** to **14/6**

It is advisable that all Dolls' Houses be packed in crates the charge for which is 6d., 9d., 1/-, &c., according to size, which should be added to order.

No. 8. Up-to-date Villa as illustration, comprising kitchen with fireplace, bedroom with fireplace and door leading to landing, large reception hall, staircase, bedroom with folding door opening on landing, 8 windows, portico with 4 turned pillars, lock and key to front door, fitted with **working passenger lift.** Roof to lift off, opens at both ends. Base 32 by 19½ in., height to chimney 46 in. Price **£5 5 0**

Dolls' House Furniture, Stoves, etc.

Japanese Furniture. Complete set packed in box, **10½**d.
Japanese Washstand, **6½**d. Post 2d.

Loose Furniture.

Assorted Designs and Woods.

Chairs, **6½**d., **8½**d. Tables, square, **10½**d., **1/-**, **1/3** Tables, round, **6½**d., **7½**d., **8½**d. Writing tables, **1/-**, **1/6** Sofa, **1/3**, **2/3**, **2/9** Sideboards, **1/4½**, **1/6**, **1/10½** Cabinets, **1/10½**, **2/6** Stools, **6½**d. Pot Stands, **6½**d. Cosy Corner, with Mirror, **2/11** Screens, **6½**d. Easy Chairs, **1/-** Rocking Chairs, **10½**d. Bedsteads, **6**d., **1/6** Chest Drawers, **1/-** Dining Tables, **1/6**, **1/10½** Clocks, **6**d. Washstands, **1/6** A large assortment to choose from always in stock.

Carriage extra.

Stove for Dolls' House, **10½**d. Postage 2d.

Stove for Dolls' House, **1/4½** As illus., **1/9** Post 2d.

Toy Mangles .. .. .. **6**d. and **10½**d. Postage 2d.

Miniature Washing Machine, with Tub complete .. **6/6** Carriage extra.

Superior Quality Furniture, each kind strongly made and finished in Up-to-Date Style. Drawing Room, **7/11**, **10/6**, **12/6** Dining Room, **12/6** Bed Room, **7/11**, **10/6**, **12/6**, **17/6**, **18/6** Carriage and packing 3d. to 1/-

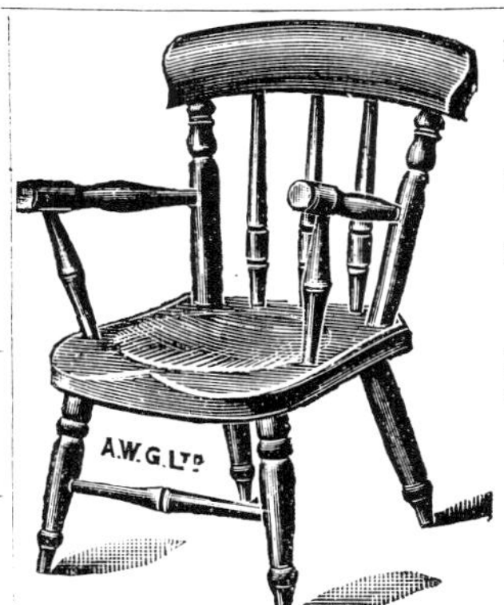

Dolls' Windsor Chairs.

10½ in. high to top of back.

No. 1 Plain Chair without arms, **6**d.

No. 2 Ditto, stronger make, with arms as illus., **10½**d.

No. 3 Arm Chair on Rockers, **1/4** Post 3d.

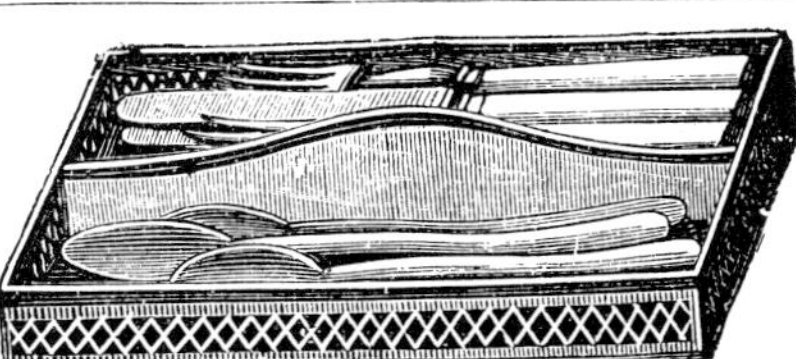

Toy Knives, Forks and Spoons. In basket, **1/-** Post 3d. In basket as illust., **2/11** Superior quality and finish, complete, **3/6** Post 3d. In plate box, **5/6** Complete Set Knives, Forks, Spoons, Serviette Rings and Knife Rests, **12/6**

Dolls' Deck Chairs .. .. .. **4½**d.
" " " with canopy, **6**d. Post 2d.

White Wood Dolls' House Furniture, containing 6 pieces, **3/11**, **4/11** Containing 9 pieces, **7/6** Post 6d.

Dolls' Toy Furniture.

Our Collection this season is from all the best markets, and comprises all up-to-date styles, and the finish is of the very best. Complete Sets, Drawing Dining, Kitchen and Bed Room packed in box. **10½**d., **1/4½**, **1/10½**, **2/3**, **2/11**, **3/6**, **3/11**, **4/6**, **5/11**, **6/6**, **7/6** **8/11**

Strong Miniature Wardrobe for Dolls' Clothes, **1/6**, **2/6** Do., superior quality, as illus., **8/11**, **12/6** Carriage extra.

Kitchen Furniture, in strong box, **10½**d., **1/6**, **1/9**, **2/6** Large size white wood Kitchen Furniture, **7/6** Do., as illustration, **2/-**, **3/6**, and larger size, **7/6** Carriage extra

Bentwood Furniture, very strong, packed in box. **10½**d. **1/3** **1/6** **2/3** **2/9** Postage 3d.

Chest of Drawers, 10½d., **1/4½**, **1/10½** Strong Oak, 2 drawers, 3½ in. high, 4¾ in. wide 2 in. top, as illus., **4/6**, **6/6**, **10/6** Carriage extra.

Miniature Cooking Stoves.

Strongly made and japanned Spirit Cooking Stove as illustration.

No. 1. Complete with lamp, 1/4½

No. 2. 1/9

Carriage 3d.

SPECIAL LINE.

Toy Stoves, with Spirit Lamp and 2 Cooking Pots.

Size 5 in. by 3¾ in. by 3 in.

10½d.

Postage 3d.

Cooking Stove, as illustration. Best make and finish, **5/11** Postage 6d.

No. 7. Superior quality nickel and japanned Spirit Cooking Stove, with oven, 5 utensils, and lamp with 3 burners, brass fittings, 11 in. long, as illustration, **7/6** Postage 6d.

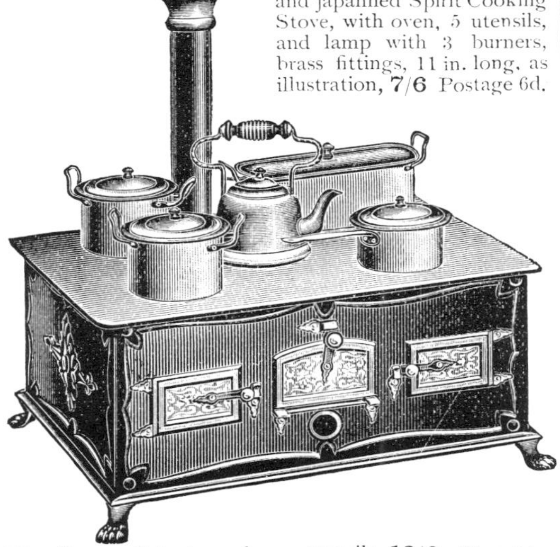

No. 7a. 14½ in. long, larger utensils, **12/6** Post 6d.
,, 7b. 17 in. long .. .. **20/-** Carriage free.

The [illegible]ignon Washing Machine. A novel toy for children and also a useful article for ladies to wash small articles. Size 9½ in. by 5½ in. by 12½ in. Price 5/6 Carriage extra.

No. 3. Highly finished nickelled and japanned Spirit Cooking Stove, as illustration, complete with all utensils and lamp .. **3/6**

No. 4. Larger, **4/6** Postage 6d.

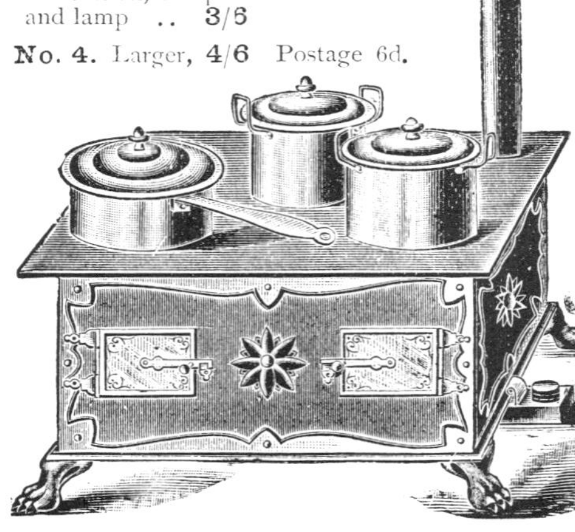

Toy Stoves for Spirit Heating,

With front & side walls enamelled grey granite.

Toy Stoves, with new Spirit Lamps, elegantly finished, with polished top, fine nickelled mountings, doors and feet.

Size 7 10½ [illegible] ¾ by 5¼ in. 2 pots, 1 saucepan, boiler and oven **..10/6** **Size 9** 12¾ by 9¼ by 6½ in. 2 pots, 1 saucepan, 1 tea kettle, boiler and oven **..17/6**

Size 11 17 by 12½ by 8 in. 2 pots, 1 saucepan, 1 tea kettle, boiler, oven, and 2 spirit lamps .. **25/-**

No. 674N. Model of Up-to-Date Gas Cooking Stove, with oven, frying pan, 1 bacon plate, 4 utensils, 3 lamps with 4 gasifying spirit burners and regulator, high heating power radiator, stand for smoothing iron. Nickel fittings. Length 14¾ in. .. **37/6** 17 in. .. **42/-**

Latest Novelty—Complete Range, as illustration, complete with improved heating lamp. All utensils strongly made and bright parts nickel plated.

No. 3,	Size 13 by 8 by 13 in.	**25/-**
,, 4,	,, 15 by 10 by 15 in.	**30/-**
,, 5,	,, 18 by 11 by 15 in.	**37/6**

Miniature Brass & Copper Models for Dolls' Houses

Shallow Brass Pan.

Solid Brass. 3½ in. wide. Price **4½**d.

Postage 1½d.

Set of Kitchen Utensils.

As illustration.

Price **10½**d.

Postage 2d.

Coal Cauldron.

Heavy Brass Miniature Coal Cauldron. Price **6**d. Post 1½d.

Small size. Splendid Model Price **4½**d. Postage 1d.

Brass Candlestick.

No. 2. Heavy Brass.
Size 4 in. ... Price **5**d.
,, 5 in. ... ,, **6**d.
Postage 2d.

Miniature Brass Kettle.

Gas Stove Kettle. Size 3in.

Price **5**d. & **10½**d. Postage 1½d.

Ditto with black handle, **5**d. Post 1½d.

Brass Bucket.

Solid Brass. Useful for matches. 3½ in. high.

Price **5**d. Postage 1½d.

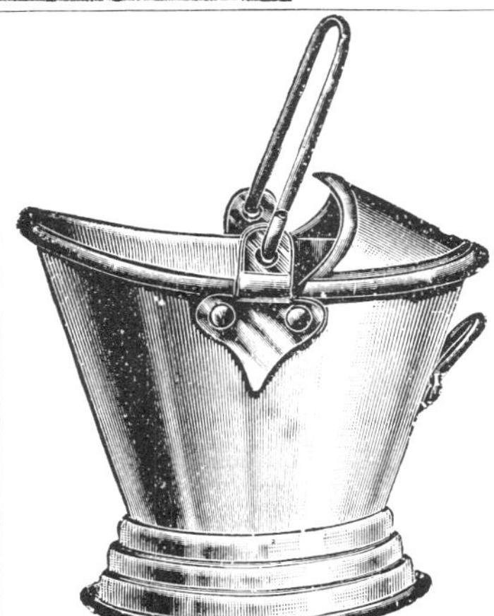

Brass Coal Scoop.

A perfect model.

Price **9**d.

Post 1½d.

Coffee Pot. Price **5**d. each. Post 2d

Toy Stoves for Spirit Heating.

Brass Tea Pots.

Solid Brass. 4 in. high. Price **9**d. Postage 1½d.

All these Articles are very Strongly Made and are perfect Models.

Fine and extra strong finish, sheet iron stamped and black japanned, with gold bronzed ornaments, polished top, new safety spirit lamp, with high-class brass mountings, guard rails and doors on solid iron base, on folding stand, sheet iron, black japanned, the side trays of the stand can be extended or folded up. With fine enamelled cooking utensils, outside light blue, inside white, consisting of 2 saucepans, 1 stewpan, 1 tea kettle, 1 retinned boiler with tap.

Miniature Vases.

In Polished Copper.

For dolls' houses, fern pots, flowers, pins, &c.

Price **4½**d. each.

4/- doz.

Postage 2d.

M 2123/11. Stove 18¼ in. x 13¼ in. x 8 in. with 2 spirit lamps, stand 14¼ in. x 12½ in x 35½ in. (extended) .. .. each **25/-**

M 2123/10. Stove 16 in. x 11¼ in. x 7¼ in. with 1 spirit lamp, stand 14¼ in. x 10½ in. x 30½ in. (extended) .. ..each **21/-**

Toy Shops, Scales, etc.

2098/3

Grocer's Shop, made very strongly in various designs.

Price **1/6 1/11 2/11** Postage 3d. and 4d.

Large assortment of **Shops,** comprising Butchers, Grocers, Milliners, &c., &c., in all qualities. From **1/6** to **63/-**

2320/1

Grocer's Shop, as illustrated, made of hard wood.
Price .. .. **6/6 7/11** and **9/11**
Carriage 6d., &c.

Butchers' Shops in various styles. Price **2/11 4/11 6/6 7/6**
Carriage 3d., 4d. and 6d.

Shops Fitted with Spiral Staircases, and Finished in Up-to-Date Styles, with Telephones, &c.
Price **10/6 13/6 16/6 22/6**

Market Stall, with Umbrella Cover, complete, **3/11**
Do., large size, **7/6**
Postage 4d.

Grocers' Shops finished in best style, nicely painted.
Price **5/11 9/6 12/6 14/6 37/6 & 50/-** Postage 6d.

Empties for Stocking Shops, consisting of Bottles and Boxes with labels for Bovril, Odol, Mustard, &c.
Price .. **9d.** per dozen. Postage 3d.

No. 750. **Toy Scales.**
As illustration. Price **6d.** Postage 2d.

No. 10,851. **Toy Grocer's Shop.**
(Cardboard.) Made to fold up.
Price .. **9d.** Large size, **3/6**
Postage 3d. Postage 4d.

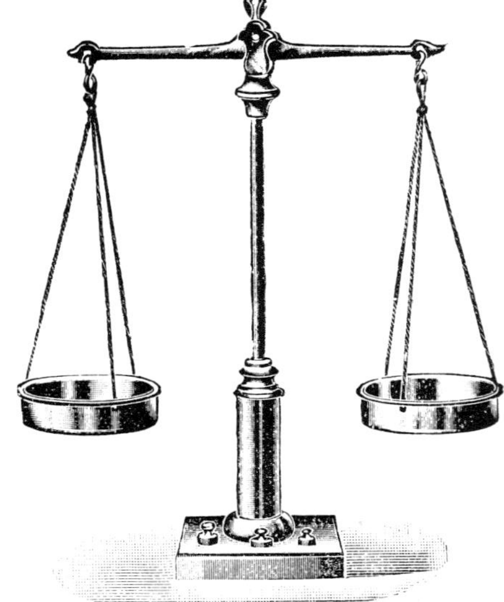

No. 752. **Toy Scales,** with Pillar.
As illustration. Price. **10½d.** Larger, **1/10½**
Postage 2d. and 3d.

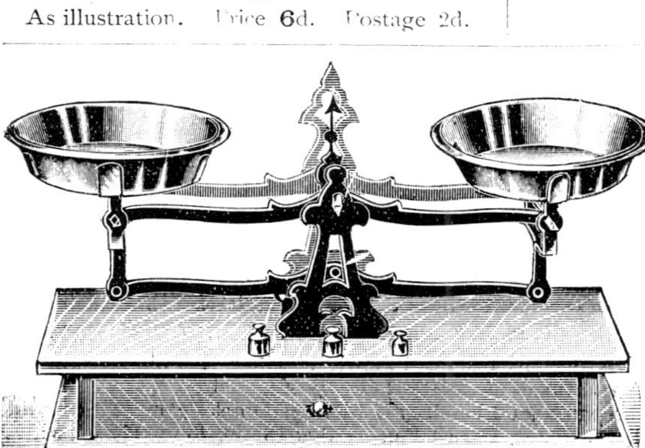

No. 526. **Toy Balancing Scales**

Price		Postage
..	**6d.**	2d.
,,	**10½d.**	,, 2d.
,,	**1/4½**	,, 3d.
,,	**1/10½**	,, 3d.

No. 573. **Toy Scales.**
As illustration.
Price .. .. **10½d.**
Postage 3d.

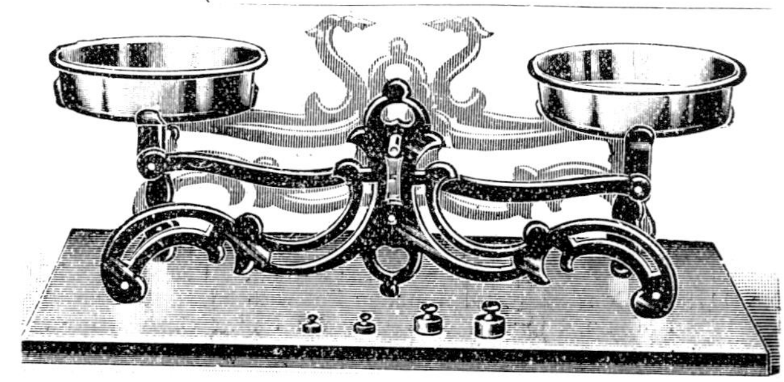

Theatres, Punch and Judy Shows, Opera Houses.

Shadow Theatre.
Box containing Showing Sheet and 6 different movable figures, **2/6** Post 3d.

Amusing Shadow-making Game, **9d.** and **2/3** Post 3d.

Miniature Opera Houses.
Complete with Characters and Plays.

No. 0, 29in. high, $23\frac{1}{2}$in. wide, 18in. deep, **21/-**
$29\frac{1}{2}$in. ,, 27in. ,, 20in. ,, **28/6**
31in. ,, 27in. ,, $21\frac{1}{4}$in. ,, **33/6**
Each packed in a box.

Special Line Small Theatre.
Size 13 in. wide, $16\frac{3}{4}$ in. high, 7 in. deep, **2/6** Post 4d.

Pandean Pipes.
Superior quality, **3/6** Post 2d.

Punch and Judy Shows.
Best quality.
Handsomely finished in colours.
Complete with Figures and Text Book.

No. 1, with 2 figures .. **3/6**
2, ,, 3 ,, .. **6/6**
3, ,, 5 ,, .. **9/6**
4, ,, 5 ,, .. **13/6**
5, ,, 6 ,, .. **17/6**

Larger sizes.

No. 6, with 6 figures .. **21/-**
7, ,, 6 ,, .. **25/-**
9, ,, 6 ,, .. **45/-**

Punch and Judy Figures.

Set of 2, **1/-** Set of 3, **1/6** Post 3d.
,, 4, **2/6** ,, 5, **3/3** Post 4d.
Set of 6, **5/6**, **7/6**, **10/6**
Post 6d.

Theatre, with Footlights.
The best Miniature Toy Theatre in the market. Strongly made and fitted with properly working curtain, English pattern, footlights to burn oil, beautifully Lithographed Characters, mounted on cardboard and cut ready for use. These Theatres have complete set of characters, &c., as per book.

No. 1a, 18 in. high, $14\frac{1}{2}$ in. wide, 8 in. deep .. **5/11**
2a, 20 in. ,, $14\frac{1}{2}$ in. ,, 12 in. ,, .. **7/11**
3a, 24 in. ,, 17 in. ,, 14 in. ,, .. **11/6**
4a, $25\frac{1}{2}$ in. ,, $20\frac{1}{2}$ in. ,, $15\frac{1}{2}$ in. ,, .. **13/6**
5a, .. **16/6**
6a, $32\frac{1}{4}$ in. ,, $29\frac{1}{2}$ in. ,, $21\frac{1}{2}$ in. ,, .. **37/6**
Postage 4d. under 20/- in value.

Extra Plays. Including Book of Words, Figures and Scenery, complete.

Suitable for Theatres	Red Riding Hood.		Snow White, William Tell, Sleeping Beauty.	Cinderella.
1, 2, 3, 4 & 6	**3/11**		**5/11**	**6/11**
5	**5/6**	Postage 3d.	**8/6**	**8/11**

Pantomime, with Moving Figures. Very novel and amusing.
Price **2/9** Post 3d.

Farmyards, Boxes of Animals, &c., &c.

Poultry Farm.
As illustration. Price **2/11** Postage 3d.

Boxes of Poultry.

Price **6**d. and **10½**d.

Postage 3d.

Larger size **1/6** Postage 3d.

Farmyard. Complete, with animals, buildings, &c.
Price **2/6** As illustration, **3/6** Postage 3d.

Zoological Gardens.
Price **1/10½** Postage 3d. Large size, **5/11** Postage 4d.

Fine collection of **Farmyards, Sheep Farms, Zoological Gardens, &c.**

Price **4/6, 6/6, 7/6, 7/11, 12/6, 21/-**

Postage extra.

Pastimes or **Farmyards.**
Containing well-modelled Animals, &c. Price **6/6** **7/11**
Postage 4d. and 6d.

Carved White Wood Animals.
Price .. .. **3/3** **4/6** Postage 3d. and 4d.

Superior quality **Farmyard Sets, Wild Animals Domestic Animals, &c.**

12/6 **17/6** **21/-** **30/-** **35/-** &c.

Plain White Wood Animals (in boxes).

On wheels ..	10½d.	1/4½	2/6
Without wheels ..	10½d.	1/4½	2/3

Postage 3d.

Menagerie (As illustration), **8/11**

Post 6d.

Also a large collection of **Fancy Arks, Menageries, &c.**, on show during Bazaar.

Boxes of **Coloured Animals.**

Price .. .. **10½**d. and **1/4½**

Postage 3d.

GAMAGE'S FOR ARKS.

NOVELTY!

Miniature Arks.

Price ... **6**d. each.
Postage 3d.

No. 73. **Noah's Arks.**
Boat shaped. Containing White Wood Animals.
Prices ... **10½**d. **1/6** **2 6** **4/-** Postage 3d. to 6d.
Ditto, Painted Animals, **10½**d. and **1/6** Postage 3d.

No. 1229½. **Noah's Ark.** White Wood Animals. Ark containing 23* Animals, **10½d.** 36, **1/6**; 62, **2/-**; 96, **2/11** and **3/9**; 152, **5/11** Postage 3d. to 6d.

No. 1228.
NEW DESIGN.
Rustic Roof Ark.
Prices **4/11** **6/6** **8/6**
Contains about 104, 112, and 134 Animals. Postage 3d.

No. 34.
Arks with Rustic Roof.
Containing 64 Coloured Animals.
Price ... **1/11**
104 ditto, **3/3** Ditto, **4/6**
Postage 3d.

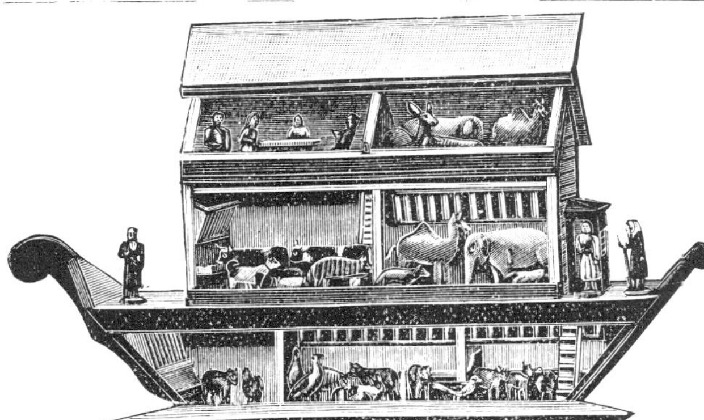

No. 38.
New Stable Ark.
Open out as illustration. Fitted with 36* Animals, 8 Attendants, and Furniture complete.
Prices:
8/6 **12/6** **21/-**
Carriage:
6d. 9d. Free

No. 31. **Painted Boat-shaped Arks.**
Similar to illustratn.
Containing:
100* Animals **4/11**
152 „ **7/6**
No. 29.
Ditto, with Polished Animals, **10 6**
Carriage 6d.

A Large Collection of Fancy Arks to select from.

No. 1227. **Fine Ark.** Containing 26 Skin and Felt-covered Animals and 8 Figures. **22/6**

No. 1231½. **Wooden Ark.** With White Wood Animals. **7/6** **12/6** **15/-** Carriage 6d.

*** Exact number of Animals not guaranteed in any of the above Arks.**

ROCKING HORSES, HOBBY HORSES.

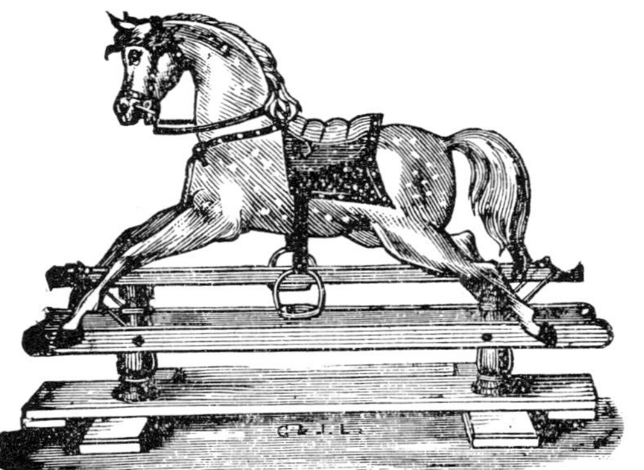

Gamage's Celebrated Hobby Horses.

Very strongly made and finished in best style. Quite safe and practically unbreakable. Painted in various colours.

No.	About height to saddle.	Length of Stand.		Price.
1	2 ft. 3½ in.	3 ft. 0½ in.	..	18/9
1B	2 ft. 5 in.	3 ft. 2½ in.	..	23/6
2	2 ft. 7½ in.	3 ft. 8 in.	..	26/6
2C	2 ft. 8 in.	3 ft. 10 in.	..	35/-
3	3 ft. 0 in.	4 ft. 4 in.	..	38/6
4	3 ft. 4½ in.	4 ft. 9½ in.	..	46/-
	Superior quality, large size.			
4D	3 ft. 0 in.	4 ft. 6 in.	..	50/-
4E	3 ft. 3 in.	4 ft. 10 in.	..	63/-

English-made
Real Skin-covered Hobby Horses.

Sizes as above. No. 1, **34/6** No. 2, **47/6**

Gamage's "Bronko."

Safety Hobby Horse.

(Regd. No. 467,670).

This Horse is specially constructed to our own designs.

Fitted with cowboy saddle and stirrups which not only give it an elegant appearance, but render it a much safer horse for child than the old style.

Made in 4 sizes.

No.	Height to saddle.	Length of Stand.	
B	29 in.	38½ in.	32/6
C	32 in.	46 in.	42/-
D	36 in.	54 in.	63/-
E	39 in.	58 in.	75/-

Strong Wood Rocking Horses.

No.		Height of Saddle.		Length of Rocker.				Extra carved, best finish.
0	..	2 ft. 2 in.	..	4 ft. 4 in.	..	13/9	..	17/6
1	..	2 ft. 6 in.	..	5 ft. 0 in.	..	18/6	..	24/6
2	..	2 ft. 11 in.	..	6 ft. 3 in.	..	25/6	..	34/6
3	..	3 ft. 2 in.	..	6 ft. 6 in	..	35/-		

Improved Hobby Horse.

With 2 end Chair Seats.

For 3 children.

Very strongly made in best quality only.

No. 2C .. **47/6**

Size as No. 3C Hobby Horse,

62/6

1906 NOVELTY.

Strong Wood Rocking Horse.

No. 1. .. **32/6**
No. 2. Height to saddle, 2 ft 11 in., Length of rocker, 6 ft. 3 in. .. **37/6**
No. 3. Height to saddle, 3 ft. 2 in., Length of rocker, 6 ft. 6 in. **47/6**
Saddle Panniers and Straps. No. 2, **10/6** No. 3, **12/6** extra.

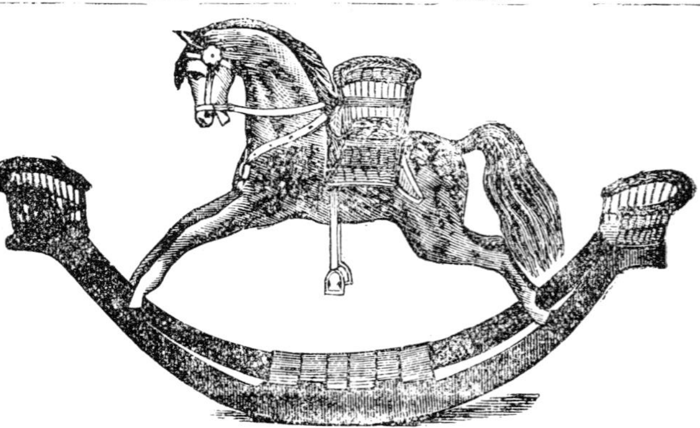

Nursery Yacht.

Perforated Seats to seat 3.

Height 2 ft. 6 in., length 5ft. 6in.

45/6

Other sizes to order.

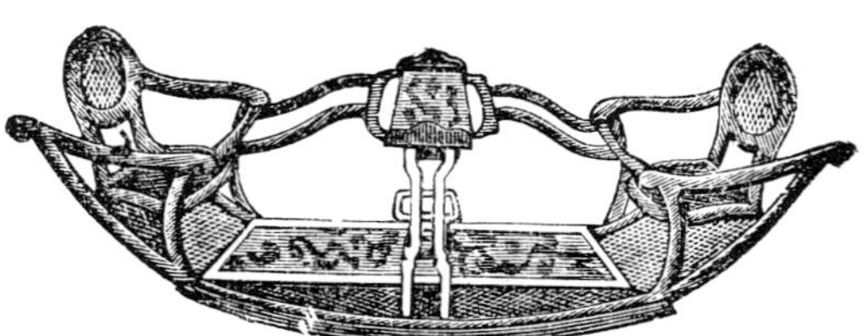

GAMAGE'S Patent "Galapa" Horse. *Canters, Gallops, Answers to the Reins.*

Patent No. 7379.

The Patent "Galapa" Horse is entirely new, and comprises all the advantages of both the Cycle and Rocking Horse. It is fitted with two independent sprags. When the horse is rocked gently, these sprags engage on the backward motion and drive the horse forward on small rollers let into the rockers. If the rocking motion be increased, the pace of the horse is increased. The guiding and stopping is carried out by merely pulling the reins in the usual way.

A **50/-** B **57/6** C **70/-** D **90/-** E **110/-**

Carriage and packing extra on all Horses outside London delivery radius.

Felt and Plush-covered Animals.

The Celebrated Jointed Toys. No CHILD should be without one.

Mrs. Fatty.

A LARGE SELECTION OF Quaint Felt-covered Toys.

Felt-covered Jack Tar, Frenchman, Nigger, Fat Captain, Hooligan, Mrs. Fatty, Grandpa .. 2/6
Postage 3d.

Sunny Jim, 1/11½ Fat Cook, a most striking Toy or Tea Cosy, 3/9

Humpty-Dumpty 3/6

Fat or Lanky Policeman or Postman, 10½d. 1/4½
Postage 3d.

Sailor or Soldier, 10½d. and 1/4½ Postage 3d.

Sunny Jim.

Jointed Monkeys
Covered with Coloured Plush. Green, 7/6
Red, 8/11 Brown, 12/6

Puss in Boots.
Plush-covered, 6/11 Post 4d.

Jointed Plush Bears,

Very strongly made with movable limbs.

Yellow—
4/3 7/6
10/6 18/6

White—
3/3 5/11
8/11 14/6

Special Line in Jointed Bears,
10½d. 1/9

Postage 2d.

Jointed Plush-covered Monkeys.
Price .. 3/3 4/6 5/6 6/6 7/11
8/6 9/11 12/6 16/6
Felt Covered .. 1/11 2/6

Jointed Plush-covered Cats or Pomeranian Dogs, 2/- 3/3 5/11

Brown or White Plush-covered
Jointed Bear,

Price—
2/3 3/3 4/11
6/9 10/6
15/6 18/6

Jointed Plush-covered Elephants.
The most popular and up-to-date Toy.

Price—
1/11 3/3 4/11
7/11

Jointed Donkeys.
2/6 3/6 4/11 7/11

THE EVERLASTING TOY.
On wheels. The Child's Favourite Toy, 10½d. 1/11
3/6 4/6 5/6 7/11 11/6 16/6 Postage 3d.
Grey Plush-covered Elephant, 5/11 9/6 12/6 18/6
Elephants Covered Felt, strong made, on elastic, 10½d. 1/4½ Postage 3d.
White Cloth-covered Elephant, nice soft Toy for Baby, 10½d. and 2/6

Postage extra on all above under 20/-

Jointed Plush-covered Spaniels.
A very fine Toy for any Child, 4/9 8/6 12/6
16/6

Toy Stables, Skin-covered Horses, etc.

Strong Stable, with Horse and Waggon, &c. **3/6**
Ditto (as illustration) .. **5/11**
Postage 4d. and 6d.

Special Cheap Line of Stables.
Price **1/6** Postage 3d.

Special Line.
English-made Stables, Horse with clothes, **25/-**

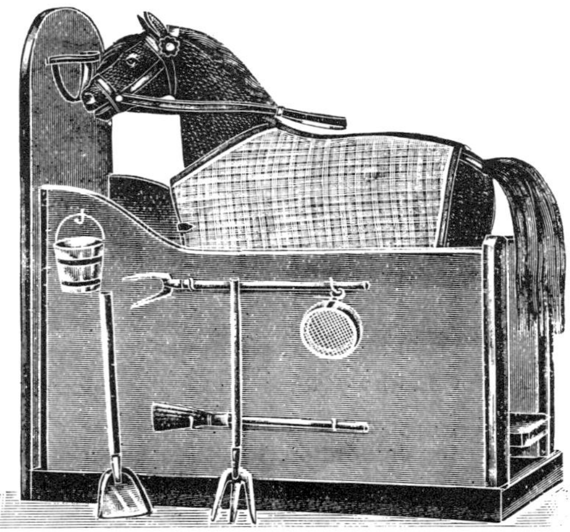

No. 1147. Stall with Horse and Stable Utensils.
Price .. **3/11** Postage 4d.

Strong Stable, complete with Horses, Waggon, &c., as illustration, **10/6**

Carriage and Packing extra on all Stables under 20/-

No. 2533/4. **New Design in Toy Stables.**

Prices	**2/11** and **4/3**
As illustration	**6/11**

Postage 3d., 4d., and 6d.

No. 712. **The Hunter's Stable.**
This Toy, by its interest and strength, should make a suitable toy for any Boy or Girl. The fittings included are: One finely-shaped Horse on board and castors, with Clothing and all Harness to buckle on and off, finely-modelled Saddle and Stirrups, Harness Room with Cupboard, Harness Table, Stand, Chair, Lamp, Brass Manger, Dandy Brush, Curry Comb, Shovel, Broom, and Fork, &c.
Price complete, as illustrated, **23/6**
With 2-Horse Stalls and 2 Horses, &c. **40/-**
Size of Single-Stall Stable, as illustrated, 20 in. high, 22 in. wide, 23 in. deep.

No. 4043. Stable as illustrated, well made and finished.
Price **4/-** Postage 4d.

Skin and Felt Covered Horses on Wheels, Push Horses, &c.

Skin Horses.
Harnessed, on Wheels—

No. 505/5	505/6	505/7	505/8
5/11	**8/6**	**10/6**	**12/6**

Saddle, ditto, **2/11** **3/11**
Postage 4d.

No. 1002/12.

Brown Felt-covered **Bears.**
On Wheels, with Chain, **3/6 6/6 8/6 12/6**
White or Brown Felt ditto, on Wheels,
3/6 6/6 8/6 12/6 16/6

Large Assortment of Stables,
In addition to those illustrated.
Prices:
3/6 5/11 8/6 9/6 10/6
12/6 14/6 16/6 21/- 30/-

Best Quality Push Horses.
Covered with Plush or Skin.

Skin	..	**15/6**	**16/6**	**17/6**
Plush	..	**12/6**	**13/3**	**14/6**

Ditto, on Stands with Wheels.

Skin	..	**20/-**	**22/6**	**25/-**
Plush	..	**16/6**	**17/6**	**18/9**

Real Skin Covered Horses. No. 506 ☞
With Harness complete, **21/-**

Plush Covered Horses.
6d. **10½d.** **1/4½** **2/11** **4/6** **5/6**

Strong English-made Toys. Best Quality only.

Strong Wood Omnibus.

No. 1 .. .. **7/11**

No. 2 .. .. **9/11**

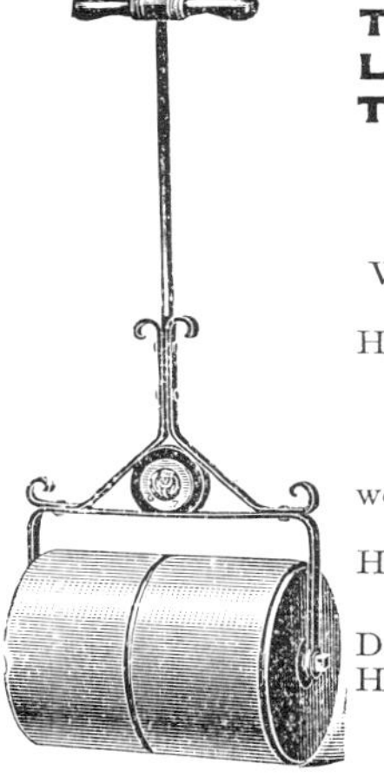

The Latest Toy—

Children's Garden Roller.

Wooden Barrel, 3½ by 5½ in., Height of handle 2 ft. Price **3/6**

Metal Barrel, wood ends, 7 by 9 in., **4/9** Height of handle 2 ft. 3 in.

Do., 12 by 9 in., Height of handle 2 ft. 9 in. **6/9**

Baker's Barrow. On Rubber Wheels. Well painted. Made to open. Price **13/9**

G.P.O. Cart. On Rubber Wheels. Well painted. Top opens both sides. Price **12/9**

Wood Engines.

Handsomely painted, on Strong Wheels.

No. 0, **1/9** 1A, **2/11** 1, **4/3** 2, **5/3** 3, **7/6**

Engines on Spider Iron Wheels, 4, **8/6** 6, **12/9**

Ditto, Rubber Wheels **13/9**

Trucks to match,

No. 0, **1/4** 1A, **1/9** 1, **2/3** 2, **2/6**

Gamage's Special

G.N.R. Coal Trucks.

Painted grey and lettered .. **2/11**

Strong Wood Steam Roller.

Latest Novelty. Well Finished.

Price .. .. .. **6/6** Postage 3d.

STRONG WOOD ENGINES AND TRUCKS.

Best quality Wooden Train.

Engine as illustration .. **9/11**

Saloon **7/11**

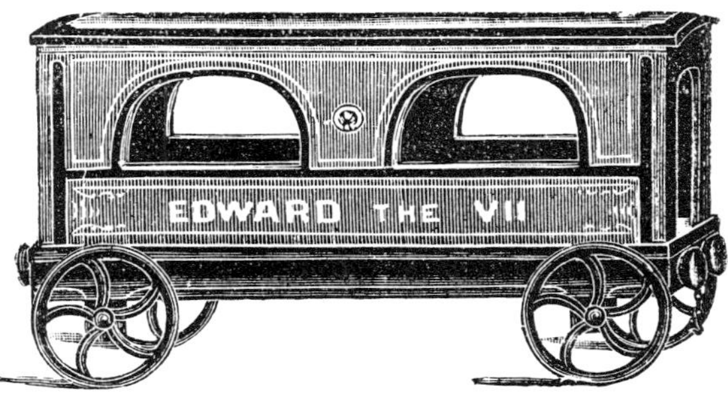

Strong Wooden **Tram,** with Iron Wheels .. **9/6**

Do., Rubber-tyred Wheels, nicely enamel painted.. **12/6**

Wood Horse Tram Cars.

Strong Wood Tram Cars with Horses. Complete as illustration.

No. 1 .. **4/6**

No. 2 .. **5/9**

No. 3 .. **8/11**

American TOY WAGGONS, &c.

No. 31. **The "Daisy,"** as illust. American Pole Cart with whip, strongly made and well finished and decorated. 36 in. long, 18 in. high. Price ... ... **13/6** with Seat. Carriage extra.

Strongly Made.

Imported Direct from United States.

No. 32. **"Express" Waggon,** as illust., very strong and nicely painted with name, etc. Length 26 in., width $13\frac{3}{4}$ in. Wheels $15\frac{1}{2}$ and 10 in. diam. Price **6/6** with seat. Carriage extra.

No. 38. Painted and Varnished **"Express"** Waggon, strongly made and well finished. Length 28 in., width $13\frac{3}{4}$ in. Wheels 11 in. diameter. Price **9/11** Carriage extra. With seat.

No. 112. **Large American Express Waggon.**

As illustration. Very strongly made, well finished, and decorated. Length 39 in. Width $18\frac{1}{2}$ in. Wheels 15 in. Price **25/-** With seat. Carriage extra.

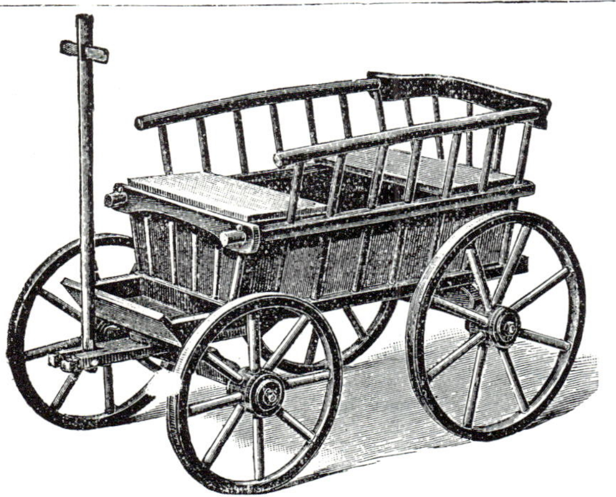

Strongly-made Waggonette (as illustration). Price .. .. **18/6** Carriage extra.

Tilting Sand Cart. Nicely japanned on solid forged iron frame with strong iron wheel, detachable handle and eyes for fastening a cord on both ends so that the cart can be pulled along. All parts made of forged iron, body of cart made of strong sheet iron, tilting, with adjustment for fixing.

No. 14198/1. Frame $20\frac{1}{2}$ in. long, $8\frac{1}{2}$ in. wide, Body $12\frac{1}{4}$ in. long, 10 in. wide, height of truck $13\frac{1}{2}$ in. **9/6**

No. 14198/2. Frame $22\frac{3}{4}$ in. long, 10 in wide, Body $14\frac{1}{2}$ in. long, 12 in. wide, height of truck $14\frac{1}{2}$ in. **12/6**

Pull Metal Train. A very strong toy for Children. No clockwork to get out of order and no danger **4/6** **7/6** **14/6**

WHIPS.

Strong Wood and Leather Handle Whips. Well made.
Price .. **6½d.** and **10½d.** Postage extra.